RAISING HAPPY CHILDREN

RAISING
HAPPY
CHILDREN

*What Every Child Needs Their Parents
to Know – from 0 to 11 years*

Jan Parker and Jan Stimpson

HODDER

MOBIUS

Hodder & Stoughton

Copyright © 1999, 2004 by Jan Parker and Jan Stimpson

First published in Great Britain in 1999 by Hodder and Stoughton
This revised edition published in 2004 by Hodder and Stoughton
A division of Hodder Headline

A Mobius Book

11

A CIP catalogue record for this title is available from the British Library

ISBN 9780340734643

Typeset in Baskerville MT by Palimpsest Book Production Limited, Polmont, Stirlingshire
Printed and bound in the UK by CPI Mackays, Chatham ME5 8TD

Hodder and Stoughton
A division of Hodder Headline
338 Euston Road
London NW1 3BH

Jan Parker is a journalist and writer specialising in child and family issues; an accredited parenting group facilitator; and an honorary member of a Child and Adolescent Mental Health Service family therapy team. She writes for many newspapers and magazines, including the *Guardian*, the *Independent* and *The Times*. She has three children.

Jan Stimpson is a leading parenting adviser and facilitator for the charity Parentline Plus. She runs courses and workshops in community centres and schools, and works privately with parent groups. She has two sons.

Our thanks to our families and friends for their invaluable support, and to all the parents and contributors who made this book possible.

CONTENTS

FOREWORD

By Dr Dorothy Rowe

Being a parent takes up a great deal of time, effort and expense. Even if you only do the basics – keep your children fed, clothed, healthy and provide a good education – you put a great deal into the whole exercise. What is the reward for all this? A few parents might be able to boast later that their son kicked the winning goal in the World Cup or their daughter was Prime Minister, but is all that most parents can expect a few hugs and kisses and a Christmas present?

No, it isn't. The reward can be the best prize of all – a close, loving relationship with another adult. When all the business of being a parent or a child is left behind what remains is two adults who see one another as equals, who share a history, who know and accept one another. They keep in touch with one another, not out of guilt or a fear of what other people might think if they don't, but because they love one another and are always interested in what the other is doing and thinking.

Such a relationship does not occur automatically when the child reaches a certain age. Many parents and children never achieve it because the basis of the relationship has not been laid down in the early years.

Babies are born wanting to love their parents. They are primed to love those one or two people who are with them often and who smile at them and talk to them with kindness.

In fact, parents have to work very hard to stop their children loving them. Babies always try to make the most of what's on offer, and older children will try again and again to win their parents' love and approval. Nevertheless, many parents do succeed in withering their children's love. They do this by controlling their children through fear, and fear drives out love. Love is open and fearless, and thus you cannot love someone whom you fear. Many children grow up telling themselves that they love the parent whom they fear, but what they feel is guilt, which they think is proof of love, and a sad, painful longing for the parent they never had.

I like to think that such tragedies will be fewer in the future because so many young parents see their role very differently from the way my parents' generation saw theirs. In my family my father was under constant criticism from my mother and other relatives because he was pleasant to his two daughters. He never hit us or even yelled at us.

Meanwhile my mother slapped me, sometimes hitting with great force when she was very angry, not so much with me but with herself and her life, and she was constantly criticising me and denigrating me. My big sister joined in this criticism and denigration, and was not corrected by my mother. (In my work in later years I found that this was a very common family style of communication.) Yet there was nothing my mother did which other adults found strange or reprehensible. At school, I and others were hit by the teachers using their hand or a cane. It would not cross a teacher's mind to be concerned about how a child might feel. The attitude of adults was that children should think what they were told to think and do what they were told to do.

Thankfully, views are changing. Hitting children was never an effective way of teaching them and is now increasingly recognised as such. Treating children as human beings deserving respect, dignity and being listened to, is the best way to bring up children. As *Raising Happy Children* illustrates so clearly, it is possible to provide the discipline and guidance all children need without resorting to physical punishment.

Bringing up children in this way is not easy, but the rewards are huge. It does not require you to be the perfect parent, but a considerate, loving and respectful one. If parents were perfect, children would never need to grow up. If you were able to read correctly every need and wish of your tiny baby and were able to fulfil that every need and wish, your child would have no desire to become independent.

Children will forgive their parents' fallibility if they are certain that their parents accept them as they are. If they believe that their parents never wanted them, or they had them only to make use of them, or that they can never be the kind of person their parents really want, they will always have cause for grievance. However, they can accept that their parents sometimes lose their temper, or get tired, or don't pay attention, or get involved in other things, or get things wrong if they know with the certainty that night follows day that their parents love them simply because they exist.

If this is the basis on which you operate as a parent then all you need to help you on your way is guidance about what to expect as children develop, and constructive, informed ideas and approaches about how to tackle the issues which arise. *Raising Happy Children* is not about spoiling children, but about how to help children to grow up feeling comfortable with themselves and with other people, and having the courage to face the inherent difficulties of life. Such children are indeed happy children.

Dr Dorothy Rowe

A DIFFERENT PATH

Nearly ten years ago, two friends – one a parenting adviser, one a journalist – were watching their children play in a garden. The conversation turned to parenting books. How come most big sellers were prescriptive manuals, advocating rigid baby-training or child-taming regimes? How come so many made parents feel guilty if the 'one-size-fits-all' tactics happened not to fit their circumstances or their child? Where was warmth? Where was real life with real children? Where was support and information on a whole host of crucial issues that matter to parents, but which are roundly ignored by most 'parenting' books?

That's how this book began. Now a bestseller, translated and sold across Europe, it's clear we weren't the only ones asking those questions.

Raising Happy Children is very proud to be a different kind of book for parents. It won't tell you how to live your family life or attempt to impose a child-rearing regime. Instead, it offers insights into how we can understand, support and guide our children as individuals, and nurture happy, healthy relationships with them from birth and on through their primary school years. It is this understanding and relationship-building that's too often ignored but which is key to our children's futures – how they feel about themselves, how they feel about others, how they communicate, behave, learn, develop, delight in life's joys and cope with life's knocks.

We're also proud to have created this book in a different kind of way. It sprang from our conversations and work with families but, conscious that no one individual, group or field of learning can have the monopoly on wisdom, we cast our net wider. We interviewed hundreds of parents from all walks of life, from those with everyday difficulties to others facing extreme problems. We spoke to family support professionals of world renown and leading academics involved in some of the most valuable research of our day. We read, we wrote, we checked back, we travelled the length of the country listening to people's stories of life with their babies and children – the difficulties they'd faced and what helped them most.

At the request of readers, this new edition features an expanded age range to eleven, and offers even more real-life examples, respected research and insights into problems and potential solutions. Our very heartfelt thanks, as ever, to all who've shared their experience and experiences so honestly and generously.

The result is a wealth of invaluable insight and knowledge that affirms our core beliefs: that understanding and respecting each child's unique strengths and vulnerabilities, capacities and needs, will help us support them and guide them as they grow. That wherever parents may be in their relationship with their child, whatever the child's age, whatever difficulties they may or may not have encountered, the positive steps parents take can make a huge difference to their child's life and their relationship together.

The understandings offered in *Raising Happy Children* are rooted firmly in the real world. And in the real world, happy babies are those whose needs are respected, understood and responded to, not those trained to be quiet by being ignored. Real parents are caring, concerned, often overstretched, and, like the rest of humanity, sometimes mistaken.

In the real world, children may be sad, unreasonable, angry, demanding and damned hard work as well as often loving, exuberant, hilarious and joyful. Happy children are not those trained to 'perform' impeccably or allowed to do just as they please. They are children who are loved and loving, whose feelings are respected, who are allowed to be children and who are given the guidance they need to flourish.

They are children:

— who are loved for who they are
— who appreciate their worth and the worth of others
— whose feelings, needs and development are understood
— who are guided by effective, clear and educative discipline
— who develop confidence and competence
— who have resilience to deal with problems and the capacity to delight in life

Raising Happy Children respects the resourcefulness and needs of parents and children, and aims to boost parents' confidence in their abilities and understanding. It is warm, thought-provoking, often touching, often funny, and genuinely supportive and helpful.

We've enjoyed working on this second edition very much, revisiting old friends and making new ones. We hope you enjoy it, too.

Jan Parker and Jan Stimpson

CHAPTER ONE

BABY'S NEEDS, YOUR NEEDS

How is life with your baby? Here are a few words parents have used to describe their first weeks and months: 'magical', 'terrifying', 'numb', 'warm', 'scary', 'exhausting', 'sublime'. It can be all these things, and usually is, in varying degrees and at various times.

It's heady stuff, so it helps to get straight down to essentials. At the moment and for a very long time to come, you are the most important person in your baby's life.

What your baby needs – and what you need once you've had your baby – will change over time and sometimes take you by surprise. Understanding and responding to those needs is key to your relationship together, now and for the rest of your lives.

Getting to know each other

I think the reality is shocking. So much time in the pregnancy is spent preparing for labour. Even if all the baby bits are bought, unpacked and washed, actually putting the baby into them is overwhelming. Babies don't come pre-packed and they do all sorts of odd things. Most parents, when they take baby home, feel they don't know what to do. It can take them a few days, a few weeks, even a few months to settle down to having a real live baby as opposed to a romantically imagined child.
Ann Herreboudt, midwife and family therapist

In the hospital after my first was born I even called the midwife to ask if I could pick him up. I literally didn't know what to do with him.
Christine Chittick, NCT ante-natal teacher

The highs are higher and the lows are lower than I ever imagined.
But my limits are also more flexible than I thought, sometimes out of
necessity, sometimes out of love.

Clare H

You have all been on an incredible journey, you to parenthood and
your child from the womb to the world. You each need time to recover
and to nurture and delight in your developing relationship.

So many factors influence this bonding process, from the birth
itself to a new baby's temperament and the support we receive, that
there can be no 'average' experience. Yet most parents and infants
appreciate skin-to-skin contact so they can touch, smell, hear and
respond to each other more easily and get to know each other better.
Setting aside time simply to indulge in a little mutual adoration is also
essential.

Allowing ourselves this time may seem difficult, especially when

 # *Beginnings*

Some love affairs begin at first sight, but not many.
None can be forced, most take time to grow and a
parent's love for their child is no different.

He was hauled out by a doctor called Martin and placed into my arms.
And I wasn't hit by that overwhelming feeling of love I'd been led to expect.
He was flesh and bone and blood and slime. His skin was scarlet and
he had a pointy head. His feet were still blue. He had dark hair and
enormous wrinkled hands that reminded me of my grandfather's.
He was real. It was extraordinary. But it wasn't love.

David F

When Matthew was born, at first I was too exhausted to
feel anything like love.

Mary C

With my first child I had a long and difficult labour, but the moment
I saw my little baby and held him I felt a rush of love so powerful I knew
instantly I would never, ever be the same again.

Jane R

life intervenes to disrupt the best of intentions. In the first weeks, it can take all our wits and resources to look after our baby, drink that cup of cold tea and think about getting out of our pyjamas. But try to make it a priority.

In our fast-past society, so much emphasis is placed on 'achieving' at speed that life's essentials sometimes get lost in the rush. By slowing the pace and spending calm time together you will be fostering your present and future bond with your child. In these first weeks and months, there's little that matters more.

You may already be astonished at the intensity of emotion you feel for your baby. If not, remember this is the beginning. If you are responsive to your baby, feeding, holding, comforting and helping them feel safe and loved, the relationship between you is already unfolding.

We so often just expect these things to happen and if they don't we tend to get more frantic and do more. So the key to this process is the 'undoing', the slowing down, quietening down and waiting. It is about giving time. You may be feeling quite damaged, and there does have to be time for the mother to heal. Sometimes mother and baby need quiet warmth to 'undo' all that before they can move on.
Barbara Dale, parenting counsellor and psychotherapist

For the first two to three months it is best for the baby to stay with the mother as much as possible. Once their senses become a little more developed, a baby can feel their way into the world, but initially their world is their mother and they are set up to see her and get to know her first.
Peter Walker, author, yoga teacher and physical therapist specialising in mothers and babies

Understanding your baby

Babies are very social beings and they are in need of 'conversation' as much as they are of being held and being provided with food and warmth.
Royal College of Paediatrics and Child Health[1]

Babies are born ready to communicate and interact with adults, so ignore anyone who repeats the tired old myth that infant expressions of pleasure in the first six weeks are only due to wind.

Our babies communicate their feelings and needs to us through gestures, noises and expressions (see First 'Conversations', p.12). As we spend time together – cuddling, listening, watching our baby's actions and reactions, playing and enjoying each other's company – we will interpret and respond to these signs, often without even realising the process is happening. Through this responsiveness – echoing back our baby's sounds, mimicking their movements and expressions, feeding and holding them and beginning to understand their likes and dislikes – confidence between parent and child grows and our relationship will develop and deepen.

As parents of two or more will already know, no two babies are the same and every newborn arrives in the world with their own temperament and distinct characteristics and needs. Some babies are robust, laid back and generally happy to take life as it comes; some are very sensitive and anxious, reacting dramatically to seemingly minor events; most are somewhere in between. All feel most secure when the care they receive is adapted to their own particular needs and preferences.

Babies signal these needs and preferences through their behaviour. This is their 'language', and sometimes the messages are loud and clear and at other times more subtle. Even small hand movements can indicate a change in an infant's level of distress, alertness or interest.[2] By becoming more aware of what our own baby is 'telling' us, tuning into all their subtle cues, we can develop a deeper understanding of how they are feeling at any particular moment, when they need attention and when they need a break.[3]

What are the common 'messages' babies send, and what might they be 'telling' us?

THE 'SIGNAL'	POSSIBLE MEANINGS
Cooing, gurgling, smiling	No problem interpreting this one. The baby's saying 'I'm happy doing this and I'd like to carry on; or 'I want to play' (see The Pleasure Principle, p.15).
Arching back, squirming, turning head away	Parents often feel these gestures as rejection. In fact, they are ways that a baby tells us 'I'm tired', 'I'm uncomfortable', 'I need less stimulation' or 'I need a break'.

THE 'SIGNAL'	POSSIBLE MEANINGS
Crying, whimpering	'I'm hungry/frightened/wet/very tired or perhaps just overwhelmed by too much going on around me – and I need your help to do something about it.'
Yawning, sneezing, looking away, looking down, splaying fingers, clenching fists, rubbing eyes, staring with no expression, sucking on nothing	These subtle clues can be a baby's way of communicating that 'I've had enough of this for now' or 'Something is making me tense'. After a little 'time out' they may be happy to interact again. Changing their environment – perhaps lowering the light or noise in the room, or altering their position to make them more comfortable – may help them relax.
Regurgitating milk (possetting)	This may also be a clue that a baby is becoming upset. By responding now, you may prevent upset escalating into full-throttle distress.
Facial expressions	Use your instincts. A frown, for example, doesn't always indicate annoyance. With some babies, like some adults, a frown may also indicate intensity of concentration.

On a practical level, understanding your own baby's 'language' is invaluable. Once you recognise how your child shows they are getting tired – do they become grouchy? Do they stare vacantly? Do they turn away or signal by other means that they want less stimulation? – it becomes easier to avoid distress through overtiredness. Knowing your baby's tiredness 'cues' will also help you establish settling routines, which they will learn to associate with going to sleep (see Sleep Solutions, p.44). Once you recognise how your baby indicates discomfort, it becomes easier to hold, soothe and settle them generally.

On a deeper level, responding to your baby's 'signals' will also encourage a more secure and trusting relationship between you and, importantly, build your confidence as a parent.[4]

So many parents worry whether they're doing the right thing when caring for their baby. Often they don't seem to realise that the best approach is to watch how the baby's responding, to read the baby's signals and ask 'I wonder what he's

First 'conversations'

Even very young babies can engage in 'conversations'. All it takes it another person who can respond to the baby's facial expressions, gestures and vocalisations with imitations, comments and warm interest.
John Oates, developmental psychologist in the Centre for Human Development and Learning, Open University

Your baby's most important toys are your voice and your face.
Dr Joanna Hawthorne, research psychologist, University of Cambridge, and co-ordinator and trainer at the Brazelton Centre in Great Britain

Babies engage in 'conversations' with the important people in their lives in their very first weeks. They not only respond to engagement and interaction – they actively seek and initiate it.

Newborns arrive in the world primed for communication. They have already learned to recognise their mother's voice while in the womb. Only minutes after birth, they can recognise their mother's smell and show their preference for people rather than objects by turning towards a voice rather than another sound of the same pitch and intensity. Within hours, they can recognise their mother's face and within days can imitate facial expressions, simple vocal sounds and head movements.[5]

See for yourself. If your baby seems contented, comfortable and alert, try slowly mimicking their expressions, sticking out your tongue or opening your mouth, or simply exchanging gazes and smiles. Try to go at their pace, give them time to respond and be sensitive to how they are feeling. Babies, just like parents, tend not to feel much like play if they're hungry, upset or tired, and they'll indicate when they've had enough. Grimaces, glazed stares and turning away can all be signs that they're ready for a break.

At first, babies may only engage in face-to-face play for brief moments, but their interest will develop over time.

Astonishingly, there is now evidence that even *premature* newborn babies may enjoy such 'conversations' with their parents, exchanging coos in a gentle, vocal dance between parent and child that displays what Professor Colwyn Trevarthen, a world authority on infant development, calls the 'innate musicality of infant communication'.

'We have recordings[6] of a father while he is cuddling his two-month-premature baby on

Every new parent or grandparent can find the 'human' in human nature. The adult responds instinctively to the infant's spirit. Beyond needs for parental physical care or comfort, a human baby seeks to engage with a human companion.
Professor Colwyn Trevarthen, Emeritus Professor of Child Psychology and Psychobiology, University of Edinburgh

Place your face about 8–12 inches away from your baby, so your baby can focus, then move slowly from side to side and watch your baby follow you with their gaze. Watch as your baby turns to your voice. These are such simple things, but profoundly comforting and moving. I can't tell you the reactions we get from mothers when we encourage them to do this. One woman burst into tears when her five-day-old son turned to her voice, saying, 'Oh, he does know me. I didn't think he did.' New parents want to know two things – does my baby know me and does my baby like me. These are simple ways we help parents see that they do. They make parents feel far more confident that they are liked and needed.

Dr Joanna Hawthorne, research psychologist, University of Cambridge, and co-ordinator and trainer at the Brazelton Centre in Great Britain

his chest. There evolves a sort of dance, in which the pattern of the baby's sounds changes and the baby pauses for the father to echo them. In effect, baby and father are involved in a conversation, an expressive, emotional narrative.'

Evidence of babies' sensitivity to the nature and timing of our responses also continues to grow. In one study, a nine-week-old baby shown video footage of his mother's cheerful face and voice became distressed and confused. The mother's responses and expressions didn't *feel* like fun to the baby because they weren't appropriate or 'in tune' with his.[7]

So how can parents encourage infant 'conversations'? 'Parents will be doing so by affectionately responding to their baby,' suggests Professor Trevarthen. 'It is very difficult to be conscious of all that goes on because it is so intricate and registers with the parents at such a deep level. So have enjoyment and faith in the process and don't over-analyse, don't distance yourself from your intuition.'

I talk to my third baby in a way I just didn't to my first two, not for any other reason than that I simply didn't know they could be so responsive so early. He is now ten weeks, but we started from when he was born, talking to him and noticing and responding when he 'talks' back. Now, if I stick my tongue out at him, he will copy me. It's very funny. There's no great technique, it's almost as simple as recognising that babies are people from day one. It's about listening to him and allowing him time to respond to you – just as you would pause to let an adult respond in a conversation. It's also about letting the baby sometimes take the initiative and take the lead. He gets so much out of it and so do we.

Careen H

telling us?' The baby will tell us when something is helpful or pleasurable, and when it's not. Observing these subtle changes is what helps parental confidence and understanding to grow.

Dr Joanna Hawthorne, research psychologist, University of Cambridge, and
co-ordinator and trainer at the Brazelton Centre in Great Britain

A young baby may express itself more with delicate hand movements than with its voice. So we need to pay attention to the baby's dance.

Professor Colwyn Trevarthen, Emeritus Professor of Child Psychology and
Psychobiology, University of Edinburgh

Rigid and prescriptive babycare regimes that take no notice of infant individuality will rebound if, as often happens, they don't suit your baby. Parental confidence can be undermined when what was promoted as the 'right way' doesn't work.

By concentrating on what *does* seem to work for *your* baby, you'll all have a more enjoyable time. How does your baby prefer to be held at the moment – upright or horizontally or somewhere in between? How does your baby show this? Do they prefer to lie with their head on one side or another? How do they show you when they're comfortable? What startles your baby? What soothes? (See Crying, p.20.) What interests and stimulates? What is their emotional state right now – tired or alert and ready to 'play'?

These aren't questions to answer all at once but simply to be aware of as you care for your child and as you enjoy and entertain each other. Remember occasionally to ask yourself, 'What signal is my baby giving me? What might it mean?' Remember, too, that you are the world's greatest expert on *your* baby. By tuning in to your baby's interests and preferences, listening to your baby's sounds and watching their gestures before you respond in return, your understanding of your child's characteristics and needs will grow, helping you care constructively and sensitively.

We almost require a shift in understanding, so parents are encouraged to figure out what helps their baby most, and to provide an environment suited to their baby's needs. Parents can then find ways that help them soothe or engage with their particular child. This can be liberating.

Dr Joanna Hawthorne, research psychologist, University of Cambridge, and
co-ordinator and trainer at the Brazelton Centre in Great Britain

The Pleasure Principle

The purely social interactions, sometimes called 'free play', between mother and infant are among the most crucial experiences in the infant's first phase of learning and participating in human events.

Daniel Stern, Professor of Psychology, University of Geneva[8]

Playing with young babies – smiling at them, gently stroking and cuddling them in ways they like, laughing when we find something funny – is a crucial part of getting to know and understand each other.

We can take our baby's lead and be alert to their temperament and mood. Sometimes they may feel like gentle play and find anything more robust too intrusive. Sometimes they may squeal with glee if you blow raspberries on their tum. However you do it, if you can help your child experience delight in themselves and their world, you're one hell of a parent. Shared pleasures are not only vital to babies' self-esteem and therefore crucial to their healthy emotional and behavioural development (see Feelings and Fears, p.124), there is now evidence that they are good for their brains.

There is good evidence that the kind of joy which comes from having a lot of fun with somebody is very good for the brain. Chemical changes in the brain during positive emotions have beneficial effects on brain growth.

Colwyn Trevarthen, Emeritus Professor of Child Psychology and Psychobiology, University of Edinburgh

In the first three years of life, children's brains develop very rapidly, especially those areas of the brain involved in attention, memory, learning and the regulation of emotional arousal. Recent research[9] shows that how each baby's brain develops will depend to a large degree on their experiences and the emotions they learn to connect with those experiences. Babies who receive unresponsive care, or who frequently experience environments they find threatening, tend to develop exaggerated responses to stress and become less able to calm themselves. Conversely, babies who experience sensitive, responsive care and who learn to associate pleasure and positive emotions with everyday experiences develop their capacity to calm, self-comfort and learn.

We can set up opportunities for pleasure (see Baby Massage, p.16), but fun and pleasure can also be a part of what goes on in our daily routine. There will be times when we'll feel as much like having fun as flying to the moon. No person is happy all the time and the combination of little sleep and little baby makes no one feel like a party animal. There is little point faking pleasure if you are not in the mood because children have an uncanny ability to spot inconsistencies between how you feel and what you do. But whenever you genuinely feel it, show your baby that you think they're splendid, gorgeous, loveable, funny.

Baby massage

Peter Walker, author, yoga teacher and physical therapist specialising in mothers and babies

Baby massage provides a whole range of benefits for you and your baby:

— It fosters mutual trust and understanding, and develops your confidence in your ability to handle your baby.
— It can stimulate your baby's immune system and circulation, both of which are immature at birth.
— It aids your baby's digestion. It can relieve constipation.
— It is the perfect preparation for co-ordinated movement and mobility and is a natural response to your baby's inherent need for tactile stimulation.

When can you begin?

Your baby can be massaged soon after birth. Touch is the most developed of the senses at birth, and your newborn baby's prime means of communication.

Do not worry too much about how you stroke the baby – massage at this stage involves doing what feels relaxing, comfortable and right for you both. It has no set technique.

If babies are warm enough they rarely mind if they are clothed or not; however, they often dislike the process of being dressed and undressed in these early weeks. Touch and massage for a newborn can take place at any time, within natural activities and with clothes on. You can also clean and massage your baby with oils every 24–48 hours if it feels comfortable.

Ensure that:

— Your hands are warm and clean.
— You keep the oil away from the baby's face as it can blur vision if it gets into eyes.
— Your baby is lying on a soft, clean, cotton surface (the combination of wool and oil may irritate the skin).
— Your baby is not too full and certainly not hungry. Baby massage is best done between feeds.
— Remember you are doing this *with* your baby, not *to* them. Move the baby in ways they want to go.
— You stop if your baby becomes upset. Return to the massage when they are ready and willing.

If your baby is unwell or has a skin disorder, seek professional advice before massaging. Wait 48 hours after immunisation to see

The early routines and patterns of caring for young babies – feeding, changing, bathing and so on – can become enjoyable rituals which can be made special and fun. There will be recognisable stages or moments in each of them to which the parent and baby can be primed; eye contact is important as an infant can feel 'held' and recognised in this moment. Sounds and tongue responses, movements of legs and arms all express the baby's vigour and pleasure at being together with the parent. These experiences contribute to how a baby begins to discover relationships.

Judith Philo, psychotherapist, social worker and parent adviceline consultant

how they are affected before massaging, avoiding the injection site until it is no longer sensitive.

Massaging Oils

Organic grapeseed and organic sweet almond oil are best. (Many of the mineral-based so-called baby oils are made from petro-chemicals. I do not recommend their use for newborns or babies.)

Introducing a Light Massage

This can be introduced once your baby is happy to be undressed and enjoys being naked (often from about six to eight weeks).

Ensure you are comfortable. Keep your hands well oiled and shake out your hands from time to time to keep them relaxed.

1: Pull your baby's leg through your palms and fingers, hand over hand, from the thigh to foot. Give your baby's leg a gentle shake. Do the same with the other leg.

2: Now do both legs together. Place your well-oiled hands on the inside thighs and pull downwards around the back of the thighs, down the back of the knees and calves and feet.

3: Lay the weight of your open, relaxed hand on your baby's tummy and, without pressing downwards, massage in a clockwise direction This is in the same direction as the baby's digestive system. (Only introduce tummy massage once the cord has healed and the baby has straightened from the foetal position.)

4: Place your hands on the centre of your baby's chest and massage upwards and outwards, over the shoulders. Draw both arms down vertically through the centre of your palms.

5: Rest your hands on the front of your baby's shoulders and draw them downwards over the chest, hips, legs and feet.

6: Lay your baby on their tummy and stroke down the back, hand over hand.

7: With a relaxed open hand, stroke clockwise around the base of the spine and buttocks.

8: Now lay your hands on the back of your baby's shoulders and stroke downwards over the back, down the back of the legs to the feet.

Your baby's needs

Infant urgency

Babies who have not experienced a secure, attuned relationship with attentive adults have greater difficulty establishing such relationships when they are older children and adults.
Royal College of Paediatrics and Child Health[10]

My mother was always on at me to let him 'cry it out'. She would tell me to leave him even if he got distressed.
Angela C

Babies are learning about relationships from birth. Ignore anyone who bleats about making a rod for your own back. Young babies are not 'naughty' or 'manipulative', 'wilful' or 'trying to wrap you around their little finger' – they simply get hungry, hot, cold, windy, wet, frightened, tired, uncomfortable and lonely and need us to do something about it.

Responding to those needs sensitively and promptly is an investment:

1   In the short term, because babies who are comforted quickly when they are distressed tend to cry less after the first three months than those who are not.[11] By responding when our babies tell us they need something, we up the chances of us both having a happier time (see Crying, p.20).

2   In the long term, because by caring and responding we are showing our babies they are safe, secure and valued. Babies who experience this as they grow generally develop greater trust and confidence in themselves and their world, becoming more able to tolerate their mother's absence and more able to explore their environment happily and form relationships with others[12] (see Feelings and Fears, p.124).

This is a relatively short, though intense, phase of our children's lives and the urgency of their needs will gradually diminish over their first few months, as they begin to adjust to life outside the womb, we become familiar with their preferences and foibles and they learn to trust in our care.

Babies feel and express a range of emotions, and tuning in to your baby's feelings by responding appropriately helps your baby gain a sense of closeness and being understood. Showing your love and acceptance of them – when they are feeling bad as well as when they are feeling good – helps them know the mutual pleasures of sharing happy times and that comfort can be found in others. This is an important part of building what psychologists call a 'secure attachment', which research is showing has many advantages for children's later development.

John Oates, developmental psychologist in the Centre for Human Development
and Learning. Open University

Security

How we respond to our babies when we can't settle them easily is just as important as our best days together – it is a valuable lesson in the constancy of our love, that our care and regard are not conditional and that we are there for them even when the going gets tough.

This will support their budding confidence to explore the world around them – to touch, feel, look, listen, reach. Think of it in terms of their voyage into the unknown. It is bound to make them anxious at times, and they will need to keep coming back to us to 'refuel' on comfort and reassurance.

Imagining life from our baby's emotional and physical perspective may help us understand their emotional needs. How would it feel to be them at any particular moment: cuddling up to us? Crying alone in the night? Having a bath?

Putting ourselves in their shoes may also make it easier to understand why something that calmed them yesterday may be a washout today. Are they tired? Feeling off colour? Uncertain? Bored?

It is a question of recognising the interior, or emotional needs of the baby, as well as the physical needs. I think babies are sometimes given very short change. The exterior of the baby is very visible, but the interior is somehow invisible. We wipe the baby's face clean, but we don't really think, 'How do you feel, little baby?'

Ann Herreboudt, midwife and family therapist

Crying

All babies cry and and rightly so. It is their only way of expressing themselves and having their needs met. We tend to view it as a problem, and crying can do dreadful things to us as mothers, but they all need to do it.

Ann Herreboudt, midwife and family therapist

It's not OK for people to tell parents to ignore their baby's cries or to train their baby out of crying. If you ignore a baby, you are simply setting down problems for the future. In the first months especially, it's really important that parents respond.

Eileen Hayes, parenting advisor to the NSPCC

Babies cry. Some babies cry a little, some a great deal. They may be expressing a physical need, an emotional one, or both. Our role as parents is to respond.

We can't always know why our babies are crying, or prevent them doing so. Crying plays an important part in infant development, and it's important we remember this. One reason parents often find crying so stressful is their fear they may be doing something 'wrong' or that there is something 'wrong' with their relationship with their child. The truth isn't anything like so clear-cut. There are many reasons babies cry, and some aren't under our control.

Yet whatever the cause, when a baby cries they need us to respond sensitively. 'Care-by-the-clock' manuals, encouraging parents to 'train' young babies to cry less by ignoring them, have become fashionable again. This is troubling. A huge and growing body of evidence confirms that responding to a baby in their first months of life supports their physical, mental and emotional development and the 'attachment' bond between adult and child. The benefits of these are life-long. Equally, repeatedly ignoring a baby's cries can cause long-term damage.[13]

So seek to comfort and reassure your baby while you try to work out what on earth they may need. And reassure yourself that most mothers depend on nothing more than trial and error, intuition and increasing familiarity with their child's ways.

The more you meet the needs of the infant, the more you go to a crying newborn, the less they cry over time because if the baby's needs are met appropriately, the baby will come to feel secure.

Dr Joanna Hawthorne, research psychologist, University of Cambridge, and co-ordinator and trainer at the Brazelton Centre in Great Britain

The causes of crying

Babies may cry because of hunger, thirst, discomfort or pain (too hot, too cold, nappy wet, nappy rash, etc.), tiredness, wind, fear, after-effects of the birth (foetal distress, drugs and anaesthesia etc.), sudden stimulation, over-stimulation, boredom/frustration, or simply because they're developing just as they should.

As NSPCC parenting advisor Eileen Hayes explains: 'At certain stages – often around three to six weeks and again around six months – there are changes in the baby's developing brain linked to increased crying. These findings are universal. Everywhere in the world the patterns are the same, no matter what the culture or parental care. So parents shouldn't be blamed or blame themselves. The two clear messages from recent research are that there are healthy, developmental reasons why babies cry, but for their healthy development they need us to respond with comforting when they do.'

Important *Crying can also be a sign of illness. Trust your instincts – if your baby's cry is noticeably different from normal, or if you are concerned about your baby's health, contact your doctor or health practitioner.*

Soothing your baby

- Are there any obvious causes (see above)?
- Most young babies cry less when in body contact with their mother,[14] so simply holding a baby or carrying them in a sling will often soothe. Even if they continue to cry, a baby may feel better being held than not. Rocking, rhythmic and gentle patting and singing, stroking and wrapping the baby so they feel 'held' may also help (see Settling for Sleep, p.46).

Excessive crying

I get just as many calls from parents of second, third, fourth babies, who thought they had cracked it but then have a child who cries and cries. Anybody can have a crying baby. This is a great comfort to many first-time mothers who think it is something they are doing wrong, or that they haven't got the maternal instinct or the magic touch.

Louise Walters, Cry-sis helpline for families with excessively crying, sleepless and demanding babies

Nothing can prepare you for it. I felt battered and stretched to my limit. I was scared by how angry it made me feel.

Helen C

It is clear that some children do seem to like being babies more than others. Those who do not may seem frustrated and generally unhappy with their lot, despite their parents' best efforts to comfort and cheer them. The turning point may be when they become more mobile or when they are able to communicate verbally, and the root of their frustration ceases to be.

Dr Elizabeth Bryan, Honorary Consultant Paediatrician at Queen Charlotte's and Chelsea Hospital, London and founder of the Multiple Births Foundation

Around one in 10 babies cry 'excessively' in their first months, and this doesn't seem linked to how they are cared for.[15] Whatever parents do, some babies cry a great deal. The reasons are still not clear, but it is now thought that these babies may have more immature nervous systems and find it harder to calm themselves once they become upset, or they may be particularly sensitive to noise, light or movement.

Amounts vary widely but, on average, babies cry and fret for more than two hours a day for their first three months, most often in afternoons and evenings. This is hard enough, but 10% of infants cry and fret for more than three hours a day, three days a week.

If your baby is one of them, understanding what triggers your baby's distress may help (see Understanding your Baby, p.9). Also try to get some support and practical help for yourself. This is especially important if you're feeling exhausted or have other children who need your attention. Is there a trusted friend or relative who might care for the baby for a short while to give you all a break? (See Your Needs, p.29 and Coping in Hard Times, p.151.)

There are two identifiable crying 'peaks' – approximate periods when a lot of crying is common among babies. One begins around three to six weeks, and may be due to developmental changes in the brain. Very rarely, babies around this age may begin to show signs of gastrointestinal disturbance – what was once termed 'colic' – due to intolerance to cow's milk protein and other elements of breast or bottle milk. The numbers affected are very low. The second crying peak, around seven months to one year, may be linked to changing sleep needs and patterns.

If you are experiencing combined problems – i.e. crying and feeding difficulties – decide which you find most difficult. Tackling problems one at a time may help you feel less overwhelmed. Keeping a diary may help you detect emerging patterns and possible causes. Many parents report success with complementary approaches, such as homoeopathy and cranial osteopathy (see p.50).

Remember also to make the most of times with your baby when the crying has stopped. Cuddling and playing will help you both feel better, and make the tough times a little easier to bear.

Parents may give a baby everything they might need and everything they have to give and still the baby cries. This is what parents find so stressful. After a long time without positive responses from their baby, any parent can snap. In the majority of cases, the reason given for hitting babies or shaking them is that they just wouldn't stop crying. The more you get back from the baby as a parent, by mirroring, cooing, exchanging smiles, the more rewarding parenthood feels and the more able you are to cope.

Eileen Hayes, parenting advisor to the NSPCC

Without support, you may find yourself feeling distressed, exhausted or depressed. Let your partner, relative or trusted friend take over for a while so you can rest or have a break. If you don't, your stress signals will be picked up by your baby who may cry all the more.

Talk matters through with your health visitor, GP or health practitioner, or you may prefer to contact a parents' support group.

If you feel at breaking point, put the baby down safely in the cot and pick up the phone. Call a friend, your partner, the Cry-sis helpline (see Contacts, p.429), anyone who will give you the understanding, help and support you need.

The notion that parents can and should know what to do, always, is nonsense. We'd had two children, then our third was a totally new experience. She screamed her way through the first twelve months.

Professor Hilton Davis, clinical child psychologist and Director of the Centre for Parent and Child Support

My husband would come home to find the baby at one end of the sofa crying and me at the other end doing the same. I felt out of control and totally inadequate. Once she could crawl, she was suddenly happy and our lives turned round.

Karen M

It is important for parents to try to find a way through this period. Don't feel guilty if you can't find anything that works, because sometimes nothing does. If you have to put the baby down because the crying is too awful to bear, of course you will feel wretched, but that doesn't mean you are a bad parent. You are a parent going through a very bad time. And it will pass.

Louise Walters, Cry-sis helpline

*You can't be everywhere at once. That's why I found talking gently
to my baby really helped, especially when I was on the loo or getting her big sister
ready for school and couldn't actually pick her up. It let her know I was there, so
she didn't get into that panic babies do when they feel abandoned.*

Amanda T

- Take your baby's lead. Subtle changes in behaviour and expression may alert you that they're becoming upset or uncomfortable (see Understanding your Baby, p.9).
- Responding sensitively has little to do with knowing the 'right thing' to do and everything to do with understanding what works best for you and your baby. This understanding develops over time.

*Some babies find it harder to adjust to day/night patterns, or are particularly
sensitive to changes and movement. These babies may startle easily or
become distressed by everyday occurrences such as having a nappy change. They
may also find it harder to calm after becoming upset and may need more help
from parents than other babies. Premature babies are more likely to show
this response, but almost one in five healthy, well-developed babies are highly
sensitive in the early weeks.*

Dr Joanna Hawthorne, research psychologist, University of Cambridge, and
co-ordinator and trainer at the Brazelton Centre in Great Britain

- Baby massage (p.16) can be particularly effective in calming 'jumpy' babies who startle easily or who are quickly distressed. It often helps parents feel better, too.
- Try to encourage your baby's abilities to self-comfort. Some babies find this easy, some find it hard, but you may be able to help.

*One mother we saw had put mitts on her baby's hands.[16] The baby was two
days old, and when we took the mitts off the baby immediately put her hands in
her mouth and calmed down. The mother said she'd seen the baby doing this on
the scan, so she had actually learned to self-comfort in the womb but was
prevented from doing so because of the mitts and being wrapped so her hands
couldn't reach her mouth. Simply being aware of how babies self-comfort often
helps mothers support their babies' efforts.*

Dr Joanna Hawthorne, research psychologist, University of Cambridge, and
co-ordinator and trainer at the Brazelton Centre in Great Britain

- If your baby becomes more distressed the more you do to soothe them, they may need less stimulation. Some very sensitive babies need as much peace and quiet as you can provide.

Some babies are overwhelmed by adults trying to comfort them, bouncing them up and down like cocktail shakers when what they need most is peace.

Dr Joanna Hawthorne, research psychologist, University of Cambridge, and co-ordinator and trainer at the Brazelton Centre in Great Britain

- Other babies begin to want more fun as the weeks go by, and become distressed if they don't get it.

One family told me their baby was in pain. In fact he was not enjoying interactions because they were spending all their time trying to comfort him while he was trying to tell them 'I want to have fun.' This was a robust, thriving baby, crying because he wasn't getting the kind of attention he needed.

Dr Joanna Hawthorne, research psychologist, University of Cambridge, and co-ordinator and trainer at the Brazelton Centre in Great Britain

- Be pragmatic. Learning what your baby likes best involves trial and error and watching how your baby responds. Avoid trying too many different things in too short a time or you'll both feel frazzled, but if you hit on something that helps you through a particularly bad crying phase, use it. Feed your baby, carry your baby, snuggle down with your baby, consider that dummy you vowed would never enter your home, do whatever it takes to help you both get through the day; you can always return to your 'normal' routines once you and your baby are less stressed and less needy.
- No young baby should be left in distress (see Sleep Solutions, p.44). Yet some babies do cry or fret a little before they fall asleep, often more in protest than upset. If this happens, picking up your baby the instant they grizzle may over-stimulate rather than soothe. It may also prevent them learning how to fall asleep on their own (see Emerging Patterns, p.46). Listen to your instincts and respond in the way you think is right and appropriate to your baby's needs at that moment.

My first child would love to be cuddled for hours on end. When my second child, my son, was three weeks old I realised he cried less if I put him down after a feed. He'd cry for a few seconds then fall asleep, whereas when I tried to comfort

him he became more agitated because I was actually stopping him sleeping.
Every child is different.

Dr Joanna Hawthorne, research psychologist, University of Cambridge, and
co-ordinator and trainer at the Brazelton Centre in Great Britain

- If all else fails, put your baby in a pram or sling and go for a walk. The rhythmic movement may help them settle and the change of environment may help you both.
- As babies grow, their needs will change. By observing what they respond to well, and how this shifts over time, we'll be able to adapt our care.

Learning fast

Getting appropriate responses to their behaviours and feeling nurtured fosters babies' brain development. It helps them become co-operative and competent and it inspires learning and exploration.

Dr Joanna Hawthorne, research psychologist, University of Cambridge, and
co-ordinator and trainer at the Brazelton Centre in Great Britain

Your baby is taking in information about themselves and their world at an astonishing rate. As ever, you are their most important and effective teacher and your reactions and responses will have a profound influence on what they learn and how they feel about themselves and the objects, people and places around them as they grow.

By taking your baby's lead, adapting your play to what suits your baby best and being aware of what babies may enjoy at different ages and stages, you can make the most of your relaxed times together.

At around four months, many babies enjoy attempting simple gestures and 'musical' sounds in response to familiar nursery rhymes and action songs such as 'Round and round the garden' and 'This

Little Piggy' – sensing what comes next and sharing the fun. By six months, many babies delight in new-found physical skills and exuberant play, waving their arms, kicking legs and moving however they can.

Some babies need no encouragement to play, while others need lots of attention and stimulation before they perk up. The key, as ever, is to watch for all the signals each baby gives about what they enjoy and how they are feeling. By watching their responses, we can discover which games they like and how they prefer to play and how we can best encourage their exploration and enjoyment of their world.

A very active baby may enjoy robust physical play, for example, whereas a less active or sensitive child may respond better

After six months or so, babies may start to experience new fears, such as separation anxiety. The sorts of comforting they respond to is changing, too. As well as just holding and comforting, they respond well to engagement and distraction, with toys to interest and amuse.

Eileen Hayes, parenting advisor to the NSPCC

Everything changes over time, and it can change very quickly. Babies can change their habits and routines virtually overnight and, because it changes, even bad times do not last long.

Ann Herreboudt, midwife and family therapist

if introduced to new experiences more gently. Many less active children like moving to music, especially when their parents join in. We can use this knowledge to expand their experiences and confidence by, say, playing their favourite tune while playing a gentle game of ball together.

The speed and sophistication of babies' learning has surprised many researchers in the field. At six months, they already know the basics of social interaction.[17] By one year they show interest in objects and tasks that interest the important people around them, and even display rudimentary social etiquette, such as waving goodbye.

'They have a lot of favourite objects and are interested in what others do around them,'[18] says Professor Colwyn Trevarthen. 'They like to show off how they can use objects that others use, say, a vacuum cleaner or a pencil. This shared interest is the prerequisite for learning language and much more.

'Children become very clever at their mannerisms by this age, too – they can show off, clap hands, wave and so on. They are learning etiquette, conventional behaviour. They are also learning about institutions and already know the difference between, say, a shop and a play field and the different things that happen there. They have accumulated a great deal of knowledge and cultural awareness, often before they can say their first word.'

Your baby will be registering your responses to people and objects around them. As infancy researcher John Oates explains: 'Older babies make use of emotions their mothers show towards another person or object to decide what their own reaction should be. For example, if a mother shows positive reactions to one toy and negative reactions to another, their baby is much more likely to choose the first to play with.'

Consider this next time you grimace at the contents of a nappy or laugh with friends or flinch at the sight of a dog – our own positive and negative responses are some of our children's most powerful lessons in how they feel about themselves and their world.

Moments alone

Caring for and responding to babies does not require us to carry and cuddle them in our every waking moment. Some babies, particularly those who seem overwhelmed by stimulation, may relax more easily when put down (see Sleep Solutions, p.44). Even babies who delight in lots of close physical contact may be happy to spend brief periods in their own company, physically separate from their mother, as the months go by and they grow in confidence and trust.

This brief quiet time alone is important for older babies' emotional development and will help you both cope better with those times when the phone rings or the pan boils and you need to put your baby down.

Infancy is very much about responding to the baby's needs but gradually there will be times when the baby is awake and doesn't need to have anything practical done for him; when enjoyment in a quiet time may occur. As the baby awakes, ask yourself whether you need to pick him up straight away. This also depends on the infant and whether and how you are summoned, but being awake and quiet, feeling secure about being alone and being able to take in this experience and the sensations around him plays a very important part in the child's development of relationships and his sense of his own individuality.

Judith Philo, psychotherapist and parent adviceline consultant

It is a gradual process that is best not forced. If your baby is happy, for example, you might leave them in the cot for a short while rather than picking them up straight away. From around three months, as babies become more aware of their environment, mobiles and other safe cot toys may amuse them when they first wake.

Just as some parents find the extreme dependency of a newborn baby delicious and others find it difficult, so some find the first signs of their baby's fledgling independence a very bittersweet experience. Yet raising children is sometimes about 'letting go' and allowing our children to move on to the next stage when they are ready.

Some parents find these transitions hard. You may have got some kind of a routine sorted out, you know where you are, and then it's time to go into something different again. But it is part of the job of being a parent.

Paula Bell, health visitor

Your needs

At first the parents' needs may be met by attending 100% to the newborn, but soon their own needs must arise – simply having a bath or preparing a meal – so the balancing act begins. If we listen to ourselves and to our babies, we can usually mediate successfully between the two.

Barbara Dale, parenting counsellor and psychotherapist

I had to shake myself up, remember to do some things for me. Looking after yourself is a habit, I think, and one that's pretty hard to establish but I knew I must start so I could keep us all going.

Anne-Marie I

Recognising our own needs is important throughout parenthood, but never more so than during our babies' first weeks and months. Look after yourself a little more whenever you can and you and your baby may feel the benefits.

Expectations v. reality

I didn't expect it, but from the moment he was born it felt like he'd always been here. There were times when I hoped I was doing the right thing, but I never panicked. It all seemed to unfold.

Lisa F

For me, the birth was the first thing I hadn't been able to sort out, control or otherwise fix in my entire adult life. The baby was the second.

Nicola B

I was breastfeeding him in bed at night. I'm still not sure how it happened but he slipped off the pillow and landed in the wastepaper bin.

Alison Y

New parenthood is full of clashes between expectation and reality. It may be much better or much harder than you predicted, or both. Whatever your experience, it may help to remember that:

1 Babies in advertisements do not cry, scream, throw up down your back or wake at horrible times. Mothers in advertisements are usually smiling and have had time to brush their hair. Real life is not always like this.

2 As a human being you are entitled to emotions, needs, strengths, weaknesses and the right sometimes to get things wrong.

3 Life will get easier. The emotional and physical demands on new parents are huge, and the first months are particularly intense. This isn't how it's going to be for ever.

We will never be perfect parents, our children will never be perfect children, and that is as it should be. Burden ourselves with unnecessary guilt or unrealistically high expectations and we risk focusing on what isn't happening rather than what is – an evolving relationship between two unique individuals.

We need to trust our intuition but also remember that we are only human. There will be times when we misread the signs or when we don't have a clue why our child isn't settling. Sometimes life goes in ways parents cannot interpret, control or predict.

The fact also remains that some babies arrive in the world more anxious and less easy to comfort than others (see Understanding your Baby, p.9). We recognise the importance of individuality in older children and adults but, bizarrely, often expect babies to conform to predictable patterns of behaviour and response.

Children are born with their own individual characters and needs. Even among identical twins, the difference in their temperaments may be evident very soon after birth and the mother may find that what soothes one baby may not suit another, what may entertain one may annoy his or her sibling. If one approach doesn't seem to work, the mother must try not to blame herself – the technique may be a fine one, the way she did it may be admirable, but it simply may not have been the right one for that baby at that time.

Dr Elizabeth Bryan, Honorary Consultant Paediatrician at Queen Charlotte's and Chelsea Hospital, London and founder of the Multiple Births Foundation

As if caring for your new baby isn't enough, the weeks following the birth are a time of deep and powerful emotions (see Baby Blues, p.32). The birth experience leaves many women feeling shocked and battered. Some feel profoundly disappointed if it was very different to their hopes and dreams.

Most women also have to cope with new and major life changes

Who mothers new mothers?

Our experiences of new motherhood depend hugely on the amount of support we receive. Many women are cosseted and given the time and help they need to adjust, recover and enjoy. Many more are not . . .

Chinese, Japanese, many cultures insist on the new mother resting for the first month. It is often called 'doing the month', when the mother is looked after by their families. Here, the focus after birth goes straight to the baby and the mother is expected to just carry on as soon as she is on her feet. She needs to recover properly, over about nine months.

Peter Walker, yoga teacher and
physical therapist

My aunt came to the hospital and dressed my baby in the shawl and other clothes my family had made and sent, so symbolically the child was wrapped in the family's love. She brought me and my husband and child home, where my favourite foods had already been prepared. Prayers were said with a lantern and flowers, and we ate. I then fed my baby and he slept. When the sun went down, she warmed her hands on the prayer lamp and gave me a very deep massage. I was then wrapped in warm towels and she ran me a bath with the petals plucked from the flowers. She washed me and dried my hair, and put me into bed where I slept wonderfully. As well as the care it was hugely important for me symbolically. It made me feel I was welcomed into motherhood. All the customs are done as recognition of the gateway to change, to welcome and guide the woman as she has just become a mother.

Sangamithra C

I'm not good at staying in bed and I don't believe having a baby should be thought of as an affliction. But because I was up and about, my partner thought I must be OK. I was exhausted but I didn't ask for help. I somehow hoped he'd realise.

Claire T

beyond the birth of their child: stopping work, even if temporarily; adjusting to a new and unfamiliar role; coping with cuts in household income; isolation from former social networks.

Having a child can stir up memories and emotions rooted in our own experiences of childhood and our own relationships with our parents. Add to these all those changes in role, identity, sex life, money and power that can cause seismic shifts in the relationship between the new parents (see Important Relationships, p.250) and you have a highly potent mix. Understanding and recognising these pressures may help us be a little gentler on ourselves (see Consider Yourself, p.41).

I can't remember individual days or events very well from those first weeks. It's more of a blur. I do remember doing contortions in the kitchen, jiggling her up and down while I did the washing up, and those long nights and that sense of never, ever getting any time for myself. We had this unspoken fear that this was how life was going to be from then on.

Margaret S

Baby blues

Around half of all mothers experience the 'baby blues' in the first week to 10 days after the birth of their baby.[19] The symptoms, linked to maternal exhaustion and hormonal changes following the birth, usually disappear after a few hours or, at most, a few days.

The most common symptom is tearfulness. Many mothers feel very emotional and upset. Some feel anxious and tense. Other symptoms include mood swings, memory lapses, sleeplessness, loss of appetite and a feeling of helplessness and confusion – all of which may be exacerbated if you are exhausted or experiencing problems feeding your baby.

Mothers who have the blues should be allowed to cry and express their fluctuating emotions. They need as much rest as possible (the Association of Postnatal Illness recommends at least one proper rest in bed every day until the baby is several weeks old) and reassurance that the symptoms are common and usually pass quickly. Practical help in the home can be particularly useful at this time. Many mothers also find it helpful to talk through their experiences of the birth and new motherhood with someone they trust.

If you feel the symptoms are worsening or the feelings of depression last longer than a few days, it may be that you are experiencing the onset of post-natal depression (see p.36). It is important to consult your GP or health visitor.

Let me in!

It is so important to focus on the family rather than just the woman after the birth of a child. The whole family is in a period of transition.

Yehudi Gordon, consultant gynaecologist and obstetrician, specialising
in holistic health

Because they carry their baby for nine months mothers usually have a 'good start' while fathers have a lot of catching up to do. Some mothers also find it difficult to 'give up' their baby in a way that is not quite the same for fathers who, in contrast, often find it very difficult and even frightening when they have to adapt to the intense, loving and emotional arousal generated by their infant.

Royal College of Paediatrics and Child Health[20]

The mother-baby bond is intense. Other family members may feel it is impenetrable. Partners may feel like a spare part, wondering what their role should be and what relationship they can nurture with a baby so focused on mum. Older siblings can feel excluded, unaware that they had their time of infant dependency.

It took me a long time to understand that all the wonderful love between my partner and our baby was something to enjoy and not feel jealous of.

Martin S

Every member of the family needs to feel valued and supported through this huge change in family life and to feel confident they can develop an understanding and loving bond with the new baby. How we encourage these feelings of appreciation and understanding can make a huge difference to all family relationships, so it's worth taking time to imagine how life must feel for partners and older children right now – and what might help (see Siblings, p.279, and The Role of Fathers, p.253).

Being anxious is nothing to be ashamed of. First time fathers have usually not had much practice holding babies and babies are so small and fragile . . . But you can learn. Relax before you pick up the baby. Smile at the baby. Touching may be the best way of developing the bond at first.

David Cohen, *The Fathers' Book*[21]

New research shows that encouraging new fathers to 'tune in' to their infant's ways of communicating can increase their involvement and understanding dramatically.[22] (see Understanding your Baby, p.9). Sharing what you know of the baby's behaviour and feelings can help other adults and children develop a caring and loving bond and feel part of the 'charmed circle' of understanding and responsiveness. Simply pointing out the baby's responses can help all family members feel important and involved in the new baby's life:

'Look, he's sticking his tongue out. If you do it back to him, he may do it back.'

'That's his way of playing.'

'Look, she's smiling at you.'

'He's screwing up his face. Do you think he's uncomfortable or perhaps he needs a nappy change?'

'She loves it when you stroke her like that.'

Once family members become more aware of the baby's 'signals' and what they mean, they can respond more sensitively. These are the beginnings of considerate, affectionate and fun relationships. Once they understand what the baby enjoys and what makes the baby smile and chuckle, they can have their first 'games' together.

Men have major life changes after a baby is born. Their partner gets a lot of positive attention in the pregnancy and the birth, and is now focusing on someone else. Men can feel very left out and, importantly, often have even fewer places to go and talk things through. As the bond between mother and baby develops, the father can feel a sense of increasing separation from his partner, particularly if the parents had a very close relationship before the baby was born.

Ann Herreboudt, midwife and family therapist

One of the hardest things is letting my partner or my little girl care for the baby. I really do know what our baby likes and doesn't like better than anyone else and it's so hard letting someone else do it without being hypercritical.

Kate H

Help and advice

You are very vulnerable at this time and there is no great gain in pretending otherwise. You and the baby are like sponges and you need to be careful who you have around you. Learn to say 'no' kindly. In my experience 'second and third timers' keep unhelpful visits to a minimum, having learned first time round. I took tranquillisers when my mother-in-law came to visit following the birth of my first child. Second time I only let her come on my terms.

Gill Wood, NCT ante-natal teacher

It is very important for staff to understand how vulnerable and sensitive new mothers are. Sometimes staff might label the baby: good, bad, greedy, naughty, a handful. This can be incredibly damaging to the new relationship as parents do not forget what they are told. It is very important that anyone working with new babies and parents are extremely careful about the words they use.

Dr Joanna Hawthorne, research psychologist, University of Cambridge, and co-ordinator and trainer at the Brazelton Centre in Great Britain

We need to develop two skills – asking for and accepting help and advice when it's useful, plus a diplomatic method of getting rid of those who think they're helping but aren't. Don't underestimate the importance of either.

You may receive much advice. Too much. Most of it well-meant, outdated and contradicted completely by the advice you were given ten minutes earlier. Babies should be picked up, put down, carried, jiggled, stroked, sat up, laid down, across your knee, over your shoulder . . . Friends and relatives may try to extrapolate a theory from their own, very particular experiences and tell you all about what worked for them as if it should be carved in stone. They are only trying to help, but it would be most helpful if they remembered that different babies like different things and that you'll soon know what yours responds to best. Babies' needs change, so be willing to change tack and try something new if your once-successful technique now fails. But avoid trying every bit of advice at once or you and your baby will feel completely bamboozled.

What you may need most after your baby is born is practical support – cooking, washing and ironing, all the boring but essential bits – and emotional support, someone whose company boosts your confidence rather than undermines it, and who knows how to help without taking over.

Understanding post-natal depression

*Within a few days of having my second child, I was feeling very stressed out.
The feelings just grew worse. You think that if you say anything they'll take your
children away, but I knew I had to do something. In the end my health visitor
walked through the door and I just said, 'I hate my baby. What are we going to
do about it?' By this stage I didn't even want to be in the same house as him, let
alone hold him. I felt isolated and terrified. My health visitor made me see my
GP, who was very good. I also decided to tell my family and friends, who have
been so understanding and supportive. My son is coming up to a year and a half
and I feel so differently towards him, it's incredible.*

Belinda M, former PND sufferer and telephone counsellor
for the Association

Contrary to popular belief, not all post-natally depressed women have trouble bonding with their child or reject them in some way. Neither does PND always occur soon after the birth – it may not be noticeable for several weeks, even months, after the baby is born.

PND affects one in 10 mothers who've recently given birth. If left untreated, it can cause distress to mother and baby, yet PND is rarely mentioned in baby and childcare books. We owe it to ourselves and those around us to be more informed and understanding about the condition and its consequences.

The Association for Post-natal Illness is clear in its guidance: 'Do remember that this is a condition which always results in complete recovery.'[23] But the longer it remains untreated the longer it can last, and the longer both mother and baby can suffer. Three-quarters of PND sufferers will not seek any form of medical help.[24] This may be partly due to the pressures on mothers to pretend that all is rosy, and partly due to a general unawareness of the illness and its symptoms.

Most sufferers experience a combination of the symptoms listed below in varying degrees, from mild to incapacitating. All may also be symptoms of other conditions, so expert help and diagnosis is vital.

— **Depression** Mother feels depressed, despondent and unable to cope. May cry frequently, feel rejected by family and baby.

— **Tiredness** Feelings of tiredness, lack of energy and inability to concentrate. Even simple tasks feel confusing and overtiring.

— **Anxiety** Mother may feel worried about her own health and experience severe but inexplicable pain (often in head, neck, back or chest). May also have unjustified worries about the health and well-being of other family members, especially the baby. May feel too anxious to go out, meet friends or even answer the telephone.

— **Fear** A fear of being left alone is a common but passing phase of the illness. Someone close to the mother should always be with her during this time.

— **Panic** Unpredictable feelings of confusion and panic about everyday situations.

— **Tension** Unable to relax. Tense and irritable, sometimes feeling on the point of explosion.

— **Obsessional and inappropriate**

thoughts A common but frightening symptom, often focused on a particular person (perhaps the baby), a situation or activity. A mother may fear she may harm her child. Such fears are almost entirely unjustified, but she should tell her family and doctor so she can receive treatment to recover from this distressing phase of the illness. The companionship of a friend or relative may be reassuring until this phase passes.

— **Sleeping difficulties** Often, even when the baby is asleep (see Sleep and You, p.64).

— **Sex** Loss of interest in sex. A return of sexual desire is often the last sign that a depression has lifted, and great patience and sensitivity is required if a relationship is to be kept intact while the mother recovers (see Sex, p.251).

List adapted, with kind permission, from 'Post-natal Depression', produced by the Association for Post-natal Illness

Family and friends should ensure that mothers with PND receive the help and support they need from health professionals and others. If the mother feels unable to visit her doctor or health visitor, a home visit should be requested. Be aware that the illness is a temporary one, and that it is usually inadvisable to separate mother and baby as this can deepen the depression. The mother needs support and care; she doesn't need someone to 'take over'.

Mothers should try to eat regularly and rest, as tiredness and irregular meals seem to make symptoms worse. There is also growing evidence that 'listening therapy' – listening to the mother's problems in a supportive, non-judgemental way – is helpful for at least a third of mothers with depression.[25] You may find it helpful to talk to an understanding, sympathetic friend, or to another mother who's had PND and recovered (see Association for Post-natal Illness, Contacts p.429).

If you feel you are experiencing the onset of PND (also see Baby Blues, p.32), it is important to consult your GP or health visitor as soon as possible to discuss the problem and possible treatments. Many mothers recovering from PND feel very isolated. Try, when you can, to meet up with friends and other mothers of babies and young children (see Meeting Others, p.39 and Contacts, p.429).

My son was 18 months old when I was finally persuaded to go to the doctor. I hadn't felt angry towards him, or rejected him, but I was very over-protective. All my emotions were for him and I had nothing for anybody else, including myself. I had this overwhelming fear of losing him, I thought he was going to die. If he didn't finish off all his food, every mouthful, I'd worry. I hated every minute of our holiday because I hated being so far away from our GP in case something went wrong. I was having panic attacks. I thought I was going mad.
I was so shocked when I was told I had post-natal depression. I feel it is behind me now, but if anyone feels they may be suffering from it, my advice is, for God's sake talk to someone. You are not going mad, nobody will take your baby away, and you will get better.

Alison H, former PND sufferer and telephone counsellor for the Association for Post-natal Illness

It is important to realise that apparent support is only as supportive as the woman experiences it to be.

Sarah Darton, health visitor

Asking for practical help can be hard, but think of it as asking for the support you require to give your baby what they need. Asking for advice can be even harder, especially in the face of such potent myths as the omniscient maternal instinct and our ridiculously high expectations of our own capabilities and understanding.

Do not struggle on alone If you want advice, seek it. Whatever you are going through, someone will have been through it before and information and support are available that will benefit both you and your baby (see Contacts, p.429).

Be realistic It's unusual to get the right help or information on your first enquiry. Some relatives, friends and health professionals are great communicators, bursting with appropriate advice and full of understanding of your situation. Others are not. But try not to let their shortcomings put you off your search for constructive support.

Many parent support groups and organisations now have their own websites, while telephone advicelines have the advantage of total anonymity for those who still feel uncertain about seeking help. But remember that no parent can know how to deal with every eventuality. There should be no embarrassment in admitting this, and the more of us who do, the sooner the daft and damaging fiction of the perfect parent will crumble.

I'd called a helpline about my baby's crying and the advisor obviously realised I felt dreadful about doing it. She told me that it is not bad or incompetent mothers who seek advice, but ones who care enough to want to solve their problem and who are responsible and motivated enough to seek the information they need. That really helped. And the advice was invaluable, for the baby and for me.

Jo W

Meeting others

We lack groups in which parents can talk through the day-to-day situations they face. It may seem boring to someone outside the situation, but that day-to-day stuff is what people are scrabbling with, it's life and if it is a problem you can feel dragged down. If you've got the support of others in a similar situation it can help you take pitfalls in your stride.

Paula Bell, health visitor

It is easy to feel isolated when you have a baby. Where and how you meet up with other parents depends on your circumstances and your interests – it may be a parent and baby group, your local NCT branch or a group of mums who meet in the park. What matters is that you go somewhere where you may find other people with young babies, some of whom you feel comfortable with. Opportunities to talk about life beyond parenthood are important, too.

If you find it hard to mix on your own behalf, bear in mind the positive impact it can have on your child. Babies are astonishingly receptive from a surprisingly early age, and the foundations of their ability to socialise are laid by what they see their parents do and by the opportunities they are given to be with other children.

Where, once, people would have raised children within the extended family and could go round the corner to their mum, their aunt, whoever, for that all-important change of scene and the opportunity to diffuse a possibly fraught situation by just being some-where else, the chances are that network is not available now. It is very important that parents try to create networks of their own. Whatever the activity, it is a way of comparing notes, letting off steam and getting ideas from others in a similar situation.

Vivienne Gross, family therapist

Avoiding competitive parents

Part of this competitive parenting stems from the feeling that we should consider ourselves so lucky to have a baby that no one will admit to having had an awful day, to say, 'He has cried all day, and I have got nothing done.' But honest friends will understand because they've experienced it. Without honesty it all gets terribly confusing as to what is normal.

Christine Chittick, NCT ante-natal teacher

Be warned – competitive parents are out there, smiling radiantly at child clinics, beaming smugly at baby groups, offering unsolicited tips to soothe your screaming baby in the Sainsbury's queue. These are not the parents who are so happy at their lot that they can't help but show it, but those whose happiness is bolstered by the fact that their baby is fatter, longer, quieter, louder, sleepier, more alert, in fact anything more than yours. They are to be avoided where possible because they are bad for your soul and your sanity.

New parents, especially, have a habit of comparing the progress of their child with others. Eventually you will learn to laugh, understand exaggeration as an extension of pride, and ignore it. When your baby is young, however, you are easy prey.

My daughter was premature and seemed to do most things long after the other babies at my post-natal group. When they were laughing, she failed to perform apart from the occasional fart. By about six months she'd caught up, and some mothers found it hard to contain their disappointment. But I do understand that urge to compare – I've had three children and even now find myself thinking, 'Oh God, mine's got the smallest head here' or quietly swelling with pride when he claps on cue.

Clare T

Your baby is an individual who, like any other, will do some things fast and some things slower and most things in between. It is remarkably easy to start poring over developmental charts, but the routine developmental checks with your health visitor will pick up the rare instances when a child's progress is cause for concern. The vast majority of children fall within the very wide band of what is considered 'normal', and attempting to speed a child to the next developmental stage can often do more harm than good.

There is still a friendly battle between mothers as to which child will walk and talk first. Yet encouraging children to skip the crawling phase by plonking them prematurely in an upright position in a baby walker, for instance, is not good. Baby walkers are used at a time when children do not have the developmental capabilities to use them safely, and when they can, they don't need them any more. They can delay steps being taken or even lead the child to miss important parts of their development. Natural developmental stages are there for a reason and it is neurologically detrimental to leave them out.

Penelope Robinson, Director of Professional Affairs, the Chartered Society
of Physiotherapy

Consider yourself

As parents we all need encouragement to look after ourselves better, and to give ourselves treats. Without that, we risk burn-out.

Candida Hunt, Family Links

Our children won't give a damn whether their tops match their bottoms or the house hasn't been dusted for weeks. They will care if we don't eat properly or if we've had so little sleep, support and time to unwind that we're completely exhausted.

It happens, often. Most parents go through stages when, out of necessity or circumstance, their needs are completely subsumed by those of their children. The trick is to avoid this when we can, so we have the energy to cope when we can't.

Think of your body as a car, and rest and relaxation as the petrol it needs to keep going. Giving to yourself simply fills up the tank so you are able to keep running smoothly and nurturing others. Think of three things that you will do for yourself each day without feeling guilty – they may be as simple as eating a chocolate biscuit, switching the phone off for an hour, phoning a friend. But by doing this, and establishing a habit of doing this, it becomes much easier to remember you have needs, too. It is good for your self-esteem – it is saying to yourself you are worth it.

Gill Wood, NCT ante-natal teacher

Introducing our needs into the equation may be in very small ways initially. Having a trusted friend babysit may give you a rare opportunity for some uninterrupted sleep; be brave enough to ask and remember people often like to be needed. A walk in the sunshine may give your baby the comfort of your company and you the chance of fresh air, exercise and a change of scene.

Try to make at least a little time for relaxation (see Relaxation through Breathing, p.42). This is not indulgence, it is an investment for you and your family. How you choose to relax is up to you – it may be by fulfilling your need for adult company, for solitude, for exercise, for a video and a takeaway – but try to include a bit of pampering and a bit of peace somewhere along the line. If you simply don't have the time, try to work out what needs to be done to get it.

Relaxation through breathing

Lolli Stirk, pregnancy and post-natal yoga teacher

Being a parent, particularly first-time parents of a new baby or a toddler, can sometimes feel like being 'on duty' 24 hours a day. Taking time out to relax can make the difference between enjoying your baby or just feeling trapped and exhausted. Having someone look after your baby, and going out with your partner to remember who you were before the child came along is vital. Shorter, concentrated, 10-minute relaxation breaks also help, and can be as refreshing as a couple of hours' sleep. What follows is a short visualisation exercise to encourage deep relaxation through breathing.

1: Lie on the floor, drawing your knees in towards your belly.

2: Wrap your arms around your bent legs and 'cuddle' them towards your body.

3: Stay like that for a couple of breaths and then put your feet down on the floor. They should be close to your bottom, hip-width apart and slightly turned in.

4: With the next couple of exhalations become aware of your lower back releasing and dropping towards the floor. Then give yourself an enormous hug, slipping your fingertips under your shoulder blades to open the space between the shoulder blades.

5: To open them up even more, snuggle your chin down into your chest and for the next couple of exhalations feel the upper spine sinking down into the floor, drawn by gravity. Then let your arms drop heavily down to your sides, palms turned upwards.

6: For a few moments imagine you are lying on the sand on a warm, sunny beach with your feet just touching the edge of the water. Slowly bring your attention to your breath and observe how it enters and leaves your body, how it rises and falls just like the waves of the sea. Now, as you inhale, imagine you are drawing the breath like the waves of the sea, up through the soles of your feet through your legs, pelvis, chest, shoulders, head. The inhalation fills you with everything you need – oxygen, energy and lightness.

7: As you exhale feel the wave of the breath sweep down your body back towards the sea, taking with it your toxins and your tiredness and stroking you into a deeper relaxation.

8: Keep your attention focused on each cycle of breath and become particularly interested in the pause at the end of the exhalation. Let your body dictate the rhythm of your breath as it does when you are sleeping, while you observe and enjoy the benefits that come with spending time focusing on your breathing.

Baby's Needs, Your Needs: A Quick Reminder

- Discovering your baby's language – coos, gurgles, gestures, expressions – will nurture your developing bond.
- Your responsiveness to your baby is key to your relationship, now and in the future. Babies and children develop increasing independence from foundations of security.
- It's an obvious point but one too often missed: every baby is unique. Some cry more than others; some sleep more than others; some are laid back; some are highly sensitive. Recognising your baby's rhythms and how your baby expresses needs and emotions will help you respond sensitively and constructively.
- Life can feel a rush. Taking the time to play with your baby can help you both find delight in each other's company and support you both when times are hard.
- Caring for your baby may be demanding and tiring in ways you'd never imagined. You need to look after your own needs occasionally so you are able to look after your child. Be kind to yourself.

CHAPTER TWO
SLEEP SOLUTIONS

It's my weakest spot. If they don't sleep, I don't sleep and if that happens night after night after night, I begin to fray at the edges. I get ratty and unreasonable and desperate.

Ruth H

Children and parents need sleep. Lack of it can damage health and relationships, which is why we've dedicated a whole chapter to the subject. Sleep deprivation is a very effective form of torture and only those who have survived periods without it will know what this can do to your brain, your body, your patience and your sense of humour. Helping your child develop child- and parent-friendly sleep patterns will help you both have the resources you need to appreciate life's high spots and deal with its difficulties.

How you do this matters. Certain baby 'sleep-training' methods, still advocated by some childcare books, are so harsh, so early in a baby's life that they risk doing much more harm than good. Undermining a baby's trust in their parents' responsiveness can damage relationships and children's emotional and cognitive development. As if this isn't bad enough, harsh techniques aren't even a recipe for extra sleep, as insecure children tend to cry more in the long run than those whose parents respond sensitively to their needs.

So, for the sake of parent *and* child, this chapter attempts to balance the needs of all family members, offering approaches that respect and build upon the developing parent-child relationship, and offering insights into common sleep problems and effective long-term solutions.

Babies and sleep

Newborn needs Young babies need feeding and attention through the night. They have no control over when they sleep and when they wake and have yet to spot the difference between night and day.

Some people do have babies who sleep for chunks of the night from a very early age, but their ability to soothe and settle their child may have very little to do with this. Sleep patterns in the very young are due partly to circumstance – birth weight, birth experience and so on – and partly luck. Just like adults, babies have widely varying sleep patterns and needs and those of young babies can be particularly erratic.

So the first thing to remember is that your baby's sleeplessness is not your fault. If this eases some of the anxiety, frustration and sense of inadequacy most parents carry along with the baby as they pace up and down the bedroom in the small hours, it's worth knowing.

We all have expectations and when things do not happen as we expect – for example, when the baby doesn't sleep at night – we see it as something to rectify. Sometimes it is better to be able to step back and recognise that the baby is just not ready for it yet. When a couple comes to me for advice it is because they feel something is wrong – that there is a problem with their baby or that they are bad parents or wrong parents. Mostly, however, what we are dealing with is a normal developmental pattern in a normal baby.

Ann Herreboudt, midwife and family therapist

If anyone asks, it *is* possible to get a baby to sleep for twelve hours through the night from a very early age. A few babies do this naturally, the rest are programmed to do it in early infancy by being fed by the clock and trained not to expect either milk or attention at night – i.e. they learn that their cries will be ignored. To show tiny babies that their cries will not be responded to, that their need for comfort, care and love are worth little, seems a peculiar path to take.

For most parents, the first weeks are more a matter of sleeping when they can, of gradually tuning in to how best their baby likes to be settled and soothed, of recognising and responding to the baby's emerging patterns (see Understanding your Baby, p.9) and holding on to the fact that these are early days and it *will* get easier.

Many parents worry that life will always be like this, but in fact this early part of a baby's life is over so quickly. As a parent, you do need to be generous with your time.

Eileen Hayes, parenting advisor to the NSPCC

Emerging patterns

With my first baby, I was so anxious that she had a sleep routine before I went back to work that I attempted strict bedtimes too soon. It backfired – she'd be crying, I'd be crying. Second time round I was more aware of a little baby's needs for comfort before we moved on to any of that. It's never easy, but it was certainly easier, and my second child was more settled generally by the time I returned to work.

Amanda T

Settling for sleep: 0–6 months

Remembering where newborn babies have come from – a dark, warm, sometimes noisy womb where all their needs were instantly met – may help us better understand and respond to their needs in their first weeks.

Understanding each child's signals and rhythms and developing a relationship of responsiveness and trust takes time (see Understanding your Baby, p.9). Many infants will show similar patterns of rest and activity to those they had in the womb but gradually, with our help, they will develop patterns more attuned to the rest of the family. By trial and error and watching and listening to our baby's responses, we'll begin to understand what soothes them most. We'll then be able to match our settling routines to their individual preferences and needs.

It may help to consider the following:

— What does your baby like best at the moment? Every baby is different, and every baby's needs will change as they grow.

— Many babies like rhythmic rocking or gentle patting of their back, chest or bottom to mimic your heartbeat in the womb. How does your baby like to be held while rocked: upright, horizontal or somewhere in between?

— Check your baby is comfortable and not too hot or cold. Touch their tummy to gauge their temperature.

— Most babies prefer stimulation kept to a minimum, with lights low and no playing. Keep night feeds low-key and keep partners or visitors under control.

— Some babies like no noise, some like background noise, some like music or lullabies (see Crying, p.20).

— If your baby seems fretful, they may relax if you gently massage their tummy (see p.16).

— Some babies like being wrapped or

Most babies are not developmentally mature enough to sleep for long periods without waking in their first months. As the weeks go by, however, their sleep patterns gradually shift towards more night sleeping. Babies also tend to wake from sleep less frequently as they begin to take more milk per feed and the nature of their sleep changes (see Sleep Needs, p.48).

By providing the comfort, cuddles and reassuring responsiveness an infant needs, we can help our babies feel increasingly secure and settled. This security is the foundation from which more parent-friendly sleep patterns can develop as they grow. Attempting to 'train' babies by ignoring their cries at this young age merely risks increasing their anxiety and damaging their confidence in our care (see Sleep Training, p.55). So ignore anyone who mutters about 'spoiling' little babies with sensitive

'swaddled', especially newborns who feel startled by freedom of movement or jerk themselves awake. Use a thin cotton sheet to wrap around them rather than a blanket, and only as much clothing or covering as the room temperature requires. Avoid covering the baby's head and, as ever, don't place the baby on their front. Placing the baby's arms high on their chest, with hands near their face, allows them to suck on their fists and fingers and wriggle free if they need to.

— Remember babies get overtired, too. If this is avoided they're generally easier to settle.

— Many babies like gazing at mobiles with high-contrast patterns, while others find them disturbing.

— Some babies prefer to be put down to fall asleep, as constant body contact over-stimulates them. Some feel soothed by just a hand placed on their back until they drift off. Once they learn to drift off to sleep on their own, by being placed in their cot when comfortable and drowsy, they are more able to comfort and settle themselves when they wake through the night.

— If you are breastfeeding, could any foods you are eating be upsetting your baby? For example, hot, spicy foods, citrus fruit and chocolate are known to affect some babies.

Important For safety's sake it is recommended that you place your baby to sleep on their back, with their feet at the end of the cot so they can't wriggle down under the covers. Ensure they do not get too hot. Sheets and cellular blankets rather than duvets are recommended for babies under one year. The Foundation for the Study of Infant Deaths (FSID, see Contacts, p.429) also suggests that no one be allowed to smoke near your baby or in the house and that you have your baby in a cot beside your bed for at least the first six months.

Consult your GP or health practitioner if you think your baby's wakefulness or crying may be due to any medical problems (illness, allergy, etc.).

attention. This is nonsense, though sadly there's still a lot of it about.

As with all aspects of development, children vary. Some will go with the flow, drop off to sleep easily and learn the difference between day and night fairly quickly. Others seem much more sensitive to change, more anxious about settling to sleep and more distressed on waking. These highly sensitive babies can be hard to soothe. Being their parent isn't easy, but the more sensitive and responsive care we can give, especially in the early months, the sooner their distress is likely to ease and the less intensive support they'll require.

By responding, watching and listening to your baby, you'll develop an understanding of their particular likes and foibles and what helps soothe and settle them (see Understanding your Baby, p.9). You'll also recognise how they indicate tiredness (i.e. turning their head away,

---

Sleep needs

The nature of babies' sleep changes as they grow, so it is important that our efforts to encourage parent-friendly sleep patterns are appropriate to their age.

Remember that babies' sleep needs vary widely. The following statistics are offered only as a rough guide, so we do not expect too much of our babies too soon.

Newborns spend up to 60% of their sleep in dream or REM sleep (Rapid Eye Movement sleep – i.e. they wriggle and, characteristically, move their eyes under closed lids). This 'active' sleep falls to 43% at three months and to 30% of total sleep time by the time they are one year old.[1]

Average number of hours' sleep by age.[2]

Age	Daytime	Night time
1 week	8	8.5
4 weeks	6.75	8.75
3 months	5	10
6 months	4	10
9 months	2.75	11.25
12 months	2.5	11.5
2 years	1.25	11.75
3 years	1	11
4 years	0	11.5
5 years	0	11

getting irritable, gazing, etc.) If you take these signs as a cue to settle them, you'll help them gradually associate settling routines with sleep (see Settling for Sleep, 0–6 months, p.46).

This is important. We all know that young babies often fall asleep while feeding or being rocked, stroked or held. This is a delicious fact of life with a new baby and a very important part of the growing bond between you. However, if the pattern persists, babies may learn to expect and depend upon being fed, rocked, stroked or cuddled and be unable to fall asleep happily without these 'clues'.

This isn't a problem if you don't mind, but if you would like your baby to learn to fall asleep without you, look again at your settling routines and the baby's responses. Once your baby seems generally secure and confident in your care and you feel the time is right (often around three months and over), try to soothe and settle them until they are almost drifting off, then put them down and encourage them to fall asleep without your close physical contact. Singing or talking softly, placing your hand on their back until they are calm, 'swaddling' them so they feel 'held' or giving them the peace they desire may help soothe them to sleep. By trial and error and watching your baby's responses, you'll develop an understanding of what generally soothes and settles them.

This will not only help your baby fall asleep with less upset, but should also reduce the number of times they need you through the night. Babies expect to wake up in the same place where they fell asleep. If your baby was feeding in your arms or lying in your bed when they nodded off, it can come as a shock to find themselves in their crib or cot when they wake. If they fell asleep in their crib or cot, they're more likely to stay there happily.

Remember, too, that all babies and children move, wriggle and wake at night. If your baby has learned to calm themselves and doesn't depend on you for their 'sleep clues', they can fall back to sleep again on their own and cry for you only if they are hungry or really need attention or comfort.

If babies don't learn to be on their own, the problems can get worse as the baby gets older and she can fight sleep. We have endless calls about babies who cry the moment they are put down. Or you put them down, creep away and before you have even got to the door, they are crying again, because they know they are no longer in their parent's arms and they haven't learned to settle without them.

Louise Walters, Cry-sis Helpline for families with excessively crying, sleepless and demanding babies

If your baby is calm, comfortable and content, then protests a little at being put in their cot, try to resist the temptation to pick them up immediately. Babies often grizzle a little before falling asleep. This does not mean leaving them to become distressed (see Crying, p.20). Leaving babies to cry for five minutes or more (see Sleep Training, p.55) is not recommended for babies under seven months.

Establishing routines Once sleep patterns begin to emerge, try gradually to establish a bedtime routine. This can provide your baby

Complementary approaches

Many parents report success with complementary therapies for 'excessively' crying babies or those with sleep problems. The two most commonly used are homoeopathy and cranial osteopathy.

If you decide to consult a complementary therapist, it is important you choose one who is reputable, qualified and experienced in treating babies (see Contacts, p.429 for professional organisation) and only do what feels right and appropriate for you and your child. Also be aware that some children seem more receptive to certain treatments than others.

If you give it time, most of these problems will recede after birth. I would expect more than half of all babies to sort out these things for themselves. Where this does not happen, patterns can remain and cranial osteopathy help. I find mothers have a real instinct for when their baby is not settling or not quite right, and that is the best time to come.
Gez Lamb, cranial osteopath

Cranial osteopathy for babies
Gez Lamb, cranial osteopath

Cranial osteopathy (also known as paediatric osteopathy) is a very gentle, non-invasive treatment that involves holding the baby's head or body and making minute movements to correct problems. It is most recognised for correcting the effects of birth trauma, in the easing of 'mechanical' (circul-

atory, muscular, skeletal, digestive) conditions that may contribute to poor sleep and digestion in babies, and for speeding the body's own healing processes. The treatment is generally considered very safe and gentle, and most babies find it relaxing.

Cranial osteopathy can be useful for babies suffering from:

* Not sleeping/waking often

with the security of predictability, help prevent overtiredness and encourage them to distinguish night from day. A morning routine can also offer them reassurance that you'll be there when they awake.

Aim for an evening routine that suits you as well as your child. There is no reason why babies should be in bed by 7.30 p.m. if they're getting enough sleep at other times of the day, and many parents and cultures are happy for children to stay up until late in the evening. What does matter is that each evening has roughly the same structure – say food, play, bath, cuddle, book and bed – at roughly the same

---

- Excessive crying
- Digestive problems
- Restlessness/irritability
- Feeding difficulties
- Post-vaccination to alleviate shock

Homoeopathy

Edie Freeman, homoeopath

Homoeopathy can be useful for babies suffering from:

- Any after-effects of the birth
- Constant crying
- Sleeplessness
- Colds and coughs
- Teething
- Digestive problems

Homoeopathy is a gentle system of medicine that treats the whole person (mind, body and emotions) with a minute amount of a substance that is just sufficient to stimulate the body's own healing forces.

It can be useful to maintain and improve children's health in a number of ways:

1: Improving the immune response, making children less susceptible to infections and able to recover more quickly.

2: Providing alternatives to drugs, such as antibiotics.

3: Healing chronic conditions: asthma, eczema, ear infections, some speech difficulties.

4: Vaccinations i) Pre- and post-vaccination remedies to prevent and alleviate after-effects. ii) Alternatives to vaccinations if parents do not want their children vaccinated.

5: Addressing emotional and behavioural problems, particularly through times of change.

It is important that you feel comfortable with your chosen practitioner, that you have trust and rapport. Some are much better than others, and some will suit you and your family better than others.

Be aware: you will know what your child needs better than anyone else. Take your child to hospital or call a doctor if your child's temperature rises above 102 degrees, looks to be losing consciousness, or has an acute ear infection.

times. A child can't be expected to know when it's time for bed if that time keeps changing.

Playing with your baby during the day will also help them distinguish the night hours. Offer opportunities for them to play on their tummy while you're near, so they have the chance to exercise their shoulder and neck muscles in a different way. Spend plenty of time holding them as well as talking to and playing with them, so that they don't begin to think of night as the best time for physical closeness. Be led by their responses – they'll let you know when they'd like a break and when they want more (see Understanding your Baby, p.9).

Parent-friendly sleep patterns: 6 months–toddlers

Some babies have fallen into parent-friendly sleep patterns by about six months. Some fall out of them again, some don't adapt to them until much later and many need a little persuasion. The tips for settling young babies still apply (see Settling for Sleep: 0–6 months, p.46) and the following checklists may help:

Difficult settlers

— Do you have a regular bedtime routine? Try to introduce one if you haven't.
— Does your baby depend on signals from you to fall asleep? (See Emerging Patterns, p.46.)
— Could your baby be teething?
— Is your baby overtired? Have a calm, quiet time together before you attempt to settle them to sleep, perhaps looking at a picture book. Think about the frequency of naps – are they getting enough sleep during the day? Babies'

needs change as they grow and it may be that your routine needs revising.
— Is your baby tired enough? Perhaps they are having more daytime sleep than they need.
— Does your baby have a comforter? Some parents find it helps to encourage one – a toy, a blanket, the child's own thumb or fingers – if it helps the baby cope away from the mother's physical presence.

Night wakers

Consider the above, plus:
— Is your baby waking for night feeds? If night feeding is increasing, it could be a sign that your baby is ready to move on to solid food if they haven't done so already (see Feeding and Food Wars, p.66).
— Most babies of six months and over do not need night feeds for nutritional reasons, but many still enjoy them. If

Many children become particularly unsettled at around three to six weeks and again at six or seven months, when they are old enough to force themselves to stay awake (see Crying, p.20). Babies who had previously slept for enviably long stretches may wake many times in the night at this stage. According to the support group Cry-sis (see Contacts, p.429) one in three children are still waking regularly in the night at twelve months. Re-establishing routines when you are able will help you all get back on an even keel.

Three in a bed? Many mothers – out of considered choice or sheer

---

this isn't a problem for you, there's no reason to stop, although there is some evidence that excessive fluid intake at night may disturb some babies by increasing night-time wetting and waking.[3] If you feel this may be the case, you may wish to reduce very gradually the number and length of night feeds. If bottle-feeding, gradually reduce the amount given at each feed.

— Is your child sleeping in your bed/bedroom? If you are disturbing each other, consider moving your baby into a cot or another room.

— Are you jumping to attention at your child's slightest whimper and snuffle? This can disturb a baby more than letting them drift off to sleep again.

Early wakers

— Try heavier curtains or blackout blinds.

— Cot activity toys, mobiles, etc., may encourage your baby to play in their cot for a while.

— If your baby wakes for their early morning feed at a regular but ungodly hour, try to move it, gradually and in five-minute jumps, to a more parent-friendly time.

Nap refusers

— If your baby won't sleep in their cot during the day but will sleep in their sling or pushchair, try taking them out at a regular time to establish their sleep pattern. Once established, you could try the cot again.

— Do they need the nap? If your baby is at an in-between stage, refusing a nap but getting strung out without it, try building quiet times into the day so at least they are calm and rested.

I used to love being sung to by my mother and used to sing to my babies until one day, my three-year-old daughter said, 'No!' when I started their lullaby, 'I don't like the noise!' It came in useful later, though, because I could say, 'If you don't get to bed I'll sing.'

Helen D

exhaustion – let their babies sleep in bed with them. This is the accepted norm in many societies and cultures and it is an arrangement that has been around a lot longer than cots, so it is hardly a new or radical idea. There is much evidence that young babies cry less when in body contact with their mother[4] and that their breathing patterns often follow those of their parents when they're sleeping close.[5] Video studies have shown mothers instinctively protecting their babies while sleeping together, adjusting blankets and moving to keep the baby comfortable and at the right temperature. Many parents and professionals believe putting a young baby in a cot enforces a premature separation and are convinced of the psychological advantages of 'co-sleeping'.

How parents co-sleep with their babies is important, however, and there are crucial safety issues to consider.[6]

- Ensure your baby doesn't become too hot. Swap duvets for sheets and blankets; keep pillows away from the baby and do not co-sleep where room is restricted, i.e. on the sofa.
- Is your bed suitable? The mattress needs to be firm and the bed sufficiently large, so you don't risk rolling together. Some parents recommend 'co-sleeper' cots, designed to attach to the parents' bed and provide a separate yet connected place for the baby to sleep.
- Parents must to be able to respond to their babies. Avoid alcohol and drugs that make you drowsy (including medication). Do not co-sleep with your baby if you are excessively tired.
- Mothers and fathers who smoke are advised not to co-sleep.

Many parents treasure the intimacy of bed-sharing with their babies and close contact does help nurture the mother-baby bond and can also help breastfeeding. You may find nights of light sleep, while your baby breastfeeds at will beside you, more restful than nights broken by having to stagger out of bed to feed them, or you may find the very lightness of sleep together exhausting. Whether or not to co-sleep is *your* choice, but let it be an informed one. Also be aware that co-sleeping can become a fairly long-term commitment if your baby learns to depend on your physical closeness to settle (see Emerging Patterns, p.46).

It is a commitment, but it felt right and it worked for us. Nights were a
pleasure, not a battle.

Helen D

Sleep training

If you are going to do any kind of sleep management, it's so important to wait until the baby is at least six months, or even older. Before then, the potential damage to the developing attachment bond between parent and child outweighs any benefits. After about eight months, when the trust and attachment between baby and parent is securely established, it is much less damaging to leave them to cry for a few minutes.

Eileen Hayes, parenting advisor to the NSPCC

We decided to feature sleep-training methods in this chapter because we're very aware of just how exhausted parents can become. But these methods are only ever intended as a last resort. Many books advocate using these methods far too young, and too harshly, so it is also important to clarify safety guidelines.

Sleep training is troubleshooting. It can be extremely effective in older babies and children but it is NOT recommended for babies under seven months. Even after that time, it is only appropriate when other, gentler approaches have proved unsuccessful (see Parent-friendly Sleep Patterns, p.52) and you or your baby are absolutely desperate for more sleep.

Take time to consider whether these methods are right for you and your child and if they don't feel right, don't use them. Leaving your baby to cry will be stressful for you and the rest of the family, so it is important you choose a time that's right, too. If you wish to discuss your baby's individual case in detail, contact your GP, health visitor or health practitioner. They may also be able to refer you to a specialist sleep clinic if necessary, although these aren't available in all areas.

I was getting up ten times a night every night with my youngest, until he was 16 months old. I took it out on my other children because I was too tired to cope. We were referred to a sleep specialist by our GP, who made us write down everything we did, day and night. She said I needed to communicate to him that nothing exciting happens at night: no food or drink, no cuddles or play. But what she really taught me was how you have to make a decision about what your aim is, then work out steps that you can cope with to get there.

Sue B

Sleep-training techniques

I respect the fact that some parents reach the end of their tether, so it may be necessary to do this, but to say it's easier is complete nonsense. It is hugely stressful, emotionally and biologically, for a mother to leave their baby crying.

Eileen Hayes, parenting advisor to the NSPCC

I tried sleep training. The first two nights were just awful. He was so upset and I felt dreadful, but I was so incredibly tired I knew I had to do it. But the third night I put him in his cot, he made a token cry, then lay down. By the fourth night he was sleeping until morning.

Lindsay C

Remember that sleep-'training' techniques are a last resort, when gentler methods have failed and parents are at their wits' end (see Sleep Training, p.55). With all three methods mentioned here, it is important to put your child into their cot *awake*. Do not carry them to their room sleeping, as it can be very disturbing for a child to fall asleep in one room and wake up in another.

Be positive and set realistic targets, looking for small improvements over an achievable timescale rather than overnight miracles. Importantly, look after yourself and obtain as much support as you can.

The checking routine
(for children and babies 7–9 months and over)*

This method has worked for many parents who have contacted the Cry-sis helpline.

1   Ensure parent(s) and baby are well. Give yourself two clear weeks when you are not going out in the evening or going away.

2   Babies and children need a routine, especially at bedtime. Set a bedtime and stick to it. Make sure there is a good 'winding down' period: quiet games, stories and a relaxing bath.

3   Put baby to bed, tuck them in, say 'goodnight' and leave. Make sure they have any comfort objects with them before you go (soft toys can act as insulation. As ever, be careful your child doesn't get too hot).

4   When they cry, leave them for a set time (1–5 minutes) then go back, 'check' them, tuck them in and leave. Do not pick them up. Do this until they

go to sleep. You may wish to start with a short period between checks, leaving it a little longer each time.

5   If your child gets up return them gently but firmly to bed. Ensure they know you mean business and that you are not going to give in. It may help to use the same repetitive phrase and calm tone of voice each time you go in to your child.

6   Avoid drinks (unless the weather is very hot), cuddles or stories as these can be interpreted as 'rewards' for not going to sleep.

7   Be determined. If you give in now they will try much harder the next time as they know you will give in in the end.

8   If your baby wakes in the night do exactly the same as before. Go back as many times as is necessary to 'check'. In this way, you and your baby know everything is OK.

9   Be consistent. If you have the support of a partner, make sure you work together.

10 Be prepared. This is a difficult process for you and your child.

The gradual retreat method*

This method usually takes longer to work than the checking routine but is probably easier on you and your child. This time, instead of leaving the baby, you stay and sit by the cot or bed until the baby falls asleep – stroking them as necessary. Over the following nights, gradually sit further away from them until they will go to sleep with you outside the bedroom door.

The goodnight kiss/cuddle

This option may feel more long and drawn-out, but tends to be gentler on mother and child's nerves. After a relaxed bedtime, kiss or cuddle your child goodnight and promise to give another kiss soon. Do this almost immediately, then move away from the cot or bed. Shift your attention to something else in the room, perhaps quietly tidying away toys or clothes. Promise to return to give another kiss/cuddle. Leave the room, then after a short while return and kiss/cuddle as agreed. Over the following nights, gradually reduce the number and increase the length of time between kisses/cuddles. Children old enough to understand may feel more secure if you give them 'a kiss to hold' (by kissing the palm of their hand) while you're not there

*Adapted with kind permission from 'Sleep Problems In Babies' produced by Cry-sis (see Contacts, p.429).

I thought about sleep training but realised I just couldn't do it. So I decided not to view my baby's sleeplessness as a problem I had to solve but as something I had to live through, a phase that would end. I feel quite liberated. Now I don't have a problem, I just have a child who's acting his age and doesn't sleep through.

Kathy H

Sleep for toddlers and older children

The ground rules for bedtime change considerably for toddlers and older children who have moved out of a cot and into a bed.

Sometimes a child who won't get to sleep needs comfort, or perhaps to tell you what's on their mind. This is when a few minutes' cuddling is often the most caring and quickest way to settle them. But sometimes children issue demands simply because it's a good game. This is when you need to tuck them in, kiss them goodnight and tell them, calmly and firmly, that it is time to go to sleep.

Somewhere between a fifth and a third of all families say their children have a sleep problem during the pre-school years.[7] Approaches for settling young children can still be very effective (see Parent-friendly Sleep Patterns, p.52 and Sleep Training, p.55). Other points to remember include:

Be positive Children need lots of sleep and you are not being unfair or unkind by encouraging your child to go to bed on time and stay there. Children who have the sleep they need tend to display fewer behavioural problems and are less irritable than those who don't. They find play with other children less difficult and are generally better able to concentrate and cope with life's ups and downs.[8]

Be boring Be as low-key and calm as you can. If your child hates hair washing, try doing this in the morning to shift tensions away from bedtime.

Stick to routines If you have let them slip, try to re-establish them. If your child is spending time between two families, it helps if everyone sticks roughly to the same plan if possible. Quiet rituals, such as reading a book together or rubbing their back before you say goodnight, will help your child feel more calm and secure.

Look beyond bedtimes Could any event or change in your child's life be unsettling them? Children who aren't tired won't sleep, so are they getting sufficient physical exercise? Are they sleeping too long during the day? Are they eating 'stimulating' foods too close to bedtime?

Children and working parents, especially, may find bedtime is when they enjoy most warmth and intimacy, so it's hardly surprising children try to drag it out. Sharing quiet times for chats and cuddles before the bedtime routine begins may reduce the temptation to make it last as long as possible.

Be firm Try not to raise your voice, but mean it when you say it's time for bed. Remember, a child who is loved and stimulated during the day won't feel rejected by a parent setting clear limits about bedtime behaviour. If they pop out of bed again, turn them around and return them to their bedroom. Try not to let them sit with you, or make it fun. Explain that they needn't go to sleep if they're not tired (which is what they may protest), but that they must stay in their bed.

Be honest Sometimes we all forget to explain to children why we want them to act in a certain way. Even with young children this is sometimes all that is needed to turn an unreasonable order into a sensible plan (see Communication, p.89).

I'd had weeks of my twins hopping in and out of bed, and I couldn't get on with anything. Out of exhaustion more than anything one night I sat on the end of a bed and explained to them, very quietly, that I was shattered, I wanted to get to bed myself, that I couldn't until I'd cleared up and that I couldn't clear up if they were running around the place. My daughter said, 'All right then.' And that was that, no more running about past bedtime. They were only three.

Julia P

Give warning Bedtime is often greeted with less protest if it doesn't come as a complete surprise, so issue advance warning. How long before bed this warning is given depends on the age and temperament of the child; five minutes beforehand is often enough for a young child, while half an hour will give an older one time to finish whatever they are doing and have all the moans they want. Letting children choose a final activity in the time they have left may help them feel they have some control.

Allow sufficient time Rushing at bedtime often backfires. Where possible, adding an extra fifteen minutes to the routine can mean the difference between calm and hysteria.

Get a clock A child's concept of time may bear little relation to reality. Show them where the clock hands are when it is time to get ready for bed and where they are when it's time to go to sleep. Also show them the time when you think it's OK for them to get up in the morning.

Help your child let go Some children find it incredibly hard to go to sleep. Sometimes cuddles and reassurance do the trick. Children who seem lonely or frightened may fare better if they can share a room with a sibling. Some children need help to relax.

> *I help her imagine herself somewhere relaxing. She lies down still, and I tell her she's lying in a field of lavender, the sun is as warm as a hug and a soft breeze is blowing. Then she adds her own bits, like imagining she's wearing a pair of heart sunglasses. Once what she calls 'the picture in her eyelids' is just how she wants it, she's often calm enough to drift off.*
>
> Aileen M

Praise whenever you can Try to praise success rather than criticise bad nights (see Positive Power, p.115).

Food and drink Does your child eat or drink anything before bed that may be making them unsettled? Cheese, chocolate, even fruit and raw vegetables before bedtime are known to disturb some children.

Understand bed-wetting This may be one very obvious reason why your child isn't settling at night. Many children aged four and up will still occasionally wet the bed. Encourage dry nights by praising them when they occur and try to discover if there has been any upset or change in routine that might have prompted the bed-wetting. There needn't have been – sometimes it just happens. Reducing liquid intake before bedtime often helps. If it is a regular occurrence, contact your GP or health practitioner for advice.

Nightmares and night terrors

I was just so scared by nightmares I had as a very young child that I can still remember details after 30 years.

David P

I know parents who have set up problems by changing routines drastically, such as sleeping with the child on the floor in their room every night. If you respond like this you are almost saying you have got something to be afraid of. You are also breaking down the routines and boundaries they need to feel safe whilst they are experiencing ordinary fears. You could be putting them in freefall.

Pat Elliot, psychotherapist and bereavement counsellor

A child's imagination can be a scary place, and their nightmares so vivid that memories of them linger well into adulthood. We may not be able to prevent them happening, but we can provide the comfort and reassurance our children need to recover from them.

Nightmares tend to occur most in children over three, but can begin earlier. Even everyday events may seem frightening to children this age, as much of the world and its ways won't yet make sense. Nightmares often won't have any easily identifiable cause, but it is important to consider whether any change in the child's routine or circumstance may be causing upset. Video and TV viewing needs especially close supervision when children are young, as their limited understanding means even 'children's' television can be frightening. Also consider whether anything in their bedroom is making them anxious – children's imaginations can transform familiar objects into all sorts of dark and threatening creatures at night.

When you do comfort your child, try not to deny their fear by saying 'Don't be silly' or 'Don't be afraid' because they are afraid and it is much better they can express that (see Feelings and Fears, p.124). Ask open questions, such as 'How are you? I heard you crying', rather than specific ones such as 'Did you have a nightmare?' or 'Are you thirsty?' as these can be auto-suggestive. Try not to probe, but help them to tell you how they feel if they are sufficiently awake. This will help them feel understood and secure.

Looking under the bed and behind the door to 'check the monster has gone' may compound their fears. Overreacting – 'Oh! How terrifying! You must be frightened out of your wits!' – could also make your child more fearful. They depend on you to be understanding yet also calm and in control of the situation.

If they insist on you looking behind the door or under the bed, you could explain that monsters exist in stories and imagination but not in real life, and that you are checking to reassure them, not to reassure yourself. Tell them they are safe and you are near, and try to gauge what else may help. Some children like a lighter room, some a much darker one that doesn't cast long shadows. Make it clear that their dream wasn't real but you do accept they have a real fear, and that you're there to help and comfort.

My kids like to know what to do in the dream if it gets scary. We've talked together about what dreams are and how imagination isn't real, but also how they can use their imagination to help themselves. My son likes to hold a magic kiss in his hand to protect him and my daughter likes to know she can tell any imagined creepy things that her mum will sort them out if they don't clear off. It makes her laugh which takes the sting out of the fear a little.

Jane P

If your child has a nightmare and isn't fully awake, it may be kindest simply to soothe them and let them know you are there. They will, hopefully, drift back off to sleep and have no recollection of their bad dream in the morning.

Night terrors Much the same advice applies to night terrors. A child having a night terror may appear to be awake, with eyes open, but is actually asleep. They may sit up suddenly, sweat and breathe heavily, shout or even scream. They'll be unable to respond to anything you do or say because they cannot hear or see you. This can be terrifying for the parent – and for the child in that moment – but be reassured that children generally have no recollection of these episodes the next day.

Soothe or comfort your child if they will let you, but be aware that some children become more confused and distressed by this, almost as if the parent's actions become part of the nightmare. Be guided by your child's reactions and if they are disturbed by your efforts, wait until they calm down, then soothe them back to sleep.

Waiting is extremely hard, especially as the terror can last five minutes or more. But remember your child is terrified, and not in control of their actions or what they are saying. Getting angry or trying to shock them awake could frighten them more and make them hysterical, so try to keep calm, stay with them and comfort them when you can.

Night terrors generally occur between one and three hours after falling asleep, and in children over eighteen months old. Cry-sis, a charity for parents of excessively crying and sleepless children, suggests that if they occur at approximately the same time each night, it may be worth gently rousing the child fifteen minutes before they would normally begin, then allowing them to drift back to sleep again. If this is done for several nights, the change in sleep cycle may stop night terrors returning.

If you are concerned about the frequency and intensity of your child's nightmares or night terrors, contact your GP, health practitioner or health visitor, who may recommend specialist help.

It was the most frightening thing that's ever happened with my kids. My son would wake up just screaming, shouting, 'Mummy, Mummy, Mummy,' obviously terrified. I would try to get him to talk to me, saying, 'It's all right, Mummy's here,' but he never heard me. It was like a blind terror and I just couldn't reach him. Once I tried to shake him awake, and another time I tried to get him to snap out of it, being quite stern and saying, 'That's enough, Mummy's here, stop now.' But both times he went completely hysterical. I had no idea what it was and had never heard of night terrors. Once I found out that he was actually asleep, it helped me deal with it better. Now I just say, 'I'm here' in a really quiet voice, and wait until he's ready to be comforted back to sleep.

Helen P

Sleep and you

Sometimes a mother's condition can be radically improved by restoring a single, critical need in her life that has been damaged subsequent to her baby's birth. In many cases the decisive factor is sleep. Sheer, unalleviated exhaustion is one of the most commonly experienced symptoms and restoration of regular and sufficient sleep may produce a very significant improvement in a mother's condition, even when other symptoms such as depression and anxiety are present.

Simon James, the Association for Post-natal Illness

Most mothers of young children understand the joke: 'What do women want in bed? Eight hours.' But sleep is a serious issue. Go without what you need for too long and the consequences can be extremely damaging. Serious lack of sleep leads to stress symptoms such as worry, backache and being easily upset. Parents often report feeling frustrated, anxious and angry, punishing their child too harshly or 'lashing out' at them verbally when they are tired and on edge. Parental relationships can suffer under the strain. When sleep returns, parents feel generally more positive, confident, relaxed and in control.

The Association for Post-natal Illness recommends every new mother has at least one proper rest in bed every day until her baby is several weeks old. As your child grows, try to catch up on sleep when they sleep, or ask your partner or a friend to babysit while you rest. This isn't indulgence, this is family investment.

Your options are largely determined by your circumstances but try not to let your sleep slip from your list of priorities.

Sleep v. sex

A good night's sleep is more important than good sex, according to a survey conducted at 15 World Health Organisation centres around the world.[9] In a quality of life study, which involved almost 5,000 people in 15 different countries, sex was rated as one of the least important priorities. Way above it came the ability to carry out ordinary daily activities, energy, restful sleep and personal relationships. Professor Michael Power of Edinburgh University, who presented the data to the British Psychological Society, said: 'We were somewhat surprised by this finding.'

Sleep solutions: a quick reminder

- Be very wary of harsh sleep-training methods, especially with young babies. They can undermine babies' trust in parental responsiveness. They also tend to backfire.
- Babies vary widely in temperament and sleep needs. Understanding your own baby's rhythms, what soothes and upsets them and how they 'signal' tiredness, will help you gradually encourage more parent-friendly patterns.
- As your child grows, there are many ways to encourage and establish routines. Choose those that suit your child and your circumstances.
- Nightmares are a part of growing up. Children can cope best if their fears are understood and respected.
- Sleep deprivation is a form of torture and also a common experience of early parenthood. Look for constructive, caring ways to help your children sleep, and prioritise your own sleep needs, too.

CHAPTER THREE

FEEDING AND FOOD WARS

Nothing short of a revolution is required in terms of our attitudes towards food, towards ourselves and towards our children.

Susie Orbach, psychotherapist and writer

The hardest thing is being understanding when they reject a meal you have lovingly prepared. I find that really, really hard.

Laura M

How our babies feed and how our children eat can be a source of delight or desperation. The feelings our children learn to associate with food can affect their eating and behaviour for years to come, often fuelling family rows and impacting on family relationships. At a time when even primary-age children are falling prey to fad diets and obesity figures soar, how we feed and respond to our children and how they respond to food may never have been so important.

From first milk feeds to family meals, knowing what to expect and what to do if problems occur can help ease parental concerns, prevent many eating difficulties and keep food battles to a minimum. Through our own behaviour and attitudes to food we can role-model true 'healthy eating' for the next generation. This is essential action for the present and an investment for the future.

Feeding your baby

Breastfeeding is something that affects you at a very deep, very fundamental level, which is why it is so wonderful when it is going well and so upsetting when it's not.

Anna P

At birth all the baby's senses are co-ordinated around the mother's breast. It is no coincidence that the distance the baby has clear vision is about the distance from the mother's breast to her face. It is nature's way of helping the bonding process.

Peter Walker, yoga teacher and physical therapist

The evidence is conclusive: breast milk is best for babies in the first six months of life. As well as being the perfect food, it also contains antibodies to fight infection and provides protection against asthma, eczema and other allergic diseases. Studies show that babies who are breastfed may be less likely to be obese in childhood. The quantity and composition of breast milk changes to meet your baby's changing needs, and it may even help in the introduction of solid food, as it can be flavoured by what the mother eats and thus familiarise the baby with a variety of tastes. Breastfeeding can play an important part in the developing bond between mother and infant. It is also cheap, convenient and cuts down on the washing up. But it is not always easy.

Images of breastfeeding mothers are extremely potent and usually airbrushed, which can be guilt-inducing and frustrating when you feel less like Madonna and Child and more like Daisy the Cow. Many women give up after a short time because they encounter difficulties and believe they must be doing something 'wrong'. The truth is that while many mothers and babies take to breastfeeding easily, and most find it a close and loving experience eventually, many find it a struggle at first and are surprised by the effort and energy it involves. Knowing that this is not unusual may help more women stick with it.

Informed advice and support is readily available and may be all that is needed to make breastfeeding a satisfying experience for mother and baby (see Breastfeeding Facts, p.70). The support of those around the mother is also hugely important – women whose partners strongly approve of breastfeeding are thirty-three times more likely to breast-feed than those whose partners don't.[1]

Patterns and Balances

I breastfed my first child in front of my mother-in-law and he was grizzling afterwards when she leant over him and said, 'Is your mummy not feeding you properly?' I said to my husband, 'Sort her out,' and left the room. The oldest and cruellest way to undermine a breastfeeding mother is to wonder if the baby is 'getting enough'.

Christine Chittick, NCT ante-natal teacher

I remember being told to feed my daughter ten minutes on one breast then ten minutes on the other. I thought: 'My daughter is tiny. She can't take ten minutes on each side, she'll spit it up.' But despite my knowing a good deal about the feeding situation and the psychology surrounding it, I was still affected by the instruction. It took me a while to wrestle with what I wanted to do – give her what she could take, when she wanted. What if that initial advice had been given to an anxious mother or someone with an eating problem? You can see what a nightmare it could be. Set 'times' for every mother and every child are a nonsense. They act against the mother picking up the rhythms of their baby and working together.

Susie Orbach, psychotherapist and writer

Letting your baby set the pace in the early weeks is the most successful way to encourage a predictable pattern of breastfeeding. If you let them feed as often as they want for as long as they want, rather than forcing them into a pattern designed for the mythical 'average' baby, they will be getting what they need and, gradually, the gap between feeds should increase.

If the gaps aren't increasing, it may be that your baby delights in comfort sucking and would quite happily stay snuggled up your jumper for twenty-four hours a day. Once you are happy that you've both got the hang of breastfeeding, you might want to try giving them the comfort and closeness they crave without them suckling. Try carrying them round in a sling for a while once they've had a good feed, or perhaps ask your partner or trusted friend to carry them instead. Becoming more alert to how your baby communicates and more confident in interpreting and responding to your own baby's 'signals' will also help you decide whether a feed is what they really need (see Understanding your Baby, p.9).

It can take three months or more for a predictable pattern to be established. If demand feeding is working well, continue for as long as you feel able and your circumstances allow. It's one hell of an achievement and you have every right to be proud of it.

If, as time goes on, you are beginning to feel like you would kill for another twenty minutes' sleep if only you had the energy, or if other demands on you mean that you can't always feed the baby when they'd like, it may be time to strike a balance between your baby's needs and your own. Once feeding is established, you may want to give them occasional feeds before they get hungry enough to demand one. This may be before you attempt to sleep at night – feed them and they are less likely to wake ten minutes after your head has touched the pillow.

If you are worried about producing enough milk, an occasional bottle of formula milk will solve nothing as it may disturb your milk supply. However, you could take a well-earned break and let someone else give a bottle to your baby if you can express enough breast milk for a feed. Every child is different, but a bottle used in this way seems to cause least disruption to feeding patterns and meet with least resistance if introduced after six weeks but before four months. The first six weeks are crucial in establishing breastfeeding and a bottle before then may prove disruptive, but if you wait until after four months your baby is much more likely to refuse it.

I think it is helpful to occasionally get your partner involved, giving expressed breast milk in a bottle. It helps their relationship with the baby and helps you. If you are giving expressed breast milk it also gives the baby a gentler learning curve for going on to formula if and when you decide to stop breastfeeding or need to go back to work.

Paula Bell, health visitor

Looking after yourself If you are breastfeeding, it is extremely important that you have sufficient rest, food and peaceful time to feed your child. Rushing is counterproductive, as your baby will only need another feed sooner than if you took your time and allowed them to take their fill. Relax when you can. Remember, this is an opportunity not only to nourish your child but to help them feel cherished. There is rarely a better use of your time.

Feeding a baby can be draining. That's something that is rarely emphasised enough. If you don't take it on board you can push yourself too far, your milk will suffer, your baby sleep less, the more drained you will become and so it

Breastfeeding facts

Breastfeeding is slowly increasing in the UK and now stands at around 69% (from 66% in 1995). This is still one of the lowest breastfeeding rates in Europe; more than 98% of Norwegian, Swedish and Danish women breastfeed. France (50%) and the US (57%) are even lower than the UK in the breastfeeding league.[2]

UK breastfeeding rates drop dramatically as the weeks go by. Only one in five British mothers feeds her children solely on breast milk for six months as recommended by the government and the World Health Organisation. More than 45% of mothers give up breastfeeding within the first two weeks.[3] The most frequently mentioned reasons are;

— Insufficient milk or that the baby seemed hungry.
— The mother had painful or engorged breasts.
— The baby would not suck or latch on to the breast.[4]

Nine out of 10 women who give up breastfeeding within six weeks say they would like to have continued for longer.[5] As an inadequate milk supply is very rare and other common problems can usually be remedied relatively simply and quickly, it seems more women would continue to breastfeed if they had access to, or felt able to ask for, the advice and support they need.

If you are experiencing difficulties breastfeeding, contact your midwife, health visitor or medical practitioner as soon as possible (via your local health centre or surgery). Many mothers also recommend contacting specialist support organisations such as La Leche League and the NCT (see Contacts, p.429).

goes on. Mothers aren't very good at thinking of themselves, but you sometimes have to step back from the situation and see how important it is to look after yourself so you can look after your baby.

Careen H

Choosing to Bottlefeed

Success in breast- or bottlefeeding will largely depend on how happy you are with the decision you have taken and how supported you are in that decision. It horrifies me that women can come to NCT mornings, hiding their use of a bottle and feeling they have to justify their decision. Who are we to judge?

Christine Chittick, NCT ante-natal teacher

If you truly feel unable to breastfeed, or if you have tried breastfeeding and sought the advice you need and it still hasn't worked for you and your baby, then go with what feels right. Everybody's circumstances, needs and demands on them are different. A bottle and a happy mother seems a much better deal for all concerned than a breastfeeding but continuously desperate, anxious or unhappy mother. If you are unsure which route to take, it makes sense to try breastfeeding first and to seek any support and advice that may help.

Moving on to Solids

There is an important Hindu ceremony, Mook-e-bhat, when the baby reaches six months and has her first taste of solids. It means 'rice in the mouth', and in India it usually is their first taste of food because babies there are generally breastfed for so long. Family and friends bring gifts and the baby is dressed up – in her first sari, with a little golden crown and sandalwood spots on her face if it's a girl. The ceremony is a very big deal, a rite of passage and celebration that the baby has survived and is now moving on to the next stage, taking food.

Chitrita C

Some time around six months, your baby will probably show they are ready to start solid foods, either by demanding more milk feeds, remaining hungry after feeds, waking more in the night or all three.

Many mothers feel pride at their baby's first taste of food, others a tinge of regret as their child becomes less dependent on them for

---

First foods

Our baby's first experiences of foods will influence their attitudes to feeding for a long time to come.

- Begin with puréed food and introduce new textures gradually. Introduce new tastes individually, but try to introduce as many as possible in the first year.
- Avoid giving cow's milk, honey, raw or undercooked eggs, chilli, citrus fruits, strawberries, shellfish and nuts for the first year. Well-cooked eggs may be introduced after six months.
- Families with allergic histories are advised to avoid peanut products for children until they are at least three. Whole peanuts are not recommended for children until they are over five years.[6]
- Cereals and purées should never be added to milk in a bottle.

sustenance and turns from suckling babe into banana squelcher. It is, as many cultures recognise, a significant and symbolic step away from infancy.

It is also a significant and symbolic step towards mess. As a society we tend to encourage children to play with 'educational toys', and then expect them to keep their fingers out of the baby rice. This seems a bit of a tall order. Your child will want to play with their food, stick their fingers in it and smear it everywhere within reach. And within reason (i.e. up to the point you can stand), why not?

Our children's attitudes to feeding and food will be influenced by our reactions and their early experiences of it. To make the transition to solids as stress-free as possible, it may help to remember that:

1   Babies soon learn the entertainment value of parental anxiety about what and how they eat. There is much you can do to avoid this (see Food Wars, p.74).
2   Babies soon learn to use food as paint. There isn't much you can do to avoid this.

Is it an allergy?

Parental anxiety over first baby foods is often focused around possible allergic reactions. It's important we recognise the common triggers and symptoms but also important to keep the issue in perspective. True allergic reactions are rare and milder food intolerance is easy to spot if foods are introduced gradually, one at a time.

Most signs of allergy or intolerance are evident within 24 to 48 hours of a food first being introduced. Reactions can range from a very mild rash or a slight runny tummy, indicating that your child is not yet ready to take the food happily, to a true food allergy indicated by symptoms such as breathing problems, swelling of the lips and dramatic rashes. Such rare reactions require urgent medical attention.

If there is a family history or sensitivity to particular foods, or of atopic conditions such as asthma and eczema, you may wish to proceed more cautiously in the introduction of foods.

'Timing is important,' explains early months specialist Ann Herreboudt. 'It is best to introduce one thing at a time for a few days at a time so you can have a clear view of how the baby is doing. Each food should be watched. The very best thing to avoid problems is to introduce new foods gradually.'

3 Your baby needs you to be relaxed and realistic about their eating more than they'll ever need homemade papaya purée. Of course, offer good, nutritious food but don't knock yourself out in pursuit of perfection.

If you offer a breast or bottlefeed after solids, the amount of food your baby takes should gradually increase over time and the amount of milk they take gradually decrease. Some babies, however, especially those who get fretful without a breastfeed when hungry, may relax more with a milk feed before solid food to begin with.

Introducing a variety of foods gradually, say a new one every few days, will encourage your baby to enjoy a wide range of tastes and allow you to watch for any signs of allergy or intolerance (see Is it an Allergy?, p.72).

Food refusal in babies It's not worth spending a long time trying to encourage a weaning baby to take food – they will take it if they want it. If we try to force them, mealtimes may degenerate into a battle of wills. In the long run, we'll be the losers, either because our children will have discovered early that food refusal attracts attention, or because they associate eating with stress.

Babies, like the rest of the population, have different appetites and preferences. We can respect this by trying to go at their pace, and by remembering that a baby who turns their head away or holds their mouth tight shut has had enough. We can offer some other food and if that's refused, stop. Food refusal may also be a sign that a baby is feeling off colour. Consult your GP, health visitor or medical practitioner if you are concerned.

Doing it for themselves Your baby will show you when they're ready to start trying to feed themselves, usually by grabbing the spoon and smearing gloop all over their face. And you. This is when the real mess starts.

If you find mess hard to cope with, plan accordingly – perhaps have two bowls, one for your baby, one for you, and take full advantage of finger food. Try giving them only one or two pieces of food at a time, or giving them a small portion of something less messy while you deal with the runny, flickable stuff. If you give them a spoon to wave and hold, they're a little less likely to stick their fist in their food. But only a little less likely.

Many parents accept this as an important and funny stage in their baby's development. If you're finding it hard, try to remember that your baby hasn't a clue how much effort you have put into making their food, washing their clothes or cleaning the floor. They aren't dropping food or sticking it in their ear to be 'naughty' or ungrateful. They're doing it because this is how babies learn. They're learning that food can be fun and that they can do some things for themselves. So it may be messy, but it's progress. By praising them when they find their mouth and being as low-key as possible when they don't, food flinging is less likely to turn into a sport.

Food wars and how to avoid them

Eating can be a focus for conflict and tension at home and undermine the mother's confidence in performing one of the most basic tasks of motherhood, feeding the child.[7]

Jo Douglas, Consultant Clinical Psychologist, Department of Psychological Medicine, Great Ormond Street Hospital for Children

My dad's sausages are disgusting. They're the worst thing. My favourite meal in the whole wide world would be prawn cocktail crisps followed by spaghetti with the red sauce, not the funny one, and ice cream with sweets stuck in the top and squirty chocolate sauce. And apple crumble. And crisps.

Gemma, aged six

What our children eat – and how they feel about food – will have a profound effect on their health and development now and possibly for the rest of their lives.

It takes less parental effort to prepare good food for children than it does to deal with ill health and other consequences of a child's poor diet (see What's Healthy?, p.78). Yet preparing healthy, varied food doesn't mean your child is going to eat it. Most children go through phases of refusing certain foods, especially if parents tell them that they're healthy and 'good' for them or insist on their consumption. Food refusal is most common under five, but can occur at any age; a recent study found that children aged between three and sixteen

Parental behaviour and children's eating habits

Our attitudes to food are an extremely powerful influence on our children's eating habits. 'Recent research[8] shows how mothers' concerns and behaviour at mealtimes influence their child's eating,' Dr Andrew Hill, psychologist at the Psychiatry and Behavioural Sciences Unit at Leeds University, explains. 'For example, a study of mothers with eating disorders and their 12-month-old babies found significant differences in how they interacted at mealtimes compared to other mothers. They were generally more intrusive and negative, and their infants were lighter.

'These interactions were filmed and make stunning viewing. The mothers seem to be both ambivalent about giving food and also find the whole ritual of mealtimes a fuss and a mess.

'There are examples where a child is literally force-fed and spits the food out, which upsets the mother who then cleans the child . . . basically both child and parent get more and more upset. Mealtimes, instead of being good fun and a time to communicate, turn into an adverse experience with neither mother nor child responding to the other's communication. This can inhibit the child's ability to learn self-regulatory skills around food.'

commonly had an 'arbitrary and despotic dislike of vegetables' and that many children only ate the recommended five portions of fruit and vegetables a day at Christmas.[9]

Food wars are a common feature of modern family life. They can be fuelled by children's early feeding experiences and their effects can spread to other aspects of family relationships and behaviour. Yet it *is* possible to prevent them breaking out or to call a truce if the battle has already begun.

Professionals working with children with eating difficulties and, crucially, parents with first-hand experience, offer the following suggestions:

Understand children's eating habits Appetites vary between children, just like adults, and even the same child's appetite may fluctuate wildly. Children who pick at food one day may wolf food down the next. Much will depend on how they are growing and how they are feeling at the time, none of which can be predetermined in regular portions.

Understanding your child's attitude to food may not make life more predictable – what they liked last night may be what they hate tomorrow – but it may make food a less likely cause of conflict between you.

Remember, too, that some children are pickier than others. This tends to be more a matter of temperament than bloody-mindedness (see Why Children Go Urggh!, p.76). A genuinely small appetite or fussiness can't be 'cured' through coaxing or discipline. Parents should instead aim to manage the situation as well as they can, so problems don't worsen and mealtimes can become more enjoyable.

One of my kids had an amazing appetite, one was picky but would eat a fair amount, and the other one just shut his mouth and wouldn't eat what he didn't want. He was like that as a baby and he's the same now. I was lucky he was third. If he'd have been my first, I'd have panicked.

Jess T

Introduce foods early The earlier a food is introduced the more likely it is that your child will enjoy it.

A process takes place during the pre-school years, through which children decide what's food and what's not (see Why Children Go Urrgh!, p.76). If they haven't eaten a food by about four years old,

---

Why children go Urrgh!

Dr Gillian Harris, clinical specialist in children's feeding difficulties

If I gave you a sheep's eyeball, you'd go urrgh! This is to do with the categorisation of foods, a process which occurs around three or four years old. By this time children have decided what is a food and what is not for them.

That is why I like to get children into my clinic before four years old because after that their categories can become entrenched.

Children also have different temperaments; some are easy and some are difficult around food. Think of Michael Palin in *Full Circle* eating strange fried things in strange places. There are some people who will do that, who will try everything, and some people who won't want to try anything other than the things they normally eat. It may be a matter of temperament which, comparatively speaking, is inherited, rather than the result of their parents bringing or not bringing certain child-rearing strategies into play.

they won't consider it part of their usual food 'category' and are much more likely to reject it. This explains why children of four plus often turn their noses up at foods that aren't exactly as they have at home.

You may also have to persevere with new foods. A child may need about fifteen tastes of a new food before they grow to like it![10]

Understand fads and rituals Food preferences and fads may become evident between one and two years old and can pop up without warning from then on. Some children decide they don't like 'mixed-up' foods, others don't like different foods touching on the plate, or want tomato sauce on the potato but never on the peas. How you react depends partly on how it affects your life: if the requests are simple and you are happy to oblige, fine; if you feel you are being given the run-around and things are developing to ridiculous extremes, it's time to say no (see Keeping your Cool, p.80).

Avoid Lectures

Children are beautiful behaviourists and far better at it than their parents, so don't go into anxiety overdrive if your child doesn't want what you've cooked because your child will find great fun in watching your reaction and having your concerned attention. I watch mothers, especially middle-class mothers, doing it all the time; going into a long lecture to a healthy, robust five-year-old about why they should eat peas. The child sits there thinking, 'I don't understand a word she's saying but I've got her attention.' Try saying, 'Fine, the rest of us are having peas but you can go without.' It's a clear message, they can get what they need from other foods and they'll probably have peas again in six months' time.

Dr Gillian Harris, senior lecturer in Development Psychology, School of Psychology, Birmingham University, consultant clinical psychologist and head of the Feeding Clinic, the Children's Hospital, Birmingham

If you've 'good' food in the house and your child sees you eating it, chances are they'll do the same. If, however, you insist or attempt to persuade them to eat it because it is 'healthy', chances are they'll ignore you or protest loudly, especially if you don't eat the stuff yourself.

Clinical researchers have now confirmed what parents have long reported: 'Our study[11] found that if you offer a novel food a child hasn't tasted before, along with a health message, they rate it as less nice than exactly the same food they weren't told is especially healthy,' explains Jane Wardle,[12] professor of clinical psychology at University

What's healthy?

A third of the money spent on food in the UK now goes on convenience meals, take-aways, shop-bought sandwiches and 'fast food' restaurant meals – up 40% since 1980 and fast approaching US levels[13].

The occasional ready-meal or takeaway does no harm, but problems arise when they form the basis of children's diets. According to the Government's National Diet and Nutrition Survey[14], 92% of children consume more saturated fat than the maximum recommended level for adults, and 83% consume added sugars above suggested adult limits, most of these coming from processed foods, snacks and drinks.

The Food Standards Agency has also issued new salt intake guidelines for children[15] after studies revealed high and potentially health-threatening salt levels in their diet (target intake, 1–3 years, less than 2 grams daily; 7–10 years less than 5 grams daily). Parents are advised to cut down on salt in cooking and at the table. Around 75% of salt intake comes from processed foods and ready meals (including some so-called 'healthy' options), so parents are urged to check food labels before they buy.

Cutting back on the amount of ready-made and processed foods children eat may be the simplest way to reduce intake. But nutritionists also warn well-meaning, health-conscious parents that many adult 'health' foods are not appropriate for children.

One recent survey in Newcastle found that the highest total cases of children failing to thrive occurred in the poorest social groups, but the second highest was among top-income families[16] – a phenomenon researchers have dubbed 'muesli-belt malnutrition'.

No-fat and low-fat foods, including skimmed milk and low-fat yoghurts, are not suitable for the under-fives (the Department of Health advises that semi-skimmed can be given after the age of two only if the child has a varied and full diet).

Added fibre or high-fibre cereals such as bran can compromise a child's vitamin intake because of the problems they have absorbing fibre in the bowel, while natural sugars are more suitable for babies and young children than chemical sugar substitutes found in many low-or no-sugar foods and drinks.

Most young children in the UK are not short of nutrients. In recent studies,[17] the most common problems found in pre-school children were:

— **Insufficient iron** (10% of those surveyed) Iron is found in meat, green vegetables and pulses, as well as more commonly child-favoured foods such as fortified breakfast cereals and bread.
— **Low zinc levels** (14% of those surveyed) Zinc is found in cheese, eggs and bread as well as fruit, vegetables and nuts.

With this range of foods to choose from, it should be possible to provide what a child needs without too much difficulty or resistance.

College, London. 'When they're young they learn an association with "health" and something they don't want to eat. One solution is to point out that something they do like is good for them.'

In other words, food is 'good' to a child if it's enjoyable. If you're aware your child is eating too much junk, of course guide them to foods of better nutritional value, but we can do this by making it available and making it clear we find the food appetising. If you make your child a healthy meal, or pack their lunchbox full of nutritional goodies, that's great, but say you've chosen them because they taste nice, not because they're packed with vitamins or are a wonderful source of zinc. Worthy, well-intentioned lectures rebound.

Our preoccupation with what's healthy can create anxiety around food and that helps no one.

Susie Orbach, psychotherapist and writer

Avoid 'treats' If we offer food as a treat, a reward or a bribe, it will go up in our children's estimation. We tend to reinforce certain foods' special status without even thinking about it. 'Eat your carrots, then you can have your pudding' is a trap most parents fall into occasionally, but what message does this give children about which food is a chore and a bore and which food is delicious and desired? And when was the last time you saw a parent give a child an apple for keeping quiet in the supermarket? We reap what we sow.

Most damaging of all can be the use of food 'treats' as a substitute for emotional support – perhaps offering sweets to a child who's hurt. This not only suggests that real comfort is to be found in food, and sweet food in particular (which can lead to eating problems) but also that emotions are to be ignored or avoided (which can lead to many more problems in childhood and beyond). A child who is hurt or upset needs the comfort of our understanding and care, not chocolate.

What does having a bad day at school or having grazed your knee got to do with having an ice cream? How does it solve or comfort the knee or the bad day? Bad days and knees need attention. That child needs you to say 'poor you' and to listen to them, or kiss the knee or whatever. They are hungry for emotional contact, not food. An ice cream treat simply suggests that the distress can't be handled, that the parents don't know how to deal with emotion. That can frighten a child.

Susie Orbach, psychotherapist and writer

Avoid bans If using food as treats ups them in a child's estimation, banning them altogether can make them rocket up a child's 'most wanted' list.

Bans are tempting. There's a lot of heavily marketed junk around, with negligible nutritional value. Yet forbidding sweets, crisps, chips, etc. for anything other than medical reasons (such as allergy) is a sure recipe for them becoming the focus of your child's desire, sometimes to the point of obsession.

Consider the example of children with cystic fibrosis.[18] These children require a very high-calorie diet, so their parents tend not to offer them salads but encourage them to eat as many chocolate bars and other high-calorie sweets as possible. When asked by researchers to record their favourite foods, topping the list were cucumber and lettuce. Chocolate came near the bottom. The food that was withheld or discouraged had become desirable and the things their parents most encouraged them to eat were the things they didn't want.

So treat bans with care. If you really don't want your children eating certain foods, try not to have them in the house. It may also help to think in terms of good or bad diet rather than good or bad food. The occasional portion of chips, chocolate or crisps is OK if the general diet is good, and much less likely to do harm than making food a battleground.

Keep your cool This is the key to minimising mealtime battles and largely depends on us not feeling incensed and/or hurt by our children's rejection of food. It may help to remind ourselves that it is our food that is being rejected, not us, and that food fads are a very normal part of growing up.

Parents can only 'lose' in the food war if they engage in a battle, and food refusal isn't half as much fun for children if their parent doesn't blow a gasket or give them their undivided attention as a consequence.

Gauge your reaction to your child's food refusal by their age and dietary needs. If a very young child rejects a certain food, try offering something else in its place. It makes sense to offer savoury items, or they will soon learn that making a fuss brings sweet things sooner.

Once children are old enough to have established the skills of eating, and if they are generally healthy yet refuse to eat certain items on their plate, try saying, 'OK, if you don't want it, don't eat it.' If they refuse to eat any more or anything at all, calmly remove their plate. If they aren't hungry, it doesn't matter. If they are hungry and are simply playing up, it will still help everyone in the long term because they are much less likely to do it again.

Keep mealtimes relaxed. Don't bother offering the rejected food again for a while as the child may consider this confrontational and reject it as a matter of principle. Offer your child the range of foods they need, then worry less. If your child has a small appetite, or is fussy, offer foods you know they'll like as well as offering new ones. Many children need small frequent snacks through the day, and especially after school. Offer energy-boosters such as chopped banana, sandwiches, etc.

I usually have mothers say, 'She doesn't eat a thing,' and I say, 'Write down everything that passes her lips for two weeks,' and having done this they realise there is not a problem. Obviously, if it is a very young baby and they are losing weight this is different. But most of the 'problems' and anxieties are around toddlers who are fit, healthy and growing yet 'don't eat'.

Carol Ann Hally, health visitor and clinical practice teacher

Stay consistent Mealtimes are just a feature of the day, and normal rules should apply. The basic ground rules for behaviour will be clearer if you don't allow your child to do anything at the table you wouldn't allow at other times. Praise positive behaviour (see p.115) and try not to go through elaborate rituals to get your child to eat or let mealtimes drag on and on.

Use alternatives and disguises If your child declares a pathological dislike of carrots, give them other vegetables next time. If they're off vegetables altogether try disguising them, perhaps chopped small in a pasta sauce. If they wince at the mention of milk, try other dairy foods – yoghurts, cheese, custard.

As long as, over the space of a week, they eat different types of food (meat, fish or pulses; dairy foods; starchy foods; fruit and vegetables) they are likely to be getting what they need. It does not matter much if they want the same lunch day after day, as long as they get the variety they need overall.

Offer small portions Large portions may overwhelm a child by the sheer enormity of the task ahead.

Stick to deals Some children do need prompts if their attention wanders, and encouragement to take a few more mouthfuls. If yours is one of them, avoid connecting the last bites of one dish with the imminent arrival of the next: 'two more mouthfuls then you're done' is storing up less trouble than 'two more mouthfuls then you can have your ice cream' (see Avoiding Treats, p.79).

Stick to your side of the bargain. If your child takes the mouthfuls don't then up the stakes by requesting a few more – a deal is a deal. Also be willing to accept and respect your child's right to eat when hungry and stop eating when full.

Let children help

My daughter's friend wouldn't eat at other people's houses, and didn't eat very much at home. One afternoon we were making pizzas – piling all sorts of things onto the bases – and she joined in the preparation and the meal afterwards. Since then she's made and eaten sponge cake and baked potatoes with different fillings. Helping make it seems to take away some of her suspicion of food.

Amanda T

Letting children help prepare and cook food, set the table, pour the drinks, may make mealtimes more fun. This is particularly useful if mealtimes have become tense or the focus of family arguments over eating or 'manners'. Children can feel part of a process they enjoy rather than at the 'receiving end' of something they don't. It also helps children find pleasure in helping their parents, which is no bad thing.

Children of 7, 8, 9 need to begin to learn skills for adulthood. In our clubs, cooking is always the favourite. There are lots of explanations for this, but perhaps one uncomplicated one is that feeding and being fed are important aspects of nurturing. To prepare and give food to others is to be a person who can do the caring as well.

Allan Watson, chief executive, National Pyramid Trust

Choices Be wary of offering choices to very young children – some find decision-making hard and the choice between fish fingers or pasta too traumatic to contemplate calmly.

Yet choices can help older children feel they have some control over what they eat. Asking 'Do you want baked potatoes or pasta?'

rather than a question with an open-ended outcome – 'What do you want to eat?' – is more likely to result in a reply you are happy with.

Considering our children's preferences may also help us put the issue into better perspective. Inevitably, our children will occasionally dislike foods we enjoy or enjoy foods we don't, follow the food fads of their friends or declare a preference just to be different to their sibling. Food is one way children express and explore their individuality. Once they know we're fairly relaxed about that, and accepting of their right to have food preferences just like adults, they are less likely to treat every query about vegetables as a call to arms.

Are they hungry? We can't expect children to eat a meal happily unless they are hungry enough to want it. This may require us to give them a run-around before teatime or cut back on squash and juice (see Soft Drinks, Hard Facts, p.83).

Soft drinks, hard facts

Squash and other soft drinks may damage children's health and appetite. One study,[19] by doctors at Southampton, found that 15% of two-to four-year-olds were getting nearly half their recommended daily energy intake from soft drinks, and that this was disrupting the normal development of hunger between meals.

The study was initiated after doctors reported growing numbers of children displaying similar symptoms: loss of appetite, diarrhoea, stomach pains and misbehaviour at mealtimes. The researchers have dubbed this 'Squash Drinking Syndrome', where the high sugar content of soft drinks stops children feeling hungry. Parents of children in the study reported frequent disputes at mealtimes because their children refused to eat.

Consumption of soft drinks by children under five is estimated to have doubled in the past 15 years, and expensive squashes and fruit juices as well as cheaper squashes were problematic, the report stated. One of the researchers, Dr Chris Rolles, explained: 'Calories in fruit drinks are empty calories . . . If these children are getting half their calories from fruit drinks, they will miss out on the vitamins, protein, fats, calcium and minerals they need to build bones and muscles.'

The study also showed how consumption of water has plummeted in recent years: 72% of two- to four-year-olds and 50% of five- to seven-year-olds surveyed drank no plain water at all. Parents were advised to dilute squash or juice gradually over time until the child was taking it very weak or, preferably, not at all.

Where to go for help

If you feel your child has a problem eating, or if they appear very listless or not to be growing as predicted, consult your health visitor or medical practitioner.

Your GP can refer you to a chartered clinical psychologist who specialises in working with children and families. The British Psychological Society (see Contacts, p.429) has details of suitable professionals working in your area. You can also be referred to a specialist speech and language therapist if your child seems to have problems sucking, swallowing or moving food around the mouth. Your health clinic can advise you of local speech therapy services. Alternatively, contact the Royal College of Speech and Language Therapists (see Contacts, p.429) for details of suitable professionals working locally.

Children's appetites can be re-educated to expect food at different times of the day if the process is done gradually over three or more weeks, so if your child is snacking but not eating main meals it may be worth slowly reducing the amount they have between meals.

Young children who are still drinking large quantities of milk may need this reduced (a pint a day is recommended for children aged five years and under).[20]

Don't force it Forcing children to eat, by making them sit at the table until they've cleared their plate or by threatening to punish or withdraw treats, is one of the least helpful things a parent can do (see Co-operation and Discipline, p.196).

I don't believe in giving a child what they don't like because when we talk to adults about their memories of eating they can remember exactly the colour of the wallpaper when they were forced to eat mushy peas, liver or whatever. It is so traumatic and achieves so little, why do it?

Dr Gillian Harris, clinical specialist in children's feeding difficulties

Don't mention weight-reduction diets

I wouldn't mention the word diet to anyone under the age of 32! You shouldn't put children on diets at all.

Dr Gillian Harris, clinical specialist in children's feeding difficulties

I've got to lose a few pounds. I want to look good in my bikini for my holiday.
Rebecca, aged seven

We live in strange times, and it's doing strange things to children's relationship with food and their self-image (see The Eating Problem Epidemic, p.86). Our sons and daughters are exposed to screen and print images of skeletal or body-obsessed 'celebrities'. 'Teenage' clothes and accessories are aggressively marketed to primary-age children as never before. Many children are becoming body-conscious – and body-concerned – before they even know how to cross the road safely.

Perhaps it's little wonder that eating disorders and obesity levels are reaching epidemic proportions while the diet industry booms. Over-eating and under-eating are being seen in increasingly younger children as food is no longer considered something to enjoy when you're hungry but as something with which to 'treat' or 'punish' yourself.

We can't possibly censor all media images from our children, but we can make sure we don't compound the pressures they're under by passing on our adult concerns about dieting and body image. If we sit unhappily in front of salad, moan about our body shape and the need to lose weight, then guiltily eat our way through the biscuit tin, we are sending powerful messages. As ever, what we do tends to have more impact than anything we might say or advise.

Weight-reduction diets are *not* suitable for children, unless recommended and supervised by qualified dieticians or medical practitioners. They can make children dangerously anxious about food, start them on the pendulum of weight loss and weight gain that plagues many adults and, just as bad, can deny them the freedom to enjoy their childhood bodies by imposing adult values and fears.

If you feel your child is becoming overweight, consider your family lifestyle. The benefits of exercise hardly need spelling out, but we may need to start taking notice. A recent report published in the US concluded that 'a TV in the child's bedroom is the strongest marker of increased risk of being overweight'.[21] More than one in three children aged between two and seven don't reach even minimum recommended exercise levels and habits learned young tend to stick. Two-thirds of fifteen-year-old girls take so little exercise they're officially classified as inactive.

There is a danger, though, that if we attempt to force, coerce or embarrass children into taking exercise, it will rebound and become yet another threat or chore. Like food, the more of an issue it becomes, the more anxious parents and children become and the more likely it will be rejected.

Encouraging pleasurable eating and exercise for the family as a whole is a more constructive route than singling out one child for 'special', and therefore stigmatising, treatment. Children should enjoy sport and physicality, so steer clear of highly competitive games if your child finds them hard. Family activities such as swimming or playing in the park can be just as much fun.

The eating problem epidemic

Obesity and other eating problems in children have reached epidemic proportions. Around 20% of four-year-olds in the UK are overweight and 8% are obese. In England, 17% of 15-year-olds are officially classified obese. This hasn't always been the case. In the past 10 years the number of obese six-year-olds has doubled, while cases of obese 15-year-olds have trebled.[22] In the US, a shocking 30% of school-age children are now overweight.[23] High obesity levels have also been reported in Eastern Europe, Australasia, Central America and the Middle East.

Being heavily overweight increases the likelihood of osteo-arthritis, back pain, hypertension, diabetes, stroke, heart disease, sleep problems and cancer, as well as exposing children to bullying and other psychological risk factors. Seriously obese children are losing up to nine years off their lifespan, while the dramatic rise in obesity-linked diabetes means many may now be outlived by their parents.[24]

Meanwhile, more than a million people in the UK are believed to be affected by eating disorders such as anorexia or bulimia nervosa.[25] These conditions usually become apparent in adolescence and beyond, and their roots are complex, yet there does seem to be a link between even moderate dieting in younger children and the onset of eating problems later in life. One recent study shows children who diet moderately are five times more likely to develop a serious eating disorder. If they diet heavily, they become a shocking 18 times more likely to develop eating disorders than those who don't.[26]

As parents, we can't isolate our children from social and peer pressures and aggressive advertising, but we can lessen their impact by examining our own anxieties around food and weight, and by helping our children feel good about themselves (see Feelings and Fears, p.124) and good about food from their earliest years on.

'We are facing an absolute epidemic of eating problems,' says psychotherapist and writer Susie Orbach. 'I don't think it's an accident that the obesity statistics have quadrupled when we have got mums

If you think your child is becoming tubby, you can do two things: the whole family can switch to semi-skimmed milk or cut down fat if the child is old enough (over five), and you could start a family exercise programme in which you all go for a walk, you all get on a bike, you all get fit. What you don't do is start reducing the child's calories, because they will get very miserable and anxious about food and it is not going to work.

Dr Gillian Harris, clinical specialist in children's feeding difficulties

preoccupied about their body weight and unconsciously passing on all their problems to their kids.

'Mums are even anxious about food around their babies. Within weeks of the birth, they're not supposed to even look as though they've had a baby, so there are pressures and stresses around food right from the start.

'As children grow, what they observe completely contradicts what they are told. They are rewarded with garbage foods but told to eat healthy foods; they are told to eat up then see mums not eating – or stuffing or doing both. These are all part of the same problem.

'It's critical not to make a fetish of junk food. My daughter has a friend over to stay right now and they go out and eat so much junk I can't begin to tell you. Why? Because that friend is forbidden junk food at home. In my experience, kids who have food that's forbidden are the ones who have no way of self regulating it.

'I overheard my daughter saying to another of her non-petite friends, "Are you sure you're hungry for biscuits? There's ravioli, there's chicken." She was trying to encourage her friend to think of *all* foods as

potentially pleasurable, and I think that's because we've never had certain foods off-limits at home.

'What I'd like to do is neutralise food, so it's neither "forbidden" or imposed or used to reward – so carrot is the same as a Mars bar, both can be a pleasure to eat. We can model a different kind of behaviour around food, too. Eat a Mars bar in front of your children, get part way through and say, "God, I've really had enough, now I need to have some bread or something." Or "You know, I'm really hungry. I wonder what it is I fancy? Hmmm, I fancy some chicken." Or "I need a couple of bites of something sweet."

'We can make clear connections between feeling hungry and eating, so a parent could sit at the table saying, "You know that's absolutely delicious but I've had enough to eat now." That kind of modelling is very effective, because it's not about telling the kid to eat healthily, it's about showing it and doing it.'

Feeding and food wars: a quick reminder

- Breastfeeding is the best way to give babies nourishment, early experiences of different tastes and positive experiences around food. It's not always easy. Informed support is available and often invaluable.
- Babies and young children play with food. Being realistic and relaxed about this helps children have a comfortable relationship with food from the start.
- We can encourage healthy eating by eating it ourselves, and back-pedalling on lectures.
- Avoid bans. Forbidden foods merely become more desirable. Avoid mention of weight-reducing diets for children, or in front of children, and increase family exercise.
- If a child needs a cuddle, give them a cuddle. If they deserve praise, praise them. Take care not to give chocolate or sweets as substitutes for attention or affection.

CHAPTER FOUR

COMMUNICATION

Children are never too young for adults to start really talking to them and listening. Try and help them find the right words to express their needs. Listen to them: children are worthy of being heard.

Stella Ward, nurse and parent educator

*Good communication is not something we do **to** children, it's something we do **with** them, responding to them, adapting to them.*

Dr John Coleman, Trust for the Study of Adolescence

Good communication can determine the nature of parent-child relationships through infancy, childhood, adolescence and beyond. It helps us avoid potential problems and untangle those that arise. It fosters warmth, understanding, trust, respect, consideration and fun.

Sounds simple? Try telling that to anyone who has ached for their child to say what's troubling them or who has experienced the table-chewing frustration of a child's selective perception (i.e. their ears stop working when parents speak – an extraordinarily common phenomenon).

Railing against parents and grunting monosyllabic replies are all part of growing up. Poor communication and simple misunderstandings have been the root of international conflict so it is hardly surprising that they can cause friction at home. Words are complicated things, especially for relative beginners, and most families will hit patches when understanding and listening to each other seem hard.

Yet we can help our children talk and we can help them listen. And by encouraging good family communication, we can nurture closer family bonds.

First words and conversations

It is vital that children acquire speech, and good for their overall development and relationships to do so comparatively early, but the child who acquires words first is not necessarily the one who is going to have the most interesting things to say later, nor is the child whose speech is delayed necessarily 'backward'.[1]

The Commission on Children and Violence

Recent research has brought new insights into how children learn to talk. Groundbreaking studies have also confirmed the importance of responsive interaction and communication between parents and children in the development of children's emotional well-being, behaviour, schooling and social skills. The benefits of good communication are life-long, but the foundations are laid in infancy. So what can all these advances in understanding offer us in terms of practical advice? How can parents best help?

Begin at the beginning Infants know their mother's voice before they are born, and their parents' faces and sounds are their most loved and enjoyable toys. Babies also make their own sounds, facial expressions and gestures to prompt communication with their parents. These early interactions are important for speech development (see Your First Conversations, p.12). They are also great fun. By singing, talking and replying to our infants' coos, gurgles, gestures and movements, we'll boost their enjoyment and confidence in their ability to express and our ability to respond. These are great foundations for healthy family communication.

Keep talking

Talk a lot – it's really important. If you get used to chatting a lot to a small baby you tend to set up a communication channel that continues. Some people wait until the baby can talk back – it's a bit late by then.

Dr Sally Ward, specialist paediatric speech and language therapist

The skills babies need to recognise and develop speech begin at an astonishingly early age. We can encourage these by talking to our infants about all and anything. Holding your baby close so they can look in your eyes as you talk and smile will help, as will trying to 'tune in' to your baby so you are talking *with* them, rather than *to* them (see Understanding your Baby, p.9).

Recent research indicates that one-month-old infants can distinguish between subtleties of speech, such as 'r' and 'l', [2] and that some babies as young as six months know the sound and meaning of their names. [3] Certainly the fundamentals of speech awareness are in place well before one year, and evidence is mounting that the quantity and quality of parent interactions with young babies have profound influence on their later speech skills and vocabulary.

The timing and pace of speech development vary widely between children (see Getting Help, p.95), but all will benefit from hearing their 'mother tongue'. So tell your baby what you are doing and why; ask questions that begin to link words to objects: 'Where's teddy? Here he is!' Children find it easier to make certain sounds if they can see how they are made, so try to get down to your baby's level or bring them up to yours to play and chat whenever you can.

Babytalk The importance of using 'parentese' or babytalk is one of the most significant recent developments in understanding speech development (see Talking Parentese, p.92).

'Babytalk' to infants across the globe has surprising similarities of rhythm and pitch, and has been shown to engage babies' attention and prompt happy interaction much more than more adult-oriented talk.[4] Repeating single words and using exaggerated 'baby' speech seems to make it easier for them to connect words and meanings and to isolate difficult sounds.

One small step ahead Once babies begin to understand their first words (often around eight or nine months) it helps to pitch our conversation to just one small step ahead of their ability. For example, if a child is not yet saying words, using single, simple words and repetition will encourage them. When a child is confident in using single words, we can link two together ('more milk', 'Jenny's toy' etc.); when they begin to say two together, we can link three ('put it here', 'big, red tractor' etc.).

Speech specialists suggest we let our children set the agenda and try to talk about what they are doing and what they are interested in. If they are playing with the saucepan there is little point talking about the ball.

Talking parentese

Many parents use 'parentese' instinctively, though some find the shift hard. Understanding why babies worldwide respond and flourish with it may make the transition easier.

Saying 'horsy' or 'doggy', for example, emphasises the 's' and 'g' sound for the child to hear and repeat. Focusing on individual words – 'spoon' instead of 'Look, here's your spoon, let's put it in your hand' – helps a baby identify sounds and meanings and name objects more easily.

Dr Sally Ward, a specialist paediatric speech and language therapist, explains: 'Parentese is very, very important. When you have a very small baby that you know isn't understanding your words, the natural thing is just to chat and tell the baby what you're doing, as you do it, for example "I'm putting washing in here". But when the adult perceives the child is beginning to understand the words, around eight or nine months, then mothers tend to modify the way they speak. At this point, you don't continue to speak in long sentences but use much shorter utterances, for instance, "It's a cup, a cup". Mothers will speak slower and louder, hopefully, with lots of repetition.

'Basically you are helping the child map the meaning on to the words. If that modification of how the parent speaks doesn't happen, if the parent speaks to the child as they would to a much older child or an adult, then it causes big problems. Children can have a lot of difficulty then figuring out what we mean.'

Instead we can focus on what they want to talk about most, and let them tell us about it. Ask simple questions: 'Would you like milk or water?' 'Where is your shoe?' Also introduce conversation into pretend play with their favourite toys: 'Ted needs a drink. Shall we give him his bottle?'

If your three-year-old is talking in complete complex sentences, you can talk back like that; if they are at the 3–4 word utterance level, you need to respond at the 4–5 word level to help them move on.

Dr Sally Ward, specialist paediatric speech and language therapist

Quieter children may need lots of encouragement to put their thoughts and feelings into words. We can help by being alert to their behaviour and describing what may be going through their minds. For example, if we see a child looking at a toy we could say: 'That's the red truck. Shall we play with it?' or 'That's your rabbit. Shall I get it for you?' Try to phrase questions in a way that encourages response. 'I'm hungry, are you? Let's get lunch.'

Mind our body language

Non-verbal communication is the language of an infant. A pre-verbal child responds more to the music of the words and to the expression than to words themselves. Even later when there is language, non-verbal communication normally still carries most of the impact. The meaning of the words will be interpreted by the sound of the voice and facial expression. It is rather like watching a film with different music tracks. The same visual can carry very different meanings with different music, be it frightening, relaxing or whatever. The visual and audio messages override the verbal.

John Bristow, psychologist and psychotherapist

It's not just what we say but how we say it that matters (see First Conversations, p.12). How else is your young child going to know not to touch something hot unless you screw up your face and suck, saying, 'Ooch, hot!'? The word 'hot' will mean nothing, but your gestures and tone of voice tell the story and teach the meaning.

The importance of non-verbal communication in any relationship is well established; only about 7% of what we express as adults is communicated through words, the rest is through tone of voice, inflection and other sounds (38%), body language and facial expression (55%).[5] Just as you are receptive to your child's non-verbal messages, so you will use a whole raft of gestures, expressions and exaggerations to get your message across, emphasise a point or engage your child's attention – smiling, frowning, looking surprised, changing the pitch, tone and volume of your voice and so on.

Share books Books spur children's linguistic skills and vocabulary from a very early age, but the key to using them successfully is to choose ones not too far in advance of each child's age and ability.

I think we are all in danger of introducing things much too early. Good books for young children are very repetitive and about their life or environment, about the world as they know it.

Dr Sally Ward, specialist paediatric speech and language therapist

We can encourage older babies to turn pages, and take an active role by asking questions about the characters: 'Where's Spot?' 'What's going to happen next?' 'Can you see the banana?' Many local libraries run 'story times' for pre-schoolers. These aren't a substitute for sitting quietly with mum or dad, but can be a great way of showing children that others their age find books fun, too.

Quiet times

Children from homes with constant noise from TV, music or radio take longer to learn to talk, according to a 10-year research project by Dr Sally Ward for the Central Manchester Healthcare Trust.[6]

There has been a rapid increase in pre-school children diagnosed with listening and attention problems and delayed language development over the past two decades. Dr Ward's study links this to increased background noise in babies' crucial first year of life, and increased use of daytime television and videos for children.

Dr Ward explains: 'The figures are really scary. I went into nearly 400 homes of one-year-olds and discovered that 89% of them had constant background noise, and I mean constant. It was mostly the telly, and in a few instances music or radio. In some homes everyone was watching the television, the furniture was in a row like a cinema, and some places it was even dark, and the infant would be in the corner of the sofa.

'The babies weren't actually watching but their attention would be attracted if something happened visually, a change of colour, a flicker or a sound, so it was very definitely having an effect on their attention to anything else.

'The development of selective attention, the ability to focus on a sound and tune out background noise, is absolutely critical to speech development. It normally happens in the second half of the first year, but with huge amounts of noise it doesn't happen. Another precursor to speech is the parent responding to sounds the baby makes, which can be drowned out by TV. This is one of the most important reasons for having quiet times.

'I think that there have been profound cultural changes within people's homes over the last 20 years. People have not realised the deleterious effects. Of course, watching videos is the most wonderful babysitter if you want to get on with something else, but within reason, because they interrupt children's enjoyment and experience of the interaction of language. Last week I had a barrister mother who asked me if the fact that her child watched six hours of video per day had an effect on her speech!

'By the time children have language, around three years, watching time could possibly be up to an hour a day if the programmes are carefully selected and, preferably, the carer watches and talks about the programme with the child. I certainly wouldn't recommend any more than 30 minutes to an hour a day for a pre-school child.'

Turn it off Recent research has come to some frightening conclusions about the effect of our lifestyle on children's language development. The implications are enormous but the remedy is simple: babies and children need quiet times without background noise from television, CDs, radio and so on (see Quiet Times, p.94). If we want to help our children learn to talk, we need to hit the 'off' button.

Slow down Just as it is important to leave spaces for a very young baby to echo back sounds (see Understanding your Baby, p.9), so it is important to give a child of any age a chance to respond. If they can't get a word in edgeways, they may give up trying.

Avoid constant questions Otherwise known as the 'What's this? What's that?' trap. Your child will learn much more if you tell them what it is even if you think they know already.

Some children I meet can only say 'What's this?' because that's about all they have heard. It is far more helpful to tell them, because even if they know the word they need to hear it many many times in order to recall it well enough to say it.

Dr Sally Ward, specialist paediatric speech and language therapist

---

Getting help

I do think developmental checks are a useful way of picking up if there are any areas where a child might benefit from help. There is no question that the vast majority of children fall in the 'normal' range, which is very wide – for a two-year-old, for example, 'normal' would be a vocabulary of anywhere between 20 and 200 words.

Sarah Darton, health visitor

If you are concerned about your child's speech, your health visitor can refer you to a speech therapist for assessment and further help if necessary. Early intervention is very effective in turning around language development problems in children. Paediatric speech and language therapist Dr Sally Ward found that talking to a baby or young child for half an hour a day, every day, preferably one-to-one in quiet surroundings, made 'a colossal difference to their speech and language abilities'.

Avoid correction Correction can crush. Instead, we can reinforce a child's confidence with a positive statement, showing that we've understood and also teaching them how to say the word correctly. Think of these two examples from a child's point of view and imagine which would inspire them most to keep trying to get it right:

Child: 'Dup.'
Parent: 'No, not dup. Cup. Cup.'
or
Child: 'Dup.'
Parent: 'Yes! Cup, cup.'

Child: 'Miss Shones said I had to bring vis back tomorrow.'
Parent: 'Miss Jones said you had to bring this back? OK.'

Have fun By showing pleasure when a child points, shows us something, attempts a word or shows enjoyment in expression, we are boosting their confidence in their abilities and in themselves. Words and sounds make children laugh, and encouraging delight and confidence in language and communication can do nothing but good. Your child will enjoy fun for fun's sake and shared pleasure is healthy in any relationship, so find time to join in when you can.

My daughter had one word that made her collapse in giggles from about two and a half. It was 'seaweed'. She'd say 'seaweeeeeeeed' and fall about laughing.

Joanne H

Encouraging children to talk

I am incredibly passionate about the importance of a child being able to talk to somebody. If children learn from an early age the ability to talk to someone I think this is the foundation of emotional well-being.

Camila Batmanghelidjh, psychotherapist and Director of Kid's Company, a charity providing caring adults to listen to children in their school or home

As our children grow, how we talk and listen within our families will be key to how relationships develop. If communication is generally good, we will have a sound understanding of what our children are feeling, thinking and doing, and how we can best support them. If communication is muddled or blocked, minor difficulties can escalate into full-throttle conflict or major problems develop beyond an easy point of return.

Boys, in particular, may struggle to express how they think and feel[7] (see Feelings and Fears, p.124, and Gender and Development, p.302), yet all children say that being listened to and being able to express their feelings and views are crucial factors in how they feel about themselves and family life in general.

Many problems fuelled by poor communication become apparent in adolescence, but have their roots much earlier in children's lives. So the sooner we start genuinely listening and talking in our families, the better for our children and the better for us. The following suggestions and approaches can help. Some are adapted from techniques used by professionals to help children 'open up'. Others are straightforward tips and pointers that parents and professionals alike have found useful. To work, each may require not only a change in the words we use to our children but also a shift in how we feel and think about what they have to say. For any of them to be effective in encouraging children to 'open up', our children have to believe we truly want to listen to what they have to say.

Show them we are listening

In terms of a child's needs and welfare I think listening is the linchpin of parenting. If you don't make time to listen there is little hope of other communication, especially as they grow older.

Eileen Hayes, parenting advisor to the NSPCC

The main benefits of listening to our children is that it is fun and you get to know them as people.

Dr Sally Ward, specialist paediatric speech and language therapist

Imagine. You are trying to share something important with a friend or partner and they are distracted and focusing on something else – answering the phone, cooking, shouting at the dog, telling another child to put their coat on. You would probably feel unheard. You might

Are you listening to me?

Changes in pace and lifestyle are cutting in to family 'listening' time. We may have to make it a much greater priority if our children's needs, thoughts and feelings are to be heard. According to research in the US by psychologist Professor Philip Zimbardo,[8] working parents spend an average of just eight minutes a day talking to their offspring 'but it isn't even meaningful talk – it is mostly them giving commands to the children'.

In an NSPCC survey of 1,000 children and young people in the UK, most believed adults in general did not listen to what they had to say. Most said they had at least one person to talk to when they had worries or problems, and mothers were overwhelmingly the most popular confidantes. However 22% of younger children in the survey felt they had no one they could turn to.[9]

lose your thread even if you managed to keep talking. You might clam up and not bother. You might find other ways to grab their attention. Not surprisingly, children find it easier to talk and express themselves constructively if they know we are listening.

This means giving a child our full attention. Of course we can't give our children 100% attention 100% of the time. If we are having a chat about something not particularly serious, we can respond to show we've heard but we don't need to drop everything. The world can't revolve around a child every minute of the day.

If, however, a child seems to want to talk more seriously, or if we realise we haven't had a good talk for too long, it's time to focus our attention on them and to let them know we are listening. We can signal that they have our attention by:

Adjusting our body language Eye contact can show we are interested in what our child has to say, but it has to feel right for them and for us. If it doesn't, it can be very off-putting (see Ease the Pressure, p.106). A gentler approach may be to show we are listening by positioning ourselves near the child's physical level, perhaps sitting, kneeling or even lying on the floor with them. This way, the child doesn't feel as though they are 'looking up' to us. It also makes us available for eye contact should they wish it. Take their lead and ignore simplistic advice to make repeated and exaggerated attempts to catch a child's gaze if it's clear they don't want it. It doesn't help children 'open up', it does make them think we've gone a bit peculiar.

Responding so they know we've heard Simple, low-key responses can be clear but unobtrusive so they don't interrupt the child's train of thought or speech flow. They can be non-verbal, such as gestures and facial expressions to show we have understood what they are saying, or simple verbal messages: 'Really', 'Uh-huh', 'Sounds scary'. We're not commenting, judging, dismissing or reassuring, which can stop them in their tracks (see Communication Traps, p.105). Instead, we're simply letting them know that we're really listening. This is often all they need to move on and tell us what they really want to say.

We argued every single morning about getting ready on time. I would go crazy because I felt he was stalling on purpose. Then one morning, he said he didn't like school and instead of saying the usual 'Of course you do' or 'We all have to do things we don't like doing' or 'It will get better', I just said, 'Really?' It was hard to resist the temptation to say more, but I didn't. After a short while he said his friends all wore jackets and he didn't. I asked him how that made him feel and he said, 'Stupid.' All that time we'd been arguing and I hadn't known the root of the problem.

Helen S

Reflective listening

I see listening as the foundation of close relationships and understanding in families on which all other things are built. It's a way of putting love into practice.

Doro Marden, parent educator and trustee of charities
Parentline Plus and Young Voice

He would just shout and rage and storm off. He was six and this had been going on for ages, these temper outbursts. Then I tried reflective listening. I didn't say anything until he'd stopped shouting then said something like, 'You sound really angry.' There was a pause. I couldn't think of anything else to say so I just said, 'Really angry . . . Poor you. That must feel bad,' and he crumpled. I can't remember the last time he'd let me hold him like that when he was upset.

Melanie M

Reflective listening is one of the master skills of communication. It helps children feel heard, valued, respected and understood. It helps us by encouraging children to 'open up' when they are finding life hard, so we are more aware of how they are feeling and why. It is a technique frequently used by family therapists and other professionals but it can be learned by any parent keen to encourage better family communication. And it is just as effective with surly adolescents and grumbling partners as it is with young children.

Shock of the new

Learning to drive, wearing a new pair of shoes, anything new feels uncomfortable when you first try. I guess you have to go through the difficult bit to get to the good bit. But the children seemed to respond better from the start. It was hard for me but not really for them.

Kathy A

It really used to irritate me, when he'd put on a certain voice when he was using a particular listening technique. It was his 'now children, I'm your caring father' voice and it would either crack me up or drive me mad, depending on how I was feeling. He doesn't do the voice any more because he's more relaxed about it. Thank God!

Anne M

Learning new approaches takes time and practice before they feel natural. Reflective listening, for example, may feel awkward to begin with, because it involves a profound shift in how we view and behave towards our children. Yet the more we do it, the easier it tends to feel for everyone involved until, eventually, it becomes second nature. If, after about four to six weeks, there is still no positive change, the technique may not be right for you and it is probably best to move on. Not all the approaches discussed in this book will work for all relationships, because families are as unique as the individuals involved.

As parent educator Peter Mellor explains: 'Most of the skills will work for most of the children most of the time, depending on the commitment of the parents.' But you are the expert on your family and your circumstances, so you must decide what works best for you all.

When I first started reflective listening, I felt a complete idiot. I thought my children would burst out laughing, but they didn't. They talked to me. In first few weeks I found out loads of things I didn't know were going on. Now I'm much more at ease with it and do it without even thinking.

Terry S

Like so many good things in life, it may take time and energy to practise to a point where you feel comfortable. Time and energy are what most parents don't have much of, but stick with it if you can (see Shock of the New, p.100). When children are stuck or struggling to talk, it can be just the help they need.

Put most simply, reflective listening involves repeating or 'reflecting' back to a child what they have said, so they know we've been listening and we understand. What we 'reflect' back can be split into two key elements:

1   What the child said.
2   The underlying feelings expressed.

Reflecting back what the child said At its simplest level, this involves us feeding back the child's own words, adding no personal comments, observations or judgements. This lets them know we are listening and helps children carry on talking and thinking.

Child: 'I got told off today.'
Parent: 'You got told off?'
Child: 'Yes. And it wasn't my fault . . . I told Miss James we were playing not fighting but she didn't believe me.'
Parent: 'Oh.'
Child: 'No. And . . .'

As a next step, we can 'reflect back' or summarise, in our own words, the gist of what the child has said. This may feel like stating the obvious, but it shows we have understood. This can make things clearer in the child's mind, helping us all get to the root of the upset without intrusive questioning.

Child: 'Katie said I wasn't her friend any more. She said I had silly hair and my teddy had a silly name and my bike was silly.'
Parent: 'Katie was unkind to you.'

Listening in this way passes no judgement upon the teller and so encourages children to tell us what is really going on, not what they think we want to hear. It also gives them a sense that their view of a situation is recognised and acknowledged. To a child in pain or crisis, this can feel like a lifeline.

Feeding back the underlying feelings At the same time as summarising the child's words, we can briefly describe the feelings we think they may be experiencing. The above example, for instance, could continue along the lines of:

> *Child:* 'Katie said I wasn't her friend any more [and so on].'
> *Parent:* 'Katie was unkind to you.'
> *Child:* 'Yes, and she stuck her tongue out.'
> *Parent:* 'Sounds like she hurt your feelings.'

This needs to be done sensitively, without pretending we know precisely how a child feels but rather offering suggestions that may help them feel understood and make sense of their own emotions. Once that is achieved, they will find it easier to let those feelings go. For example:

> *Child:* 'I was the only one without a Chelsea kit.'
> *Parent:* 'Sounds like you felt left out.'
> *Child:* 'Yep and Michael said I wasn't any good in goal.'
> *Parent:* 'I guess you've had a tough morning.'
> *Child:* 'I hated it,' or perhaps, 'Oh, it wasn't that bad. I did a cracking free kick.'

Suggesting how children feel gives a sense that we are trying to help rather than taking over. Children quickly indicate whether we are on the right track, often with much passion. If we guess right, they will be pleased. If we're mistaken, it is much less likely to draw the conversation to a close. On the other hand, stating how children 'must' be feeling risks their incredulous scorn if we get it wrong.

> *Child:* 'I was the only one without football boots.'
> *Parent:* 'You must have felt left out.'
> *Child:* 'No. I just kept slipping over! Don't you know anything about football?'

For this reason, steer clear of comments like 'I know just how you feel' because you probably don't. Phrases like 'it sounds like', 'I expect', 'I guess' and 'I imagine' are much safer ground. When we haven't a clue what a child may be feeling or even what they are talking about, be honest. Ask: 'How did that feel?' or better still, 'I don't know what that must feel like', 'I'm a little confused about what you were doing' or 'Let me see if I've got this right . . .'

A word of warning Reflective listening is a technique to use sparingly, when circumstances are right for you both (times when you are very tired or rushed are best avoided). It is only really useful when a child needs some help to work out how they are feeling or what has happened to them. Use it in everyday conversations and situations and we risk making a drama out of a crisis. And sounding like a wally:

Child: 'Mum. Take Charlotte into the other room.'
Parent: (Trying to reflect her child's feelings) 'Take Charlotte away. Sounds like you're finding it hard to be with her right now.'
Child: 'No. She's just standing in front of the telly!'

Respecting opinions

Children should be consulted and their views respected.

Eileen Hayes, parenting advisor to the NSPCC

Children are full of ideas and opinions. If we want them to feel confident about talking to us when times are hard, they need lots of practice talking to us about everyday issues. We may also need practice in listening respectfully to what they have to say, especially if we weren't listened to as children ourselves.

Children are much more resourceful and thoughtful than adults often realise, but of course they will have some whacky ideas and suggestions. Respecting opinions doesn't mean we have to agree with them. Yet how we respond can either encourage them to offer their thoughts again, or crush their confidence through fear of criticism or humiliation.

The same holds true for adults. If you made a suggestion to your boss, how would you feel if you were ignored, laughed at or told not to be so stupid? And how you would feel if you were told. 'That's really interesting. Let me think about that'? The final decision might be exactly the same, but how your suggestion was greeted would be key to how you'd feel about offering an opinion in future.

If children seem uncertain or shy about expressing thoughts, we can help by asking their views on simple family issues: what they would like to do at the weekend; what flavour ice cream to buy; who chooses which video to rent. 'How do you feel about that, Helen?' 'Tom, I know what the grown-ups think, but it's important I know your view, too.' Once they feel they have made an important and appreciated contribution, they are more likely to make another. Once expressing and listening calmly to opinions in the family become second nature, children often find it easier to chat through problems and disputes without crumbling or battling to the death over every point. Which makes life much easier.

Seizing the moment

It is so important to be emotionally available for our children and by that I mean being around in a peaceful and responsive way. You can be certain the most important piece of information comes when you least expect it, not when you schedule 'a talk'.

Adrienne Katz, Young Voice

If I'm cooking and Josie wants me to read a book, she may say 'Mummy, Mummy' and pull at me a bit, or whine. If I get down to her level and ask her what she wants, or acknowledge how she feels by saying something like, 'I know you would like me to read that book right now and I can't because I'm cooking dinner', she is much more likely to be OK about it than if I try to ignore her or tell her to get off my leg. It is a matter of respecting their needs while also asserting your own at that moment. And you can only work out what they need if you listen.

Stella Ward, nurse and parenting advisor

Making time to talk is important, but don't expect this to be at your convenience. Life is rarely that neat. The younger the child, the less skilled they tend to be at choosing times to talk when parents can easily listen. They may decide to tell you their worries or concerns just as you're about to fly out of the door or take the dinner out of the oven. Try to keep your 'antennae' up for any signals that they want to talk. Take their lead and, whenever possible, listen.

If you do want to do something else at the same time, try to make it something you can do together (see 'Sideways' talk, below) and focus on what they are saying. If it is not possible to listen at that moment, be honest:

Communication traps

The key to getting children to talk is to listen. Some parents are very good listeners. Some think they are listening when they are not. It may help to check that we're not doing something else instead, such as:

Advising 'Lucy wouldn't let me play with her today.' 'I'd take no notice if I were you. Go and play with Polly instead.'

Criticising 'Joe took my key-ring and lied and said it was his and Mrs May believed him!' 'Well I told you not to take it to school.'

Dismissing 'Emily broke my shell.' 'Oh, it doesn't matter. We can always get another one when we go on holiday.'

Correcting 'It wasn't fair at lunchtime. You are always nicer to Jason.' 'You mean teatime.'

Ignoring 'I need Daddy to take me to football on Sunday.' 'Would you help Lucy with that balloon.'

Distracting 'I've not been picked for the school play and everyone else is in it.' 'Come and look what I got you today, that will take your mind off it.'

Reassuring 'I'm scared of the monsters in my room.' 'There's no need to be scared.'

Praising 'I hate him playing with my toys.' 'Oh, you don't mind, you're such a good big brother.'

Most parents do all of these from time to time, but none of them involve real listening and none will reap the same results. They are used most when parents have run out of patience or time, because they can be very effective at stopping a child talking. Listening does the opposite – it encourages a child to talk.

'I'm so tired/rushed I don't think I'll be good at listening right now, but I really want to. Let's have a cuddle and a chat at bedtime when I can listen better.'

or

'I want to listen to this, it's important to you. Let me just finish what I'm doing, then I can listen to you properly.'

Children can generally wait under these circumstances. But they won't do so often unless they know they'll be heard eventually. A deal is a deal, and children need time to talk as soon as we're able to give it.

'Sideways' talk

Often parents want to talk about the burning issue when children are not able or ready. When children reject the offer to talk, parents can get frustrated and annoyed which makes the child close up further. Using different ways to approach the subject can help. It is often a question of being available and not forcing the

Ease the pressure

Vivienne Gross, family therapist

I think car rides are wonderful. You can talk about things, with the environment flashing by and with a lot less intensity, and the child might appreciate that.

Don't just sit children down in a room eyeball to eyeball and say, 'Dad and I have been thinking, we need to get close to you right now.' You don't want to leave them with a feeling of no escape, or they may stop listening and talking altogether. Little children actually put their hands over their ears if they don't want to hear something. Older children may not use their hands but they may still stop listening if the conversation feels over-intense. You may have to come up with different ways of getting a message across. Reading books together and other 'slightly to one side' ways of talking can be very effective.

It is not a matter of doing either one thing or the other, but actually paying attention to what you all feel is right. It can be that a child almost floats off, that you realise three weeks have gone by and you haven't a clue what they've been doing at school or whatever, and that you have actually lost your focus on them because there's been so much other stuff happening. You can sort that out by having a relaxed chat in a relaxed situation without being too deliberate or intense about it.

issue. Often in therapy I find it useful to have an outside focus, to be doing something together with the child so you have 'sideways' talk at the same time. A lot of eye contact can be too intimidating – waiting and listening for openings is the most important skill.

Jim Wilson, systemic psychotherapist and director of the Centre for Child-Focused Practice at the Institute of Family Therapy, London

Some children find face-to-face conversation too intense, especially if they have something difficult or uncomfortable to say. If you are worried that something is troubling your child, or if you have had a conversation along the lines of:

Parent: 'How did it go today?'
Child: 'Fine.'
Parent: 'It doesn't look like you're fine.'
Child: 'Well I am!'

try easing the pressure and doing something together: cooking, going for a walk, playing football – anything that reduces the intensity of the situation. This will allow you to bring up the subject sensitively, with a light touch. Or it might help a child relax enough to bring up the subject themselves.

If we have more than one child vying for our attention, it sometimes helps to allocate each a little time every day to do some activity together – reading, playing, pottering about outside, anything that means each has some undivided, relaxed attention. Even ten minutes a day can work wonders. It helps to set up some activity for the child who isn't being focused on at the time – drawing, construction kits, cooking, a burst of a favourite video – whatever it takes for them to feel noticed rather than ignored, and to allow their sibling some attention without interruption.

It is so often difficult for children to talk because an adult is looking at them and asking or demanding them to. It comes down to spending time and doing things with them – making a cake, doing washing up, painting. Whatever you are doing the focus is on something else, something enjoyable and that has a way of cutting down the tension.
Camila Batmanghelidjh, psychotherapist, Director of Kid's Company

Let children tell us anything

Be tellable. Your children need to be able to tell you anything and know it won't get them into more trouble than they are already in.
Steve Biddulph, psychologist and author

There were things in my growing up that I could never have told my mum and dad, not because I thought they'd be angry but because I thought they'd be so upset, so disappointed that my childhood and adolescence weren't as happy as they'd hoped or that I wasn't who they thought or hoped I was. So I kept a lot to myself.
Chrissy M

Our children need to know we will listen, however uncomfortable we find what they have to say. For our own peace of mind, our children's safety and the richness and honesty of our relationships, children need to be able to describe their thoughts and experiences and we need to be able to listen.

This is not the same as agreeing with or approving of what we hear, and it does not mean we won't want to do anything about it. But it does mean that we shouldn't do anything at that moment. That moment is for listening and for listening only, not jumping to conclusions or pronouncing judgements. Do that and the child may clam up. And often the most important things for our children to tell us are the hardest things for them to say.

Think back to the way you communicated with your own parents. Did you feel that they listened to you and that you were able to express anything that worried, concerned or even interested you? Were there reasons why you did not tell them more? Was it to avoid disapproval? Punishment? Disinterest? Humiliation? Did you do it to protect them because you thought they would be unable to cope? Or be disappointed? Or hurt? Or value you less?

The key skill for getting a child to talk is listening in a very non-judgemental way. If you are going to listen you are actually saying to the child that they can tell you negative things as well as positive, otherwise it cannot be an honest and full dialogue. Otherwise it is like tricking the child, saying, 'I want to listen to you but I do not want you to say anything that is upsetting to me.'

Camila Batmanghelidjh, psychotherapist, Director of Kid's Company

Resist interrupting Listening to all our children have to say involves us putting aside our needs temporarily, even those inspired by the best of intentions – i.e. the need to interrupt, to express how we feel, get more information, give advice, make it 'better', pass judgement or finish that half-completed sentence. (See Communication Traps, p.105.)

Many children find it hard to focus on a concern for a length of time and are easily pushed off track by questions and interruptions. Once a child trusts that they have our full attention, they may also need time to collect their thoughts and find the right words. Gaps and silences in their conversation can help them become clearer and calmer and put issues into perspective. This isn't avoidance or naughtiness, but simply a reflection of their age and stage.

If you do fill silences with your words, try to ensure it is because you are responding to the child's needs, not your own.

Parents are often so anxious about correcting their children's behaviour or having a 'good' child that often they push essential information and communication underground. Listening is not to say we approve of everything children do, but

listening time isn't the time to step in and correct. Behaviour education can come later. This keeps the channels of communication more open. Often we do not listen to our children because we cannot bear to hear, especially if they are in pain.

Camila Batmanghelidjh, psychotherapist, Director of Kids Company

Use open questions and statements We generally ask questions for our own curiosity – 'Was Rachel there?' – or to pass judgement – 'Why did you do that?' When we genuinely need more information to understand or to encourage a child to continue talking, it helps to ask 'open' rather than 'closed' questions. Consider which of the following are likely to elicit more useful information:

Open question: 'What were the best and worst bits of school today?'
or
Closed question: 'Good day at school?'

Feeding back incomplete statements also encourages children to continue: 'You said John was mean to you . . .'

Help children describe emotions With our help, children can develop a wide vocabulary of words describing feelings and experiences. These are the tools they'll need to express themselves clearly and

---

Opening up conversations

We can help our children 'open up' by responding sensitively to the words they say and the signals they give.

If you think something is bothering your child, you could say: 'You look sad/angry/worried . . . anything you want to talk about?/ did something happen today?/ I would like to listen if you want to talk about it.'

If they begin to founder or struggle, having started to talk 'Looks like/feels as if it's really hard to talk about this'; 'Sometimes it takes a while to talk about things'; 'Seems like this is confusing for you.'

If a child is silent, or 'signals' or says 'Leave me alone' 'I am around if you want to talk later'; 'Let me know when it would be good for you to talk.'

If your child's meaning or messages are confused or unclear 'You know, I'm not really understanding this. Could you tell me again?'; 'I would really like to help but I'm not sure how. Can you tell me again what happened?'

constructively, and the simplest way to equip them is to talk about feelings as they arise in everyday situations: 'It is upsetting when you have to leave somewhere nice'; 'Are you're disappointed because you wanted a balloon?'; 'Looks like that hurt'; 'You've found your homework. What a relief!' Parents sometimes fear that talking about feelings will escalate them. In fact the opposite is true. By identifying and expressing feelings, children are less likely to 'act them out' in their behaviour and more likely to understand them, manage them and move on (see Feelings and Fears, p.124).

Beware adult word play Irony, sarcasm and the like are way above children's heads until they are at least five or six, and even then can cause confusion. Superior, adult reasoning powers can also inhibit a child's confidence in conversation. Of course we can express our opinions more clearly and effectively than our children, but that does not deny them the right to have their views respected and considered.

She was two and a bit and had wiped the paint all over the table top and I remember saying something like 'Oh great! That's just marvellous' and her little face! When she turned round she was beaming, she really did think I thought it was great.

Suzanne T

Mirroring

I thought it was weird, but I was desperate enough to try anything and I have to say it seemed to work. It seemed to reach him when I was at a loss what else to do. It calmed him down. Me, too.

Mark O

This is not an everyday technique and is another to hold in reserve until a child really needs help to unlock genuine distress and talk about problems.

To do it, simply copy the child's body language and position. For example, if they are sitting on the stairs feeling sad, sit with them. Be available for eye contact if they want it, but don't push things. An upset child may shrug off hugs or even a touch, in which case, sit by or near them and match what they do. If they are hunched, hugging their knees, hunch and hug yours. If they are holding their head in their hands, do the same.

This is the body language equivalent of reflective listening (see p.99), showing that you acknowledge how the child is feeling, that you are respectful of their emotions and willing to go at their pace, taking their cues. Once the child sees you are not going to impose or invade, physically or emotionally, they will often begin to relax. As they adopt a more 'open' position, you can, too, until you are both relaxed enough to get closer, either to hug or talk or both, whichever seems right at the time.

Keep it up If we can listen well in everyday, ordinary circumstances our children are more likely to talk to us when a problem or extraordinary situation arises.

Children who visit counsellors and family therapists say they feel more relaxed about talking when the focus is not only on their difficulties, but on themselves as people – what they are doing, what they are interested in, what's fun for them, what's not.[10] Exactly the same is true in families. The more we talk, the easier talking becomes. If parent and child are used to talking and listening, there are far fewer barriers to effective communication around the tough stuff.

Encouraging children to listen

Listening is an essential skill for our children to develop, not only because it helps us all get through the day but also because listening to people's opinions and suggestions will help them understand others, untangle disputes and resolve conflicts.

Clearly, their most important lesson in listening is our own example. Children learn much more easily if they are listened to themselves, so all the points discussed above are key. They are also more likely to listen if we:

Mean what we say This is particularly effective for getting children to co-operate (see Co-operation and Discipline, p.196) but will help get any message across. At its simplest level, it requires our body language, non-verbal signals, feelings and words to match. If they don't match – perhaps we are trying to smile sweetly while we are seething inside, or trying to be stern when we feel like laughing – children will spot the conflicting messages and won't know which to follow.

There is little point in trying to feign interest, concern or resolve when we really couldn't care less because children can spot insincerity at twenty paces. A limp 'That's lovely' or 'That's interesting' will cut little ice when we are really thinking, 'What shall we have for lunch?' or 'If I see another trading card, I'll scream.' If we say 'No' when we're not sure, children will pick up our uncertainty and push to get their way. If we save 'No' until we really mean it, we are far more likely to stay calm and clear and our children are far more likely to get the message.

When I first heard about matching the messages it was like a light going on in my head. Because I've got a sweet tooth I always found it hard to say 'No' to my kids when they wanted sweet things. They'd sense that and would just go on and on until I either gave in or blew my top because I really didn't want tea spoiled again. Once I realised I had to sort out how I felt, then let them know clearly, it was much easier. Did I want them to have one or not? If yes, then OK as a treat and none of this posturing. If no, then I really meant no and I had to make sure they got the message. It sounds so obvious, but it worked like magic.

Sophie P

Stay close by This is such an obvious point that it tends to get overlooked. Children find it much harder to ignore what we are saying if we are in the same room, speaking calmly, rather than shouting from somewhere else in the house. Many parents who've switched tack, from shouting instructions to standing next to the child and talking, report a dramatic upturn in their children's ability to hear what they are saying. The morning rush, in particular, is often conducted with fewer frayed nerves and lost tempers.

This has been life-transforming. I used to shout up the stairs endlessly every morning. 'Get ready. Get your shoes on. Have you brushed your hair? Come on.' And none of them took a blind bit of notice. Then I went upstairs and stood in their room as I said what they needed to do, and stayed until they took notice. They get on with it themselves now. It's been much quicker and much less stressful than the old shouting routine.

Leslie M

Encourage turn-taking Taking turns at speaking, and being quiet when others speak, sounds so simple but is so hard for children to achieve. Young ones may be bursting to say their piece. Children of all ages can battle for available airtime, so no one is easily heard.

Simple turn-taking games can help children appreciate that everyone will have their 'turn', and that their 'go' will come round faster if they don't butt in (see Play and Learning, p.324). As our children grow, we can be very clear about the rights of all family members to have their say, praising any signs of considerate listening. We can also stress the mutual benefits of listening: it helps us all see situations more clearly and ups the chances of others listening to our point of view.

Pitch what we say to the child's level Language is complex and how much of it children understand will depend on their age and ability. If our words and means of expression are way over a child's head they will, quite understandably, stop listening.

Try not to witter on Less extreme but much more common is the trap of overwhelming a child with words. It is very tempting to jabber on with instructions, information and expressions of frustration, especially when faced with their inaction. But it rarely works. Children can feel angry, confused or intimidated by verbal bombardment. They can't listen to what we say if we give them too much to take in at one go. They need pauses in which to think and respond.

She's five, and I was having a go at her last week for not listening to what I'd asked her to do when she shouted back, 'I'm trying to tell you I'll do it but you won't shut up.'

Martin G

Say the child's name before telling them what we need them to hear. A teachers' trick, and especially useful for attracting a child's attention when there is a lot of background noise. Simple, but usually effective. If that doesn't work, gently touch them, say their name and look directly at them as you speak.

Pick the right moment Times of upset or heated argument are the wrong times to expect a child to listen to much we have to say. When there are important issues to discuss, wait until they are calm.

Message Received?

I must have asked my son to put on his trousers six times and he said 'OK.' I guessed he wasn't really listening so I asked him to repeat back what I'd asked and he replied, in all earnestness, 'Yes, I want peanut butter on my sandwiches'! At least then I knew why he wasn't getting dressed and he knew why I was getting wound up!

Anne M

Sometimes a child won't listen because they don't understand, and sometimes our words simply seem to go in one ear and out the other. If we're not sure a child has listened, it helps to check.

Try to avoid the 'What did I just say?' approach which can sound like a reprimand and make children unnecessarily anxious or lose the thread. Little children can be helped by direct questions: 'Put this in the bin . . . Where does this go? Yes, put it in then. Thank you.' Older ones may respond best to a straightforward 'Can I check what we have agreed here?'

Use different ways to communicate If a child doesn't seem to listen to a word you say, not using speech may help. A note in their lunchbox saying you love them can get an essential message across, especially if they're going through a tough patch at school. A note by their bed, reminding them of an agreement struck the day before, may push a point home.

As ever, do not presume that because an approach makes sense to you it will make sense to your child or work every time. Many parents report success, but there will be glittering exceptions.

I tried leaving a note by her bed. It asked her to clear up her room, like we'd agreed. Next morning I gave her enough time to tidy up, then went upstairs all eager to see how it had worked and saw she'd stuck her own note on the front of her bedroom door. It said one word. 'No'!

Claire H

Take care Children don't always listen, but they often hear what's not intended for their ears. Most have an uncanny ability to home in on parental expletives. Much more importantly, they will also pick up any conversation about themselves. In particular, try to avoid criticising a child within their earshot. Every word you say may be remembered for a very long time to come.

Positive power

What messages are we sending our children by what we say? Different words evoke different responses, and if we think and talk positively with our children, they are far more likely to behave positively and feel good about themselves.

Descriptive praise

Its effect was like getting a drink when you are really parched. It turned things around from a situation where we were at each other's throats, when you ask yourself, 'How did this all go so horribly wrong?' to one in which you re-establish the links with your child. It was the most fabulous tonic for both of us at a time when everything seemed hopeless.

Kate K

Instead of noticing what she hadn't done, like eaten all her carrots, I said what had gone OK, like, 'You've eaten two sausages already, you're doing well.' It affected her behaviour around food straight away, which I hadn't expected. Instead of pushing her food around, she ate more than she had in weeks.

Lindsay M

Praise is a great boost and motivator. The most effective and appreciated form of praise is descriptive – saying exactly what we like and why. This shows our children that we have really noticed them and what they have done. It also lets them know why we'd like to see such behaviour repeated.

It may seem simple, but the shift in how we view and speak to our children can bring profound changes to our relationships with them. It can help us begin to 'reconnect' if we've hit a rough patch, and it can encourage every aspect of their behaviour, from the way they clean their teeth to the way they treat friends. It may take practice until it feels comfortable, but it is worth every bit of effort (see The Shock of the New, p.100).

Consider the following examples. Which provides your child with the most useful information and helps them feel best about themselves?

Descriptive praise: 'Thank you for putting the glass on the side, it stopped it getting knocked over.'

or

Non-descriptive praise: 'Clever girl.'

Descriptive praise: 'It was kind of you to kiss Matthew, he was feeling a bit sad.'

or

Non-descriptive praise: 'Good boy.'

Repeated, non-specific praise of the 'Good boy' type soon loses its currency. An absent-minded 'Oh, lovely, dear' or 'That's nice' when shown your child's latest picture, especially when you've not taken the time to look, conveys little more than disinterest. 'That's beautiful' will not mean as much to your child as 'I love the way you have done the mountains so big and the people so small.' Children know when you haven't paid attention, and this can be worse than not noticing at all. It is usually safer to be honest and say, 'I'm up to my eyes at the moment, but I really want to see it. Can you show me after tea when I'll have more time for a proper look?' (See Seizing the Moment, p.104.)

We can use descriptive praise whenever a child has done something worthy of a mention; painting a picture, sitting for a meal, finding school shoes, putting the toothpaste back, considering someone's feelings. Look hard enough and any step in the right direction can be appreciated and commented upon. The approach is particularly helpful when:

— A child is 'stuck' in a pattern of behaviour.
— Their confidence is low.
— They are getting lots of negative attention.
— They have done something they previously found difficult.
— They have turned their behaviour in a more positive direction.

As ever, don't fake it. Insincere, overused or inappropriate praise at best won't work and at worst undermines a child's trust in your honest opinion.

Children do know the value of the praise they are getting and some know that whatever they do they will be praised by their parents and thus it becomes meaningless and is a waste of time. 'Mum, I've just murdered someone'; 'Oh that's marvellous, darling.' Praise is also often used to cover some sort of deficiency in the child or his environment. If used in this way, to compensate for not being very able or suffering a loss, a child will know this.

Dr Dorothy Rowe, psychologist and writer

It's getting the balance that's the tricky bit. Between noticing and commenting on the good things and not going over the top and saying, 'Wow! You've picked up your toy!' That can sound so insincere. It's got to be somewhere in the middle, so you're comfortable with it. But once you are, it really works.

Anne M

Stating the positive

If you describe to the child what you would like from them rather than what you do not want, it gives them an image of what could be, so it is quite creative.

Barbara Dale, parenting counsellor and psychotherapist

If I say don't think of a kangaroo, what happens, you think of a kangaroo!

Candida Hunt, Family Links

Children's lives are filled with instructions of what *not* to do. This is a great shame, because if they were told what *to* do they would be much more likely to do it. Kicking the 'no' habit takes time and practice but can bring about dramatic improvements in a child's self-esteem and behaviour. Compare the following responses to the same situation. Which response criticises, and which gives support and information?

'No, not like that, you'll cut yourself!'
or
'If you hold the knife like this it keeps it away from your fingers.'

Even the most urgent instructions can usually be given positively and effectively. Compare:

'Don't cross the road!'
with
'Stop. Now!'
or
'No, don't run off with those matches.'
with
'Put the matches in the drawer.'

Count up the number of times in a day your child is criticised or told what not to do, and the times they receive a positive comment. The results may surprise you. Yet simply turning around your language won't work unless you also believe in your child's intention and ability to co-operate. Children can spot insincerity and tend to do what is expected of them, not simply what they are asked to do.

Talking positively can be a hard shift to make if you've previously considered a child to be 'troublesome' or 'difficult', but it is worth the effort. Children may see little point in improving their behaviour if the worst is always seen and mistakes always highlighted.

Negative instructions have a nasty habit of turning into self-fulfilling prophecies: 'Don't! You're going to drop it on the carpet!' can undermine a child's faith in their ability to do otherwise. Instead, we could say: 'Hold the cup tightly when you carry it.' An anxious or angry 'Don't do that! You'll fall!' may jolt a child into doing just that. Instead, we can tell children what they need to know, specifically and positively: 'Turn around and come down the stairs backwards.'

Telling children what not to do also risks giving them the idea in the first place. 'Don't you dare throw that water over me!' may introduce an option they hadn't even considered. Negative comments can also be more provocative, especially for older children. 'Don't think you're going to come in here and drop your things all over the floor, young man!' is far more likely to result in conflict than 'Put your things away before you go out.'

Avoiding 'no' and 'don't', like all skills, is not appropriate to every occasion. Negative language – especially 'No!' – can sometimes be the quickest and most effective way of getting a message across. There will be other times when you don't use positive messages as well or as often as you would wish. No one's perfect. But we can aim to increase the positive and reduce the negative comments in a child's day. This is what matters most.

This is so important, I can't stress it enough. We always tell parents it takes three positive comments to every one negative comment to change behaviour. It's not easy – it's not very British to accentuate the positive, after all. We tend to just tell children off when they're not behaving. But then they get most attention for being 'bad'.

Jenny Oberon, pupil behaviour management consultant

Ripping up labels

When children's behaviour is unacceptable, adults should criticise the behaviour, not the child. They should say 'That noise is giving me a headache', not 'You make me ill'.

The Commission on Children and Violence[11]

I got so sick of being the 'good' one. Still am.

Julia M

The language we use about our children can damage their self-image and influence how others respond to them through their childhood and beyond. Labelling children – 'bad girl', 'clumsy child', 'the sporty one', even 'clever boy' – can limit how they are viewed, and obscure their needs and potential.

Avoiding labels is hard, but it is a core skill in positive and healthy family communication. It is acknowledged by all respected professionals dealing with children's issues as one of the most effective ways to protect and promote children's self-esteen and encouraging them to manage their behaviour.

But before we can do this, we need to understand why labels are so harmful:

Labels describe the child rather than the behaviour A child may think you disapprove of *them* rather than what they have *done*. This can crush, confuse or even scare them and result in more negative behaviour, not less.

Labels can stick If children begin to feel *they* are, say, 'bad', 'stupid', 'lazy' or 'slow', they can begin to feel unloved or even unloveable. If

Why label a child?

John Bristow, psychologist and psychotherapist

Labelling must be put in context. We are not perfect parents, all of us can easily slip into it at times. However it is a very low-level form of influencing, controlling, conditioning and educating our children. You have to ask yourself what your aim is.

If the behaviour of a child is over-generalised – for instance 'You are a bad boy' – that child may enter another experience thinking 'I am bad' and will therefore not behave very effectively. Then the child will feel even worse about themselves. If it remains generalised, expectations are built that things are not going to turn out well, the child becomes more anxious and therefore does not perform well. It is a vicious circle.

Very often as parents we find ourselves behaving as our parents did or even hearing our parents' words and being quite shocked by that. Parents may also label as a vehicle of emotional release, like a swear word – it is often considered more acceptable to say 'You idiot!' than 'Oh bloody hell!' if a glass of milk had gone over the carpet.

Yet specific praise and criticism, focusing on the behaviour rather then the person, can be a much more useful tool to help educate children's behaviour whilst maintaining their self-esteem (see Descriptive Praise, p.115). We do have a responsibility to both educate our children about the world and help them feel good about themselves in their interaction with it.

repeated or reinforced over time and in different situations, the label can become part of a child's view of themselves and therefore self-fulfilling. It may convince them that they really are 'stupid' or 'thoughtless' or 'crazy', so they will begin to behave accordingly.

A label does not communicate anything helpful It fails to tell children what it is we approve or disapprove of in their behaviour, or how they could do things differently.

By placing a label on a child we take away their ability to put the situation right If they see the problem as who they are rather than what they are doing, they may feel powerless to improve matters.

But if ripping up labels is so liberating, why do so many parents use them? The first and most obvious reason is their familiarity – it is the way we were brought up. They are also a shorthand means of expression, which saves time and effort. And they can be used as an emotional release to make us feel better, almost like swearing: 'Oh you stupid girl!' or 'Naughty boy!'

The most commonly used labels are negative These tend to be used in times of exasperation: 'bossy', 'lazy', 'stupid', 'selfish', 'naughty', 'rude', 'cheeky', 'bad'. You may have been called a few of these yourself as a child.

Adults feel angry or hurt if value-judged in this way, and so do children. If they feel unable to express that anger, they can become resentful, unlikely to want to listen and even less likely to want to co-operate.

Even positive labels can have negative consequences These can be restrictive, inaccurate and potentially damaging for similar reasons. Our children need to know when we think they've done well (see Descriptive Praise, p.115), but will suffer if they believe our love and attention is conditional on them being a 'good girl' or a 'brave boy', the 'funny one' or 'the clever one'.

Children may feel manipulated through overuse of generalised praise, of the 'Oh you're such a good boy, I'm sure you'll let your sister have your new book' kind. This can lead to resentment and resentment can lead to rebellion. You have been warned!

It can be very unhelpful when children get polarised in families into being 'the good one' or 'the troublemaker' or 'the child from hell' or even 'mummy's little sunshine boy'. Children pick these labels up and it is very restricting. We don't see the half of our children's qualities. We tend to focus on a few and then narrow them down into a very constrained role.

Vivienne Gross, family therapist

Avoiding labels This requires much understanding and practice and many parents find it easier to proceed in steps.

1　**Separate the doer and the deed** In other words, comment on the behaviour rather than the child. For example: 'Your bedroom is a mess' rather than 'You are so messy'. You have communicated what you need to without labelling.

2　**Describing behaviour** If you have managed to label your child less often, you are doing well. The next stage is to stop labelling their behaviour and to describe it instead. A specific description of what you see and hear – for instance, 'You have split the milk on the carpet and it's made a mess' – gives a child much more information about what is wrong than saying 'That's so clumsy' or 'Clumsy girl'.

The technique can be effective with young children: 'Leave it! It's hot!' gives them more important information than 'No, naughty!'

In the same way, 'You're so rude' might make an older child feel crushed or humiliated. Either that or they'll ignore you completely. On the other hand, 'You are shouting and I cannot hear what Grandma is saying' tells them exactly what it is you dislike and why. This increases the chance of them putting it right.

Without specific descriptions, the world can be a confusing place. A child may be praised as a 'Good boy' for putting a cup by the sink, only to be told he's a 'Naughty boy!' two hours later because the same cup is now full of hot tea. A simple description of why you approve or disapprove would be far more constructive. For instance, 'The cup was empty. Thank you for putting it there,' and later: 'The tea is hot (taking it away). Look.'

Specific descriptions of behaviour may feel strange. Surely we are just stating the obvious? Yet most children respond constructively when given this sort of information. They often talk more because they feel less threatened and co-operate more as they have understood the effects of their behaviour.

3   **Describing the consequences of a child's actions** This will give your child an even greater understanding of how and why a situation should be put right, or why they should avoid the same thing happening in future.

'You have forgotten to feed the rabbit and he is hungry,' gives the child more to go on than, 'John, you're so selfish, that poor rabbit!'

'You've poured your breakfast down your school uniform and I'm going to have to wash it again,' might help a six-year-old understand why you are gnashing your teeth far more than a rhetorical cry of 'What have you done!'

How actions affect the feelings of others is another important consequence for children to understand and consider, so try to include these in your description when appropriate. This is how they can begin to understand that a specific action is not always the problem but rather who is doing it, where and when it is done, and who it is done to. How else is a young child to understand that you love to be tickled, but baby brother does not; or that you love to be tickled, but not when you are eating; or that your sense of humour plummets when you are tired?

Such guidance can be used in praise as well as criticism. Compare 'There's a good boy' with 'Thanks. Grandma really appreciated you being quiet tonight because she had a headache.' (See Descriptive Praise, p115.)

This is complex and sophisticated territory for children, but by communicating the information they need in a way they can accept, we can guide them through.

Communication: a quick reminder

- Good communication is at the heart of healthy, happy relationships. It equips us to avoid or untangle problems and helps us support our children as they grow.
- We can encourage our children's confidence in communication by playing, talking, singing and responding to them from birth; turning off background noise; pitching our responses to their age and stage and boosting skills through praise.
- We can help our children talk by listening. Reflective listening, in particular, helps children put feelings into words and find their way through problems to possible solutions.
- Encouraging our children to express themselves and to listen helps them assert their own needs and consider other people's.
- Telling our children what we want them to do, rather than what we don't, boosts their self-esteem and willingness to co-operate.
- Descriptive praise tells our children precisely what we appreciate and why. It builds their confidence in their own strengths and values.
- Labels and rigid roles within families limit a child's view of themselves and their potential. We can rip up labels by describing specific behaviour, and avoiding generalisations about the child.

CHAPTER FIVE

FEELINGS AND FEARS

Children need to have the opportunity to express their feelings and be valued for who they are and how they feel, not who they have to be to gain the love or approval of their parents.

Kitty Hagenbach, transpersonal and child psychotherapist

If we cannot tolerate our children's upset, they will learn this and not tell us when they are upset. So the line of communication will be blocked. And if we can't handle the upset, how the hell can a child?

John Bristow, psychologist and psychotherapist

Responding to our children's emotional needs is the heart of parenting, the core issue from which so many others flow. The insights we gain by trying to understand our child's emotional world can lead to profound shifts in our attitudes and behaviour as parents, and in the nature of our relationships with our children.[1] With this understanding, we can help our children feel good about themselves, respect the emotions of others, cope with life's highs and lows and better understand and express their own feelings. These abilities are crucial to their behaviour and healthy development.

Building self-esteem

Self-esteem is a bottom-line sense of self-worth. It is not the same as bumptiousness or precociousness, or being selfish or self-absorbed. It is the kernel, the child's core belief in their own value. It is not about telling your child 'you are a marvellous baseball player' or whatever, it is about your child having masses of experiences that enable them to appreciate that their life has value, that they are a worthwhile person, that their opinion has some validity and that they have an entitlement to a place in society.

Vivienne Gross, family therapist

Simple pleasures

Think about treasured moments of your own childhood. What made you feel loved and special? Often it's not the grandest days out, the biggest presents or the organised activities that make the most impression, but the more simple times when child and parent can find delight in each other's company.

Being with our children to enable such moments to unfold is not only a matter of time, but of being emotionally available. Parents may be with a child 24 hours a day and still not tune in to their needs or actually share time together, talking, going for a walk, rolling around the carpet, cuddling up with a book, playing football in the park. Precisely what we do matters much less than that our children know we have enjoyed being with them. This isn't about po-faced parenting, this is about pleasure.

I always had the feeling that my mother loved an idealised version of me. That felt quite fragile. My father, on the other hand, seemed to know me warts and all and still love me. So it was him I talked to and turned to most.

Amanda T

If we are emotionally warm with our children, show them that we love them unconditionally and that they and their feelings matter, we will boost their sense of their own worth. From this will spring the confidence and security they need to understand their feelings and manage their behaviour, to get along with others, grow in independence, seek assistance when they need it, cope with life's knocks and imperfections, and to love. In other words, it sets them up for life.

Much research now confirms that children whose emotional needs are chronically rejected will begin to distrust others, have difficulties forming friendships and stable relationships, have more problems at school and be at increased risk of mental and behavioural problems (see Moving Closer, Building Bonds, p.148). At the extreme, children subjected to insensitive care and harsh treatment are more likely to develop severe conduct problems and display aggressive delinquency in adolescence and beyond.[2]

This knowledge doesn't require us to grin benignly at our children in all circumstances, ignore their misdemeanours or be a slave to their every whim. It does require us to:

— Love our children for who they are, not who we'd like them to be.
— Recognise and respect how they feel.
— Encourage them to express emotion.
— Listen to what they have to say and show that their opinions matter (which is not the same as agreeing with them all the time).
— Understand that grotty behaviour is often a normal and necessary part of growing up (see Horribly Normal, p.166).
— Show we dislike certain behaviour, but love them.
— Notice and praise our children when they behave in ways we like.
— Help our children negotiate problems, but not always negotiate them on their behalf.

Experiences of loss, deprivation and other circumstances beyond our control may impinge on the way our children view themselves and their world. Yet even in extreme situations, we can influence our children's self-image and their future (see Coping in Hard Times, p.151). We can make a difference.

How we respond to a child's worst moments will shape their self-esteem and behaviour just as much as our responses when they are deserving of praise. Our role is to respond to their needs – and all children need to know what behaviour is expected of them and when they have overstepped the mark (see Horribly Normal, p.166 and Co-operation and Discipline, p.196). Yet we also need to let our children know that our love is not conditional on their 'good' behaviour.

Let your child know they are allowed to make mistakes and you will still love them. If a child feels they are in a loving, caring environment but not one in which they are over-protected or stifled, if they are allowed some independence, allowed to make mistakes, that speaks volumes about the sort of person the child will turn into.

Hugh Foot, Professor of Child Psychology and Social Development, Strathclyde University

The more a child is made to feel good about herself, the more she will want to be good. The more she is humiliated, made to feel tiresome, wicked or helpless, the less point she will see in trying to please.

The Commission on Children and Violence[3]

This message of unconditional regard can be reinforced throughout our children's lives, from their very first weeks when we help them feel secure and valued by responding to their cries, caring for their needs and showing pleasure in their company (see Baby's Needs, Your Needs, p.18).

Crucially, children also need to be accepted as unique individuals

---

Your self-esteem matters

I think too much attention has been focused on the birth. When you think 40% of families in the UK will be split within ten years of the birth it is clear there are much more important issues to address. We are so abysmally uneducated about the importance of emotions in our lives. The single most important thing we can do for our children is to strengthen and develop our own self-esteem. This equips us with huge resources to draw on when the going gets tough as a parent and provides a role model for our children to feel good about themselves in the world. Little is more important than this.

Yehudi Gordon, Consultant gynaecologist and obstetrician,
specialising in holistic health

If you wish to show your child how effective good self-esteem can be, consider how good you feel about yourself and how you could treat yourself better. If you work at your own sense of worth, the job of boosting your child's self-esteem will be that much easier.

Feeling good about ourselves in a role as devalued by society as being a parent isn't always easy. It may help to reflect on the qualities it requires and the opportunities it brings. 'Many parents, especially mothers who opt to stay at home, feel they're achieving nothing compared to their peers without children. They feel devalued,' explains Angela Gruber, a transpersonal psychotherapist. 'Yet parenthood calls them to develop qualities such as love, patience, self-discipline, self-control, self-sacrifice, understanding, dependability – the list is endless. Our children teach us constantly. As my own children move into adulthood, I feel a deep sense of gratitude to all that they have taught and continue to give me. Parenthood is a precious opportunity to unfold hidden potential within us all.'

If a parent has low self-esteem they are likely to place greater expectations and demands on their children to behave in a way that will reflect positively on themselves; they will be less accepting of their children as they are.

Kitty Hagenbach, child psychotherapist

rather than a reflection of our wishes and aspirations. Our relationships with our children may be the only opportunity we have to love
unconditionally, but do we really know who it is we are loving? You
may have imagined your child sharing your pleasure of sport and they
turn out not to like it. You may have wished for an academic high-
flyer and your child may not be made that way. You may appreciate
calm and quiet and have given birth to a firecracker. Loving and
supporting our children requires us to tolerate and appreciate the differences between us, and to show them they shine in our eyes. It requires
us to create opportunities for each child to feel good about themselves,
developing *their* potential and helping them make the most of *their*
world.

I was never quite good enough. Even when I did something right there was
always a mistake pointed out, a something I could have done better,
another hurdle to jump.

Doug C

We need to help children become skilled, find what they are good at and build up
a self-esteem bank from which they can draw at times when they're not able to do
something particularly well. One of my daughters was poor at anything sporty but
over time we found she loves singing and drama. Because she excels at these things
it gives her the ability to cope in areas she is not so good at.

Eileen Hayes, parenting advisor to the NSPCC

A bedrock of love, understanding and appreciation is crucial to each
child's sense of worth. Specific approaches to help us boost their self-
esteem are detailed later in this chapter, but our respect for our children's feelings and individuality and the efforts we invest in recognising
and responding to their emotional needs will be what turns these
approaches from potentially confusing bolt-on extras with a short shelf-
life into effective strategies with profound benefits, now and for years
to come.

Understanding emotions

It's not what he feels but how he expresses it that really winds me up – it's moan, moan, whinge, whinge. He just presses all my buttons. It's not my one-off reaction that concerns me but the cumulative effect of me getting irritated and saying, 'Oh, for God's sake'. That does worry me. Is he going to think he shouldn't let me know how he feels?

John T

I think parents these days have this expectation that their children have to be happy all the time and you feel something is very seriously wrong if they are not, but it is just life, it involves happiness and sadness, ups and downs.

Marina C

Aaaaaaarrrrrrrrrrgggggggghhhhhhhhhhhhhhhhh.

Joe P, five, on being told to turn out his light

Our children's ability to recognise and express their feelings constructively helps them and helps us. We need to know what they feel and why, within reason, and they need to be able to communicate their needs and control their behaviour.

How children express their feelings can sometimes be a problem – for them and for others. If they express them in ways that are too aggressive, too timid, too loud, too confused or simply inappropriate, they risk being told off, fobbed off or ignored. Yet with our guidance, they can learn to show their love and assert their needs and opinions without going haywire.

To do this, a child first needs to know what emotions are, how they feel, what they are called and what can be done with them. Sounds obvious? Remember we are adults with adult experience and grasp of language. A child may never have felt such jealousy, hate, fear or unbridled joy before, or at least not so intensely or mixed in such a maelstrom of other emotions. Even if they have, they may not know what the feeling is called or even that other people feel it. If we identify, name and describe an emotion, we show our children that we know this feeling, too. We've handled it, and so can they.

Remember not to wait until a problem or crisis is looming, but bring feelings into everyday conversations. Naming positive as well as negative emotions makes talking about them feel less intense.

The best of parenting is when you are helping children recognise their emotions and express them on a day-to-day basis, not just when there's a problem. If they come hurtling down the slide and they are shrieking with delight, you can say, 'That looks fun!' You can talk about what is going on for them all the time so they are able to name their emotions, and express them, so that when they come to express anger it is not the only emotion they have had to express.

Vivienne Gross, family therapist

Parents can help children express emotions effectively if they:

Allow children to feel Avoid telling a child not to feel or how to feel. Think how many times children are told 'Don't be sad', 'Don't worry', 'It doesn't hurt', 'You do like it', 'Don't be daft' . . . They trip out of our mouths before we've had time to think, but if used too often they can make a child feel misunderstood, confused, ignored or rejected. Acknowledging a child's feelings may be all the help they need to begin to deal with them.

Talking about emotions

The emotional support we give our children will enrich their lives and our relationships way beyond their childhood years. US psychologist and author John Gottman's 20-year study of 100 families[4] indicates that children of parents who give emotional support and advice have better health, fewer behavioural problems and better academic results.

Helping children find words for their emotions is a fundamental part of this process, says psychotherapist and author Susie Orbach. 'I think part of the job of a parent is to help children have access not to just their biological processes but their emotional processes, and being able to name

feelings is really crucial. There isn't just one word for upset or anger, there are probably 30 or more, and if we don't name feelings or receive them then they don't find a place in people's lives. They either get repressed, cut off, or have one dominant feeling.

'For me the important issue is how we find words which help a child digest the feeling, rather than attempting to divert feelings with food treats or whatever. Feelings are what make us who we are. There's nothing wrong with them. Without them we'd be pretty empty and lost. Being sad is part of life and faking or imposing synthetic happiness is complete and utter crap. That's not going to feed our children emotionally.'

Robert fell over, I was in a rush and my first response was 'Oh, you're all right, come on, we've got to be quick' and he started howling and going into one. So I tried again. I said, 'That must have hurt' and he stopped crying and nodded. If you try to squash their feelings, they can explode right back at you. Once he realised I knew how he felt, he calmed right down.

Leslie B

The emotional needs of sensitive, highly reactive and anxious children may surprise us, especially if they struggle in situations other family members take in their stride. But their feelings are no less genuine and in need of appropriate support. Talking through potentially tricky situations in advance, and encouraging them to problem-solve, may help them feel understood as well as developing their own resources to cope: 'We're going to Tom's party this afternoon. I know you sometimes find it hard to be in a room with lots of excited children. What would make it easier?'

If we tell children repeatedly not to feel, they may stop telling us. Children whose emotions are denied may also, over time, lose confidence in their ability to recognise their own feelings, which makes them more likely to be easily led and influenced by others. Ultimately, and most destructively, they may withdraw from emotional relationships.

So try to take your child's expression of emotion as a compliment, even if it is an emotion you could do without at that moment. Most children show behaviour and feelings to their parents that they wouldn't show to others because they trust their parents' love. This is how it should be.

Accept 'negative' feelings

Babies and children can manage pain, anxiety and anger more easily if they know that adults know and accept how they feel. It is important that alongside nourishing and sharing the love and pleasure that children need, we also accept normal 'bad' feelings.

National Children's Bureau[5]

With the very best of intentions, parents often try to steer children away from expressing anger, or unhappiness. Yet stopping the expression won't stop the feeling. The sooner the feelings are expressed and accepted, the sooner they can be dealt with and disappear. Feelings that are ignored do not disappear. They simply hide to erupt again another day, often in ways that are harder to handle because neither parent nor child can locate their root cause.

Happy families are not happy all the time. Disagreements and conflict are a necessary part of living closely together. Both love and hate are to be expected in the intensity of family life but it is the way that negative emotions are handled that makes a difference.

Royal College of Paediatrics and Child Health[6]

Help children identify emotions

All scrumblywumbly.

Bea, three, when asked how she felt about her first day at nursery

You will need to acknowledge a child's feelings. For example: 'It sounds as though you are upset about something.' Labelling emotions is very helpful to children. Specific names for emotions can help them recognise, acknowledge and manage their feelings.

John Bristow, psychologist and psychotherapist

Children sometimes need our help to identify what it is that they are feeling and why (see Reflective Listening, p.99): 'I can see you're angry because Kate broke the bike,' for example, or 'You seem frightened of going to school today.'

When we're not sure what a child is feeling, or when they seem to have a mixture of conflicting emotions, it may help to say so: 'I guess you're feeling lots of things at the moment. Perhaps you're a bit excited and a bit scared?' or 'I'm confused. Could you tell me a bit more about how you feel?' Even describing the situation – 'This must be hard for you. Your toy is broken' – shows understanding and encourages the child to explain.

Talking about the feelings of people and characters in stories and programmes encourages children to explore emotions openly and easily. Even toddlers may enjoy discussing people's feelings and why they behave the way they do.[7] As our children get older, talking with them about emotions can help them develop a sense of perspective about their own feelings and encourage them to see the difference between a temporary upset and a more serious problem.

Once children recognise their emotions, they can begin to manage them and marshal them in pursuit of a goal rather than being hampered by them. They can also learn to recognise emotions in others. This is essential for healthy relationships.

Candida Hunt, Family Links

Show we understand We can let our children know we understand what they are feeling, even if we don't agree with the reasons why. One effective way of doing this is to 'reflect back' emotions, in context (see Reflective Listening, p.99). For example:

Child: 'I hate her.'
You: 'I can see she was getting on your nerves.'
or
Child: 'I hate you.'
You: 'I know you're angry that I made you tidy your room.'

We are not saying the child should not feel the emotion, neither are we agreeing with their response. We are simply saying 'message received' which, with any luck, will stop another louder message following on.

There may be times when it's simply not possible to discuss a situation in detail with a child. Letting them know we understand how they feel will help them cope until we have got time to talk. Compare these three exchanges.

1   *Child:* 'I hate Miss Adams!'
    Parent: 'No, you don't.'

2   *Child:* 'I hate Miss Adams.'
    Parent: 'Oh darling, do you? Poor you. Are you all right to go to school?'

3   *Child:* 'I hate Miss Adams.'
    Parent: 'You hate Miss Adams right now. Can you tell me why?'
    Child: 'She told me I wasn't trying and I was!'
    Parent: 'That must have been hard. We have to get to school now but let's talk about it again this afternoon.'

In the first exchange, the child's emotions were contradicted. In the second, the parent collapsed under their weight. In the third, the child's

Exploring emotions

It helps if the underlying message is that when you are faced with difficulties you are courageous and do the best you can; that the world is an interesting place and even though bad things happen, lots of good things happen, too. All the old fairy stories show that even though you are a little person, you are strong and courageous and so these are wonderful to share with children.

Dr Dorothy Rowe, psychologist and writer

We cannot accept and acknowledge our children's emotions until we know what they are. But what if they cannot put their feelings into words? Sharing stories can help children explore, identify and understand the feelings of others, which may help them understand and express their own.

Some parents encourage their children to paint or draw how they feel. This can be very effective and reinforces the message that even 'negative' emotions can be expressed non-aggresively. It may be more appropriate for less violent emotions such as sadness or longing, however, or after the storm has passed. Few children in full-throttle rage would respond well to a parent suggesting: 'Would you like to draw how you feel, darling?'

Try to be alert to times when your child describes feelings through symbols, images, even gestures, when they don't yet have the confidence or vocabulary to use specific words.

This mother's story is a graphic example of how parental responses can help a child struggling to understand emotions and experiences. 'We were chopping vegetables and my son (six) said, "You know there's a difference between this time this year and this time last year? Like someone with a big axe comes and chops time into two different bits?" We had no idea what he was talking about but I knew he was trying to tell us something important, so later I asked him how he felt about the two "bits of time". Asking how he felt rather than what he meant seemed to help. It turned out he was talking about his new teacher. This year he feels understood and understands, last year he felt neither. His experience is so different, to him it felt like time had been split into two bits – then and now.'

Once children have expressed an emotion, it is much easier for parents to help them cope.

The reassurance needs to come after the emotion has been released, as the child cannot be receptive while the emotion is still present. Be led by your child and wait until you are 'invited' to offer reassurance or comfort. Be clear you are responding to the child's need, not your own.

Kitty Hagenbach, child psychotherapist

emotions were acknowledged but not inflated, and avenues were left open for further conversation.

Letting our children know we've had similar experiences may also help children feel less angry, fearful or isolated, and provide living proof that problems can be overcome:

'Oh, that must have hurt. Sometimes it helps me if I hold my knee after I have banged it. Do you want to try?'

'I didn't like the dark when I was your age. I know now that there's nothing to be frightened of, but I did feel scared when I was young. What would help?'

Be guided by your child's response. If they find this annoying rather than helpful, they'll let you know!

Let children know that feelings are OK, but there may be better ways of expressing them It is important children know their feelings are valid, but that this doesn't give them free rein to express them in any way they choose. Our children will need our guidance on what behaviour we find acceptable. You can explain that being angry is OK but hurting is not, for example, or that you understand why they are disappointed, but shouting in your face is not going to help them or you. How else could they let you know how they're feeling?

Suggesting different ways of releasing emotions can be helpful if children seem stuck for ideas (see Exploring Emotions, p.134). Some like drawing or painting pictures, some may need to get physical – running, jumping, thumping the bed, kicking a ball – before they feel calm enough to talk.

When we don't like how a child is behaving, we can tell them and ask them to think of a better way: 'I can see you are angry and tired of waiting for your turn *and* you know it is not OK to pull Katie off the swing. How could you let her know you're angry without hurting?' (see Co-operation and Discipline, p.196.)

How and when to express how we feel is a balancing act we all get wrong sometimes, so don't expect perfection. The important message for children to receive are that feelings are OK, and they have a choice in how they communicate them. Also, that they will sometimes make mistakes that will affect others, and they have the capacity to put many things right. This balanced sense of themselves will encourage them to take responsibility for their mistakes and do something about them rather than relying on the constant approval of others, denying their mistakes, blaming others or becoming aggressively defensive.

Over time children do understand the concept of appropriate behaviour, i.e. it is OK to have feelings and it is only OK to behave in certain ways with those feelings. So even, for example, the joy of splashing through puddles in the park can be separated out at quite a young age so that this same behaviour is not OK in different circumstances, e.g. on the way to school.

Pat Elliot, psychotherapist and bereavement counsellor

Try not to confront but to talk Acknowledging and naming our children's emotions requires us to be calm. If we are confrontational, children will clam up, won't talk and won't hear. They might shout, but they won't listen.

Imagine We can do more than think what it must feel like to be in their shoes. We can imagine what it must feel like *to be them* in this situation – at their age, with their temperament, vulnerabilities and needs.

Thinking about how he must feel has helped me stop flying off the handle so often. I see him more as a kid who's tired, nervous, muddled, or angry and not just a kid who's being horrible and getting on my nerves. It's also helped me explain things more clearly. I used to just say 'No, don't'. Now I'll say something like, 'I know you are feeling such a way but you are not allowed to hit your sister, just like she's not allowed to hit you.' It has helped.

Dave G

Be honest There will be times when we are justifiably angry, and these aren't the times for calm and considered discussions about emotions. We can tell our children why: 'I can see you're angry and so am I! I'm too angry to talk right now,' or 'I know you're furious, but if we talk about this now I'll lose my temper and I really don't want to. Let's talk about it later.'

Find time

People today are always in a rush. The enemy of love is hurry. Love returns when we spend time together. If you want things to go well with your children you need to win back some time. Children are in the here and now.

*If you talk to anyone who has had something scary happen with
their children, they all say 'Enjoy them now.'*

Steve Biddulph, psychologist and author

This is at risk of sounding like magic wand-waving. Talk to most
parents about having more time for their children and the most polite
response is 'Chance would be a fine thing.' Time is what many parents
have much too little of, often for reasons way beyond their control.
Yet that does not deny its importance.

If you can grab some, hold it tight. The importance of spending
sufficient time with our children to enjoy their company and understand them and their emotions is obvious. Time and timing are different
matters, of course. Our child might be desperate because the head's
fallen off their toy just as we're getting off the bus with them and the
weekly shop. Not a great time for calm and supportive conversation.
But we will need to find time as soon as we reasonably can: 'I can
understand why you're upset. Let's get home and see what we can do.'

Allowing our children time to go at their pace and work through
their feelings and thoughts can also make life easier, for them and for
us. We're so used to hurtling from one job to the next that we can
forget the importance of slowing down. But a tantrum-prone toddler
is far less likely to blow a gasket if given a bit of wobble, allowed to
take great interest in every gate hinge on the way to the bus stop,
allowed to walk to the shops and back for once or choose their own
jumper after great deliberation. A few minutes' playing with a child,
starting off a game or rigging up a sail at the end of the sofa can bring
more peace than ignoring their cries that they've nothing to do. Relaxed
one-to-one time also allows relaxed conversations to unfold, and helps
children express what they need at a pace they find comfortable.

Clearly, this is not going to work every day. Rushing against the
clock is often unavoidable. But rushing ups the emotional stakes with
children of any age, which means they are more likely to stop talking
and start expressing their feelings through their behaviour. A greater
awareness of this may help us all make extra time a greater priority.

*Almost everything with children requires effort, time and giving. You will either
give it up front or after the event, trying to sort out conflicts and upset. In my
experience, it's easier to take time to think and head in the right direction than
head off in the wrong one and have to turn everybody around.*

Claire H

Common fears and anxieties

Doubts, fears and anxieties are there in life. The important thing is to equip a child to cope with them.

Pat Elliot, psychotherapist and bereavement counsellor

I used to see a snake in my wall. My parents would tell me not to worry, there weren't any snakes in my bedroom. That didn't help at all. Years later I realised it wasn't a snake but the light from the lamppost outside, shining through the curtains. We left that house when I was four, and I can still remember that snake.

Sean C

Children can cope far better with their anxieties and fears if they know those feelings are recognised and accepted by those who care for them[8] (see Separation Anxiety, p.140). Far from exaggerating fears and encouraging weakness, as many parents once believed, acknowledging their worries actually helps children be more resilient and better able to cope. It helps them recognise and work through their anxieties themselves.

Every child will have their own fears and vulnerabilities, some of which may be obvious, others less so – dogs, loud noises, new places, the list is as varied as children themselves. Looking at situations from the child's perspective may help us understand their response and how best to proceed.

Let's take the example of one very common infant fear – the bath. Forcing the issue means ignoring and inflating the child's distress, which will make parent and child feel terrible. Looking from the child's perspective can prompt possible ways forward: perhaps skipping the bath for a few days, washing in between, until things calm down enough to carry on. We could then get in the bath with the child, or encourage water play with toys, or put in just enough water to let them splash but not feel overwhelmed. Playing in a quiet swimming pool can re-assure older babies and children that water can be fun. Imagining and acknowledging how it might feel to be scared can help us explore solutions gently, while ignoring genuine upset can turn everyday situations into battlegrounds and undermine children's trust in our care (see Separation Anxiety, p.140).

A fundamental fear?

Peter Wilson, child psychotherapist and Director of Young Minds

I think, right from the outset, children are terrified of not belonging to anybody. You can have different names for it, but basically infants are frightened of not being fed or nourished. Then they also fear there is nothing out there for them that cares about them, that the things they need – the nourishment, the pleasurable experiences, the sense of attachment, the sense of feeling held and protected – will not be there, and they will be left abandoned, isolated, uncared for, unheeded, unacknowledged and unfed.

These are the primary fears and underlie others – fear of the dark, of separating from Mummy, of parents arguing and rowing, of what's going to happen to them.

At a higher level, the fears are: not being approved of, being rejected, being humiliated, put down, being made to feel no good, being hurt or damaged, fears which build on each other the more the child is aware of the world. But behind them all is the fundamental fear of being left.

If children get very frightened usually something has happened – perhaps they have slipped badly in the bath or anxiety for their safety is being communicated by the parent. It is better to give them less water and more freedom than lots of water and still the need to hold on to them. It is very wrong just to keep going in an effort to overcome fears. We do have to expose children to things they are frightened of but in a safe, gentle way.

Carol Ann Hally, health visitor and clinical practice teacher

Children are astonishingly sensitive to adult anxieties, and often worry about 'adult' concerns, from family breakdown to street crime and war. They need us to recognise this and support and reassure as necessary rather than dismissing their concerns as inappropriate to their age – the 'Don't worry your little head about it' trap. This doesn't mean providing our children with information they don't need or which may disturb them further; it does mean that appropriate honesty as well as positive reassurance and listening to their concerns are often the best policy (see Protection v. Exposure, p.379).

Wherever possible tell your children the truth and go for the straight line because in the long run your children will trust you. I think you can protect them best that way. If a child asks, 'Can a burglar get in?' we can say, 'We've locked up, it is

very unlikely. I really don't think it will happen.' That reassures but acknowledges
it is a small possibility

Peter Wilson, child psychotherapist and Director of Young Minds

Beware ridiculing fears. Even well-intentioned, gentle ribbing of the 'You silly sausage, there's nothing to be afraid of' variety may sound loving to you but can be devastating to a child who is trying to express a very real anxiety. Children experience intense emotions and wild imaginings: it is obvious to you that a strange swamp thing couldn't fit into the bottom of the airing cupboard, but not to your child (see Nightmares and Night Terrors, p.61); you know from experience that a bath is a safe place to be, but to a baby still getting to know the world, it can be a very scary place.

Separation anxiety

We expect 18- to 30-month-old children to begin exploring with the absolute certainty that they can return to their carer in a group situation. They are often desperate to get in there and play but they need to know they are not on their own and they can run back to 'Mummy' when they need to. There would be cause for concern if the child will not leave the side of the carer at all, and I would be equally anxious if a mother says her child just runs off without ever batting an eyelid.
It is perfectly understandable that a young child would not want to stay with strangers.

Carol Ann Hally, health visitor and clinical practice teacher

Separation anxiety at your absence is a perfectly normal and healthy response from a young child. You are their emotional anchor and they are bound to feel sad and confused without you.

The importance of acknowledging a child's distress is one of the most significant findings of new research into handling separation anxiety. Many parents and carers try to stop children expressing their sadness at separation, which may help the adults but does not help the child (see Choosing Childcare, p.290).

Think of it from the child's point of view and this makes great sense. If they are comforted by a key carer they know and trust, they know they are in a place where their feelings matter. If they are encouraged or told to hide how they feel, they are not only without their parent but also in a place

Far better to respect how children feel and respond to their needs rather than ignore, dismiss or fuel them. Compare these responses:

Child: 'There's a witch in the cupboard.'
Parent (dismissing fear): 'Don't be silly, there are no such things as witches.'
and
Child: 'There's a witch in the cupboard.'
Parent (ignoring): 'Lights off now.'

Child: 'There's a witch in the cupboard.'
Parent (fuelling): 'I'll scare her away for you.'

where people do not understand their sadness.

'Nurseries sometimes view a child upset at this time as an indication that there is a problem or that something has gone wrong rather than seeing it as a normal reaction to the stress of separation,' state childcare researchers Peter Elfer and Dorothy Selleck.

They have studied the anxieties children feel when they are brought to nursery, and how parents and staff can handle these sensitively.[9] Their findings throw much light on managing children's anxieties in general, and on adults' tendency to brush them under the carpet.

'Sometimes staff consider that the best strategy is to move the child away as quickly as possible. We have seen many examples of staff wanting to distract a child by showing him something out of the window or wanting to distract him with a toy.

'Where we did see examples of staff who were able to "tune in" especially skilfully to a child's emotional needs, they would instead take the child to a quiet part of the nursery and just reassure them gently that they would be OK, that Mummy or Daddy would be returning at whatever time, and they would talk about what Mummy and Daddy may be doing whilst the child was in the nursery.

'It really is better that the distress is acknowledged, tolerated and managed. It is not helpful to pretend it is not here or not real or too dangerous to be talked about. It is upsetting to say goodbye to someone you love and that should be recognised. A very young child may not have a real sense of when their mother is going to return and they do need comforting and reassuring about that.

'It is important to remember the pressure on nurseries to appear to be happy, jolly sorts of places – you can understand that from a business point of view. But the transition into nursery is a very important one and the nursery and parents need to think through how it is best managed.'

and

Child: 'There's a witch in the cupboard.'

Parent: 'That's a scary feeling. Witches are in stories and thoughts, though, not real life. What would make you feel better?'

Explaining to children that different people are afraid of different things, and how we felt as children in similar situations may help them better understand their own experiences and show them that there's nothing to be ashamed of in admitting fear. We need to be careful, though, not to suggest that our fears and experiences are identical, because they won't be, or to focus more on our past than their present.

After her first morning at school, my daughter was such a whirl of contradictory emotions that she tried them all out for size in rapid succession. She sang, shouted – at me – then announced that she hated her drawing paper, then had an astonishing tantrum and ended up sobbing. We cuddled, then I told her about how strange I'd felt on my first day at school, because there were some bits of it I liked and other bits that felt very odd and other bits that were scary. I didn't know all the people and I wasn't even sure where the loo was. She seemed amazed that I ever was a child, then said she'd felt a bit like that, too. It seemed to help her calm down enough to talk rather than explode in all directions.

Lindsay C

Whatever our child's age, they need us to try to listen to what they are telling us, either through their words or their behaviour. Even if we can't take away the source of their concern, knowing we understand their fears and take them seriously will help them cope.

Our feelings as parents

Our emotions have a right to be acknowledged, too. We all get angry, happy, sad, confused and if we do not show our children how we deal with those feelings, we deprive them of an important role model.

Anger, for example, is an emotion most parents experience, often with good reason. We can show our children that anger is not the same as aggression and that it can be expressed constructively and used positively, as a prompt to change situations for the better. If we can express our anger in ways that show we are controlling it, rather than it controlling us, without becoming abusive, blaming, threatening or crushing our children in the process, we will have taught them a powerful lesson.

Clearly, some issues are not appropriate to share with our children and it is important we respect their age, vulnerability and understanding (see Coping in Hard Times, p.151). Neither should we blame our children or burden them with responsibility for our happiness (we can, for example, say 'I feel angry/tired/sad,' rather than 'You make me angry/tired/sad'). Remember, too, to tell them when we're feeling great, not just when we're feeling angry or low.

The catch, of course, is that we can't let our children know how we feel unless we know ourselves and are able to admit it. This is not something that comes easily to everyone. Go at your own pace, but try to reflect on how you are feeling and why.

Being emotionally honest with ourselves will help us:

- **Better understand our relationships with our children** How we are feeling will influence how we respond.

Parenting involves an almost endlessly diverse and shifting mixture of care, affection, control, and stimulation. All this is supported by a complex array of feelings and interactions that reflect partly the parent's internal world and partly the child's temperament and reactions.[10]

Christine Puckering, clinical psychologist, Senior Research Fellow, University of Glasgow, and co-founder of Mellow Parenting

- **Better manage our responses** These will take us less by surprise if we are aware of our own emotional state. Not admitting how you feel, even to yourself, will make you more tense and increase the chance of you blowing your stack in ways you don't wish (see Boiling Points, p.146).

The first stage for parents to do it differently is to become aware of their own emotions sufficiently to moderate them while experiencing them. We may learn many tactics and skills but not be able to use them because of our state of mind. Being in touch with our own feelings is in a sense a master skill. Without it, we cannot use others.

John Bristow, psychologist and psychotherapist

Communicating our feelings appropriately and constructively will help our children:

- **Express their emotions** Instead of bottling up and lashing out, our children will learn the confidence and the vocabulary to say how they feel and to recognise and consider other people's feelings in what they say and do.

We need to accept feelings and be flexible in the ways these are expressed. Families who have problems around expressing anger tend to fall into one of two groups. One group is where everyone is angry all the time and the other is where no one ever gets angry whatever happens or admits to the slightest bit of irritation. It would be more helpful to talk to our children about how we feel and give guidance on how to behave with those feelings. It is helpful to show different ways – shout, go quiet, write a letter to those we cannot challenge directly. It is important to show children different ways to express anger.

Dr Dorothy Rowe, psychologist and writer

- **Boost their understanding** Knowing how parents sometimes feel gives children a more realistic view of the world and of people's strengths and vulnerabilities. This allows them to be more accepting of their parents' inability to control the universe (as important a knowledge for an eleven-year-old who wants new trainers every month as it is for a toddler who wants the rain to stop). It also gives children the opportunity to view themselves in a more accepting light, warts and all.

You can't learn Japanese from someone who doesn't speak it. We can't teach a child emotional literacy without being emotionally literate ourselves.

Candida Hunt, Family Links

- **Ditch unnecessary guilt** Appropriate communication and explanation of our feelings can help children understand that they aren't to blame for everything that happens in families. This will help protect them from the potentially devastating responsibility children may feel when something very painful or serious happens in their lives (see Coping in Hard Times, p.151).

I thought my mum had left home because I was untidy and she was so unhappy about that. I had no understanding of her real feelings or reasons for leaving.

It is not protecting children to hide how you feel if they still have to cope with the consequences.

Jane S

- **Get the message** If we say one thing and feel another, our children will sense the contradiction and not know which to respond to – the words or the feelings (see Communication, p.89). Smiling while saying, 'Come on, sweetie, let go of Grandma's curtains,' as you fume inside will only confuse. This is likely to result in a child gripping on tighter, until *what* we say and *how* we say it communicate the same, clear message – i.e. 'Let go now.' It is far easier for our children and for our nerves if our feelings are clear from the start.

Let them know how you feel. Without this, it can just feel like a nag. If you find what they are doing a problem – perhaps they are being unbearably loud or playing football in the house – explaining how you feel will help motivate them to change their behaviour because they understand the consequences for you.

Brigid Treacy, parenting advisor

- **Exploring the roots of our emotions**

I've realised that when me and my wife hit a bad patch, I see the worst in my son. It's like all the anger and sadness that's not getting sorted out elsewhere gets stuck on him.

Mark T

The intimacy of our relationship with our children, and the amount of time we spend with them, means they are sometimes at the receiving end of parental feelings they have not caused, but merely tapped or unleashed. Exploring where our feelings are rooted may help us understand and manage them more easily. This is especially important when we are aware of being snappy or sad around them, or blaming them without justification. We owe it to them and to ourselves to try to untangle the knots.

- **Memories of our own childhood**

Becoming a parent can sometimes raise issues that stem from one's own experience of being a child. Distressing memories or gaps in one's own parenting can surface, stirring powerful feelings and making it difficult to relate to one's own child. At these times, it is very important to sit quietly and listen to the child within the parent that is longing to be heard. These feelings and memories are nothing to be ashamed of but need to be approached with warmth and compassion. It helps to talk about them with someone you trust and who is supportive.

Angela Gruber, transpersonal psychotherapist

Just as having a baby can stir thoughts and feelings about our relationship with our own parents, so bringing up children can stir feelings and responses rooted in our own childhood. We may feel drawn to responding as our own parents did to us, or to reject out of hand our parents' approaches to raising children. Yet neither may be appropriate. Far better to consider what works best for us in our relationships, and to choose appropriate and helpful ways to respond to our own children's feelings, thoughts and actions.

Recognising and reflecting on the emotions stirred in our childhoods can be an important step in learning to respond sensitively to our children as unique individuals, rather than to echoes of our own early experiences, feelings and fears.

Thinking about our attitude to emotions is important, too. Have we tended to regard emotional expression as somehow weak, unnecessary, indulgent, embarrassing or explosive? Where have those attitudes come from? How might they influence our responses to our children? Are they something we want to continue or to do something about?

Boiling point

We can learn to recognise our own build-up of anger. It's then sometimes possible to take action before we reach our flashpoint.[11]

Candida Hunt, Family Links

Prevention is clearly better than cure, but if you feel angry to the point of explosion, do something. Expressing how you feel and why may help you feel calmer and more in control: 'I am really angry because I've asked you twice already to pick up your clothes and they're still on the floor.' Even counting to 10, breathing slowly to slow your heart rate or leaving the room for a few minutes may help you cool down enough not to snap.

There are times when I just need five minutes to recharge, to get to grips with the situation. I will tell them I need five minutes on my own and go in my bedroom, shut the door and read a magazine.

Ros L

In our view there are no 'bad feelings', though there are many painful ones.
All feelings are OK, all feelings are valid. This challenges traditional social and
religious views. Generations of boys, for example, have learned that they
'shouldn't' feel upset, sad, shy or frightened.[12]

Candida Hunt, Family Links

• Scapegoating

Children are extremely sensitive to parental stress and too often the butt of our moods. If a problem is overwhelming us, they may suffer (see Coping in Hard Times, p.151). This happens to most parents sometimes, but by being emotionally honest with ourselves, we can aim to keep such times to a minimum.

Occasionally, one child in particular may become the target of upset, sadness or anger that lies elsewhere, often being blamed or 'scapegoated' as 'the' problem in the family for a long period of time. The effects of this can be devastating and life-long, damaging the child's sense of their own worth, their behaviour and their trust in relationships. If we become aware of a child feeling they can't do anything right, or if they make us fly off the handle with little provocation, it's time to consider what else is making us feel bad or sad. It may be time to address the real problems, and love the child.

• Who do you remind me of?

One of my children looks just like my dad. His mannerisms are similar, too.
I'm sure that's one reason why he irritates me most.

Fiona M

When a child reminds us of someone else, our responses may be fuelled by our feelings towards that person as well as to the child themselves. And feelings can be prompted by more than physical appearance or behaviour traits. Gender, position in the family, temperament, sense of humour, particular aptitudes, difficulties, and much more may remind us of ourselves and others, and inform our feelings and reactions. Acknowledging the similarities we see and the feelings they evoke and, crucially, accepting our children as unique and separate individuals, is essential if we are to liberate them from our presumptions and our past.

Moving closer, building bonds

'Strong attachment and bonding between parent and child enhance their relationship together and the child's other relationships inside and outside the family,' explains child psychotherapist Kitty Hagenbach.

'But the bond between a parent and child is not made of cement. It can be lost and it can be created or strengthened as a child grows. To bond, both the parent and the child need to feel safe and relaxed. It is based on trust.

'The optimum time to bond is at the birth, but the process can start in the womb and the opportunities to bond continue long after the birth. For example, I thought I was fully bonded with my first son. Then at 12 years old he went into hospital for appendicitis and that experience created an even stronger bond between us. The difference was palpable and beautiful and it has changed our relationship since.

'As parents we need to stay in touch with our children but also with ourselves, to make sure we are present for them emotionally and physically and that we deal with the things that can get in the way, such as grief or depression, or the experiences of medical intervention at birth. Sometimes we can do this ourselves, sometimes we need help.

'If bonding has not occurred around the birth, we must remember that opportunities continue. The bond can always be healed. Even as an adult, if we can find the voice to share our sadness or anger with our parents and they receive this and are sorry and wish to reconnect and make things better in the present, we can bond. It is so important to take the opportunities to reconnect with our own children. It shapes so much of our ongoing relationship with them, and how they see themselves and the world.'

- **Emotional dependency** Children thrive in atmospheres where emotions are appropriately and constructively expressed. They don't thrive when parents use children as emotional props or confidants or overload them with inappropriate information (see Divorce and Separation, p.262).

- **Emotional distance** The rhythms of human relationships mean that sometimes we may feel very close to our children, and sometimes less so. Sometimes we may adore them, and occasionally we won't find much pleasure in their company. That's family life. Problems arise when relationships become 'stuck' in a phase we're not happy with, and when problems seem entrenched and long-term.

As ever, being honest and admitting to ourselves how we feel is the first step to turning things around (see Moving Close, Building

Bonds, p.148). The next is to do something about it. Spending relaxed one-to-one time with any child we feel less close to, boosting their sense of worth and building up a bank of shared happy memories, is a simple and effective way of nurturing the relationship.

All of this becomes much easier if we have the support of others to talk to and to turn to. If we want to invest in our relationships with our children, we also need to invest in our other relationships inside and outside the family. These will boost our resources and resilience to negotiate the emotional journey of parenthood.

The problem with 'perfect' parents

Christine Puckering, psychologist and co-founder of Mellow Parenting

Life will present us with many frustrations, and learning to deal with frustration and disappointment in small ways is a very good stress inoculator for later. Children who have never experienced any frustration don't know how to handle it; they have not learned to negotiate.

Respecting a child is not the same as giving in to their wishes all the time. In fact it is not good for a child to have what they want all the time, so I have no problem with telling a child, 'I know you want two biscuits but one is enough.' They need these useful lessons. It is important to acknowledge and validate their feelings and wishes, but not necessarily to grant them.

We followed a group of women who had depression when their children were two years and some of those mothers were being 'the perfect mother'. They got up at five o'clock in the morning and did all the housework so when the child got up at 7.30 they could spend the whole day with the child. They had very warm, very intense relationships with their children. Observing them at two, I thought, 'Gosh this child is the happiest child, what a wonderful childhood.' When we saw them again at entry to playgroup these same children had absolutely no idea how to deal with frustration.

There was a group of bigger boys who were playing a bit rough and I remember vividly one of these children who had had this wonderful relationship with his mother going up to these kids and expecting to just get what he wanted. They hit him and he did not know how to handle not getting what he wanted. He just kept going back for more.

It is forgiving for parents to know that having the odd bad day and their children surviving it is actually quite useful. If they haven't learned to cope with people in bad moods they won't know when to stand up and be assertive and when to let this one go, when it is best to stay clear. This little boy standing up to four bigger boys when starting school hadn't really learned it. It is a huge social and survival skill and you do not learn this if you get all your needs met instantaneously.

The Problem with Perfection

Some advice to parents – that you should respond immediately to your child's every need is quite persecuting and can make your own self-esteem low because you know you can't be like that all the time. You are a human being and children need to know that you have your limits. You are not going to prevent them from ever feeling neglected or misunderstood and they have to be able to cope with that. As your child grows older, you have to counterbalance being responsive and listening to their unique needs as an individual, with letting them experience age-appropriate frustrations and postponing gratification, in other words, letting them wait for their needs to be met. This is socialisation.

Vivienne Gross, family therapist

So you're not a perfect parent? Join the club. We can beat ourselves up and burden ourselves with guilt because we've fallen short of how we'd ideally like to be with our children at all times. Perfect parenting is a myth that can distract too much emotional energy from exploring ways to do the best we can.

And want some good news? Imperfection is good for children. This has nothing to do with being harsh on them and everything to do with not being harsh on ourselves when we don't act as well as we'd wish or can't do immediately all that our children desire or require.

Being honest, human and fallible helps children understand that life doesn't always go as we want and helps them cope when it doesn't. This is crucial to their ability to know how to behave in difficult situations without feeling swamped by anger, upset or outrage. Children have to learn how to cope with adversity and frustration, and it is much safer to learn this from people they love and who love them.

Learning that sometimes parents get it wrong is an important lesson in life. Learning that other people have needs that occasionally have to take priority is essential for children's emotional development. Learning to wait for non-material and material pleasures increases their value, as they become invested with the pleasure of anticipation.

When children's parents and their own experience tell them that they will always get what they want, they may blame themselves when things go wrong that are outside their control. This notion can blight a child's life. Even children brought up to believe that good always overcomes bad, that the truth will always be told and that the guys with the white hats always win, can be deeply shocked when real life doesn't work that way. Those with a more balanced experience better understand that this is not a reflection on themselves.

Every relationship hits rough patches and there are bound to be times when, with hindsight, we realise we could have handled situations better with our children. We should learn from these moments, but we should put them in perspective. Children need parents to be warm, responsive and loving, not perfect.

It is my observation that many well-meaning parents bring up their children badly. If a child is brought up to believe that the world is a fair and just place to be as an adult, he or she will be disappointed. Some adults can never really get over this. Just think about how unpleasant the business world is. You need to be prepared for that. We need to stop pretending the world is a perfectly fair place but rather an interesting one in which we can encourage children to take on challenges and face problems with as much courage as possible. It is important to educate children on what helps them survive life.

Dr Dorothy Rowe, psychologist and writer

Coping in hard times

All studies world-wide of children of misfortune have found that the most significant positive influence to be a close, caring relationship with a significant adult who believed in them and with whom they could identify, who acted as an advocate for them, and from whom they could gather strength to overcome their hardship.[13]

Froma Walsh, professor of psychiatry and co-director, Center for Family Health, Chicago

We cannot eradicate all upset from our children's lives or sidestep all painful situations. But we can help ourselves and our children manage and negotiate hard times and minimise their potential for damage.

Helping yourself so you can help your child

Wherever you live or whatever your situation, being a parent is not easy. Many parents feel exhausted and overwhelmed by the stresses of family life. It is even more difficult if family or friends are unable to offer you support and a breathing space when you most need them. Some parents lose confidence in their ability to cope and most can remember days when they would have liked someone to turn to. Everyone needs a hand sometime.

Brian Waller, chief executive, Home-Start

The pressures on parents and families can be huge, but there may be ways to reduce the risks of us snapping under the strain.

Feeling miserable, tired, washed-out, tearful, being bad-tempered, snappy or unresponsive are all possible indicators of high stress and warning signs for parents to take action. It may help to identify those everyday situations we find difficult to handle. They may be unrelated to the root cause of our anxiety, and this will need to be addressed,

If you hurt your child or fear you may

He was still pretty helpless, about 15 months. It was the middle of the night, I was so tired. His cry really irritated me, it got to me at irritation levels you couldn't believe. I just wanted him to leave me alone. I lost it, I leaned over him on the nappy changing table, I yelled at him and shook him at which point my husband came into the room. I sat on the tube next morning thinking they're going to take him away, or take me away. I can still remember the look of fear on his face, when it was happening it was almost as if I was watching myself doing it. You imagine you will be endlessly patient because they are your kids, but it is scary how close to the edge you can get, how that point is not far away. It didn't happen again. It scared me so much, I knew it was an isolated incident. Thank God for my support systems, my family and friends. How people cope who haven't got that kind of support I'll never know.

Laura C

If the choice is between you hurting the baby or child or leaving him to scream until someone can come and help or you can calm yourself, it is better to leave the child to scream. In that extreme instant, mother or father need to look after themselves first in order that they can then look after their child.

Linda Connell, trainer in communication and group work skills for parents and health professionals but these 'triggers' or 'flash points' also need to be recognised and dealt with for everyone's sake. Bathtime, the school run, mealtimes, bedtimes, homework sessions, Friday afternoons, Monday mornings – each family will have its own set of situations which can compound other problems or heat tempers to boiling point.

So what might help us handle them differently? Perhaps more sleep, or a night off, a talk with a friend or tackling some aspect of

---

Shaking a baby or hitting a child can terrify and confuse. It can cause physical harm, sometimes brain damage or even fatal injury. If you ever feel close to hurting your child, first deal with the immediate crisis:

1: STOP.

2: Remove yourself from the situation. Put the baby in the cot, or leave your child in a room and take time out. The child may scream but do not go back until you are calm.

3: Wait. Are you calm enough to return? It might help to call an adviceline (see Contacts, p.429) or a friend. Perhaps you could get someone to take over for a short while? Try to remember a time when your child made you laugh or smile or melted your heart. You are the same people.

4: When you return, your child may still be screaming or behaving in a way that annoys or upsets you. Be prepared for that – you have reached a state of self-control, the child may not. Think of some ways you might help your child cope with their distress.

When the immediate crisis has calmed, consider what you must do in the longer term:

1: What help and support do you need? Make getting this a priority.

2: Is there anything you can change about what you do and how you live to reduce stress?

3: If you haven't contacted your health visitor, GP or a helpline for support and advice, try to do so now.

We are talking about very complex factors, here. Perhaps a parent has inadequate support or too many demands on them. There might be other factors that push them to the edge. Circumstances can weave themselves together in a way that isn't helping and you need someone outside the situation to help untangle it. It could be a neighbour, a friend, a professional person. If you feel at the pitch where you have shaken a baby or hit a child, or you fear you may, don't try to do it on your own. Ask for help, get the support you need.

Vivienne Gross, family therapist

our child's behaviour. Perhaps a relative could help with the bath-time/bedtime routine for a night or two. Maybe we need to reduce what we expect to achieve in a day or to ask for more support. Whatever you choose, try also to carve out some time to relax, think and have a break from your routine (see Your Needs, p.29).

Without taking care of ourselves and our needs we can easily become resentful. This inhibits our ability to hear our children or be with them without feeling so over-demanded. We begin simply to see how our children are behaving, not why.

Stella Ward, nurse and parenting support specialist

There is a popular view that people who physically or emotionally abuse their children are other people, at the 'psycho' end of society. But most are parents like

---

Stress points

The potential effects of high stress on children include:

Behaviour problems Children's social and learning skills are often dented if they feel stressed and their confidence is low. This can result in 'testing' behaviour they know to be wrong. They may have difficulty in making or keeping friends or in concentrating and reaching their potential at school.

Physical problems Stress can be a factor in headaches, migraine, asthma, eczema and other conditions. It may even affect children's growth.[14]

Mental health problems, including depression. How can parents spot when their child is stressed? 'There are obvious signs, like children being more fretful or more clingy, not wanting to go to school, bed-wetting and nightmares,' says Peter Wilson, child psychotherapist and director

of Young Minds. 'I think their persistence is key. We all have bad days, bad weeks, but a month or more of that and I would be worried.

'Listlessness also shows you something is wrong. Children who are well are happy, curious and alert. I would watch children who are really not interested or unable to really lose themselves in what they are doing. They do need to be absorbed at times, say when they are playing with their dolls or building something. When children can't do that I think it is a sign that they are stressed.

'Finally, parents need to look for changes in a child's behaviour. If he's been playing with lots of children and suddenly he's at home alone all the time, beginning to wake at night or becoming extremely fretful of going to sleep, all these things should alert a parent.'

*you and me who have snapped under stress and done something they really didn't
want to do. You have to recognise you are stressed and do something about it.
One of the best ways is to recognise your flash points and walk away from those
situations or, better still, make positive changes in your life to help you avoid those
spirals that lead you to behave in a particular way. Whatever you need, the
important thing is to act.*

Eileen Hayes, parenting advisor to the NSPCC

Helping Children Cope

*Whatever a child's circumstance, what matters most to a child's view of
themselves and the world is the relationship they have with their parent. We have
questioned 4,500 young people [15] and, while differences in background, family
structure, poverty or education levels affected 'can-do' attitudes, the most significant
difference related to their family's parenting style. Parents who 'listen to my
problems and views' were the most likely to be associated with high
self-esteem in children.*

Adrienne Katz, Young Voice

*Long-term problems occur when the parenting style fails to compensate for the
inevitable deficiencies that become manifest in the course of the 20 years or so it
takes to bring up a child.*

from Child Protection, Messages from Research[16]

How our children respond to hard times and problems in their lives
will depend on their circumstances and experiences, their temperament, their social environment and how we as parents equip them to
cope.[17] This requires us to recognise situations they may find hard to
handle and to understand our pivotal role in helping them through.

The pressures many children experience on top of the 'normal'
demands of growing up are huge, from family crises to chronic social
and economic deprivation, and no one should underestimate their
impact. Yet young people themselves have identified a positive relationship with their parent(s) as a crucial supportive factor.[18]

Whatever our children have to face in life, from the extreme to
the everyday, we can provide them with the support and skills they
need to increase their resilience and ability to cope. Supporting children in this way is much more within the reach of most families than
a life free of problem times.

Knowing the times and the signs Times of change and transition can be particularly unsettling for children, as what they have come to recognise as familiar and safe disappears and their future feels uncertain.

All children need adult help to negotiate major changes and crises, such as divorce, bereavement or becoming part of a stepfamily (see Important Relationships, p.250), yet most will also need support through changes that are simply part of life and growing up. Situations many children find stressful include:

— Moving house.
— Starting or changing nursery or school.
— Falling out with friends.
— The birth of a sibling.
— Moving from one developmental stage to another, experiencing new feelings, abilities and freedoms (see Tantrums, p.174).
— Illness in the family.
— Separation, divorce, moving into a stepfamily.

Understanding how a child's stress may be reflected in their behaviour and even their health (see Stress Points, p.154) will help us spot times when they may need more support.

Growing up is an anxious business because by definition you don't know what is going to happen next. Children can quickly find themselves in trouble or out of their depth, or in pain in new situations. This is all part of finding their own way, trying to establish their own identity. As parents we should be constantly vigilant but you do have to let them make mistakes. You don't need to be hovering around your kids but you do need to be available and to be responsive when they need you. They must know you are there, almost like a backstop.

Peter Wilson, child psychotherapist and Director of Young Minds

Keeping communication channels open If our children know they can talk to us about their problems and feelings, we will be better able to support and guide them (see Communication, p.89).

Try to build in times just to be with each other. This is easily forgotten in the whirl of conflicting demands, especially in periods of family stress, but better communication and understanding often springs from simply being relaxed and happy in each other's company.

Helping them through

Mary MacLeod, chief executive, National Family and Parenting Institute

A child can cope so much better when things go wrong temporarily, including bad times in their own relationship with a parent and bad times in the relationship between the parents, if they feel a parent loves them and is on their side.

What they cannot survive so well are stresses from the outside world, not having enough food, clothing, etc. Not meeting those basic needs overshadows almost everything else. Some families do manage very well but we should never underestimate the stresses they create.

Generally, it helps if parents acknowledge the bad times and don't pretend that everything is always good and wonderful for their children or for themselves.

1: **Say that in some way it has happened to you** This can be really important, especially between fathers and sons. It is very hard for boys to admit to being bullied, for example, and this really helps.

2: **Say sorry and mean it when we get it wrong** 'I screwed up there' or 'I absolutely shouldn't have done that' etc. This is terribly important in families, however we do it.

3: **Talk and listen** Parents have to be alert to when it is the right time to listen. So often the really important stuff gets said indirectly and sideways and you do need to recognise these times and keep spaces for them, whether that is lying on their bed at bedtime, taking the dog for a walk, cuddling in front of the TV, or whatever. We need to seize the moment when our children need to talk to us, to give them that time.

Helping a child understand There is fear in the unknown. Much avoidable stress and anxiety is caused by children not understanding what is going on in their lives. Why are they feeling as they do? Why are they in this situation? Where will it lead? Confusion can bewilder, frighten and crush a child's ability to find their own way through tough times.

Talking with children about any significant or imminent change in their lives will help them negotiate it more successfully. Try not to inflate difficulties beyond their reasonable significance or to tell children what they will or should feel, but rather give them the information they need to understand what is happening.

Talk to the child about the situation in advance, talk about it while it is
happening, and check back after a few days.

Vivienne Gross, family therapist

Story-telling may help communicate difficult concepts such as loss and
separation (see Exploring Emotions, p.134) while role-playing or
replaying scenes may help a child clarify a difficult situation and their
place in it (see Setting out Situations, p.159). Through these, they may
see how they might handle a problem differently next time or, equally
important, see that they are not to blame.

Self-blame can blight a child's life. Liberating a child from it is
sometimes simply a matter of helping them see how they could not
have influenced the outcome of events. Parental divorce or a grandparent's death, for example, would still have happened whatever the
child did and however they behaved.

Children often receive an implicit message that they cause problems and can often
blame themselves for what happens. By running through a story, you can help
them see where responsibility lies. You can offer the child other perspectives and
nudge them towards a more expanded, less critical, less blameworthy view.

Jim Wilson, systematic psychotherapist and director of the Centre for
Child-Focused Practice at the Institute of Family Therapy, London

Other children can also provide important support and reassurance,
particularly if they have had similar experiences. This need not be on
a formal basis. Opportunities to mix, talk or simply play with other
children, without a parent always listening in, can be hugely helpful.

Adults experience this feeling of 'Why me?' This feeling that you are the
only one in the world to whom this has happened. Children are no different.
Linking up with other children who share experiences can help them come to
terms with situations.

Professor Hugh Foot, specialist in child psychology and social development

Showing the way We are our children's most powerful role models
and they will cope much better in difficult situations if they see us coping.
We can show them the benefits of asking for support from others when
necessary, of relaxation and of making time for pleasure in life.

Where a child in a distressing family situation sees that the parent remains able to
cope and that the structure of their daily world, though changed, hasn't actually

fragmented and broken down, that child is much better able to cope. Where children are told their parents have found a way of sorting out a dispute, even if the children don't directly see them doing it, that still helps them cope much better.

Gill Gorell Barnes, Honorary Senior Lecturer, Tavistock Clinic, family therapist, researcher, co-author of *Growing Up in Stepfamilies*[19]

Setting out situations

Dolls and other playthings can be used to act out scenes and help a child better understand new or confusing situations.

If your child does not initiate the game themselves, you could set out the scene and its key players – perhaps a first day at school or a child visiting newly separated parents in different homes – then step back. The point of the exercise is to understand your child's version of events, not to impose your own.

Initially they may find it easier to talk about their feelings in role – 'This little girl is very sad because her daddy has gone away' – and we need to respect this. We can respond to what they say and make it clear we are listening and that we understand: 'Oh she does look sad.' We can also answer any questions without taking over or putting ideas in their head.

Once they have created and described their 'scene' they may go on to talk about how they feel directly, especially if they love your full attention and feel heard. There is no need to push them to do this – you can continue to acknowledge how the 'little girl' feels (or your child directly if they are ready/willing/able), even use the playthings yourself if it helps. You can also show them different possible ways of handling a problem or show them that a situation is not their fault or responsibility.

'It is important to follow the child and reflect the child but not to join in or take too much initiative yourself,' explains Pat Elliot, a bereavement counsellor and psychotherapist. 'Rather than saying, "I'll be this and you do that," just let her do it for herself and observe and feed back what you see. This helps her know she has been understood, and this will help her move on.'

Jim Wilson, systemic psychotherapist and director of the Centre for Child-Focused Practice at the Institute of Family Therapy, London, explains: 'It is for the parent to respond to the child's questions in a particular situation, not the parent to tell the story of how it should be.

'The core idea is to help children quite literally to look down upon themselves and see themselves as part of the overall situation. It allows children to begin to reflect on their own experiences.

'A child needing to develop social skills, for instance, could talk about a situation they have experienced recently and what was difficult for them – e.g. being left out of games in the playground – and what they could have done differently to help themselves. The child choreographs the scene, and the role of the adult is to encourage the child to do that for themselves.'

Get help if you need it If you think your child is depressed or upset in a way neither of you can manage, seek help. This is not a sign of failure or defeat but of a parent who cares enough to want to help their child through a difficult time. Many organisations can provide emotional and practical support (see Contacts, p.429). Your GP may be able to advise you on which kind of support may help most in your particular situation.

We need to be our child's advocate, who else is going to be? We know as parents when something is not right, we need to act on this as soon as possible and access the services our child may need if help is needed.

Lisa Blakemore-Brown, chartered educational psychologist

Supporting grieving children

I lost my dad when I was seven years old. I remember it all, I was so aware of the loss, the big gap. I felt very sad and angry and I couldn't put it into any perspective. When he died my mother told me, 'You are not going to see your daddy any more,' and I remember thinking, 'Has he gone to prison?' I couldn't work out where he had gone. As it was I could still see him walking down the road.

Linda H

Helping your child talk about death

A major ChildLine study[20] revealed that most 10-year-olds who had lost someone important in their lives and who called the helpline had not spoken to anyone about how they were feeling. Many reported having a powerful delayed reaction to bereavement, often triggered by another event such as an argument at school. The report concluded that: 'This may be more likely if they did not have the opportunity to think about how they felt and talk about the loss at the time it happened.'

'Children do not seem to be encouraged to talk directly about death,' explains Mary MacLeod, chief executive, National Family and Parenting Institute. 'We need to work with parents on this, to reassure them that children do not need huge protection from feelings of sadness. They are feeling anyway.

'Indirect means of exploring the realities of loss, through films and stories, can be very helpful. Singing sad songs with our children is another way to allow sadness and tension to get expression and evaporate.

'Talking about the person keeps them real, not in terms of only blame or only praise, but talking about them as a real person with all their lovely parts and all the bits that made us fed up. All this can help a child talk about death and the dead.'

My wife died when our children were seven and four. I made them each a memory box of things that were hers, photographs of them together, letters that she wrote. They look at them every so often. It prompts questions and stories and memories, and I think that's helped.

Philip D

The relevance of this section spreads far beyond the needs of bereaved children. We chose to focus on this issue because so many children experience the death of someone close. But exploring ways to support them may also help us support our children through other sad or traumatic experiences in their lives.

As a parent of a grieving child, be prepared for the wide range of emotions they may display, from apathy and withdrawal to rage and anger. When a child feels overwhelmed by grief, the bond between you can feel like a lifeline. Tell them you love them very much. They need to know. We can also help by:

Preparing our children Preparing children for bereavement can begin years before we foresee them ever having to deal with it. The more questions they can ask before it affects them directly, the better they may be able to cope when it does.

The idea that death is for ever is often in conflict with what children see in the media. We really do need to prepare them better for bereavement and one way is to challenge these media images of the hero never dying, or being killed and then coming back to life. Around three and four years, we can introduce awareness by using the natural world. It provides many different examples to show how death is different to absence – the death of flowers, insects, leaves falling in autumn. Another way, however macabre it sounds, is having and losing pets. This can be a huge preparation. We need to introduce understanding of death in a gentle way.

Pat Elliot, bereavement counsellor and psychotherapist

Being honest Children need to know what has happened and what we believe happens next. It may also help them to know that people have many different ideas and beliefs.

What any one child will need to know about what happens after death will vary enormously, largely depending on culture and religion. Manage the conversation as honestly as you can based on what you believe, but in the context that others believe differently, so that the child can find their own place. A little boy I was

very close to was three and a half when his father was killed in a climbing
accident. A year later we were in a church in front of a painting of the
Resurrection and he said to me: 'Do you think people come back from the dead,
Mary?' I said to him: "To be honest, Christopher, lots of people do, but I don't,'
and he said, 'I do,' and I said, 'That's great.'

Mary MacLeod, chief executive, National Family and Parenting Institute

Using clear language and concrete information Young children can take euphemisms literally, if they understand them at all.
'Taken by the angels', 'gone to sleep', 'slipped away', 'resting' and so
on can at best confuse and at worst terrify, because the child may fear
the same will soon happen to them. Children may hold themselves
responsible for the loss of someone close so it helps to state explicitly
that no one is to blame.

Children aged five and under often have difficulty accepting the
finality of death and that the person won't one day come back. It
helps to keep explanations very simple and clear. Explain that when
a person dies they stop breathing, eating, walking, also feeling pain or
hunger or worry. Be prepared for them to ask the same questions, over
and over again, until the issue is clear in their own minds.

Slightly older children may understand more but this may trigger
a fear of their own death or of losing others close to them, and they
may need our help to put this in perspective. They may also tie themselves in knots trying to see the reason or purpose behind the death.
If you have no religious views to draw on, it often helps to state simply
that death, like many things in life, is not fair.

With little children you need to be as concrete as possible because that is how they
understand things. Not until 10, 11, 12 can they really think in abstract terms,
which is why discussion of heaven and the spirit is so difficult. But let's face it,
do any of us really get it? Humankind has grappled with it but we each fill the
gap with our own faith.

Pat Elliot, bereavement counsellor and psychotherapist

Encouraging children to talk Children can find it very hard to
talk about what has happened and how they are feeling. It is important that a child only talks when they want to, that we do not push
them before they are ready or attempt to impose our own feelings or
agenda. Our children may feel differently to us, and they need to be
able to express this.

We can help by example, raising the subject and talking about the person who has died and how we feel, in a way that respects the child's age and vulnerability. Ask them if they would like to tell their friends, or whether they would like someone else to do this (the school or nursery should be informed). Talk to the child to help them express their feelings, but try not to burden them with the responsibility of making you feel better.

It is important to show some grief in front of the children but also to find adult support for yourself. I have seen quite a young child become the carer of a grieving parent. That is really sad and not really fair.

Pat Elliot, bereavement counsellor and psychotherapist

If we find it too painful to talk and listen to our children as they need, we can ask another close and caring adult to do so. Bereavement counselling may help all family members come to terms with your loss (see Contacts, p.429, or contact your GP).

Answering questions A basic rule of thumb is that if a child asks the question, they need to know the answer. The stream of questions may seem endless but encourage children to keep on asking, especially as their concerns and understanding will change as they grow.

It is important to make it clear they can ask any questions they like. The child may ask for a lot of details, sometimes in quite a gruesome or even macabre way, and it is important to give them these. Children also want to know details about illness and whether it is likely to affect them. Even in suicide it is very important to be honest because they will find out the truth over time and that is far worse. You do not have to tell them everything all at once; give them a little bit a time and respond to their questions.

Pat Elliot, bereavement counsellor and psychotherapist

Providing physical comfort Most children will need extra physical comfort at this time – cuddles, hugs, being close. Some may also regress and need more physical care than previously. Observe and respond to what your child is showing you they need at this time.

Staying true to life The urge to talk only good of the dead is understandable, but idolising them can cause problems. An idolised sibling

Should children attend funerals?

Pat Elliot, bereavement counsellor and psychotherapist

Attending funerals gives children an opportunity to be part of the public grief, valuing the person who has died and grieving as part of a community. The ritual is also sometimes a way things can be expressed that cannot be said. It can be an emotional release.

It is a delicate balance, though, between allowing children to show their feelings and being faced with a formal ritual which by definition involves things that you do in a certain order and a certain amount of holding yourself together. It is ideal that children be given some choice, they may prefer to have a ritual on a smaller scale at home with loved ones for example; they could make their own ceremony of saying goodbye then later visit the grave. It does always help to say goodbye.

If a child is to attend the funeral of a very special person, for example a parent, and the parent who is left is barely able to cope with his or her own pain, it can be very helpful to have a chosen adult at the funeral who knows the child well to be there particularly to support that child. In my experience children are far more often upset and hold it against their parents when they haven't been allowed to go. So if it is difficult, specific support at the funeral may be key.

may be an impossible act to follow; an idolised parent may not tally with the child's own memories. All can cause hurt and guilt.

How can you not always compete and fail against an ideal child who has died? How can you separate and become independent of a mother who is not there any more and who was perfect? It is so helpful to remain realistic.

Pat Elliot, bereavement counsellor and psychotherapist

Keeping to familiar routines As far as possible, keep to usual family routines, mealtimes, bedtimes and so on. These may seem trivial in the circumstances but can help children feel that, though they have experienced great loss, their entire life isn't in free-fall.

Letting children grieve Rather than 'protecting' your child from grief or steering them away from it, give them permission to express their thoughts and feelings. Their way of grieving may not be as you would like or even as you think appropriate, but it is what they need to do.

*Children can often go one of two ways: very withdrawn or almost frenetic.
I think you need to be as natural as possible with your feelings and this
allows children to be the same. Their grief may show itself in a different
way. Children often go in and out of grief more quickly, so to be upset one
minute and playing the next does not make the grief any less real and valid.
You have to go with their flow as much as you can.*

Pat Elliot, bereavement counsellor and psychotherapist

Allowing your child to be happy Children can feel very guilty at
feeling happy or laughing when those around them are sad. It is important that they know that grieving does not mean having fun has to
stop or that you have to feel miserable all the time.

Feelings and fears: a quick reminder

- What we show and teach our children about emotions can boost their
  sense of worth and their ability to form rewarding relationships, now
  and for the rest of their lives.
- We can't prevent all hurt and pain in our children's lives, but we can
  build their resilience to cope.
- Talking about feelings gives our children language to identify and
  express emotion.
- Accepting and acknowledging children's emotions – 'That must have
  hurt', 'You seem angry' – will help them deal with them. Telling children *not* to feel or *how* to feel – 'That didn't hurt', 'Don't be angry' –
  won't make the feelings go away.
- We can let our children know their feelings are OK but there may be
  better ways of expressing them: 'I can see she's upset you and you
  know it's not OK to hit.'
- Understanding how children may express distress, sadness and confusion will help us respond sensitively and constructively.
- Communicating our feelings appropriately helps children feel safer and
  more able to express their emotions constructively. Emotional honesty
  can release pressure, prevent feelings rooted elsewhere damaging our
  relationship with our children, and stop us blowing our stack.

CHAPTER SIX
HORRIBLY NORMAL

Parents have a huge vested interest in their children being a credit to them and therefore anything their child does to show them up they find really hard to handle. This can be a huge problem for same parents.

Eileen Hayes, parenting advisor to the NSPCC

I used to lie when my first child hit any other children – 'I can't believe he's done it, he's never done it before.' He'd been doing it for months but I wouldn't admit it, especially to other mothers.

Mel M

I've got four wonderful kids and all of them have had bouts of difficult behaviour. At the moment, my 11-year-old daughter has more than a passing resemblance to Harry Enfield's Kevin.

Kate W

Much of the child behaviour parents worry about most is prefectly normal. Horrible, but normal.

Most children lie, cheat, bite, snatch, hit and have tantrums for the simple reason that they haven't yet learned how to behave differently. Many also steal, swear, provoke and offend along the way. It's up to us to provide them with the direction and experience they need to know better – and to keep a healthy sense of perspective (see When to Worry, p.169). A child who dabbles in whopper fibs is not destined to become a compulsive liar; the child who stuffs stolen banknotes up his jumper in a game of Monopoly is not a cheat for life; the child who bites is not Vlad the Impaler.

It is not good for children to be good all the time. They need to 'test' where we draw the line and to know what will happen if they go over it. This is normal, healthy development. All children need clear and positive parental guidance and patience if they are to under-

stand the effects of what they are doing and how to do things differently. And parents need occasional breaks and a sense of humour. It
also helps to:

Be realistic If we expect too much of our children too soon, we will
be frustrated and they will have less incentive to achieve because our
aims are out of reach. Guiding children's behaviour is a process that

Highs, lows and outbursts

*My son seems to need refuelling with food every
couple of hours. If he doesn't have a little to eat,
often, he gets grumpy.*
Anne M

*I heard a foster parent on the radio. She took the kids in her care for a
daily trip to the playground because, she said, kids with excess
energy are much more unruly than ones who've had sufficient exercise.
I tried the same with my kids and it's really helped. They still fight,
but it's much less frequent.*

Sandra B

Your child is most likely to behave in ways you find difficult when they are bored, frustrated, rushed, tired, hungry or poorly. Or when you are bored, frustrated, rushed, tired, hungry or poorly and therefore less able or willing to be guide, nurturer, entertainer, cook, social secretary, servant and butt of any low-flying frustrations.

If you recognise and respond to such needs, including your own, the chances of your child behaving as you'd wish improve dramatically.

Some children have energy dips during the day when they are more likely to become belligerent and bloody-minded. Some school-age children have particular times of the week or term when they need extra sleep if they are not to fray at the edges. Others have astonishing bursts of energy and may need to play outside like puppies at least once a day if there's any hope of them settling down.

If you have children with wildly different physical needs, it may be worth organising your home as well as your routines to take this into account. A room in which rough play is not allowed can be a sanctuary for a child who feels swamped or threatened by a sibling's exuberance. It can also be a sanctuary for you.

starts young, takes time and involves a great deal of repetition (see Co-operation and Discipline, p.196).

It is an age thing, mostly. Almost all children really start to understand why and how things are wrong after the age of three or four years.

Carol Ann Hally, health visitor, clinical practice teacher

Children of any age can go through patches of grotty behaviour. Development isn't a straight line but a bumpy track with twists and turns along the way. Sometimes what's happening in our own lives can also make our children's behaviour feel extreme. There will be times when it drives us demented, but that may be more down to our moods than the child's actions (see Our Feelings as Parents, p.142).

Be clear Children are often unaware their behaviour is wrong. They need educating, not punishing (see Three Important Questions, p.170).

A very young child may bail out the bath or bite your backside because they think it's fun. So much fun that they think you'll enjoy it, too. Leave them in no doubt that you don't, but avoid being too harsh or severe as this can confuse or terrify to a degree you never intended and still leave them unsure of what they did wrong. They may even try to cheer you up by bailing out the bath again. Older children may not realise why it matters so much to us that their toys are put away, say, or their clothes are picked off the floor, unless we tell them (see Challenging, p.219).

Be positive Child psychologists have identified a link between child development and tantrums or other forms of difficult behaviour. Children often seem to have periods of regression just before an important developmental leap in their thinking, emotional or physical skills.[1] So it's painful, but it's progress.

Children often have these difficult times prior to leaps of development. It is not always the case, but it is my conviction that they very often precede a big leap, say from not being able to walk to walking, from apparently not being able to read at all to being able to. It's almost as though the child is thinking, 'The world is not how I thought it was, but I'm not yet sure what it is.' It is an awareness of the problem before they find the solution, which often brings frustration.

Professor Hilton Davis, clinical child psychologist and Director of the Centre for Parent and Child Support

When to worry

Many parents worry whether their child's 'difficult' behaviour is 'horribly normal' or evidence of a more serious 'behaviour problem'. It is important to remember that most children behave appallingly sometimes. Three key signs that more serious 'problem behaviour' may have developed are when:

— **It has been going on for a long time.**
— **It is extreme**, having a very negative impact on the child or others, on their education and/or their relationships.
— **It seems out of control**. It is not showing signs of improvement and occurs at 'inappropriate' times.

'No behaviour is abnormal by simple virtue of it happening. That's important for parents to know,' explains Hilton Davies, Professor of Child Health Psychology at King's College, London, and director of the Centre for Parent and Child Support. 'Almost everything that could be described as abnormal behaviour in a child actually occurs in normal development. Behaviour only becomes abnormal in its frequency, its chronicity and its intensity. So parents should ask themselves how often it happens, how it is developing and whether it is hurting the child or anyone else.

'An adult might be deluded on occasion, thinking, "God, they're all laughing at me." That doesn't mean they are psychotic; the frequency and intensity of the experience is well within the band of "normal". In the same way, if something's happened that worries you about your child's behaviour, don't panic but wait to see how and if it develops. It might well just go away.

'As part of that process you also need to be able to go to someone and say, "Hey, what do you think about this?" It may be a friend, your health visitor, someone you can be honest with about your concerns and who may be able to provide helpful advice.

'Unfortunately there is still a stigma attached to seeking help. We are seeking to change that, to say we know it is difficult raising children, that everybody needs support and that support ought to be available to parents very easily and in a way which isn't stigmatising.'

The National Family and Parenting Institute (NFPI) has leaflets and a website offering information and details of further support available for parents worried about children's behaviour (see Contacts, p.429).

Finding out more, and talking honestly to other parents, made me realise his behaviour wasn't particularly extreme. It helped me tackle it more constructively because I wasn't in a panic.

Dawn R.

We can shorten the journey to better behaviour by building children's self-esteem and their ability to express feelings without going bananas (see Feelings and Fears, p.124, and Communication, p.89). We can make it worth their while to behave better by praising them when they succeed (see Descriptive Praise, p.115).

Learning to be 'nice' or 'good' often means that a child must learn to act against her own best interests: if she does not snatch the last cake, she will not get to eat it. If he does not hit his friend on the head with that toy brick, the friend may snatch it. It is up to adults to balance cakes and toys with praise, hugs, gold stars or whatever constitutes the 'feel-good factor' in their particular group.

The Commission on Children And Violence[2]

Be understanding Children who are unable to express their frustrations and feelings through words often do it through their actions. Difficult behaviour can be just as much a sign of distress as tears or tummy ache (see Feelings and Fears, p.124).

Three important questions

What did they think they were doing?

So often, behaviour we find unacceptable was never intended to hurt, upset or offend. Perhaps the child didn't realise, got over-excited, didn't think, or simply made a mistake. Perhaps they didn't know another way.

When faced with children's worse moments, it can help to think about their motives: what did they mean to happen? Did they realise how others would feel? If we can see their intention was reasonable and their understanding of the consequences limited, it is much easier for us to respond calmly and appropriately, while also pointing out the effects of their actions. Children generally respond well once they understand *why* their behaviour was hurtful, offensive or annoying to others.

Thinking about our children's intent can prompt an important shift in how we view and respond to 'misbehaviour'.

If children feel genuinely misunderstood and blamed for something they had not intended to happen, they may simmer with a sense of injustice and are less likely to learn anything positive from the experience. If, however, their intent is acknowledged, they can often learn quickly and turn their behaviour around.

What were they feeling?

Children's misbehaviour can be a sign of

Be observant It's important we let our children know when we don't like what they are doing, and why. Even very young children care if another person is hurt, but they may not realise it is their own actions that caused the pain. It is up to us to tell them (see Biting, p.182).

Children suffer natural empathetic responses to another's distress. Parents' failure to confront the child about actions that harm others may extinguish such concern.

Professor Diana Baumrind, research psychologist[3]

Be active Children need to release energy, and if they don't, they may explode. Bored children are more likely to put the remote down the loo or spice up their lives with a spot of sibling bashing. Taking a few minutes to set up an activity that may keep them engrossed for a long time seems a pretty good investment. A trip to the park or a quick game of footy may be all they need to settle down and behave better.

Be sociable Children as young as 22 months have been found to

upset or distress in other parts of their lives, their way of saying, 'Notice me. I need your help.' Their conduct is unlikely to improve drastically until the root cause is addressed (see Feelings and Fears, p.124).

What were we expecting?

Our expectations sometimes outstrip our children's capabilities. We can then respond too harshly, presuming they have misbehaved. New situations are particularly hard for young children to negotiate successfully.

Examining what our expectations are, and whether they are reasonable, will help us give our children the guidance they need.

The three-year-old who kicks a ball in the hallway and breaks the mirror, for example, may not have understood the possible consequences. They need to be told why we are upset and why footballs need to be kicked outside. A 10-year-old who does the same should know that already and be prepared to face the music.

The boys had been playing dressing up. Somehow my late grandfather's hat had got muddled into the dressing up stuff. They cut off the front because they didn't want the feather. I was devastated as it was my closest reminder of how my grandfather had been in life. I began crying, tried to explain why, and the boys were more upset than me. They really hadn't meant it and I was so relieved I hadn't gone ballistic.

Amanda S

'work' at friendships and change their behaviour to influence their friend's responses.[4] This awareness of how their actions and moods affect others is how children begin to understand the importance of acceptable behaviour. Providing opportunities for our children to mix with other will help this understanding develop (see Play and Learning, p.324).

Pre-toddler mood swings

He does these cartoon leg-pedals when I pick him up from where he shouldn't be. He has an iron will, an iron grip and has perfected a screech like a dog whistle when he's not getting what he wants. And he's not yet 16 months.

Paula C

As babies edge towards toddlerhood, they begin to put their dawning sense of independence to the test and try out their developing physical capabilities. And sometimes these just won't work the way they want them to.

As children become more aware of what they can do, they also become more aware of what they can't. They want to crawl forwards but their body goes backwards. They want to walk but they fall down. They want to climb on a chair but they just can't reach. They try to open the fridge door and an adult shuts it. Where once they were easily distracted, they may now grip on to objects as though their life depended on it, and shout at every attempt to untangle their fingers.

Growing up is often confusing and frustrating for a child who begins to realise they can't control the world, other people or sometimes even themselves. How children respond to this realisation will depend largely on their temperament but also how we handle this stage in their development. Some babies take frustrations in their stride, are quite content with their lot and seem to wait for the world to come to them. Others want to go out and grab it and become desperate when it's beyond their reach. How soon this phase begins can also take parents by surprise – you often see tears of frustration or flashes of steely will and determination in children under one year.

Fuelled by powerful feelings Little children experience powerful and passionate emotions. What may seem fickle, farcical or 'put on' to an adult is a child's very real and fluid emotion, whether it be frustration, rage or joy. To them, at that moment, dropping a toy may be The Worst Thing.

This passion is a driving force behind their development; if they care enough about the brick they will attempt to crawl across the room to get it. Extreme emotion is not always negative – watch a child's thrill at a new-found skill, see them race around in delight at their new mobility.

The emotional seesaw Your child may swing dramatically from wanting to be with you to wanting to strike out for independence. They are not being 'naughty' or 'difficult', but simply haven't a clue what they want most so end up wanting both with equal passion – hence the child who doesn't want to be picked up but doesn't want to be put down. Your child is on the cusp between infancy and toddlerhood and will have practice runs at progress then regress into needy dependency. It's all part of growing up.

Comfort and reassurance Children experience new fears and anxieties as they become more aware of their world and their place in it. From around eight to nine months, for instance, your child may become wary or scared of strangers and cry or protest when they see you leave the room (see Separation Anxiety, p.140). In time, with reassurance, understanding and patience, they will become more confident and independent.

Encourage when appropriate If a child is attempting a task that seems beyond their capabilities, help but try not to take over; they may surprise you and be able to do it. If they have no chance of success, it may be best to encourage them to try something else.

Perfect the art of distraction A few well-placed toys could save you both the anguish of further frustrations. For a short while. Tempt them with a favourite game, show them the aeroplane, the bird, your watch, how you can touch the end of your nose with your tongue. Consciously shift the focus of your attention and your child is much more likely to shift theirs.

A nanny I met told me a trick. It's a box of special, little things that's only brought out on special occasions or when I really need to get things done.

We've got a toy box full of plastic so this is full of natural things or things made of natural materials that are good to feel — some wood, wool, a little loofah. Little ones are intrigued by it.

Helen O

Tantrums

Embarrassment in supermarkets? I have been there and got the T-shirt. My children thought they could do anything in supermarkets — demanding this, that and the other and protesting loudly if I refused — because they picked up that I would be embarrassed. Once they got the message that I was not going to be embarrassed any more and that regardless of what they did I was not buying it, they stopped trying it.

Vivienne Gross, family therapist

It wasn't the confrontation but the fact that he seemed so angry and desperate that I found so hard. It felt like I couldn't reach him. He wouldn't even let me touch him when he was in the middle of a rage. It was like he found life so hard in a way I couldn't understand and couldn't make better, and that made me so sad. Once I just sat on the bottom of the stairs and cried.

Caitlyn M

Tantrums can be rooted in confusion, fear, frustration, anger or simply tiredness, when the slightest mishap feels overwhelming.

They vary hugely from child to child, in type, intensity and timing. Healthy toddlers are bound to be wilful occasionally, but will differ in how they express this. Some children never seem to rage, some wait until later, and others have storm-force explosions from around eighteen months. However and whenever they manifest themselves, children need to learn for their own safety and healthy development that they are loved, listened to, understood – and can't always do what they want, when they want. And they won't like that bit. They may scream, shout, kick or roll around the floor, often do all at once and usually perform best in public. This is hard on you, and hard on your child.

Prevention is clearly the best option, but if tantrums do erupt it's generally best to let them blow up and blow over. Tantrumming children tend not to calm down until they've got it all out of their

Tidal-wave tantrums

Kitty Hagenbach, child psychotherapist

After the tantrum, children often need a hug and call out for mummy. At that stage the child just needs to be hugged unconditionally without any 'No, you've been a naughty boy'. They just need to be held. Then if things need to be talked about or boundaries set, leave a space, wait until everyone is calm, then talk about it.

I think there is a tendency towards tantrums in toddlers because there are few other ways to release their aggression, frustration or anger – they can't just take themselves outside and kick a football. Also, when they are in their twos, their feelings are so much a part of their bodies and a tantrum shows itself like this with kicks and screams and flying arms.

Often, if they are allowed to have the tantrum, it's like a wave of energy that is then gone. If this is stopped it can get pushed down and maybe this leads to later problems.

It takes someone with good self-esteem and maturity to allow a tantrum, especially in a public place.

---

system. And only when they are calm can they really hear what we've got to say.

Sometimes it's vital we hold a firm line on behaviour, and this may flip a wilful child into rage. Your child may like running away in the street, for example. They may not even know the difference between this and a chasing game, until you let them know. But when you do they may get very, very angry at being controlled. So be it. You have to ensure your child's safety and they have to be shown where the limits on behaviour lie.

Our task is to help our children master their increasing powers and skills and to let them know they are not master of the universe. By not giving in to their every request we will begin to teach them where limits lie and that other people and their needs also matter – essential if they are to socialise happily with others. Generally, though, it helps to avoid battles over the irrelevant stuff of life so we make sufficient impact over the big, important issues. We need to balance firmness with consideration and understanding. Taking life a little more at our children's pace, and imagining it from their perspective, may help:

— Young children don't have the language to communicate all they want to express, especially when excited or upset.

— They can't predict or control much of what happens in their lives.
— They are beginning to be more independent of their parents and aware of this separateness, which can be pretty frightening as well as thrilling.
— Their abilities won't always match their desires.
— Their world is bewildering, with new freedoms and a growing consciousness of limits to that freedom.
— Adults tend not to look at the world through children's eyes, so often misinterpret their intense focus and feelings and unawareness of time as naughtiness or deliberate obstruction.
— On top of all this there is the unpredictability of their needs. Young children may swing between needing and rejecting their parents, clinging to them for reassurance then refusing to hold their hand.

It can be tough being small.

The important shift for me has been not locking horns and making a big deal out of everything. I used to think his behaviour was unreasonable, a wind up, and feel I had to show who's boss. Now, if he wants to take his shoe off and put it on again and I've got time to wait, that's all right. If I haven't got time, I explain and think of something else we can do and it's generally OK. I'm not battling with him all the time so he doesn't fight me every step of the way. Life's a lot easier.

Tom C

Prevention

Our evenings were hellish. I'd rush to the childminder's after work, but couldn't get there until gone six. He'd then fall asleep in the car on the way home, get hysterical when I got him out of the car, and sometimes carry on screaming and protesting until he fell asleep again. But I couldn't stop work, so we had to think round it. I tried to get him to bed on time so he didn't start the day tired and my childminder restructured her day a bit to allow him an extra nap. She also built in quiet time in the afternoon, where the kids sat down with her while she read them a book. It really helped.

Claire M

You do have to maintain yourself as parents. You need enough rest and enough breaks to be able to stay calm when things are not easy.

John Bristow, psychologist and psychotherapist

Children, just like their parents, need sleep and food in the right amounts at the right times if they are to stay in a reasonable mood. Timing shopping trips and other high-risk activities to fit in with your child's feeding and sleep needs can reduce tantrums dramatically. But life isn't always that neat, so other tactics are also necessary.

1 **Allow your child to be physically active** Few toddlers will sit happily in a buggy or car, then happily in a supermarket trolley, then happily in the buggy or car again for the journey home. Before you go shopping, walk around a little, go to the park, have a disco in the kitchen, anything that uses a little of your child's energy reserves.

2 **Avoid unnecessary confrontations** Saying no can become a habit. Often children explode in frustration because they haven't been heard and their pleas have been met with 'just wait' or 'not now'. By cutting back on unnecessary 'no's and taking more notice, we can help them see that positive behaviour gets them most attention (see Positive Power, p.115). Aim not to refuse reasonable requests and, at other times, try rephrasing replies to accentuate the positive, especially when asking a child to wait. To them 'just a minute' means 'never' unless we make it clear that we really do intend to act. Compare:

> *Child:* 'Can I paint now?'
> *Parent:* 'No, not yet, I've got to . . .'
> and
> *Child:* 'Can I paint now?'
> *Parent:* 'Yes. What a great idea. I'll just do xyz then we'll get the
>   brushes out.'

It's the same message, but the different emphasis makes it more likely that your child will understand. Offering manageable and realistic choices may also sidestep unnecessary battles over small things and give children a sense of some input in decisions: 'Do you want to brush your teeth before or after your bath?'

3 **Plan a trip to the shops as you would a long car journey** Take nibbles, your child's favourite book, a drink, a sandwich. Involve them: let them hold things, count things, chew things. Talk to them about what you're doing, ask their opinion, let them choose the bananas.

4 **If trouble is brewing, try to find out what the problem is** while there's still time to talk through or round it.

5 **If this isn't working or there simply isn't time, divert attention** Quickly. The 'Oh! I almost forgot! I've brought your crayons' trick sometimes works. Two Crayolas and a small scribble pad can mean the difference between peace and pandemonium.

6 **Avoid difficult situations** What these are will vary widely between children. Getting to know what makes your child angry and agitated, and how they express that, can help you avoid 'trigger' situations. If going to the supermarket is unspeakably awful, try to time trips when your child can cope best, or go at a time when a trusted friend or relation can babysit. If you're having a *really* bad day, try to make do with what you've got in the house. This isn't cowardice, this is survival.

7 **Set clear rules and expectations** It tends to be far more effective to tell children what we want them to do rather than what we don't want them to do (see Communication, p.89). Compare 'Don't make such a mess' with 'Pick up your clothes please.'

8 **Encourage children to ask rather than to demand** (see I Want It and I Want It Now!, p.181.) This not only equips them with an important social skill but is also less likely to wind you up.

9 **Keep out of view any sweets, biscuits etc.** that you do not want to buy.

10 **Make sure you have enough support and rest** Dealing with tantrums is hard enough without adding your emotional or physical exhaustion into the equation.

Action

A baby is hard work to look after but there is no mystery – they are dependent and we have to be dependable. Then it changes, somewhere around 18 months to two years, when a child sends out their first message that they need their first bit of limit-setting. It is almost an invitation from them. In some way or other, with a look, a gesture or a phrase they say: 'What are you going to do about it?' They want you to engage them. They begin to need attention, guidance, limits and discipline. It should be a relaxed struggle through this stage – with you relaxed and them struggling! That's the point.

Steve Biddulph, psychologist and author

Most children have tantrums sometimes, and may need to have them to express their emotions in the only way they know how. If prevention has failed, attempting to stop tantrums in their tracks rarely works.

Instead, we can handle them constructively and use them as an opportunity to teach our children other ways to express how they feel.

Ride the storm A child may feel overwhelmed and frightened by the intensity of their emotions. Our role is to show they don't overwhelm us. Which means not matching the child's behaviour, shouting over them or crumbling under the force of their temper.

Speak quietly and explain Try lowering the temperature by lowering your voice and expressing your confidence in their ability to behave better. If they are screaming, save your breath until they've calmed down because they won't hear you.

Avoid giving in to unreasonable demands Standing firm helps re-educate children's behaviour; giving in may encourage it big-time. After all, if it works once, they'll do it again.

Go to a quieter place Ensure the child can't hurt themselves. If the tantrum is in public and that bothers you, go to a quieter spot where you are both less likely to be embarrassed by other people's reactions.

Acknowledge your child's feelings This shows that you don't disapprove of your child's emotions but rather how they have chosen to express them. Simply stating the obvious – 'I know you feel angry' – shows not only that you've understood but also that you can deal with your child's anger without hitting, stamping or screaming (see Feelings and Fears, p.124). This is a powerful lesson.

I went to seek advice about my daughter's tantrums because they seemed so extreme. She was three, nearly four so I thought she would have grown out of them by then. I was told that all periods of transition are hard for kids because they are unsettling – she'd just started nursery and I'd just had another baby. The advice I was given was not to always meet the tantrum head on or always try to control it, but let it come out and say, 'I understand why you are feeling angry, it must be very hard for you and you must be feeling very scared.' It's hard, but I am trying and it has helped me understand more what's going on for her.

Maggie C

Express how you feel If you are angry, tell your child calmly but firmly, and reflect this in your tone of voice and body language. If you pretend to be unaffected while you are seething inside, your child will pick up two conflicting messages and become even more confused and volatile. Recognising your feelings also helps keep them under control. It is hard – try counting in your head or slowing your breathing to slow your heart rate if you feel about to blow a gasket.

Ignore behaviour? Depending on what's happening and why, your best response may be to ignore your child's excesses. You are the best judge of when this may be appropriate. Acknowledge their feelings, state your case, then avoid eye contact until they have calmed down.

Hold your child? Some children respond well to being cuddled when distressed. Others may be in such a rage that a cuddle will only make matters worse; they want to be heard, not soothed.

When the tantrum is over Once your child is calm, they may be willing to be cuddled. If not, at least explain gently that you are pleased it has passed. When the time is right, children also need to know:

— They are loved.
— We are on their side.
— We understand how they were feeling.
— We do not like that behaviour.
— We are not going to give in to things we know to be unfair, unsafe or unreasonable.

Talk about different ways children might show they are angry or upset without having a tantrum: 'You couldn't go to Ella's house and that made you angry. Shouting and screaming didn't make things better for you, and I didn't like it either. Next time, how could you let me know how fed up you are feeling?'

Talk about words they might use or even faces they could pull (always a good one for taking the sting out of post-argument atmospheres. When the mood's right, try pulling a face, too, or doing them together in a mirror).

If tantrums are happening often and with great intensity, think whether anything may be disturbing your child – simple changes of routine can sometimes knock a young child off kilter. Also ask yourself whether you are expecting better behaviour than they can deliver.

Perhaps you need to loosen up a little and allow your child to act their age, or perhaps tighten the reins a touch and establish clearer boundaries. Only you will know the answer. Think it through, sort out the possible from the unrealistically perfect, and try again. Crucially, remember this is a phase. It does get better.

I want it and I want it now!

A tantrum happens when a child *loses* control. Sometimes children of all ages want to *take* control. They may try to do this by screaming, shouting, sulking, whingeing, demanding, siding with some family members against others, issuing orders or generally trying to run the show.

Most children will occasionally dabble in dictatorship. It is part of how they learn what they can get away with. Some children are temperamentally more assertive; some learn to be bossy by watching those around them. Go into any 'early years' class and you'll spot the two-foot despots. It's a phase many children grow into and out of again. As a general rule of thumb, the less we give in to loud, whingeing, demanding and controlling behaviour, the less it will happen. If children see that it works, they'll do it again.

Difficulties can arise, however, if children habitually attempt to control friends or family members and their behaviour is harming relationships. The roots of such behaviour often lie in insecurity; if their world feels shaky they may feel driven to impose their own order.

Children can feel insecure about many things: their parents' love for them; the solidity of family ground rules for behaviour; upset in the family or at school, and much more. Spending relaxed one-to-one time with them will help them feel valued and allow much-needed conversations to unfold. Actively listening will help them feel heard (see Communication, p.89). They also need to feel their parents are in charge, not them (see Coping in Hard Times, p.151). This doesn't mean being harsh; it does mean being clear about what's allowed and what's not and why. Children know what they want, but it's our job to ensure they get what they need. This is true from their first year to and through adolescence.

He was a compulsive climber and would get really angry when I stopped him climbing on to the table. That's what he wanted. What he needed was me to ensure he was safe, and to give him opportunities to exercise. So I'd take him off the table, put up with his screams of frustration and take him to the playground or for a walk up the road.

Alison Y

Wants and needs Thinking through the difference between wants and needs may help us give our children the support, clear love and guidance they require. A child beside themselves with tiredness, for example, may demand more cuddles, yet you may know what they need most is sleep. A child may demand a biscuit, yet you may know that will only pacify them in the short term and what they actually need is a meal or some focused attention. An older child may want yet another pair of trainers, but what they may need is to develop a more realistic view of family income.

Even if you give the tired child cuddles and the demanding child biscuits or trainers, they will keep demanding more because their real need (for sleep, food, attention or more mature understanding) remains. Only when you ensure they get what they need will their demand cease.

I think a child's need, as opposed to a want, is something essential to the child and thus essential for us to understand. It is something that won't go away if it's not provided. As parents it can take far less energy to meet or acknowledge that need than for it to become internalised or expressed in another way. And I do mean acknowledging. I can't always meet the need right there and then, I'm not Superwoman.

Stella Ward, nurse and parenting advisor

Biting

I've got a picture of my twins as babies with what look like glorious rosy cheeks. They're bite marks. They'd go for each other like terriers.

Jane P

All my children have gone through biting and out the other side and they always bit other children they loved passionately. It was funny, they never bit people they were not sure of.

Anne M

For many children, biting is as much a part of growing up as trying on their first pair of shoes. So is hair pulling, thrusting digits up a parent's nose and taking exquisite delight in pinching. If you turn a blind eye or otherwise condone it, you'll be pulled, bitten and pinched all the more, but your response should be guided by your child's age and understanding.

If a baby or toddler bites you They may be doing it because their gums hurt, or because it's great fun watching people go 'Ouch!' Either way, we have to start teaching them it is not OK. Show your disapproval by putting the child down immediately. If they have hurt you, show it.

If they bite another Remove your child or, better still, leave them where they are and remove the victim so they do not receive extra attention for unacceptable behaviour (see Remove the Victim, p.228).

Either way, calmly acknowledge their feelings and very firmly tell them what they have done and that it is not to happen again: 'That hurt! I know you are angry and you know you are not to bite.'

Watch for 'trigger' situations your child finds difficult to handle, and consider motive. Some children bite because they are angry or frustrated or simply don't know it hurts; others because they are over-excited and lose control. Once we've a clearer idea of why and when they are doing it, it is much easier to guide and support them effectively.

Please don't bite back. It may stop your child in their tracks but sends such a confused message ('My parent says this is wrong yet does it to me/my parent thinks it is OK to hurt me') that it can do much more harm than good. It is up to us to show our children different ways of responding to provocation.

The defence to biting a child back — that they need to know how it feels — is just not valid. They do not know that a flame hurts but we are not going to stick their hand in it to teach them, neither are we going to stick them in front of a moving car. If a toddler is hitting, kicking or biting because they are angry or frustrated, the best way to deal with this is to acknowledge their feelings and show other ways of behaving in that situation. For example: 'I know you are angry because you wanted to play with what Johnny's got and you can't bite him. The next time you want to play with a toy he has, you ask him.'

Sarah Darton, health visitor

Hitting

I didn't hit my first child. I always found him very easy to reach. There was never any need to. So by the time my second came along we had a house rule – no hitting – and it worked. I used to be able to say, 'I do not hit you, you are not to hit me,' and it really helped. I felt lucky to have it so well established because my second is so much wilder and it has helped stop me lashing out at him.

Abby H

A lot of toddlers hit out in frustration. It is also very common between siblings. Of course it will occur more if they see this behaviour around them. Sometimes even in a household where hitting is only used in play, it can still be a bit confusing to a young child. It takes quite a while for children to learn limits and appropriate rules.

Carol Ann Hally, health visitor, clinical practice teacher

The advice on biting applies here, too. In general, however, hitting can remain a problem for much longer and the reasons are fairly obvious: children are surrounded by images of heroes who hit, they may see their siblings or even parents hit, they may be hit themselves. It can be a quick way for them to get what they want – a toy, more attention, a release for their anger or frustration.

If it is allowed to continue unchecked, the risks increase for the hitting child as well as those hit. A key predictor of violence in adulthood is violence in childhood,[5] so parental disapproval and action is vital if the child is to be spared long-term problems (see Checklist for Non-violence, p.185).

If your young child hits, try to keep it in proportion (almost all do sometimes) but do act (they must be taught to stop). Show your disapproval in ways appropriate to the child's age, remembering that

Checklist for non-violence

The Commission on Children and Violence[6] was convened to review the known causes of child violence and to make recommendations about violence prevention. Its members – all leading experts in childcare and welfare – commended the following basic principles:

1: **Expectations of, and demands made on, children should reflect their maturity and development.**

'Children's development is a process, not a race . . . Children cannot do, or be, what is developmentally out of their reach. Adults who have unrealistic expectations of children therefore jeopardise the positive relationships on which non-violence depends and lack the basic understanding they need to keep children safe.'

2: **All discipline should be positive and children should be taught pro-social values and behaviour and non-violent conflict resolution.**

'Negative discipline takes violence in the relationships between adults and children for granted by focusing on "bad behaviour"; expecting it, watching out for, and punishing it. In contrast, positive discipline leaves violence on the sidelines by focusing on "good behaviour"; expecting it, making sure it is modelled, understood and achievable, and rewarding it.'

3: **Non-violence should be consistently preferred and promoted.**

'It is useless to tell children not to fight (or snatch and grab, hit or kick) without giving them effective alternative ways of getting what they want or holding on to what they have. All children should be taught to use (and to respond to) verbal requests and protests. If children are to listen to each other, they must be confident that adults will listen to them.'

4: **Adults should take responsibility for protecting children from violence done to them, but also for preventing violence done by them.**

'Although adults perpetrate the extremes of violence in society, adults also represent children's only hope of safety from it, because without adult supervision and control, children's lives can be dominated by each other's violence.'

very young children who hit have no idea it hurts (see Co-operation and Discipline, p.196).

All children can benefit from very clear messages – 'We use words in this house, not fists' or 'Being angry is OK, hitting is not' – and very clear instructions on alternative ways to behave – 'Yell if necessary but do not hurt'; 'If you feel angry and you can't sort it out, find me and I'll help you' (see Feelings and Fears, p.124). Older, school-age children can begin to think of ways to be assertive without being aggressive and to resolve conflicts peacefully and constructively (see Assertion v. Aggression, p.368). Acknowledging when a child shows self-control will motivate them to do so again: 'You did really well saying "No" instead of hitting your sister. I could see you were angry.'

The most important way to teach a child not to hit is to not hit them (see Smacking isn't the Solution, p.241). No additional approaches will cut much ice if you do.

Refusing to share

This is very normal, especially between about 18 months and three years, yet parents have very high levels of expectation. They want children to grow up quickly, easily and be perfect. Children do not often come with all these social skills built-in, they need guidance and training.

Carol Ann Hally, health visitor, clinical practice teacher

This is a phase all my children have been through. It begins when they start realising they are a little person in their own right – before they have realised other people are too!

Anne M

Expecting your child to share everything seems unrealistic. Most adults would happily share their food, their hospitality, even their clothes but might draw the line at their car or their mother's wedding ring. Children have precious objects, too, and it seems only fair that these are accorded special status and the rules explained to siblings and friends: 'That blanket is her most special thing and no one can take it without her permission.' Keeping it out of sight of others is the easiest way to avoid disputes, especially when children are too young to understand the rules.

Most children find 'turn-taking' an easier idea to grasp than sharing. For them, sharing may imply giving up something they really want. Turn-taking implies everyone has 'a go' but ownership remains clear. This is especially important if we are encouraging children to let others use their toys. Most children have a highly developed sense of property rights and won't release their grip on a prize possession until they know they'll get it back.

Simple turn-taking games can help young children get the hang of the basics: 'Roll the ball to me, then I'll roll it to you'; 'Michael's turn, then Amy's, then Michael's again'. If it doesn't work out, leave it for another day. They'll get into the swing eventually, and when they do their turn-taking skills can help them develop others, such as waiting their turn to talk: 'Tom's going to tell me his side of the story, then you can tell me yours.'

If children start squabbling, we can express our confidence in their abilities to resolve the issue and also re-state ground rules of acceptable behaviour:

Parent: 'Let go. I'm sure he will let you have a turn when he's finished if you ask rather than grab.'
Child One: 'Please can I have a go?'
Child Two: 'OK then' (possible) or 'I haven't finished yet' (more likely).

Your possible options now include:

Counting This isn't counting of the 'I'm going to count to three and if you don't hand it over I'll . . .' variety, but rather 'OK. I know you want to play with it a bit longer and I know Miles wants to play with it, too, so let's count to twenty (or whatever number the children agree), then you hand it over. That's fair.' Twenty seconds is a long time in child politics. By then they may feel they have made their point and be happy to hand it over.

Encouraging them to sort it out for themselves Say what the problem is, how the children may feel about it, and encourage them to find their own solutions: 'OK, you're both upset because you both want to play with the guitar. How can you sort this out so everyone's happy?' or 'Two girls, one scooter. That's annoying, but I expect you two can think of a way round it' (see Co-operation and Discipline, p.196, and Siblings, p.279).

Children as young as three may be able to work out simple compromises and resolve disputes amicably if encouraged and given a little guidance along the way. Older children can often display great generosity and creativity in working out solutions, if given the chance: 'I know it's your CD, but Tom's really upset. Can you think of what else he might like to listen to?'

Avoid asking older children always to give way to younger ones as there is nothing more likely to breed resentment. The rules of sharing and turn-taking are complex, so it helps to be patient, understanding and encouraging. We can demonstrate the mutual benefits through our own behaviour, and provide plenty of opportunities to practise by encouraging our children to mix with others.

Parents can too easily pander to a younger child's needs because it is easier when you are under stress. For example, a toddler wanting the older child's toys all the time and the parent saying, 'Just give it to her, she is your baby sister and she can't understand.' Parents should try to avoid this. For a child to hear, 'I understand it is your toy and you have every right to play with it. I can also see your baby sister wants a go very much. When you're ready, perhaps you'd give it to her,' is so much more helpful.

Brigid Treacy, parenting advisor

Stealing

A very young child may take something that does not belong to them because they don't yet realise it is wrong. A warning sign with an older child, who knows it is wrong to steal, is repeated, secretive behaviour. I have seen examples in schools of a child stealing from coat pockets, even stealing other children's lunches. They were not hungry, but the theft was an expression of a need. It may be they felt they had nothing, so wanted to take extra. They may have the material things they need, but feel neglected personally. Or they may be feeling that other children are better than themselves and so they want to deprive them of something. It is these feelings that need to be addressed.

Vivienne Gross, family therapist

It's the game my boys enjoy best. Stealing the biscuit tin from under my nose and dashing upstairs with their spoils. I only know they've got it because it goes quiet.

Clare M

Your response to your child's light fingers will depend on their age, their understanding and the circumstances.

If your child is pre-school or younger, remember that most very young children have no notion of property or, when they do, their notion is that all property belongs to them. If you overlook incidents, however innocent, you are wasting an opportunity to explain and educate, but try not to go overboard if it appears they didn't know their actions were wrong. Instead, talk about favourite things and how stealing hurts people's feelings. Express your confidence in them leaving other people's things where they belong.

If you suspect your school-age child of stealing:

— Try to establish the facts.
— Let them tell their side of the story (see Communication, p.89).
— Keep a sense of proportion. Many children take things that don't belong to them at least once.
— Calmly make your disapproval clear.
— Tell your child you love them and want to help before the situation becomes more difficult.
— Discuss how people feel when their things are taken (books may help if direct discussion of the incident stops your child talking).
— Avoid labelling your child a thief (see Ripping up Labels, p.119).
— Look at the wider picture. Stealing and other disruptive behaviour can be a wake-up call that your child is struggling with life and needs your help. Perhaps they are having a problem at school. Perhaps they simply need more of your time and attention. If this is the case, the most obvious cure is your understanding, support, clear boundaries, positive attention and praise.
— Let them decide what they could do to improve matters (apologising and returning any property seem good starting points. If they don't suggest these themselves, raise them as options to consider).
— Be vigilant, and also let the matter drop once the issue is dealt with. If you keep bringing it up your child will feel they can never leave it behind, which gives them little incentive not to do it again.

She was always taking her older sister's jewellery and bits and squirreling them away in her room. I was getting worried because whatever I said or did didn't seem to make a lot of difference, then it struck me that her big sister was actually quite clever and cutting and always got the last word. Perhaps taking her things was her only way of getting back at her? So I had to tackle the way both girls behaved.

Claire T

Lying

You might be worried that your three-or four-year-old appears to tell lies. Children of this age find it hard to separate reality from their fantasy world and may quite genuinely believe in something which they may have been daydreaming about.

Eileen Hayes, parenting advisor to the NSPCC

I told whoppers, I think mainly to make my rather normal existence more exciting and exotic. I told friends my dad was in jail, even though they could see him coming home from work every night, that my mother used to lock me in a cupboard and push my food in through a trap door on a stick and that my brother was a smuggler.

Michelle C

Lying and spinning yarns is something most children grow into and, generally, grow out of again. Within reason. Very few adults tell the truth all the time yet very many expect their children to display total honesty – except when Grandma asks if they liked the jumpers she knitted.

A healthy dash of realism will help you keep your children's trans-gressions in perspective. The reasons children lie are as varied as the reasons adults do it: to impress, embellish, dodge, conform, please, protect, provoke, delay consequences, because they don't understand the line between fantasy and reality or because they don't understand the question.

Very young children rarely lie; until they are old enough to realise that other people have different experiences from themselves, there's little point. The first step in the fantasy league is usually imaginary play (from one year), then vivid dreams, daydreams and nightmares (especially around three years), then denial that misdemeanours or broken ornaments have anything to do with them (around the time they realise they may get away with it). By the time they have had a year or two at school, most children have witnessed the art of telling whoppers even if they are not skilled practitioners themselves.

It is very important that our children know the difference between fantasy and reality, that they tell us the truth when it matters (i.e. most of the time) and that they feel they can tell us anything. If nothing is unspeakable, the incentives to lie reduce dramatically. To achieve this, it helps to:

Talk about lying Be clear that telling the truth is important. Discuss how lying can hurt others and hurt the person who lies. Tell the story of the boy who cried 'Wolf' so many times when it wasn't true that he wasn't believed when it was.

Recognise the power of a child's imagination Wild imaginings are not lying and are best not treated as such. We can talk about dreams and thoughts, explain what is real and what not, and help our children see the difference.

Encourage truth-telling It's important we don't punish our children for telling the truth, however hard it is for us to hear (see Communication, p.89): 'If you were to tell me that you broke that vase, I would be sad because I liked it, but I would also be very pleased that you admitted it.'

Set the example This requires us to admit mistakes (see Know you'll Sometimes get it Wrong, p.233).

Avoid 'cover-ups' Think long and hard before covering up a deliberate, self-interested lie for your child; it is usually far healthier in the long term for children to face the consequences of their actions.

Let them know we know This is important, as lying and story-telling can become a habit. If they are making up harmless stories, let them know gently: 'I used to wish things like that happened, too.' If you know something to be a lie, say so clearly and calmly. 'I saw you hit her. What do you want to do to make things better?'

I say 'Ouch' and pretend I've got poked in the eye by a long nose if one of the boys starts spinning a tale. It's just a good-humoured way of letting them know I've got their number. They usually stop.

David Y

Know how literal children can be Some young children can be so excruciatingly literal that they tell the truth but miss the point. The only solution is to be aware that this may happen and to ask very precise questions, including the all-important one: 'OK, you tell me what happened.'

My son was told off for running in the corridor at school. He denied it, the teacher said she saw him do it and so he got into trouble for lying as well. I was stuck in the middle, with my son insisting he didn't run and her insisting he did. About a week later, when he was still really upset, he said, 'I was not running.' So for the first time I asked him what he was doing and he replied, 'Skipping!'

Jane P

Know that children rarely lie about sexual abuse If a child indicates they have been abused, we must take it seriously. Let them know that you love them and will help. Contact a helpline immediately for guidance and support (see Contacts, p.429).

Cheating

The moral high ground of playing fair rather than playing to win is unfamiliar territory to many children – and many adults. It's our job to teach our children not to cheat, as there are few more certain routes to unpopularity among peers and classmates, but be prepared for a few tempers and loud expressions of outrage and frustration along the way.

— Let them know that games are more fun if people stick to the rules – and make sure they are clear what the rules are.
— Encourage children to think how they would feel if someone cheated on them.
— Explain how to win and lose well: congratulating opponents, not gloating at victory, saying if they found the game enjoyable even if they didn't win. Most children appreciate clear guidelines for behaviour in, what to them, can seem tough situations.
— Put a stop to cheating when you see it, but try to avoid humiliating the culprit: 'Oh, I think you've picked up one too many cards by mistake.' If the cheating persists, have a quiet, private word with the child involved and say you will stop the game if you see anyone not playing by the rules. Keep to your word.
— Play board and other games with them until they learn how to behave. It may help to have an adult on each 'team' to begin with.
— Praise children who do not cheat. It is very tempting, and those who do not do it deserve to be told how well they have played.

Swearing

Children can bring home all sorts of unpleasant things from school. Colds, nits, smelly sports kit and a selection of swear words are among the most common. Almost all children will occasionally display the playground's choicest grimaces, gestures and expletives. They are surrounded by language many find offensive – it's in the media, in song lyrics, on T-shirts – so it's hardly surprising that they pick it up. How we react will depend on our own beliefs and our children's intent. They really don't know what they're saying sometimes (see Three Important Questions, p.170). But it is part of a parent's job to equip children with the knowledge that many people find certain words and gestures offensive.

It is also important to keep minor misdemeanours in perspective. Sniggering with friends about 'rude' words and body parts is a perfectly healthy and almost universal part of growing up. If we overreact, we simply confirm the words' potential to shock. It's generally far more effective to keep a sense of humour and be calm, clear and unimpressed.

There was a tree in our playground and we used to dare each other to climb up to the top, shout 'bum', then all run away.

Christina C

We made up our own swear words. We had one – horhors – which meant poo and we thought it was hysterically funny. We'd say it endlessly and fall about laughing.

Angela S

If our children utter something we find offensive or which we know will offend others, first check whether they know that what they've said or done is not acceptable. This does not mean we have to explain the literal meaning of the word or gesture. This is sometimes appropriate for older children but for younger ones can be confusing and counterproductive. But we can explain the cultural meaning attached to certain words and phrases: i.e. that they are used to offend, so if you use them people will presume you meant to be offensive/hurtful/aggressive. This is why they can provoke such an angry response and this is why you have a house rule that those words (whichever you chose) are not said.

Clear rules are also needed for other sorts of hateful or offensive language, such as racist terms or name-calling, again often picked up from peers before children have any idea of their meaning: 'We don't call people names in this family. If you have a problem with him, tell him what it is and what you'd like done about it.'

Obviously, if it's something we say, our children will say it too. To work, house rules need to be followed by everybody and parents need to be able to say, 'I don't speak to you like that and you don't speak to me like that. OK?' House rules can also apply to our children's friends, who may be allowed to swear in their own home in ways we don't want repeated in our own: 'We don't use that word in our house. Every family has different rules and that's one of ours.'

If a child is knowingly and repeatedly rude in ways that worry or offend, it's time to look at what else is happening in their lives. Keep the rules of acceptable conduct clear (see Co-operation and Discipline, p.196) and think through what they may be trying to tell you through their behaviour: 'I know you're angry and you know I won't have that language. When you're ready, let's talk about what's making you angry' (see Communication, p.89).

I'd always been told never to make a fuss when a child swears. That worked until he was about six when he came out with a phrase that I find really offensive. When I said I didn't like it his friend said, 'My dad says it.' I said something like, 'Well, every family has different things they like and don't like and I don't like that.' Neither have used it in front of me since.

Laura F

Saying they hate you

It should be OK for them to hate you in the moment. The love-hate relationship you can have with your siblings or children is actually the same for your child towards you. Just as you hate their behaviour rather than them, they are protesting and hating what you are doing, rather than hating you.

Brigid Treacy, parenting advisor

Your child saying they hate you in the heat of the moment is usually nothing more than a healthy, passionate and instant response to you doing your job. Not every child says it aloud, but most show it at some stage with a withering look, a curled lip or a slamming door.

Parents sometimes don't follow consistent rules with their children because they are worried about the child not loving them, yet a great deal of what goes with the territory of parenthood is being the person your child can hate. Having them tell you that they hate you is what you are there for, in a way, just as much as putting the fish fingers and baked beans on the table. It is much safer for you to take it than for them to tell their teacher that they hate them or the policeman on the corner because you are also the one doing the loving and the care-giving. Their relationship with you is where your children work out how to deal with aggression and restraint.

Vivienne Gross, family therapist

A parent's job sometimes involves drawing lines and taking action that our children don't like. Some of their worst excesses of behaviour will be kept just for us and that's as it should be. At least it shows they know our love is unconditional.

Horribly normal: a quick reminder

- It's not good for children to be good all the time. Grotty behaviour is a normal and necessary part of growing up.
- Understanding why children behave as they do, and how we can set boundaries and support and educate them in better behaviour as they grow, will save us all much time and emotional energy.

CHAPTER SEVEN
CO-OPERATION AND DISCIPLINE

To an extent, children can be trained like rats or dogs by punishing and rewarding their behaviour. But much more importantly, children can also internalise rules, adopt them as their own and understand them. When this happens, children behave for the right reasons, not because they are scared of punishment or withdrawal of love but because the reasons for behaving in certain ways make sense to them and they want to co-operate.

Dr Gavin Nobes, senior lecturer in Developmental and Forensic Psychology, University of East London

This chapter focuses on constructive and effective ways to guide and improve children's behaviour. It details ways we can help our children understand what's expected of them, why it matters and how it benefits themselves and others. It also features discipline approaches that can turn behaviour around when things go pear-shaped. It includes firm guidelines and clear consequences. It does not include punishment for the sake of it.

Our aim is to encourage children's development of social awareness and self-discipline, helping them face challenges, handle their strong emotions and consider themselves and others. To do this, we do not need methods that hurt, humiliate, frighten or shame.

As a first step, we can remember the very basic needs that may lie behind a child's more ghastly moments: attention, warmth, reassurance, guidance, even sleep and food in the right amounts can go a very long way (see Highs, Lows and Outbursts, p.167).

Beyond this lies a long, rich process of education and relationship-building – the foundations upon which all effective discipline approaches are built. Clearly, this requires parental time, effort and understanding, but it's an investment that pays huge dividends.

Focusing on prevention as well as problem-solving will reduce outbursts of mind-numbing misbehaviour and save all family members much time and emotional energy. And the more investment we make, the easier and happier our relationships and our children's behaviour can become.

Encouraging co-operation

This wasn't how I was brought up, but it's how I feel right bringing up my own children. It helps me see the best in them and the best in me.

Sue W

I felt stuck, like we were travelling round the same circle going nowhere. We still go back to our old ways occasionally, but we're learning new ones and life's getting better. It's like we've let the love back in.

Marina T

Parents sometimes find it hard to believe, but children are essentially co-operative. They want to behave in ways that make them feel good

---

In our children's shoes

Real empathy involves more than putting ourselves in our children's shoes, it involves imagining what it is like to be that child in their shoes.

Candida Hunt, Family Links

Imagining how our children are feeling and why can help us gauge how best to respond. Are they tired? Poorly? Upset? Too young to know better? Or indulging in anti-social antics that need to be stopped? Sometimes the most constructive response is a very definite 'No'; sometimes what children need most is a gentle explanation or a cuddle.

'When you are backed into a corner what comes out is usually what you are familiar with, how your parents treated you,' explains Christine Puckering, psychologist and co-founder of Mellow Parenting. 'You end up saying the things your mother said after swearing that you never would. Once you are able to put yourself in your child's shoes, you can learn to do things differently. Different approaches would suit different situations and parents need the choices and skills to work out their own solutions, but first they need to be able to imagine how their child feels and to do this the child has to be respected and related to as an individual.'

and their parents feel good. The key to encouraging positive behaviour in our children is to build on this natural desire to please (see Ready to Care, Keen to Please, p.200).

To do this, we need to listen and talk with our children, understand their feelings and how they express them and have a realistic sense of their capabilities (see Communication, p.89; Feelings and Fears, p.124; and Horribly Normal, p.166). We can then boost our children's understanding and capacity to behave considerately and co-operatively by being:

Clear Children need to know what is expected of them, where, when and why.

Caring A child who feels loved, appreciated and respected is more likely to behave better than one whose self-esteem is low (see In our Children's Shoes, p.197).

We cannot expect children to attach value to people and objects in the outside world if they themselves do not feel valued and wanted.

Royal College of Paediatrics and Child Health[1]

Positive By behaving and talking positively with our children, they are far more likely to behave positively and feel good about themselves (see Positive Power, p.115). If we notice and praise considerate behaviour, we'll see more of it. If we point out why and how it has helped, children soon understand why such behaviour matters: 'You picked up all the toys so now we've got time to play. What would you like to do?'; 'You saw I was tired and you kept the volume down. That was really considerate. Thanks.'

Try to think positively, too. Life as a parent can challenge us in ways we'd never imagined, especially when we're trying to cope with too many things at once (see Our Feelings as Parents, p.142). Yet whether we're trying to make a good relationship better or finding our way through problems, we can always take steps forward. And small steps can make a big difference.

Having different, constructive ways of approaching this is like beginning again, both having another chance.

Jacqui C

Consistent However we want our children to behave – and this will vary between families and cultures – all children require predictability of expectation and response.

But let's get real. No child should be expected to behave impeccably at all times because that's not what people do. Burden ourselves and our children with unrealistic expectations and we could tie ourselves in knots (see Horribly Normal, p.166). More importantly, we could also make a child feel a 'failure', which will make them even less likely to behave as we'd wish.

The approaches that follow offer constructive ways to encourage positive behaviour, but don't expect to get the hang of them all at once. Some involve a little thought while others require a lot of practice; some will help in specific situations while others can change family life dramatically. Decide which you and your child need most, do what you can, when you can, and reap the benefits.

Rules and boundaries

Without boundaries a child is completely at sea. If they push those boundaries and they collapse, this is a very scary situation for a child to be in. They can become very aggressive.

Brigid Treacy, parenting advisor

Kids need to have some control, but it is distressing for children to believe they have ultimate power. If they feel they can do anything, they are terribly unhappy because the world then becomes a frighteningly uncertain and unpredictable place. Part of being a parent is allowing your child to experiment, to test what the boundaries are and where they lie, because your relationship is the safest place for them to do this. Much, much better that they do it with their mum or dad than outside.

Professor Hilton Davis, clinical child psychologist and director of the Centre for Parent and Child Support

Setting limits on our children's behaviour and making it clear where we have drawn the line is crucial to our relationship, their future and our sanity.

Some parents feel uncomfortable about setting limits and establishing rules, fearing that it veers towards authoritarianism and outmoded codes of social conduct. Yet without limits our children

Ready to care, keen to please

For children to develop positive, considerate behaviour, they have to recognise and appreciate the feelings of others. Incredibly, this capacity is evident in a newborn child.

Dr Gavin Nobes, a leading specialist in children's social behaviour and moral development, explains: 'Newborn babies can show a capacity to empathise with others. For example, babies will often cry when they hear another baby cry. This response to others' distress is similar to an adult's who sees another person or animal in pain.

'By two or three years most children show frequent signs of empathy. A toddler who cuddles another child who is distressed shows a sensitivity to other people's pain.

'So it seems likely that humans are born with a capacity to recognise other people's emotions. Their understanding of others gradually increases through infancy and childhood by observing people's actions and responses.

'Parents also help children understand and interpret what people do and what they mean through clear and consistent explanation and communication. So children arrive with an innate potential to acquire social understanding that parents can build on.'

Your child is not only increasingly sensitive to other people's feelings, they also want you to feel good about the way they behave. 'What gives you a handle on your children's behaviour isn't simply a neat set of behavioural techniques,' says family therapist Vivienne Gross. 'If things have gone more or less well between you in your child's early years, in terms of you paying attention to their needs, the sleeping, feeding, changing, keeping them warm, cuddling them and so on, your child will want to please you. They have become "attached" to you, the caregiver, and this allows them to think about you, as well as themselves.

'It shouldn't simply be that children are like prisoners who obey the prison guard for fear of punishment, but that they have a regard for you, from which all sorts of other social and relational possibilities ensue. If there isn't that attachment credit in the bank, it is going to be far harder to impose a behaviour regime that works. If you do it in a cold state rather than there being warmth between you, these regimes can feel very uncomfortable for you both.'

can't learn expected and appropriate behaviour, and this will damage their relationships inside and outside the family. Think of them as a safety net – without them, children can feel insecure and anxious. Establishing ground rules is not a sign of harsh parenting or lack of love, but rather a natural extension of our love, concern and regard. It is not the opposite of warmth, nurturing and mutual respect, but part of it.

Of course, our children won't see it that way. Part of parenthood is being the butt of a toddler's outrage at not being allowed to stick their toy down the loo or of an eleven-year-old's eye-rolling contempt when it's time for bed. Yet children themselves tell researchers[2] that family rules are an important part of parental care. They may not always like them, but they understand their importance.

What matters is the mix, between being firm enough to guide our children's behaviour and not being a doormat to their will and whim, while also helping them feel loved, cared for, appreciated and respected.

- **Decide rules** Every family will have its own expectations and rules to guide their children's behaviour, so first decide the boundaries that matter in yours.

  Boundaries are the guiding principles, for example: 'Children need to be safe'. These principles do not change as your child grows.

  Rules are how these principles are put into practice, for example: 'Leave plug sockets alone.'

  Try to keep boundaries and rules simple and few. A small number of basic and age-appropriate ground rules that everyone can remember and agree are far more effective than 101 things to forget by breakfast.

- **Explain** We need to explain and demonstrate what the rules and boundaries are if our children are to grasp what's expected of them. You could, for example, explain that they are not to hit (rule) because in your family 'We don't hurt people unnecessarily' (boundary).

  Children as young as three can generally understand language well enough to appreciate simple explanations. Remember that abstract terms such as 'safety' and 'care' are of no use if our children haven't a clue what we're talking about. They need simple, clear explanations, with plenty of specific examples.

I sometimes tell my kids, 'I love you too much to let you do that,' and then explain that part of my job is to keep them safe and that's why I won't let them play football on the pavement or go over the road without holding my hand. It seems to make it less of a power struggle. It doesn't mean they always like it, but it helps them accept it a bit more.

Debbi B

- **Remind** Children need reminding of rules again and again until they get the message: 'Remember, no hitting', 'We have a rule about that, can you remember what it is?' Assume your child is basically co-operative but not quite getting the gist of what you are saying – this will help you stay patient and realistic. Sometimes children protest or ignore it because they don't like the message, sometimes because they've forgotten it and sometimes because they still don't understand it. Check which it is – if it is the latter, explain again. If not, keep it simple: 'You know we keep the balls in the garden.' Over-wordy or over-worthy explanations tend to be ignored.

  If you have been able to communicate and reinforce these rules as your child grows they may only need occasional reminders. If, however, you feel you have all lost the plot, it may help to draw up a list of rules with your child so you have a chance to discuss what they mean and why they matter. Stick the list somewhere where every family member can see it, if you think it would help. Remember, though, that the most important and effective reinforcement is your own good example, your positive response when rules are followed and your firm-ness when they are broken. There's little point having the house festooned with lists that even you take little notice of.

- **Update** Rules need updating as children develop and their needs and our expectations alter. Many rules that apply to a toddler, for instance, would be totally inappropriate for a child of six. If rules are right and relevant to the child's age and stage, they are easier to stick to.

  What stay firm are the principles from which those rules spring, and this is where your child's understanding of these really helps. For example, if children know that one important principle is their safety, 'Always hold my hand as we cross the road' can change, eventually, into 'Look both ways as you cross the road' without any contradic-tion, because the general principle remains. All that has altered is the most age-appropriate way to put it into practice.

  Applying boundaries in ways that best suit each child may also help us negotiate sibling complaints: 'I know you're angry that he goes to bed later but the younger you are the more sleep you need to stay healthy. You go to bed when you need to, and he goes to bed when he needs to. When you're his age, you can stay up later.' Different rules, same principle, no contradiction.

  Updating rules is very different from caving in under the pressure of a child's temper or your own indecision. To make it clear to your child that you have revised a rule because you think it is right to do so and not because of their fuss or protest, it helps to:

1 Avoid changing the rule on the spot. Giving way in the heat of the moment may give children the impression that a good outburst will see off any rules they happen to dislike.
2 When the situation has calmed down, explain that you have thought long and hard and decided that the rule needs updating. Include the child in deciding the new limit, where appropriate. The child then feels you've responded to new circumstances rather than to their negative behaviour. They will also feel they've had a voice in the rule-making process, which will increase their sense of responsibility.

Consistency

Lack of consistency is the main reason why rules sometimes don't work. We can minimise the risk by:

Standing firm Children need to test, be unreasonable and sometimes say 'No' to their parents' eminently sensible requests. This is how they learn how far they can go – and it is up to us to teach them.

This requires us to stand firm and not cave in to unreasonable protests, rages or whines. A child's very act of pushing against the limits often reflects their need to know that their world is secure and does not crumble or break down if challenged. It is hard to believe when faced with a full-throttle temper, but children often need us to say 'No'. If their behaviour makes us wobble from what we believe to be right, we are creating an environment of uncertainty which neither parent or child will enjoy.

The limits a parent sets and sticks to are essential for growing up. We all know how painful people are who didn't get this parenting at a key stage and still think they are centre of the universe. They have not learnt that other people have feelings, too.

Steve Biddulph, psychologist and author

Try to keep listening, for the sake of kindness and safety. Standing firm is not the same as ignoring our children's feelings and views. These can alert us to genuine problems and injustice, and give us vital information. The child who's protesting about the lack of a biscuit one minute may the next be shouting, 'Isobel's fallen in the fish pond.' Without listening we may never know the intent behind our child's behaviour, and without knowing the intent we risk responding too harshly or inappropriately (see Three Important Questions, p.170).

Developing our self-discipline If we set new rules or drop them at a whim, children become confused about which rules matter, if any.

I was pretty erratic over this, for all sorts of reasons that had nothing to do with the children. I would insist on something one day and let it go the next, or suddenly blow up about something that hadn't been an issue before, like clearing away the table or taking their shoes off. I apologised for contradicting myself and expecting them to mind-read and we managed to get back on track. But I know I made what was a bad time for me a bad time for them, too, because they never knew where they stood. Things calmed down once that predictability was re-established.

Jeanette R

Consistency between adults

We are so different in what we expect of our children, and this will vary between cultures, families, even within couples. There are so many arguments between couples, for instance, about how long you can expect children to sit at a table and eat a meal. That is a real old chestnut.

Vivienne Gross, family therapist

I know, I know, I know. We're supposed to show a united front, never disagree about discipline in front of the children, divided we fall and all that. But she thinks I'm too strict and I think she lets them get away with things too often. We don't agree and when tempers are high that's pretty obvious, I'm sure.

Mark D

Consistency between significant adults makes a huge difference to children's behaviour for the very obvious reason that one message is easier to follow than many conflicting ones. Widely differing expectations of behaviour can rock a child's sense of security and leave them unsure how best to proceed.

Inevitably, most parents will disagree with the stance taken by a partner or another carer on occasion. That's life. But we can aim to build on common ground by discussing approaches and priorities. This reduces the risk of children spotting the gaps between their parents, or of one parent becoming the 'bad guy' for taking discipline seriously and the other becoming the soft option.

What's your style?

What might your parenting style[3] be telling and teaching your child?

1: **Authoritarian** This parent is overly strict, tending to criticise their child for every minor misdemeanour. They are often harsh and sometimes aggressive, depending on their mood. They are likely to impose rules on their children with no explanation other than 'Because I said so'. Their children are unlikely to be involved in making decisions or agreeing rules.

2: **Permissive** This parent is not strict enough. They pretend not to have seen or heard even serious misbehaviour, either because they are unsure of how to tackle it or, for some other reason, don't want to. They often become resentful. Their children are usually sheltered from the consequences of their actions.

3: **Assertive** This parent is vigilant in observing their child's behaviour and responding appropriately. They are usually calm, assertive rather than aggressive and have good self-esteem. Their words and body language convey an expectation of compliance. They tend to believe every family member has a right to be considered and heard, explain and discuss rules with their children and revise them where necessary.

Children raised in authoritarian households are likely to miss out on opportunities to develop the skills of negotiation, co-operation, sharing and competition. They will also tend to see rules as absolutes that are imposed from above and must be followed without question, regardless of whether they are fair, in order to avoid punishment. They are unlikely to understand the point of rules and so will break them if they think they can get away with it. Children do have the potential to develop an understanding of rules as agreements and of right and wrong. How this potential is developed is largely a function of how they are parented, and whether they are encouraged to talk about rules and occasionally challenge them.

Dr Gavin Nobes, lecturer in developmental and forensic psychology, University of East London

If you really can't agree, it may be helpful to be honest: 'Table manners don't matter to me so much, but Dad really cares about them. That's why he wants you to hold your knife and fork properly'; 'I know Mum's OK about the CD player being so loud, but I really don't like it. Turn it down please.' Once different opinions are discussed openly, children may be a little less inclined to attempt to play one parent off against the other.

Making exceptions Most good rules have good exceptions. If we take the time to explain why and how an exception is being made, the general rule can still hold good.

Experience and example

> *Stop shouting!*
>
> Parent, shouting

> *It is accepted that children get their ideas of right and wrong, including their attitudes to violence, from important, caring adults, but they get them first and foremost from adult behaviour that they can see; only secondarily from adult words that they may not understand.*
>
> The Commission on Children and Violence[4]

We can run but we can't hide. Our children will echo our behaviour and reactions and, from birth, we are their greatest role models. How we respond to our child and to others has a far stronger impact than anything we say (see What's your Style?, p.205). If we want our children to stop shouting, for example, we'd better do the same. If we stick to agreements, our children are far more likely to trust us and stick to agreements themselves.

Clear messages

> *I realised I had to be more precise with my instructions after the baby was born and I found my daughter dragging him down the hallway by his feet. This very sorry child said, 'But you told me not to carry him when you weren't in the room. I didn't carry him. I pulled him.'*
>
> Jane P

The clearer your message the more easily and quickly your child can respond. Being brief and to the point, making sure your body language matches your verbal message, leaves less room for debate and negative reaction. Compare:

'Deborah, where's your coat? You know you have to put it on so
    what are you doing looking at your comic?'
with
'Deborah – coat.'
or
'How many times have I told you not to do that? I can't believe
    you're still at it.'
with
'Joe – stop.'

Children can be excruciatingly pedantic. Giving simple, positive messages about what we want them to do rather than negative ones about what we don't want to happen usually leaves us less vulnerable to contradiction and nit-picking. 'Keep the noise down, Joe's sleeping' sends a clear message. 'Don't shout' risks a reply such as 'I'm not shouting, I'm singing.'

Be as specific as you can – 'Time to pick up your toys' – and avoid vague requests to 'be nice', 'be tidy', 'be kind'. Also avoid dressing up instructions as requests. Ditching the niceties of social etiquette can be hard, yet 'Please' or 'Would you?' may give children the impression they have an opt-out clause. 'Would you brush your teeth, please?' can be less effective than 'Time to brush your teeth.'

Also try to avoid two common parent traps:

Talking above children's heads Children's sense of right and wrong may be more sophisticated than generally appreciated, but it is also easy to overburden them with complexities when they're still getting to grips with the basics. Life throws up imperfections and dilemmas, and these can be discussed as they arise if your child seems ready or interested, but it is probably best not to overwhelm them with real-life exceptions to rules until the rules are set in place.

With young children, where you have a clash of moral issues things become more difficult. For example, to say you love the jumper your grandmother has knitted when you clearly don't, throws up the moral dilemma of deciding between lying and not hurting somebody. This is quite complicated and it is not really fair to expect young children to understand.

Dr Gavin Nobes, lecturer in developmental and forensic psychology,
University of East London

Such morally ambivalent and adult concepts as 'white lies' are likely to confuse young children. As they grow up, try to keep explanations clear, simple and positive. For example, you know it is good to tell the truth and you also know it is good not to hurt people's feelings unnecessarily. Sometimes we have to decide which matters most.

Children are very concrete. You will probably have to say to a child of five, 'Tell me what you saw happen.' If you say 'Tell the truth', it is loaded with values and moral imperatives they may not understand.

Vivienne Gross, family therapist

Absolutes As in 'never', 'always', 'the worst', 'the easiest' etc. Best avoided, unless you know you can stick to them yourself. 'Never lie' may rebound in a way that 'It is wrong to lie' or 'It is important to tell the truth' may not. 'We don't hit in this house' holds no water if you sometimes do. Simple statements like 'Sorry is the hardest word' may trip you up if your child finds a harder one. 'Sorry is very hard to say' leaves you less vulnerable to contradiction.

If you say 'always tell the truth', the moment they see you break from the 'always', the whole scheme is broken, and life isn't like that, it is much more graduated. Most days we fall from our own standards by some percent. Parents should try to help children see there is something to aspire to rather than to see life in terms of either all good or all bad, or associating doing something your family prefers you not to do with being a bad person.

Vivienne Gross, family therapist

Choices

At its simplest, this is a trick – giving a child two options, both of which you are happy with. As in 'Would you like a bath with bubbles or soap?' What your child is not offered is no bath at all. This is useful in areas where you have clashed in the past, as it helps children feel they have some say, but you set the parameters. Choices are much

Your child's moral sense

Dr Gavin Nobes, lecturer in developmental and forensic psychology,
University of East London

We know that even young children are much more morally sophisticated than we used to believe. Even 20 years ago it was thought that children under the age of 12 had no real understanding of why things are right and wrong and that they obeyed rules simply to avoid punishment and gain rewards.

We now know that children as young as three show surprising understanding. Many will say that not hitting someone is a more important rule than, for example, not eating with your fingers. Many five-year-olds can tell you that social conventions – rules about eating, dressing and being polite, for example – can be changed and that moral rules – rules about not hitting, stealing, lying and so on – cannot.

We used to believe that children could not make these distinctions and that they thought all rules were equal in importance. Now we know they are aware that hitting is wrong not just because there is a social command to not do so, but also because it causes distress.

Parents can help children understand what is right and wrong by explaining clearly and being consistent. It is also important to use simple language and ideas. We should expect children to sometimes forget rules, especially ones that are hard to understand, and try to explain rules rather than punish children for making mistakes.

more likely to elicit co-operation than commands, which many children take as a cue for resistance. Compare:

'How would it suit you best to do your homework? Before or after supper?'

and

'Do your homework.'

'It's cold so you need a coat. Would you like help with the buttons or to do it yourself?'

and

'Put on your coat.'

At a deeper level, giving choices helps children become aware of the consequences of their actions and find their own solutions, both crucial if they are to grow to be self-reliant and self-disciplined.

Even choices such as 'Would you like carrots or broccoli?' or

The value of values

Our beliefs about social values, about what is decent and fair, are created in our family of origin.

Royal College of Paediatrics and Child Health[5]

By their early school years most children have a sophisticated understanding of right and wrong and an awareness of other people's feelings.

The challenge for us as parents is to recognise and develop this understanding and so equip our children for a life of increasing experience, independence and choices. This gives them the capability to make the right choices even when we are not there to guide them. Equipping them includes:

Developing children's self-esteem and self-awareness They are more likely to understand and value others if they value and understand themselves.

Encouraging respect of other people's feelings Only then can they fully understand the consequences of their actions.

Establishing consistent, firm and fair ground rules for behaviour, encouraged through praise and the controlled use of sanctions.

Helping children build and enjoy relationships with others

Encouraging them to articulate emotions and opinions, helping them better understand their decisions and take responsibility for their actions.

Developing children's ability to handle frustrations and tackle mistakes Help them view these as temporary situations to be dealt with rather than matters to overwhelm or devastate.

Encouraging children to question, reason, consider and think for themselves, so they not only know how but why they need to behave considerately.

Which may all sound absurdly optimistic if your sophisticated six- or 11-year-old sometimes sighs in exasperation at the mere sound of your voice. But remember, happy children are not perfect and neither are their parents or their families.

If you have managed to create a family in which human fallibility is understood and in which self-esteem is nurtured, in which your unconditional love is a given, children are respected and communication is open and honest most of the time, your child will have already learned a huge amount about tolerance, compassion, co-operation, respect, responsibility and consideration.

'Would you like Helen or Christopher to play tomorrow?' can show a child their opinion is valued and can influence events. At their most effective and educative, choices inform children of the natural consequences of their actions, for example: 'If you stay in the bath there won't be time for stories. Are you staying in or getting out?'; 'You decide. If you eat your grapes now, there'll be none for your packed lunch tomorrow.' (See Consequences, p.225.)

Life is full of choices, and an important part of growing up is learning to face these, think issues through and decide what we feel to be right in the circumstances (see The Value of Values, p.210). By noticing and praising our children when they've made a good decision, we can boost their pride and confidence in working through dilemmas. Remember not to wait for the big issues. To a child, everyday events throw up tough choices: 'You could have eaten that yourself but you decided to share. That's really thoughtful'.

What we pay attention to is what we get more of. So if we pay attention and compliment children when they make good choices, we'll get more.

Candida Hunt, Family Links

Explore issues together With our encouragement, primary-aged children can develop a sophisticated sense of right and wrong. This lies at the root of self-regulation, of their ability to manage their own conduct even in our absence and to choose for themselves the best way to behave, even in difficult or challenging situations. It is fundamental to their ability to respect and consider others as well as themselves, and to them developing the resilience and confidence they'll need to cope with life's ups and downs.

Children as young as five – sometimes younger – can discuss dilemmas and moral choices in stories and the world around them. Clearly, exploring these in ways children enjoy and understand means avoiding anything that smacks of knitted brows or ponderous instruction. TV soaps, newspaper stories, books, films, videos and songs can all prompt playful discussions (see Tales for Explorers, p.212). By inviting children's curiosity and opinions – 'How do you think that character feels right now?'; 'That's a tricky situation, what would you do?' – we can show interest in their views and give them much-needed practice in forming and expressing opinions (see Your Child's Moral Sense, p.209).

Tales for explorers

Carol Munro, primary headteacher

Stories encourage understanding and make issues come alive for children. You can draw them in through their imagination and their own experiences and encourage them to explore new situations and considerations – How would you feel if . . . ? How did they feel when . . . ? What could she have done . . . ? What will happen now . . . ?

In this way, stories can be used to develop children's moral sense. Through them they can reflect on what they know or feel; put themselves in somebody else's shoes and broaden their understanding of other's experiences and emotions; examine actions and consequences; explore moral dilemmas; challenge their own experiences and view issues from a distance when sometimes personal experience is too close to unravel.

Most reception-age children will take stories at face value, but that's OK. Important messages are still going in. By year one (age 5/6) children are able to analyse and consider, understand and feel. The more sensitive and brighter ones in particular really benefit from this kind of interaction.

Thinking time

Adults don't respond well to ridicule or loss of face, and neither do children. If we want to avoid confrontations, backlashes and damaging humiliation, we need to avoid shaming or embarrassing our child in front of others unless absolutely necessary.

Time is a useful face-saving device that encourages thought rather than knee-jerk rebellion. When giving children a choice or instruction, we can often give a little extra time for them to comply or think matters through. Some children respond best when parents then turn away to lessen the sense of head-to-head confrontation; others when parents stay put to indicate they expect compliance without further fuss (see A Six-step Plan for Co-operation, p.221). Much will depend on the child's temperament and the particular circumstances. Very young children may forget what they are supposed to be doing if we leave the room, but school-age children often respond well if told, 'I'll be back in a minute to see how you are getting on/what you have decided.'

For similar reasons, advance warning of a situation may save public clashes and be all a child needs to remember ground rules and think through how best to behave. 'We are going to Grandma's house soon.

Can you remember the deal we made: if you take the toys out of the shed you put them back again before we leave?'

Doing it for themselves

Don't do anything for children that they can do themselves, including their thinking. Children are not grateful if you do. Their natural urge is to become self-reliant and we as parents become resentful if we do not allow them to be.

Noel Janis-Norton, Director, New Learning Centre

Children can help themselves and help us. Encouraging language may be all that is needed to prompt them into action. Compare:

> Parent (irritated): 'Didn't I tell you to put your shoes on? Do I have to keep telling you?'
> and
> Parent (calm): 'What's next? Is there anything else you need to put on?'

> Parent: 'Do I have to do everything myself? You haven't washed that plate properly.'
> and
> Parent: 'You've washed the bowls really well. Those plates can be tricky. Show me how you can rinse that one clean.'

If children are to do things for themselves as they grow – putting on their shoes, buttering their own bread, tidying away, setting and clearing the table – they have to learn how. And learning involves making mistakes. They may take longer than we would, often won't do it as well and may make more mess along the way, but it will be worth it in the end.

We can guide gently, help when requested or when a child seems overwhelmed by the task, and attempt to build regular activities, such as clearing up, into daily routines so they meet with less resistance (see Helpfulness and Care, p.214). It makes sense to save rules and high expectations for things that really matter. Remember, too, that no one likes to be taken for granted. We need to try to stay alert to displays of helpfulness even when it becomes a habit. A little descriptive praise (p.115) goes a very long way.

I always have to do the washing up again once he's gone to bed, but he's having a go and that's great.

Fiona P

Children may need some help clearing up their room, for instance. Sometimes it gets so bad that the child doesn't know where to start. You might say, 'You do 10 minutes and I'll join you', or 'You do this bit and I'll do that bit', or help them put everything in a black bag from which they can take the things one by one and put them in their right place. Sometimes it just gets overwhelming for a six-year-old to do on their own. Sometimes it gets overwhelming for a 36-year-old!

Vivienne Gross, family therapist

Helpfulness and care

Being kind and considerate to one another and taking care of one another are qualities children can and do learn when they are very young and on into their primary school years.
National Children's Bureau[6]

If we can bring up our children to help and pitch in with family tasks, we'll all benefit. They will have important lessons in working co-operatively and collaboratively. Feeling needed and useful can also boost children's confidence and sense of worth. Jobs need to be age-appropriate, unforced and much appreciated, and we'll need to do chores with them until they get the hang of things, but the child who helps set the table or do the dusting aged five may grow to be the 11-year-old who helps clean the car or empty the washing machine. Occasionally.

'Most children will respond very positively if given the opportunity to do something that is good for somebody else, especially their parents,' says Professor Hugh Foot, specialist in child psychology and social development. 'The whole process of helping in the home, helping Mum, helping Dad,

helping brothers and sisters and understanding it will be reciprocated is a good, constructive attitude to engender within families.

'The worst thing is children who have everything done for them and who never have to lift a finger, who have not had to strive for anything and who have not had the opportunity to learn the pleasure of doing things for other people. Little children love to help with cooking, even if it is just stirring flour and water together. So they make a mess in the process, so what? They have enjoyed it and the parent is paving the way for the child learning family obligations and responsibilities, which makes it a lot easier later on to get the child to help with routine housework such as washing up without having to be bullied, coerced or bribed into doing it.'

Effective discipline

The shift for me has been realising that I can be loving and firm, that one doesn't extinguish the other.

Martin P

I like to talk about soft love and firm love and the need for both. Soft love is the very patient sort of love, the kind you ideally have around little babies. Firm love is the capacity to really hold the line with your child. It is done in a loving way but it is firm – 'It is not OK to hit your sister'. This is a tricky area for most people, particularly those who grew up with very harsh parenting.

Steve Biddulph, psychologist and author

Books that concentrate solely on preventing problematic behaviour miss the point that life isn't always that neat. No matter what we do and how hard we try, all children behave appallingly sometimes. Handled constructively, these times are opportunities to teach them better ways, encouraging them to think through the consequences of their actions and how they could behave differently in future.

Managing these times so children's behaviour improves can be difficult and stressful, but nowhere near as difficult and stressful as leaving the behaviour unchallenged. Only by showing our children where we draw the line can they ever know which side of it they should be on (see Rules and Boundaries, p.199).

Our own responses will teach our children powerful lessons in handling tough situations without aggression. We will sometimes need to be gentle, sometimes firm, often both. This has nothing to do with being harsh, frightening or threatening and everything to do with being caring, responsible and responsive enough to help our children develop control over their own behaviour.

To do this it may help to consider the differences between discipline and punishment:

1 **Discipline is a tool** It educates. It encourages children to think through what they have done wrong, the consequences of their behaviour and how they could modify it. It thus increases their understanding of what is expected of them and why. It is an investment that develops self-discipline and motivates children to behave better. Discipline is not

a soft option for parent or child, and can be astonishingly effective in turning around problematic behaviour.

2 **Punishment is a weapon** It aims to shame, frighten, bribe or otherwise force children into compliance without them necessarily understanding why. It does not encourage them to think through the consequences of their actions on themselves and others, or better ways to behave in tough situations. Punishment does not encourage self-discipline. It simply teaches children why they shouldn't get caught misbehaving, not why their behaviour needs to change.

Understanding the difference between the two approaches and their likely outcomes is a first and important step away from punishment and towards effective discipline in families. Take care not to wait until tempers explode or children's behaviour degenerates before consid-

---

Comfortable with discipline?

Steve Biddulph, psychologist and author

We have lots of trouble with discipline in our society, because this is a generation that has emerged from some pretty terrible and oppressive discipline – of hitting, shaming and blaming. We are keen to find more loving ways, but when our children are difficult, it still presses all our buttons. Without discipline methods and listening skills, we tend to back down at first, let the child get really out of hand, rely too much on reasoning, which has limited effect on someone as self-centred as a two-year-old child. Then we tend to finally lash out, getting angry and quite scary. So there is a volcanic quality to a lot of 'enlightened' parents.

If we get comfortable with discipline as a regular, on-going teaching need, it is less of a worry. The most miserable children I know are the children of well-meaning, over-permissive parents who condition the child to think they deserve everything they want, that their feelings rule the world.

People mistake discipline for punishment, but discipline actually means teaching. The big lesson for the two-to-six age group is learning that they are not the centre of the universe – learning that other people matter, too, and learning how to get along with others. It's natural that a child should need lots of teaching and make mistakes; discipline is just helping a child figure out how to proceed. It acknowledges what they are feeling, what they need, and shows them how to get it effectively. It needs lots of repetition; you need to be good-natured and have a sense of humour.

ering options. These are the hardest times in which to think straight. Making positive discipline a general part of family life will make it easier to deal calmly with a child's worst moments, and reduce the risks of us reacting in ways we later regret.

To do this we need to:

Check our responses Is the child's behaviour unreasonable or are you so tired or stressed you are overreacting? If it's the latter, try explaining how you feel in a calm, non-confrontational way they can understand: 'I'm too tired to do that at the moment. Let's do it later when I can concentrate,' or 'I know it's not your fault but I can't bear that noise right now. Can you keep it down a bit?' (See Feelings and Fears, p.124, and Who has the Problem, p.218.)

If it's the child who's being unreasonable, the calmer our response, the more we model how we'd like them to behave.

Choose approaches that feel right As ever, choose those that feel right for you and are appropriate to your child's age, understanding and temperament (see Comfortable with Discipline?, p.216). If any strategy doesn't work as you hoped, doesn't feel OK or loses its effectiveness, change it. Think of the approaches outlined below as a tool kit. You are the expert on your family. Select those tools that best suit you, your child and your circumstances.

Take one step at a time Wherever we are in our relationships with our children, whatever their age, whatever regrets we may have to date, it is never too late to start building stronger, warmer bonds and encouraging better behaviour. Tackling every behaviour issue at once could confuse your child and exhaust you, so focus on whatever concerns you most and remember that most change comes in small steps rather than great leaps.

I'm a single parent with two children and a full-time job, so there's not a lot of spare time or energy. The best way, I find, is to focus on the biggest problem at any one time and put the others to one side until that's sorted out. Too much at once and I'd end up giving up.

John M

Use our power sparingly This requires us to pick our moment, our issue and our strategy with care. Inappropriately tough approaches

Who has the problem?

You want your child to co-operate but you're not sure how to help them. What next? Standing back from a problem and working out who is affected by it often makes it easier to choose an effective solution.

If it is your problem You will need to say what the problem is, why it bothers you and what you want done about it. Simply telling your child to pick up the school bag from the hall, for example, doesn't indicate why doing this is important. It doesn't bother them, after all. Instead, try: 'Your bag's in the hall. It could trip someone up, which worries me, and it looks untidy. Put it away now, please.'

If it is your child's problem. Let them work out how best to proceed, with your help (see Searching for Solutions, p.222). If, for example, they haven't been invited to a friend's party, encourage them to talk about how they feel and what, if anything, they would like to do about it (see Feelings and Fears, p.124 and Reflective Listening, p.99). Resist the temptation to make it your problem, too – ringing up the mother and asking why your child wasn't on the guest list won't solve the situation.

If it is a problem for both of you You need to negotiate. If the morning mayhem makes you late for work and your child late for school, you both need to consider ways to ease the situation. Maybe you could lay your child's clothes out if they would agree to try to dress themselves.

---

can shock a child into surliness or silence and also increase the chances of you cracking under the strain of your own excess. Standing firm for thirty minutes only to cave in after another five will confuse and/or delight your child and could mean it will take twice as long to stand your ground next time.

The discipline strategies below are for use when the going gets tough. Over-use them and they will lose their impact. Picking up every little problem with your child's conduct can also crush their confidence or willingness to listen. Effective discipline is as much about parents managing their own anger as it is about children managing their behaviour.

I'd heard he'd been rotten to a girl at school, calling her names and pulling her hair, and I came down on him like a ton of bricks. I was very angry, very stern. He just grunted 'I dunno' to everything I asked, so I sent him to his room. My brother was bullied so I was determined no child of mine would ever do that.

Weeks later I found out it hadn't been my son at all. I was so incensed, I'd not stopped to listen to his side of the story.

Anna C

Notice when behaviour improves If we tell a child off for throwing bricks, for example, we also need to praise them when they play with the bricks without throwing (see Descriptive Praise, p.115). This shift in what we see and respond to in our children not only motivates them to continue but can also help parent and child feel warmer and closer. This will help reduce misbehaviour rooted in insecurity (see Break the Cycle, p.229). A win-win situation.

Learning to challenge

A lot of destructive situations happen when people are confrontational and don't use assertive, positive skills. Assertive discipline, as opposed to hostile or pleading discipline, is calm, measured and fair. It involves you modelling the behaviour that you want the child to use and giving them the information they need to put things right.

Anne Cowling, advisor to Leeds Healthy Schools, Education Leeds

This changed how I do things as well as how he does things. It's helped us both turn a corner.

Leslie C

This is a core skill for turning around a child's behaviour. It is simple, very effective and often takes practice before parents feel fully at ease. Try to hang on in there. To those who have never tried it, it may sound too 'reasonable' to work in the heat of the moment, but parents, professionals and children themselves vouch for its ability to stop children in their tracks and bring about long-term improvements.

It works on the principle that most children, from three or four years to teenagers, will stop behaving unacceptably if they are told in no uncertain terms how it is affecting others and are given the opportunity to change course without loss of face (for younger children, less 'verbal' strategies are more appropriate; see Horribly Normal, p.166, and Remove the Victim, p.228.).

Challenging makes children examine their behaviour and its consequences and decide for themselves how best to proceed. They feel part
of the solution and not just 'the problem'. Importantly, it also helps
parents be assertive rather than aggressive. As such, it involves everything that effective discipline requires: information, education and
respect for the child's need not to be crushed by criticism and the
parent's need for the unacceptable behaviour to stop.

If delivered in a firm and loving way, it is far less likely to provoke
a defensive, knee-jerk reaction than more confrontational approaches.
You be the judge.

Challenging unacceptable behaviour

(Adapted, with kind permission, from Parentline Plus, see Contacts, p.429)

To do this we need to be firm, disclose how we feel and keep in mind
four important aims:

— We want to change the behaviour.
— We want to avoid bad feelings with our children.
— We want them to feel good about themselves.
— We want them to learn to take our needs into account in future.

To achieve these aims, we need to get into the habit of describing
what we see and how we feel about it. The easiest and most effective
way to do this is to remember to use 'I' when speaking to the child:
'I feel . . .' rather than 'You make me feel . . .' It is less confrontational, makes a clear distinction between the behaviour (which we
don't like) and the child (who we love), and encourages children to
reflect on the impact of their actions on others.

This can be done in four steps, though these can be in any order:

1 **Describe the offending behaviour** Stick to the facts of what you
   see and don't label the behaviour or the child: 'Your clothes are on
   the floor' rather than 'You are so messy.'
2 **Tell the child how it makes you feel** Perhaps you feel used and
   resentful. If you are really upset, show it. If it is only a minor problem,
   react in an appropriate way. If you are not 'straight' with children
   they will either mistrust you or not take you seriously.
3 **State your need** For example, 'I need help keeping the house tidy.'
4 **Ask the child to help you solve the problem** Say something

A six-step plan for co-operation

This approach may prove useful when your child is not listening to your requests or when you are in a hurry and need your child's co-operation quickly.

'The six steps are for parents to do, not the child,' explains Noel Janis-Norton, director of the New Learning Centre. 'They are:

1: The parent needs to stop what they are doing and look at their child. This immediately rules out shouting at a child who is upset.

2: Wait until your child stops what they are doing and looks at you. You literally wait – nothing else. These first steps are respectful so by the time you get to step 3 the child is much more likely to be listening because they are not being told off or feeling invaded. The steps are calming. They allow you to collect your thoughts and ask clearly and calmly without shouting or nagging.

3: Tell the child what you want them to do: clearly, simply and only once. Parents find it hard to believe but the child or teenager will most often do what is asked. Parents are so used to leaving out steps 1 and 2 and starting on step 3, which is much less likely to work.

4: If steps 1–3 have not worked – and this will be for a small minority of children – ask the child to tell you in their own words what it is you have asked them to do. Somehow saying what needs to be done seems to make it much easier for them emotionally to just get up and do it. It is almost that they have a moral obligation to do it once the words have come out of their mouth. What often happens is the child won't actually repeat it, they will just get up and do it. Steps 5 and 6 are for the very tiny amount of resistance that is left.

5: Stand and wait until your child has done what you want them to do. Most parents feel far too busy to do this. But if we do, the child knows we are serious and that what he is experiencing is not scolding and nagging but calm and reasonable.

6: Notice and praise everything the child does in the right direction.

'The six-step plan is an investment in time. It pays off much more rapidly than parents expect. Be realistic about how much energy and time you already spend nagging and repeating and reminding, justifying and bribing, which is putting in the time after something has gone wrong. This is never as valuable as putting in the effort before, where you have the benefit of prevention or early intervention, "nipping something in the bud" rather than waiting for a crisis and then somehow finding a way to manage it.'

like: 'I don't like what is happening and need your help,' or 'I have a problem with this. Will you help me?'

A simple way to remember this in practice is to say:
'When you . . .' (describe behaviour)
'I feel . . .' (state feelings)
'I need . . .' (state your need)
'How can you help me?' or 'What could we do differently?' (Ask child to think).

Examples:
'When you leave clothes around the house I feel really fed up because it makes extra work. What can we do differently so it doesn't happen?'
or
'I feel angry when you splash your paints around it because it splats on to the furniture and it's hard to clean. How can you help?'

Searching for solutions

We can easily overpower a child's ability to find their own way simply from our own desire to fix things quickly.

Camila Batmanghelidjh, psychotherapist and Director of Kids Company

My two were hitting each other over the head with plastic spades and both came running, blaming the other and shouting. I'd had enough. I said I was going to the kitchen to have a cup of tea and I didn't want to see or hear them until they could tell me what they were going to do instead of hurting each other. Honest to God, they came back a few minutes later, best of friends, and said they'd decided to play golf with the spades instead. I always try to remember now – they can often sort things out themselves with a bit of encouragement.

Fiona W

If children are allowed to work out for themselves how best to proceed in a new or problem situation they can often find creative and construc-tive solutions. This not only gives us a break from acting as family judge and referee, but also helps develop children's self-discipline and social skills. Once they have decided for themselves how to resolve a problem:

1 **They are more likely to put their conclusion into practice**
They have thought the matter through and understood it more fully
than if solutions were imposed by their parents. This helps them resolve
the immediate issue and teaches them how to avoid similar ones in
future.

2 **It is habit-forming** Once children realise they can work their way
through a situation without their parents telling them what to do, they
are in a far stronger position to face the next tricky situation thrown
their way.

Our role is to support the decision-making process, not to impose our
own opinions and judgements. We can help by giving children plenty
of practice in decision-making and thinking through everyday issues
so they are better equipped to cope with the tough stuff. We can also
define the problem and express our confidence in their ability to work
it out for themselves:

> 'OK, so your teacher's told me you've been skipping spelling home-
> work. She's really cheesed off. You're good at thinking of solutions
> to problems. How are you going to sort this one out?'

Children as young as two or three can often come up with solutions
to simple, everyday dilemmas with sufficient parental guidance. Most
children will be able to work through increasingly tricky problems as
they grow. If they seem stuck, we can offer alternatives but allow them
to make the final decision, so they claim it as their own:

> 'It's not OK to throw balls in the house. Do you want to put the
> ball away or play with it outside?'

> 'Painting's not allowed on the carpet. It makes a mess. Where else
> could you paint?' (If the child can't answer . . .) 'On the table or
> on the kitchen floor, with lots of newspaper?'

If children's emotions are running high, remember to acknowledge
their feelings. Once they know we've got the message about how they
feel, they may no longer need to express it through their behaviour
and can calm down sufficiently to think. Having a structure for this
approach can help you stay calm in the storm:

1   **Identify the problem** ('You hit him')
2   **Acknowledge the child's feelings** ('I know you are angry')
3   **Draw the line** ('. . . and you know hitting is not OK')
4   **Think it through** ('How can you sort this out without hurting?')

This is an exercise in thinking, not shaming and blaming, and children may need time to calm down and consider issues properly. Tell them to let you know when they've thought of more constructive ways to behave.

I asked one girl how she was doing and she said, 'Oh I'm in trouble because they can't control me.' I said, 'What do you mean? You're the only person who can control you.' They used to think it was the parent's job and the teacher's job to control them and now they know it's up to themselves. They make their choices.

Jenny Oberon, pupil behaviour management consultant

Saying no and meaning it

Children do know when you really mean it. You have to be willing to put a lot of effort into seeing it through.

Brigid Treacy, parenting advisor

If you mean 'No', your child is likely to get the message. If you don't, your child will pick this up in your expression and body language and either ignore you or provoke you until you stand your ground more firmly. This knowledge may at least save wasted effort – half-hearted 'Nos' are rarely worth the bother (see Clear, Strong and Calm, p.225).

If you mean 'No', say it in a way that increases its effectiveness. Sometimes you may need to be sharp and stern – perhaps a child is hurting another or putting themselves in danger. On other occasions, a firm but quietly spoken 'No' works wonders, stops you getting drawn into negotiations and keeps you on certain ground. It may help to crouch or kneel down to the child's level so they know you mean business.

Children often echo their parents' emotions; staying in control in an otherwise fiery situation can help them follow suit.

Clear, strong and calm

Vivienne Gross, family therapist

I think it is very helpful to be as clear as you can about what you want. I sometimes see parents who appear to say 'Oh don't do that Johnny' in such a lame way or with such ambivalence that the child is bound to pick up that there is a big gap they could slide through.

I think when you are saying very firmly, 'I am absolutely not going to have this', being clear and showing that you are really at your last ebb with this one lets the child know where they stand.

Part of the problem with children who are out of control can be that they feel nobody can manage them, so they can't manage themselves and it becomes a vicious circle. Drawing the line, keeping the child in one spot and saying, 'No, you have to stay there until you calm down because I cannot trust you to be with your sister at this minute. You are too upset and agitated and I am going to keep you here until you calm down,' is seeing through what you have decided needs to happen. As far as physical safety is concerned you might have to interpose yourself between two children and that is part of your duty to protect each of them.

Consequences

It always surprises me that kids sometimes don't realise what's going to happen next, but they don't. It might feel like stating the obvious to us, but to my two it can come as something of a revelation. You can almost see them thinking, 'Oh yeah, maybe that's not such a good idea.'

Sarah P

My husband is always saying things like, 'Right, that's it. Any more of that and I'm putting all your Easter eggs in the bin.' What's the point? They know he won't do it. To my knowledge, it has never stopped them doing anything. It drives me nuts.

Helen P

Telling children the logical consequences of their behaviour is often all that is needed to help them think through the possible impact of an action – and stop:

Parent (firmly and calmly): 'Joe, if you throw your toys someone will get hurt and you don't want that to happen. Put it down or play without throwing.'

But what happens when you have told them the logical consequence of an action and they carry on doing it? Or when you have reminded them of a family rule and they still break it? To make it very clear where we draw the line, we may have to *impose* consequences for crossing it. For example:

The weapons rule You may have a family rule that no toys are to be used as weapons to hurt or frighten other children. This can apply equally to a stick, a pile of bricks, a doll or a paint brush. As with all family rules, you explain it to your child so they understand what the rule is and why you need it (see Rules and Boundaries, p.199). Whenever necessary, remind them of it and tell them the logical consequence of breaking it (i.e. 'You will hurt'). You may even challenge their behaviour (see Learning to Challenge, p.219). But half an hour later they hit their brother on the head with a drumstick. What next?

Imposed consequences Three strikes and it's out.

1 Any toy used as a weapon (i.e. to hurt or frighten others) is immediately removed (for an hour, for the afternoon, for the rest of the day – the older the child the longer the time).
2 If it happens again, it is removed again, for longer.
3 If it happens a third time, it is put in the bin.

In general, stating *logical* or natural consequences makes children much more aware of the impact of their actions and appeals to their sense of fairness. But let's be realistic. Imposed sanctions are sometimes necessary. To use them most effectively it helps to remember that:

— Discussing and agreeing sanctions in advance with your children will make them easier to understand and accept. If this isn't possible, at least inform them of what will happen if they continue to misbehave. For example:

'Stop poking him or you will have to leave the room. Which is it to be?'

or

'If you throw sand one more time, we will have to go home. Think about it, because I mean it.'

— Punishments imposed out of the blue, with no prior warning ('Right, that's it. I'm taking you home'), give a child no chance to behave better.

— Imposed consequences can be unwanted or even unpleasant but should not harm in any way.

— They aren't intended for use before we have tried other ways, but rather if we have and the children haven't taken any notice.

— Children need praise far more than they need criticism (see Positive Power, p.115). Remember to notice if a child turns their behaviour around.

— Say it only when you mean it, because you may have to carry consequences through. If you realise you've gone over the top and the sanction is unreasonable, say so: 'I was really angry at how you behaved, but I'm not happy about taking your bike away. Let's talk.'

— Imposed consequences should be in proportion to the misdemeanour. Overly severe sanctions are not only unkind and often counterproductive, but also run a higher risk of you not carrying them out.

— The younger the child, the sooner the consequence should follow the misbehaviour. A sanction imposed tomorrow may not impress a three-year-old for whom tomorrow is too far away to care much about.

— The closer the link between action and consequence, the easier it is for the child to learn from it. For example 'If you use a toy as a weapon it will be taken away' is more likely to be understood and accepted than 'If you use a toy as a weapon you won't go to the party.'

— Imposed consequences make it clear that problem behaviour has to stop, but not necessarily why. When the situation is calmer, it is important to work out with your child why and how such clashes should be avoided in the future (see The Follow-up, p.234).

It's an attitude thing. I'm not going to get mad or rise to it any more because I know exactly what I'm going to do and he knows it, too. Six months ago, his behaviour was off the scale. But we handle it now. We're doing all right.

Melanie M

Removing the victim, not the culprit

If two children are fighting, rather than removing the child that is doing the attacking, as is often advised, try removing the victim from the scene.
If you remove the aggressor, that child wins the attention of the moment, which may encourage him or her to demand further attention in this way. If you calmly remove the victim, explain why you are doing so and walk away from the aggressor – perhaps even leave the room – then it is the victim who receives the attention. Many parents of battling siblings have reported success with this approach.

Dr Elizabeth Bryan, consultant paediatrician and founder of the
Multiple Births Foundation

This is especially useful in educating young children not to hurt others, but can also help when older ones fly off the handle. It denies the aggressor the attention that may fuel their behaviour and also makes the victim feel safer.

If a very young child is hurting another, always explain why you do not like that behaviour and how they could behave instead. Even if they are too young to understand the words, they will understand the basic message by your tone of voice. Three-year-olds and above can start to consider and suggest better ways to behave (see Searching for Solutions, p.222).

Keeping on track

This has stopped me shouting. Almost.

Pauline F

My first two children were a breeze, really. They generally did as they were told. I got quite smug. Then came Harriet – an absolute delight but a handful. Children are so different, and what works with some won't work with others, so it really helps to have different approaches up your sleeve.

Donna M

This technique is useful when children are arguing back and not taking the slightest notice of what we say. It involves us calmly repeating instructions, over and over, until they get the message.

Avoid getting into a dispute – children sometimes prefer a row to doing what they are told. If there are matters to be discussed, this can be done after their behaviour has improved. For now, focus on your demand and repeat it, however much your child argues, whines or prevaricates. Most children soon get the message that you mean what you say.

Staying calm shows you are in control of the situation. Acknowledging how they feel shows you have listened but still mean business. Using their name simply helps to catch their attention and emphasise your point.

Parent: 'Alice, I've told you to come in. It's time for tea.'
Child: 'But I haven't finished playing . . .'
Parent: 'That must be annoying, but I need you to come in now. You can play again later.'
Child: 'It won't take long . . .'
Parent: 'Alice, come in now.'
Child: 'It's not fair. I'm never allowed to play outside [not true]. I hate you [very true at that moment].'
Parent: 'Alice. In now.'
Child (grumpily): 'Oh, all right.'

For similar reasons, try not to be side-tracked by any ghastly behaviour your child may display when being reprimanded or given an instruction. These 'secondary' behaviours include pouts, mutters, stomps, grimaces, shrugs and dismissive 'so what's. If you rise to their bait, your child is setting the agenda. If you ignore their antics, you are.

If secondary behaviour is driving you to such distraction that you feel you must show disapproval, do so quickly and simply and try hard not to stray into arguments or confrontations about issues that aren't your main concern.

Break the cycle

A parent may experience an insecure child as tyrannically controlling. Once the child's strategies are seen as arising from insecurity rather than just bad behaviour, they may evoke less anger. This can also help parents become more aware of the vicious circles that arise when an angry response makes the child even more insecure.

John Byng-Hall, Consultant Child and Family Psychiatrist, Institute of Family Therapy, London

Speech bubbles

This technique helps children who are 'stuck' in patterns of bad behaviour. It is a very clear and accessible method of helping them think of better ways to manage difficult situations, emotions or thoughts (see also Assertion v. Aggression, p.368). If your child can't yet write, they may want to talk through their answers, ask you to write them down for them or to draw pictures instead. The nature of the approach makes it most suitable for school-age children.

Jenny Oberon, a pupil behaviour management consultant, explains: 'We've been doing a lot of work on speech bubbles with the kids. We have drawings of people feeling different things – stressed, frustrated, angry, withdrawn. With each there are two bubbles – a "think bubble" for the children to write in what the person may be thinking at that particular moment, and a "speech bubble" for them to write down what that person has to say to:

1: Get the help they need.
2: Not hurt anyone.
3: Keep themselves out of trouble.

'They can put what they want in the "think bubble" and you can't tell them off for that, just as in life you can't tell a child off for their thoughts. They might be thinking that they'd like to hit, shout, swear. But it's how they deal with their thoughts that's so important. By filling in the "speech bubble" they can see clearly the difference between what they think and what's acceptable to do.

'Working through these exercises shows children the problems that can arise if they say exactly what they think or do exactly what they are feeling all the time. It shows them there are better ways of getting their needs met.'

My daughter was in real trouble at school, on the point of being excluded. I felt I just couldn't cope with her. Since she's been shown things like the speech bubbles, they took a bit of a while to get through to her, but since they did, she's been able to work out the consequences of doing things her old way and come up with something different, something that will work better. It's shown her that you can still be angry without shouting and screaming. She's decided now that she's making a turnabout, not for anybody else but for herself, and this has shown her how to do it.

Jacqui C

I've had to face the fact that having a routine of conflict just doesn't work. You feel the child is going to have one up on you, that it's a power struggle, so you go angry. But if you let it go or wait until things have calmed down, you can work on the goodwill that's created, because you've broken the old pattern.

Pete L

Families sometimes get stuck in patterns of repeated behaviour. These can range from the mildly irritating to the troubling. You know the kind of thing – the child acts defiantly, so the parent reacts angrily, so the child acts defiantly, and round and round they go. Sometimes simply recognising the pattern and how our own emotional state and behaviour feeds into it can help us do things differently. Say, for example, a child displays aggression, so the parent shouts, so the child shows aggression, so the parent shouts . . . If the parent were to shout less and show more constructive ways of expressing anger, the child may show less aggression, so the parent will feel less driven to shout.

Changing patterns involves one of the individuals within it doing something different. As we're the adults, it's generally up to us to have the humility and wisdom to break the cycle. This isn't 'backing down' or 'losing the battle', this is constructive and effective action to make family life better for parent and child.

Understanding that children often express distress or insecurity through difficult behaviour can also help us give our children the mix of warmth, attention and guidance they need to thrive. Sometimes the most important step towards untangling problematic behaviour is spending more relaxed time together not focusing on the problem, so conversations, mutual pleasure and emotional connectedness can grow.

Maybe a particular environment, time or even seems to trigger the annoying or destructive cycle. Pinpointing this may help us stop the 'trigger' point arriving. Looking for exceptions can also help. When does the destructive pattern not occur? What else goes on around the child when they behave more co-operatively? When do you manage to handle situations differently? What happens instead? Can you do more of this?

A man who I'm working with just now says, 'My son drives me crazy. He won't give me any space. For example, when I come home at night I just want to read my newspaper and he always takes the paper from under my arm and runs off with it.' I suggested he hid the newspaper and, if his son did find it, to playfully hit him over the head with it. It works because it interrupts the daily routine and the argument that by now is on automatic pilot and the humour interrupts the emotional tone of the interaction between father and son.

Jim Wilson, systemic psychotherapist and director of the Centre for Child-Focused Practice at the Institute of Family Therapy, London

Stand back

Sometimes the very best thing a parent can do is to do less. If we react to every misdemeanour we could spend most of our time reining in our children's behaviour, which, by the law of diminishing returns, means they will take less notice and we will become increasingly frustrated and angry.

Liberate yourself by choosing times not to react immediately. At the very least, this will allow you time to assess what you want your child to do and how important it is that they do it, or whether you can let it go. If it is behaviour you feel you must challenge, a considered response is generally much more effective than a knee-jerk one.

I was on at him the whole time until he felt he couldn't do anything right. Once I stopped the constant nagging it felt less like a battle. That helped us both.

Tom B

Know when to stop

Any approach can be abusive if you use it too much or use it in particular ways. You do have to be honest about your motivation – any discipline should be to help a child learn, not to humiliate them. It is so important to know when to stop. Once you have discussed it and sorted it out, that is the end of it. You should not keep going on and on or keep standing over children when things have moved on.

Sarah Darton, health visitor

If you have made your point and the message has got home, try not to use this success as a platform to comment on every aspect of your child's behaviour that annoys you. It is this 'and another thing' habit, the urge to remind them of what they did last Tuesday, which can stop children listening to their parents. Best avoided.

Once an issue is over, move on. Try to show confidence in your child's ability to act better next time and allow them to start each day afresh unless the misdemeanour is extremely serious.

As important is the ability to know when you are on a hiding to nothing. Most parents get locked into a downward spiral of argument with their children at some time. The trick is to recognise this and call a halt: 'This is getting out of hand. We should stop and talk about it later when we're all calmer.'

Know you'll sometimes get it wrong

Some parents say you should never apologise or make up with your children. Wouldn't you like your children to know what to do when they have made a mistake? How are they going to learn that except by example? To hear you say 'I am sorry, I am having a bad day and am very uptight but this is not your fault' is hugely helpful for children. It is an opportunity for them to know we have limits, we are not perfect and to see how to repair mistakes.

Christine Puckering, psychologist and co-founder of Mellow Parenting

In a warm, supportive home, it may be better for a parent to get very cross with an errant child and later apologise than do nothing at all. However, in families low on warmth and high on criticism, negative incidents accumulate as if to remind a child that he or she is unloved.

From: Child Protection, Messages From Research[7]

I apologise to my kids and I need to. Sometimes I am horrible.

Anne P

All parents occasionally explode when they shouldn't, overreact, pick the wrong issue to tackle or the wrong time to tackle it. Saying sorry can relieve you of some of the guilt cranking up your stress levels and also teach your children how to cope when they have done something they regret. If our relationships are usually warm, loving and supportive, they will be resilient enough to cope with a smattering of parental mistakes.

Most close relationships involve occasional rows and conflict and our children need to learn how to cope, how to apologise when they are in the wrong, and how to move on. We can teach them by example how to admit mistakes calmly and constructively. For some children, this can be key to them overcoming an otherwise debilitating fear of failure.

Try to remember that every day is a new opportunity. Each new day that something good happens between you and your child is another layer of their life experience. If you have a period of problems, hopefully you will move on and put down more layers of the kinds of experiences you would like your child to have.

Vivienne Gross, family therapist

The follow-up

This is essential. Even if your child has stopped misbehaving and has co-operated, it is important to work out ways together to avoid such clashes in future. Try to untangle the root causes of any problem behaviour and discuss between you:

— What happened.
— How your child felt about it.
— How you felt about it.
— What the child could do to make things better now (apologise, replace broken items, talk to a sibling to resolve a row; what helps will depend on the circumstances).
— How they could handle situations differently next time.

You may also need to consider what you might do differently to encourage constructive change. What was it that made you react? Was it your mood, your child's behaviour, the particular circumstances in which it happened? Did your discipline approach prompt the child to reflect on their actions and how they could behave better in similar situations?

Short cuts and quick fixes

It helps to have a few quick fixes up our sleeves for those moments when we need to turn around a child's behaviour but really haven't the time or energy to invest in longer-term approaches.

'Quick-fix' methods usually involve 'training' a child to behave in acceptable ways. They can be useful for breaking a pattern of nega-tive behaviour but tend not to develop a child's understanding or self-discipline. So these approaches are not the whole story. They are best retained for emergency use only and followed up with one of the more constructive, educative strategies detailed above. But everybody needs short cuts sometimes.

Rewards

The best rewards are the non-material ones. The most rewarding thing children receive is descriptive praise. You need to start noticing and mentioning all the things a child does well.

Noel Janis-Norton, Director, New Learning Centre

I don't want to knock the government and schools when they are finally taking seriously the need to build in some kind of emotional relationship to children. Using a star chart system, for example, may help children feel rewarded. But we need to go deeper than that in order that children begin to internalise their own values.

Susie Orbach, psychotherapist

Many parents and teachers have used reward systems to help children break patterns of difficult behaviour. They are often cited as an effective

---

Warning: rewards can backfire

Elizabeth Newson, Emeritus Professor of Developmental Psychology, University of Nottingham, researcher and author

I feel that if you reward a child with something that has nothing to do with the key issue it's a complete waste of time because they get so hooked on the reward they stop even thinking. I remember doing some research years ago which involved doing a task with four-year-olds and someone suggested I rewarded them with Smarties, which sounded like a good idea. I took Smarties along and these poor little kids got so focused on the sweets that they just simply stopped thinking about my task and certainly stopped enjoying it. I gave it up after one trial because it took their minds off what they were doing. I thought it was a very negative thing.

I am always looking for ways to make *the action* itself rewarding, which is the key thing; in other words to look for intrinsic rather than extrinsic rewards. I don't like the use of rewards for doing well at school, for example. I think there are all sorts of good reasons for doing well or not so well at school, which cannot be related to rewards.

means of modifying children's conduct and they can work well in the short term.

However, they are not a long-term solution because they lose their potency over time and offer such limited scope for a child to learn, is a child complying because they understand why they should, or because they want the reward? (See Warning: Rewards can Backfire, p.235.)

On their own, therefore, rewards are not enough to encourage self-discipline. Yet if they help you both feel good enough to take a next, more constructive step, they may be useful.

There are four basic types of reward for behaviour:

1 **Material rewards** For example, a toy, a sweet, a fun day out. These are bribes. If you need to resort to them out of desperation, use them sparingly. They are a high-risk strategy because the child who is bribed soon becomes the child who demands, the child who ups the stakes or, even worse, the child who loses self-motivation.

2 **Tokens** For example, a star, a sticker, a home-made Superstar certificate for behaviour or achievement. These are sometimes useful as tangible evidence of parental appreciation, but it is the appreciation that counts most.

3 **Acknowledgement** If a child's behaviour results in adult praise and acknowledgement, the child has a powerful incentive to behave that way again. Being told the positive effects of their actions on others (e.g. 'Thanks for sharing your toy, that made Joe feel very welcome and happy') and themselves ('Because you put your toys away so quickly, we've got time to go to the park. Well done.') will boost their self-esteem and give them a powerful lesson in the positive consequences of positive behaviour.

4 **Internal** When a child feels good about doing something because they know it is the right thing to do. This is the core of self-discipline.

As a rule of thumb, if you use reward methods 1 and 2, aim to move towards 3 and 4. If you need to use material rewards and tokens:

— Be alert to the dangers of mixing rewards and sanctions (i.e. putting crosses on star charts, making targets unattainable or withdrawing rewards once won). Reward systems aim to shift the focus on to the positive, not remind the child of 'failures' or misdemeanours.

— Remember these are short-term options with limited value. Even if they succeed in breaking a behaviour pattern, you can then look to other, more educative methods of building on your relationship with your child and equipping them for the future.

Some parents pay their children to do routine, everyday tasks like the washing up or even setting the table. I think that is appalling. What sort of partners are they going to make? If you are paid to do something then intrinsically you view it as not a normal thing to do because you know you have to be bribed to do it.

Professor Hugh Foot, specialist in child psychology and social development, Department of Psychology, Strathclyde University

Counting

It works for reasons I don't understand because I never say what's going to happen when I get to 10. Maybe it just shows that the mood has switched, I'm serious now. Having said that, it only works for two of them. My daughter counts with me then blows a raspberry at the end. She's never taken any notice of it at all.

Jenny T

Counting – as in 'You have until I count to three/ten/whatever to get in the bath/get into your pyjamas etc' – can work well, especially as a way of getting children to focus on what they are required to do and to communicate the fact that you are serious and reaching the end of your patience. But its success depends largely on the temperament, mood and age of the child involved.

As a way of helping parents keep their cool, however, counting can be invaluable (also see Time Out, below). Whether you count aloud or to yourself, it imposes a pause for thought and can make all the difference between managing your child's anti-social behaviour calmly and flying off the handle.

Even counting to 10 can give parents the chance to avoid the automatic response, which might be to lash out in frustration. Most parents say, 'I don't hit my child because I think it's a good thing. It's because I've run out of other strategies.'

Christine Puckering, psychologist and co-founder of Mellow Parenting

Time out

I have heard of children pulling the wallpaper off when they are kept in their room because they are so angry and then the parents get even angrier with them and so it goes on. There are downsides to every strategy. But if you need to separate children, creating space between them even for a short while can be helpful as it helps you collect your thoughts and think about what you want to do next. You have to keep control of the situation. Actually locking a child in a room to teach them a lesson, however, can feel like abandonment to that child. To my mind, it is too extreme.

Vivienne Gross, family therapist

If everyone is getting upset, the most important thing is to separate everyone and then talk to each of them on their own. They will need to be in separate rooms, think about what's happened and suggest a way to put this right. It works for us.

Emma P

Some children have a great time if sent to their room, others find it intolerable, some find it helps them calm down, some seethe with rage and frustration. As ever, how this works and whether it is appropriate will depend on the situation, your child and you. Sending a child to their room can be a vital safety measure if you are extremely angry (see Coping in Hard Times, p.151). It can also be a useful means of separating sparring siblings. But it is not educative. It does not teach considerate behaviour or encourage self-discipline. And if used too harshly or too often, it can make children feel unheard and unloved. This can seriously damage their trust in us, and they may express this hurt in more problematic behaviour. So do everyone a favour and use Time Out very rarely, if at all.

Remember that young children may need your presence to calm down. They are certainly not going to calm down quickly if Time Out makes them frightened or hysterical, or they simply don't under-stand what's required of them (see Tantrums, p.174). If you need a child to think things through and join the rest of the family once they have done so, the 'thinking spot' need not be a bedroom, but a quiet, boring place not so far away. The bottom stair might do the same job with fewer risks.

Clearly, it's not OK to lock a child in a room – it can be terrify-ing and dangerous.

Shouting

Once you are behaving on their level it just goes downhill. Don't get me wrong, sometimes I need to shout at mine. I can't go nicey nicey when he's trying to put a brick in his brother's head. There's no point going all 'Oh daaarling, don't do that.' But this shouting, bawling and screaming at the kids, like we've all done sometimes, doesn't do any good.

Julie M

In a perfect world parents would never need to shout, the sun would always shine and the birds would always sing in the trees. In real life shouting is occasionally necessary and can be a very effective means of attention-grabbing when your child's safety or your sanity demands it. Yet children themselves say shouting can be shocking, humiliating and scary.

Imagine for a moment how you would feel if someone bigger and stronger was bellowing at you. You might feel like running away or you might want to defend yourself or bellow back, but you probably wouldn't be able to think straight. The bottom line is that the more we shout, the more we increase the risk of our children shouting back or switching off. If it goes too far, shouting can leave a child fearful and crushed.

So if you do raise your voice, try to drop back to a quieter level as soon as possible. If you quickly revert to your normal voice, you show you are angry *and* in control of the situation. A parent talking quietly in the middle of an argument may also surprise a child into listening.

Shouting can serve a purpose – to get attention. It's also natural and healthy for a family to have a bit of a shout and an argument from time to time. But to yell and shout and blame children when we are under stress is a different thing altogether, especially if it is used as a form of attack. Children hate this with a passion, and it makes it very hard for them to hear what we're saying.

Eileen Hayes, parenting advisor to the NSPCC

Holding

This means using your physical superiority to control a situation – something many parents feel uneasy about. It should be saved for urgent situations when drastic measures are needed.

The intention should never be to hurt but rather to hold, reassure and not let go until the child's rage has subsided. Some children respond well to being held like this while others simply get more angry (see Tantrums, p.174) and only you can judge whether and when it will help. There may be other times when, like it or not, your child will need to be held for their safety or the safety of others. This is basic protection and a fundamental parental duty.

Using physical restraint is the hardest thing for me. I hated it but I don't think I could have done anything different – he was much too angry to let loose on his brother. But that whole thing of using all your strength to hold back your own child is incredibly disturbing. I try to balance it out – if I've had to be a human barrier I make sure we all have a hug later on.

Jane P

This is just a tip, really, but I found it easier to hold my child from behind. I could then fold his arms over each other and hold him firmly without having to grapple with him. It also reduced the chances of me getting hit.

Pauline T

The yellow card

This approach, and any variant of it that suits your child, works on the principle of warning. It provides the child with physical, tangible evidence of your intention to act if they do not improve their behaviour. Once its significance is understood, it saves you having to tell your child in detail what will happen next because they'll know. This can help children feel they are taking control of their own conduct.

In football, the referee gives a yellow card to a player as a first warning. If the player misbehaves again he is given the red card and sent off. It may be a way of getting through to your children. If they are pushing the limit you say, 'Right, I'm getting the yellow card out. Any further behaviour of that type and you will be sent to your room.' I know a boy who used to get into terrible fist fights in the playground. He and his family developed this yellow card system and eventually he was able to take the yellow card with him in his pocket to school and when he felt himself getting riled he would feel the card to help remind him not to get involved. It reminded him that he would be suspended from school if he got into any further trouble. Sometimes a simple, physical thing like a bit of yellow cardboard can help get the message across very clearly.

Vivienne Gross, family therapist

Smacking isn't the solution

There is now a large and growing body of research evidence on the effects of physical punishment and the message is clear: while it might stop misbehaviour in the short term, we can be almost certain that physical punishment does not improve behaviour in the longer term. Indeed, it now seems very likely that physical punishment leads to an increase in misbehaviour. In particular, children who are physically punished tend to be more aggressive. Some researchers have recently suggested that physical punishment increases the chances of depression and even reduces intelligence. And it seems that even moderate levels of physical punishment – the occasional smack that is typically used by most parents – can have these effects.

Dr Gavin Nobes, lecturer in Forensic and Developmental Psychology, University of East London

Very substantial research evidence highlights negative, violent and humiliating forms of discipline are significant in the development of violent attitudes and actions from a very early age.

The Commission on Children and Violence[8]

This book is unashamedly anti-smacking for the simple reasons that smacking is:

— damaging
— unnecessary
— counterproductive
— an abuse of power

This is a highly contentious issue so, as the hackles of the smacking lobby rise once more in indignation and defence of parents' rights to do as they damn well please, it may help to look calmly at the facts.

1 **Smacking damages children and it damages our relationships with them.** Children deserve and need our respect.
2 **Anti-hitting does not mean anti-discipline** Positive discipline is essential for a child's healthy development, so it is extremely important that a parent's chosen method of discipline works effectively.
3 **Smacking does not work.** It may interrupt a child's difficult behav-

---

Parents' voices, parents' choices

'I have never hit any of my three boys, who are now in their late teens and twenties. They've turned out fine, but I'm astonished at the number of colleagues and friends who simply do not believe me. They don't believe it is possible to have boys, especially, and never had occasion to hit or slap them. We've had almighty arguments, but they have never been hit. What's the point?'
Bill S

'Now I feel strongly about not hitting children. I didn't always. I have hit my eldest three or four times and my younger daughter a lot more. I have flung her across the room, I have dragged her across the floor. It is horrible, it really upsets me.'
Pete L

'As a smacked child I hated it. For me it is not on. It does not work, it can make children deceitful, defiant and really angry. I remember looking at my mother and thinking you can hit me all you want and I will not please you, I will not cry. I have managed never to hit my children. They are grown up now and are very disciplined within themselves.'
Bridget T

'Six months ago I was feeling really violent towards him. I was so angry with him, I hated him because he was doing stuff to get me going all the time. I felt he was like my enemy and I'm telling you

iour in the short term, but in the long term it is likely to lead to an *increase* in misbehaviour.[9] There are far better, more effective ways of teaching a child right from wrong.

A recent round-up of worldwide research into the effects of physical punishment on children[10] showed consistent negative outcomes, including:

— Increased aggression in childhood and adulthood
— Less capacity for empathy (i.e. less able to imagine how someone else feels)

he'd have been in care, he'd have gone. But we've both learned different ways of handling it. Now we both know what will happen if he starts up, and I just don't need to smack him one like I used to.'

Melanie M

'My parents never hit. Physically, they were very gentle and kind. But my father could lash us with his tongue, just tear us apart, slowly and precisely, when he was angry. I think sometimes the smacking/not smacking debate can be too simply put. I am passionate about not smacking, but I am passionate about not terrorising and humiliating children in any way, and I think that can include what you say to a child as much as what you do to them.'

Helen F

'I'm sure I could get my toddler to stop throwing his food much quicker if I slapped his hand every time he did it. But I don't want to go down that road. If it takes a bit longer for him to get the message, that's OK. We'll get there in the end. I just don't want to start slapping for this and smacking for that.'

Mandy N

'I've never hit at all because for me it's a very clear line to draw and stick to. If you allow yourself to tap your child, what happens when you're really mad? Does that little tap become a harder one? And what happens when a slap doesn't work? I think it can crank up and I'd rather not get into it in the first place.'

Graham P

- Less internalisation of moral aspects of discipline (i.e. less able to develop their own sense of right and wrong)
- Increased probability of antisocial and criminal behaviour in adulthood.
- Evidence of compromised mental health

A huge amount of research[11] confirms that physical punishment backfires by making children more aggressive and less able to control their own behaviour, inside and outside the home.[12] Put bluntly, children who are hit learn to hit others.[13]

Smacking does not encourage family communication or considerate behaviour. It does not inform or encourage children to think about *why* their behaviour was wrong and *how* they could behave differently in future. If children stop their actions through fear of being smacked, rather than accepting *why* their behaviour needs to change, they'll simply do it again once we've left the room or they think they can get away with it. Even parents who have used physical punishment admit it is not an effective or enduring means of control.[14]

Research on huge numbers of children shows that those who were hit grow up with all sorts of negative outcomes, for example they grow up to hit their parents.[15] New research even suggests children who were hit decrease in cognitive ability, i.e. their IQ goes down.[16]

Dr Dorothy Rowe, psychologist and writer

Clearly, smacking is not the only form of punishment or parental behaviour that can harm a child. Any that involves humiliating, shaming, frightening or hurting falls seriously short of what children and parents need – effective discipline methods that enhance family relationships, not undermine them. Yet smacking is still so vehemently defended by so many, it deserves our particular attention.

The excuse that children need to be smacked to 'understand discipline' is feeble and insulting to children and parents. The same used to be said of women: it was OK to hit them to keep them in check and show 'who's boss'. We find these views abhorrent now. We look forward to the day when physical punishment of children is also viewed as disturbing and unnecessary.

Let's be clear. We are not anti-parents who have snapped and smacked. Smacking is a mistake, and people make mistakes sometimes. What we are very much against are those who still promote smacking

A very English vice

Francis Wheen, journalist and broadcaster

Spanking is known throughout the world as 'The English vice'. It was entirely predictable that Britain should be the last country in Europe to ban corporal punishment in state schools, in 1987 – and then only because the European Court of Human Rights gave us no choice.

The former Archbishop of Canterbury, George Carey, once advised his flock that: 'You say "Don't do this", "You mustn't do that" and you gently slap them if they transgress and there is nothing wrong with that as long as it is done with love and firm discipline within the family set-up.' He went on, 'We older people must practise what we preach . . . We actually live the kind of discipline we are wanting a future generation of people to grow up with.' Oh really?

I find it inconceivable that the Archbishop would take a swipe at an Archdeacon who had been 'misbehaving'. Why, then, do we believe we are setting children an example and preparing them for adult life, by administering 'loving slaps' every time they stray from the path of righteousness?

The other distinction, some may say, is that the smacking of children is administered in a 'private, loving family context'. Following that logic, we might as well legalise wife slapping and granny bashing.

as a basis of happy, healthy family relationships and a positive method of guiding children's behaviour. Smacking does not help parents or children. Those who support smacking are denying parents the support, information and constructive alternatives they need to nurture and discipline children effectively and build better family bonds.

Of course other things influence anti-social behaviour. But . . . we found that the tendency for physical punishment to make things worse over the long run applies regardless of race, socio-economic status, gender of child, relationship with parents or level of anti-social behaviour.

Dr Murray Strauss, Family Research Laboratory University of New Hampshire, USA[17]

As parents of young children we are powerful. To a large degree, we influence how good our children feel about themselves and their capacity to handle strong emotions and tough situations. We have much control over our children's routines and activities, how much

Physical punishment in the UK

Research has proved that hitting children does not improve their behaviour or make life easier for parents. Indeed it's shown that the opposite is true: whether a child starts out 'good' or 'bad' physical punishment actually makes it more likely that he or she will engage in anti-social behaviour, as a child, an adolescent and an adult. But those findings are not the whole argument against physical punishment. The other – and even more important – part is about children's rights. As human beings like the rest of us, children have the same rights as everyone else and that includes the right to bodily integrity; to legal protection from assault. It is not OK in this country for one adult to hit another, so how can it possibly be OK for adults to hit defenceless children?

Penelope Leach, Ph.D research psychologist and advocate for families

Recent studies have detailed the frequency and type of punishment administered to children. The shocking findings should be required reading for anyone who still believes attitudes towards physical punishment of children do not need to change.

A recent survey for the Scottish Executive[18] found that 51% of parents had smacked in the previous year and that this rose to 77% with parents of children aged 3–7 years. This echoes research by Marjorie Smith and colleagues at the Thomas Coram Research Unit.[19] They interviewed 400 families in studies sponsored by the Department of Health and found:

— 91% of children had been hit.

— 77% of them in the last year.

— 75% of one-year-olds had been smacked in the year preceding the interviews.

— Punishments parents admitted administering included 'physical restraint' (including 'wipe face with cold flannel, physically restrain child, cold bath/shower, hand/object over mouth, place head under water, shake, push/shove, throw') and 'punishment by example' (including 'pulling hair, scratch, pinch, bite/nip/chew, Chinese burn, burn/scald, put in cold water'). Over 40% of the children had experienced 'physical restraint' and 'punishment by example'. 'Ingestion' was experienced by 12% of the children (including 'forced to eat food, make eat something nasty e.g. mustard sandwiches, forced to drink salt water, wash mouth out with soap and water').

— Almost a quarter of seven-year-olds had received 'severe' physical punishment from their mothers. (Severe punishment was defined as the 'intention or potential to cause injury or psychological damage, use of implements, repeated actions or over a long period'.)

— Children who were frequently aggressive with their siblings were four times as likely to have been 'severely' punished at some time as those who were rarely aggressive with their siblings.

— About 10% of children in the study had been hit by an implement.

'I think most parents smack their children and they will justify their actions by referring to something that their child did,'

comments Marjorie Smith. 'But overall, the surprise of the research was the dominance of the parents' mood in affecting whether a child would be hit as opposed to hitting being something that was thought about and considered the right thing to do in certain situations.'

The smacks administered tended to get more severe as children grew: 'In the youngest age group (one-year-olds) parents were describing it as a tap, for example fingers on the hand, and they were saying they were not hurting the child in the main. At age four it has moved to the leg or the bottom using the whole hand and the parent is more likely to report she has possibly or definitely hurt the child.

'My feeling on this is that once you start hitting, be it tapping in a controlled way, it escalates to be the same action but with more anger and force.'

There is a perception that some cultures, especially black cultures, support or promote hitting children. But it is not true that black people beat their children more than white people . . . from the research it is perfectly clear that white people are busy walloping their children enthusiastically. Even if it were sacrosanct in someone's culture, that does not make it OK. In Victorian days in this country we had a tradition of husbands hitting wives. Self-respecting men kept their wives in order, often with a good slapping. It still did not make it right.

Mary Crowley, chief executive, Parenting Education and Support Forum

TV they can watch, what toys they can play with and more. We can use our power responsibly and effectively to guide and challenge our children's behaviour without resorting to physical or emotional threat. We do not need to hit, so why do it when there are other, far more effective and less damaging ways?

Significantly, physical punishment tends to tail off once children become old enough and big enough to resist or fight back. If parents haven't worked out other, better ways to control their children's behaviour by the time they hit adolescence, they could be in for a rocky ride.

You cannot teach a toddler not to bite by biting her (whatever you may say) or teach a five-year-old not to hit other children by hitting him . . . If you do not listen to her, why should she listen to you? If you slap his hand when it goes where it shouldn't, why should he take care not to tread on your foot when it gets in his way?

The Commission on Children and Violence[20]

But if physical punishment is counterproductive and harmful, why do so many people do it? The answer is partly cultural (see A Very English Vice, p.245). It is also closely linked to parental mood and stress levels. Research[21] has now confirmed what most parents already knew: that children get punished or chastised most when their parents are tired, angry or stressed, not when the child's behaviour is at its worst. Physical punishment therefore provides a release of adult rage and tension, but does not provide constructive discipline.

My daughter had to learn to stay in her bed, but the reason I slapped her was not because I thought that was the right way to teach her but because I was so stressed out. I needed to talk things through, sort things out, and I needed more help and support at home than I was getting.

Anne P

Understanding what provokes physical punishment is a first step towards finding better and less traumatic ways to manage children's behaviour. This requires parents to stand back and observe their children, examine their own actions, stresses and flashpoints, recognise those situations that often give rise to conflict and do something about them. All these require humility, courage and honesty.

I smacked my son once when he was little and I remember feeling so ashamed. It was my problem that had led to me doing it and I was very aware it would have been enough to tell him. I made a promise never to hit a child again. I have managed this by recognising risky times and taking action. For example, I am most prone to lose it in a very hot car. If I feel this happening I pull the car over and get out of the car with the child until we sort it out.

Steve Biddulph, psychologist and author

Attitudes about the physical punishment of children are changing. A detailed study of childrearing in the 1960s[22] found that 95% of parents hit their children and that 80% of them thought it was the right thing to do. Recent surveys show that an alarmingly high percentage of parents still smack sometimes yet, significantly, most say they hadn't wanted to. They recognise it was a mistake (see Physical Punishment in the UK, p.246).

These are small but important steps. If more parents were able to recognise how their own moods influence their child's chance of being hit, the number of children being physically punished would drop further still. This does not mean we should deny our frustrations and anger – it can be important for children to know when they have pushed too far – but rather that we learn to express those feelings in ways that are effective and not potentially harmful to our children (see Effective Discipline Strategies, p.215 and Feelings and Fears, p.124).

Co-operation and Discipline: A Quick Reminder

- Children are essentially co-operative. As parents we can build on this.
- Children need clear rules and boundaries *and* our time, patience and understanding.
- Discipline is a tool, punishment is a weapon. Punishment shames, hurts, frightens or humiliates a child. Discipline educates, guides and encourages understanding. It is far more effective in turning around difficult behaviour.
- 'Challenging' our children asserts our needs constructively, and educates our children to meet their needs effectively and with consideration.
- 'Quick fixes' are best retained for emergency use and followed up when we can with more constructive approaches.

CHAPTER EIGHT

IMPORTANT RELATIONSHIPS

Caring for our children also means looking beyond our relationships with them. What happens between siblings, parents, parents and grandparents and other carers will all influence how children view themselves and their world. Finding ways to support and encourage key relationships in our children's lives will benefit us all.

You and your partner

We must not minimise the demands on a couple. We romanticise it and we need to be more honest. Children are dependent and demanding, requiring of our time, our thought, our love, our money. They raise issues constantly: what school, what bedtime, how to discipline? Every issue requires the couple to come to some working agreement and this touches daily on the differences and sensibilities of the partnership. It does not surprise me that without a lot of back-up, many families just cannot hold it together.

Peter Wilson, child psychotherapist and Director of Young Minds

How we manage the parental relationship matters to our children. Their views of accepted behaviour and the potential of human relationships will be mainly shaped by what they see at home.

If you are raising a child within a couple relationship, be aware of its value to you and your children. Also be realistic. Creating, nurturing and raising a child together is a powerful and profound bond. Great intimacy can grow out of needing each other, trusting each other, experiencing pleasures and sharing love and tenderness towards the child. Yet the gap between imagined familial bliss and reality can be alarming.

You now have your child's needs to consider, and meeting them may sometimes drain you physically and emotionally. As parents, you and your partner will also have different experiences and therefore very different and often conflicting needs. Recognising and talking constructively together about your common ground and your differences may be important to how you both cope with the transition from couple to family, and so help you all.

We've got such different views, especially about leaving the baby to cry. Table manners with our three-year-old is another explosive issue. We just don't agree. He's only three for goodness sake. We are trying to talk about these things more, but we do argue a lot in front of the kids.

Ann M

Ensuring that you are both involved in or at least informed of the day-to-day decisions about your child's care is the simplest way of feeling like a couple in a working partnership rather than isolated individuals or even opponents pulling in different directions. Remember, also, to look after your needs as individuals and as a couple. Have some time together, preferably away from your child, to talk and relate to each other as adults again rather than simply as parents. This can be astonishingly hard to achieve and requires commitment, planning and support, but think of it as a family investment and book that babysitter.

By looking after your needs you are providing your children with a positive role model – of how to get their own needs met in a way that respects others but also respects themselves.

Stella Ward, nurse and parenting advisor

Sex

After being pulled and tugged this way and that by the children, especially when I was still feeding, the last thing I sometimes wanted was physical stimulation, someone else wanting my body. What I needed was more like sensory shutdown – moments when I could have my body back for me and do absolutely nothing with it. But it's hard to explain without being hurtful. We never did discuss it.

Lisa D

Sex after children

José von Bühler, sexual and relationship psychotherapist

There are three main psychological stresses that affect a couple's sex life after the birth of a baby:

1: The couple have to adapt to a change in roles and identity. A woman has changed from lover/wife/partner to also being a mother. For the man, too, this may be a difficult adjustment.

2: From the moment of birth the male has to cope with the woman's attention being divided between him and the new baby.

3: The woman's body has been through an enormous upheaval and this is anti-sexual. Her body may feel sore and tender while production of prolactin (the hormone related to breastfeeding) further reduces libido. At the same time, men usually feel in great need of sex and the reassurance they get from it. It takes time for the woman to start wanting sex again. So you have a shocked man and a shocked woman and no sex – it is this combination that can really add to the strain.

Practical Solutions

1: **Education** We need education for the father before a baby arrives about what the woman will go through and what his potential feelings are following the birth.

After our first baby, sex completely disappeared for months. We both lost interest. It was the last thing on our minds.

John C

Parenthood combined with broken nights and an upturned sex life can strain the best of relationships. Most couple's sex life goes on hold for a short while after a baby is born and recognition of this is extremely important (see Sex after Children, p.252).

As your baby grows, sex drive may increase but opportunities for sex may still seem too few and far between. And when they arise, you'll just be getting it together when a child will cry, wet the bed, come in for a cuddle or decide now's the time to tell you the name of the school caretaker's cat. A sense of humour is important, as is considering ways to negotiate these huge shifts in your relationship. Having no sex can be habit-forming and you may need to act to break the pattern.

We also need information about what is normal sexually following the birth. We are all different so there can be no guide as to the number of times you have sex, etc. But it needs to be understood that normal means possible change and that there will be temporary loss of libido in the woman. It is helpful not to be surprised by this or take it personally.

2: **Communication** The woman needs to explain what has happened to her, and the man needs to listen. The man also needs to explain how he is feeling and ask questions about what he does not understand. This is intimacy. If this vital reciprocal communication happens the woman can say for example: 'At the moment I feel like this. I do love you and I just need some time without sex. I am not rejecting you.'

3: **Intimacy of touch** A couple can use this if there are sexual difficulties. It involves a shift away from sexual touching and towards intimate touching. After the birth the couple need to start touching each other but non-genitally, rediscovering the healing power of touch and the togetherness it brings.

Later, touch can become genital but it is important to go gently, in stages negotiated between you. Some women will not want to be even touched for a while and even when the process of touch begins again, it is essential to feel OK about not having sex until both partners are ready. The worst thing is for the man to put pressure on the woman for sex.

Both verbally and physically this process is reassuring for the couple until such time as the woman is ready to come back to full sexuality.

Sex in the first few months is intermittent, possibly absent, and tends to come back to normal in the latter part of the first year, six months onwards. By 'normal' I don't mean as before but to an acceptable pattern in the couple. In my experience it never goes back to exactly how it was before the baby, there just isn't the time, there isn't the energy. Particularly for women, with breastfeeding and the hormonal changes, the sex drive lessens. Also, having the baby so close means she doesn't have the same need for physical contact.

Ann Herreboudt, midwife and family therapist

Reviewing the role of fathers

There's been so much talk about men in crisis, men losing their traditional role in society, but that misses the point. We've also got new opportunities. My dad never spent much time with us as we were growing up. He regrets it but it's too late. I don't have to make that mistake. I'm much more involved in my children's lives, and I love that.

Adam M

I have been a single parent and looked after my children for the past 10 years. It has brought home to me just how important it is for both parents to have a relationship of trust with their child because anything can happen.

Peter Walker, yoga teacher and physical therapist

This section is relatively small because most of this book is addressed to fathers and mothers. We've taken care to consult and quote men from many different backgrounds and with differing experiences, and do not want in any way to marginalise their role. However, there are specific issues that relate to men's experiences as parents, and it is important we acknowledge these.

The level of support, understanding and care a father brings to family life may be crucial to the happiness of all its members and to the success of the parental relationship.[1] Every family is different and couples' expectations vary, but for most the same truth holds: the more the father is actively involved in the children's lives, the more everyone will benefit.

Paternal warmth, emotional closeness and playfulness seem particularly significant in fostering successful father-child relationships, and have been linked to children's improved school performance, social adjustment and even to their employment patterns in later life.[2] Dads, more so than mothers, tend to encourage children to take risks and try things for themselves, which may explain why studies point to a link between strong father-child relationships and children's improved problem-solving and thinking skills[3] (see Play and Learning, p.324). The more active and physical style of many dads' play may also explain why children of 'involved' fathers tend to have greater tolerance of stress and frustration.

The time children and dads spend together is severely limited by the culture of long working hours. British fathers still work among the longest hours in Europe, and the phenomenon of the hard-working but rarely seen dad remains a feature of family life in much of the industrialised world. Yet attitudes and behaviour are changing. Recent studies suggest that fathers spend more time caring for their children than previous generations[4] and would like to spend more. Many want to be far more than family breadwinners and increasing numbers are

Shift parenting

Parents are often required to meet the demands of parenting whilst juggling their time between their children and their workplaces. Many also face the challenge of trying to make ends meet while raising children in poverty. The society we live in is not child friendly, and only rarely, explicitly or implicitly, recognises or supports the important job of parenting.

Royal College of Paediatrics and Child Health[5]

Many parents are now staggering their working hours[6] to make ends meet and to share childcare responsibilities. This has led to a rapid rise in 'shift parenting' and anti-social work patterns which are playing havoc with family relationships. More than 20% of British mothers and 40% of fathers now start work between 6.30 a.m. and 8.30 a.m., and 25% of mothers and 45% of fathers regularly work in the evening. Night and weekend working has also increased significantly in recent years.

Time that parents have as a couple has been the main casualty, since parents give priority to time with their children and the family as a whole. However 32% of mothers and 46% of fathers working unusual hours say their job significantly limits the time they can spend playing and reading with their children and helping them with their homework (compared with 12% of mothers and 18% of fathers who work 9 to 5).

Parents today need affordable, good quality childcare and work practices that are genuinely 'family-friendly'. There is no evidence that workplaces are any less productive if these are in place. In fact research suggests that people with access to such policies make better, not worse, employees.[7]

centrally involved in child-rearing.[8] It's high time social policy and attitudes caught up with parents' wishes by introducing more family-friendly work practices. There have been major and very welcome advances in recent years but there's still a very long way to go (see Fathers under Pressure, p.258).

In the early months of parenthood, many fathers feel on the periphery of the action while some other being they've only just met has first call on their partner's heart, mind and body. Yet fathers do have a crucial role to play in their child's first months. This cannot duplicate the role of the mother: the intensity of the mother/infant relationship springs, in part, from the experiences of pregnancy and birth and the physical dependency of the baby if breastfeeding. Yet the involvement of the father and the support he provides is invaluable.

With the break-up of many extended family networks and traditional support systems, the father is sometimes the only person around to provide the support both mother and baby require.

The biological and physiological differences between mothers and fathers often means the way in which they bond with their baby differs. This can be exaggerated by the additional time the mother spends with the baby in the early weeks. One way of dealing with this difference positively is for the father to take care of the mother while she takes care of the baby. This is where his input

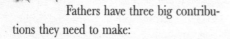

Father and child

Steve Biddulph, psychologist and author

Fathers have three big contributions they need to make:

1: **The first is time** You cannot be a good dad if you work a 60-hour week. Kids need you for several hours a day – not just playing with them, but cooking, working, doing things together. They need time to download your qualities and feel close to you in many moods. A workaholic father will harm his daughters, but he will cripple his sons. This is the big lesson of recent years. Dads are irreplaceable.

2: **The second is to be a real equal parent – not be a lightweight dad** Some dads just do the fun stuff, and leave discipline to their partners. Be sure to help with the discipline: supervise homework, organise tidying up or laundry.

3: **The third thing is the opposite of the second – to loosen up**. Some dads are never any fun. Often if our dads were stiff and remote we find it hard to get down on the rug and play.

Even to give a hug or a kiss is hard for some dads. So take a few risks and loosen up. You'll find it wins your children's hearts.

So it's a balance. There is great fun to be had from parenthood and great pride from discovering that you can really change the course of your child's life.

What is so helpful for building all relationships is to ensure there are opportunities for one-to-one relationships between all family members. For example, dad and daughter could go off for the weekend together, basically so every pair relationship can find its own rhythm. Traditionally there has been a tendency for the mother to be the relationship fixer. This can mean the father always relates to the children through the mother. We recommend that the mother takes off for a weekend with her friends once in a while so that the father can find his own footing.

*is invaluable and he may also bond with the baby in the process of taking care
of the mother.*

Yehudi Gordon, consultant gynaecologist and obstetrician, specialising in
holistic health

The father's sense of exclusion usually diminishes as his own relationship with the baby develops. In a recent Canadian study[9] all fathers
– from those who expressed an immediate love for their child to others
who said their love grew over time – said a crucial factor in the development of this relationship was when the baby smiled and 'spoke'
back to them. Research in the UK[10] confirms that fathers who were
helped to understand infant communication and their own baby's
'signals' felt a strong and growing bond. One father told researchers:
'My baby knew me . . . I've also now become more patient and tolerant
of my baby's needs.' On the other hand, fathers who weren't encouraged to understand and respond to their baby's cues felt they didn't
have much of a caring role when their child was very young: 'He really
is still a bit of a blob . . . wasn't much of a person . . . can't wait until
he's two and I can play with him.' Clearly, an understanding of how
babies communicate, and sufficient time spent with babies to learn
their 'signals', can be invaluable (see Understanding your Baby, p.9).

Quite how the bond between father and child intensifies and
develops will depend in large part on how much time the father spends
at home and to what extent he chooses to be involved in his children's
lives (see Father and Child, p.256). The parenting 'styles' of mothers
and fathers are surprisingly similar once childcare responsibilities are
shared equally.[11] Babies and children certainly don't seem fussed about
the gender of the parent who cares for them – they would prefer to
have intimate and affectionate care from both.[12]

*In the beginning it felt like I was watching my former life disappear and I had
no idea what was going to replace it. But then an incredibly powerful love
develops. There's much talk of a mother's instinctive, natural bond with the child
but men have one, too. It may not be the same, but that's surely the point.
It's the difference that makes another parent/child relationship worth having. I
think some men have always been greatly involved in raising their children and
have got great enjoyment from it. The difference now is that more men are going
public about it and admitting not only their role but also the fun and intense
pleasure of having children.*

Russell C

Fathers under pressure

British fathers still work the longest hours in Europe.[13] One in three routinely work over the 48 hours a week limit set by the European Working Time Directive. Fathers in professional and managerial jobs work the longest hours of all and are least likely to be involved in their children's care.[14]

- In a poll for the NSPCC,[15] almost one in five of the children living with their father could not recall doing anything with him in the previous week.
- The extent to which fathers share in the care and socialisation of children is a key factor in mothers' marital happiness and satisfaction in life.[16]
- Fathers in dual full-time earner households were more likely to share in childcare and domestic work than those in other employment situations, but their contribution was reduced considerably if they worked long hours.[17]
- Most mothers are still chiefly responsible for looking after children, organising their care and doing most household chores, even in those households in which both parents work full-time.[18]
- Following the birth of their child, 80% of fathers surveyed said they felt worried, 60% said they felt lonely, 12% felt depressed and 6% said they felt jealous.[19]
- Qualities children say they require of good mothers and fathers are remarkably similar and suggest children think in terms of good 'parents' rather than differentiating on the basis of gender.[20]

Every caring dad knows that the more involved he can be in his children's upbringing, the greater difference the children will make to his life and he will make to theirs. Recent studies show that the nature of father-child communication develops with frequency of contact.[21] This isn't something to consider only at weekends or in slices of 'quality time' carved out from hectic schedules, but something that develops in everyday moments over time. Whether it's bathing or feeding or settling your baby, chatting to your school-age child about homework, going for a walk together, finding socks, playing in the garden, reading stories, life is full of simple opportunities to 'connect'.

Even when fathers live apart from their children, the time and care they give makes an important difference to their children's lives and future (see Divorce and Separation, p.262).

If yours is a family without a father, you and your child may benefit hugely if a trusted male friend or relative can become more involved in their lives, offering another role model, another voice and view, another source of understanding, listening and love.

You know what's been hardest about me staying at home and my wife returning to work? Dealing with other parents; mothers especially. Some were great but I wasn't generally accepted. We need more than laws to make it easier for dads to share in parenting, our attitudes need to change, too.

Paul D

I'm not the biological father, but I am their dad. I think that's important to stress. I'm the caring father figure in those kids' lives; it's my love they have.

Martin W

Conflict between parents

All parents and children will experience family conflict at times. This is part of everyday family life and, indeed, of children's growing experience.

Martin Richards, Director of the Centre for Family Research, Professor at the University of Cambridge

Sitting on the stairs listening to them row was as much a part of childhood as Blue Peter and Curly Wurly toffee. Some nights we were terrified. Next day we'd all pretend nothing had happened, with a lot of forced jollity and embarrassed silence.

Amanda T

Occasional arguments between parents are a fact of family life, and how we handle them can make a significant difference to how children feel about themselves. They can even bring positive benefits, providing children with important lessons in how to handle conflict and anger constructively in their own lives.

Most parents are aware that their arguments can be upsetting for their children and many of us were brought up in families where parental rows were conducted behind closed doors in an attempt to protect us. Yet research suggests this approach is not helpful.[22]

Children of all ages are very sensitive to tension between the adults they love, even if they haven't actually witnessed any conflict. What they imagine to be happening is often far worse than reality, especially if parents' attempts to suppress anger create a silent, hostile atmosphere in the home.[23] The tension this creates can fuel anxiety, often

Helping children through

There are a number of things parents can think about when they are going through a bad patch or have been rowing a lot, says Jenny Reynolds, Senior Research Officer of One Plus One, the marriage and partnership research charity.

- **Reassure children that they are not to blame for an argument** Children often feel they are the cause of a row so their self-esteem suffers. They may then become depressed or anxious. A child might also need help in understanding that he or she doesn't need to protect a parent from an angry or upset partner.
- **Avoid getting children to take sides** It can be tempting for parents to involve children in an argument by, for example, making snide remarks to the child about the other parent or encouraging them to take sides.
- **Avoid lavishing lots of attention on a child because they are a source of affection and solace** when things with a partner aren't going well. This can cause long-term difficulties because it undermines the child's relationship with the other parent. Moreover, it can put the child on an emotional roller-coaster because they cease being the centre of attention when the parents' relationship is back on course again.
- **Take time to listen and talk to the children** Listen to what they are thinking and help them explain how they are feeling.
- **Apologise if necessary** It helps children to see parents apologise to each other if they've been hurtful. There may also be times when parents need to apologise to the child, for letting anger at a partner spill over on to them or where the child has been made a scapegoat for problems in the couple relationship (see Feelings and Fears, p.124).
- **If possible, stay united on discipline** In some cases, parents in conflict undermine one another by taking a different line on issues of discipline.

'From a child's perspective, the best ending to a fight is a warm and meaningful compromise where parents are able to apologise where they've been hurtful. In reality, our arguments don't often end like this,' says Jenny. 'However, some type of resolution to the dispute, even if parents can't muster any warmth or humour, is better than things being left unresolved. Similarly, even if children don't see parents make up, it is helpful if parents tell the child that they have or give positive clues that things have been sorted out by resuming "diplomatic relations".'

expressed through changes in the children's behaviour. It also gives children the sense that disagreements are something secretive and shameful, not to be talked about openly and constructively. Research evidence and children themselves tell us this can be disturbing, even scary, especially if they feel they have to be the go-between or peacemaker to help adults communicate.

Children are very acute observers and parents delude themselves that they aren't. They also often blame themselves if things are going wrong in the partnership or marriage. If the issue is not addressed by the parents, children can feel they have to be a go-between and peacemaker. This is terribly frightening and onerous for a child. Children can become tremendously anxious but not show it because parents don't want to see it. So the child is there for the parent, but the parent is not really aware of what's going on for the child.

Dr John Byng-Hall, Consultant Child and Family Psychiatrist,
Institute of Family Therapy, London

Clearly, some forms of parental conflict are damaging to children's well-being. Intense and frequent rows, verbal or physical aggression, silent hostility and arguments about the children are particularly detrimental. Children growing up in an atmosphere of extreme parental discord may develop emotional and behavioural problems and fight more with friends and brothers and sisters.[24] Their feelings and behaviour can also take a downturn if parents treat each other with contempt or if one parent regularly withdraws during a row.

Yet if we handle most disagreements constructively and without hostility, stating our case and listening to others, we will give our children a lesson for life. Studies[25] show children can actually benefit from observing their parents' rows if those parents seek compromises, use negotiation, humour and warmth as they attempt to resolve differences,

Taking it out on the children?

Overcrowding, low income and lone-parent status does not significantly increase the risks of physical violence to children in their homes, according to UK research sponsored by the Department of Health.[26] But a third of children living with parents who had a poor marital relationship experienced severe physical punishment, compared with 7% of those whose marriage was good.

don't resort to aggression, apologise when they've been hurtful and generally make up. Even being so mad that we can't sort things out in that moment can be helpful if we handle the situation well: 'Can we leave sorting this out until tomorrow, when we're calmer?' (See Helping Children Through, p.260). These are tall orders, especially at times when relationships are strained, but simply knowing what helps our children most may help us behave more positively when we can.

If we don't make up immediately after a row, we can still let our children know when we do. Even when matters remain unresolved, discussing issues openly, making it clear that the children aren't to blame, even agreeing to disagree, can foster security in family relationships and help children learn constructive ways of dealing with disagreements in their own lives.

Letting children see disagreements resolved takes some of the fear out of conflict and teaches them the various ways in which we sort out our differences. It also gives them a realistic view of family relationships; that adults, and children for that matter, don't always see eye to eye but that doesn't mean they don't love one another or that the relationship has been irrevocably damaged.

Jenny Reynolds, Senior Research Officer, One Plus One

I think it is a very positive thing when children see parents handle a difficult situation, that they see a parent grasp the problem and deal with it. It must help them know the parent is a protector and it also shows them how to deal with their own problems when they encounter them.

Cherry H

Divorce and separation

The hardest thing was so wanting the family to stay together and the inability to do that. Then feeling judged for it, almost as if I didn't take my family responsibilities as seriously as those marriages that stayed together, as if I didn't have the same protective feelings. I would have done anything to keep it as a marriage that was OK for the children to be in but it just was not possible.

Rosie G

Divorce and separation are experienced by ever increasing numbers of children and families. Clearly, it's a painful and distressing time for all involved, yet only a small minority of children experience serious and long-term difficulties.[27] Not surprisingly, our own behaviour as parents is key to how children cope when their parents split up.

The pressures on parents experiencing family change are huge, and we don't wish to add to them by proposing unrealistic goals or checklists of required behaviour. But it is worth considering what research and families themselves say helps them most.

We're the generation that grew up with divorced parents.
We know what it's like and it's up to us to use that knowledge. We can deny that it hurt, say it never did me any harm. Or we can admit that it did and try to think of ways to lesson that hurt for our children. We do know, in a way perhaps our parents never did, and I think it's our responsibility to act on that.

John M

Two happy homes are better than one unhappy one.
Mohammed J

Family facts

Families come in all shapes and sizes, and many children experience different types of family unit as they grow. If your family is changing through separation, divorce or forming a stepfamily, remember you are not alone. Many parent support and self-help groups now offer great advice and information for adults and children (see Contacts, p.429).

— Every day more than 700 children and young people see their parents divorce or separate.
— Lone parent families now make up 20% of all families with children, compared with 12% 20 years ago.
— Official statistics do not count how many co-habiting parents separate although studies indicate the rate is higher than for married couples.
— One in eight children is likely to grow up in a stepfamily.
— One in two of these stepfamilies will have a new child of the step-couple.
— At least 50% of remarriages which form a stepfamily also end in divorce.
— 25% of stepfamilies break down in the first year.
— One in six fathers lives apart from some or all of his own biological children.
— Nearly 150,000 children a year experience their parents' divorce in England and Wales alone. A quarter are aged five and under.[28]

Parent-child relationships

Parent-child relationships, rather than family structure, are vital to how children fare during and after a transition.

Jenny Reynolds, Senior Research Officer, One Plus One

The most important contributions parents can make to the well-being of their children at separation/divorce are to tell them in an age-appropriate way what is happening; to listen to their views and concerns about future living arrangements and contact with parents and family; and to ensure children have a continuing good enough relationship with both parents and relatives on both sides

Martin Richards, Director of the Centre for Family Research, Professor at the University of Cambridge

The conclusions of recent studies are clear. Children may experience many difficulties following divorce or parental separation – including moving house, area or school and a fall in household income – but what children find most damaging of all is a breakdown in the relationship with either parent. Equally, the most important factor boosting children's resilience to the impact of divorce and separation is the relationship they have with their mother and father.

Understandably, parents may feel distracted and less available to their children when they are struggling with their own emotional distress, yet an awareness of just how important they are to their children at this time may help parents 'be there' for them as much as possible.

When children are living through the upheavals of family change, they need the important adults in their lives to be as loving, warm and responsive as they can, to listen to and understand their feelings and to provide clear and fair guidance on behaviour (see below). Whenever possible, they also need continued contact with and commitment from the non-resident parent.

It is clear that those children for whom divorce meant the loss of a valued relationship found it hard to deal with the emotional toll.[29]

Amanda Wade and Carol Smart, Centre for Research on Family, Kinship and Childhood, University of Leeds

Continued contact need not mean sharing time equally with mum and dad. Many children prefer a main 'home' and to visit or be visited by the other parent on a regular basis. Recent research also indicates that babies who spend nights in the separate homes of their birth parents may display confusion and distress at the mother's regular absences.[30] Regular contact rather than regular one-night stays away from their main home may ease their anxiety. As they get older, longer visits rather than 'single night stays' may help them settle.

Crucially, other factors found to influence very young children's ability to cope included the parents' ability to minimise the stresses of separation for the child; the parents' ability to communicate and co-operate about their baby's well-being; and the level of parental conflict.

Clearly, supporting our children can be far from easy when life is hard, but every bit of concern, commitment and consideration we offer can make a very real difference to how they cope, now and in the future.

Lessen exposure to bitter conflict

Some parents continue to be in conflict long after they've parted ways and children are often the focus of dispute. Unless parents are careful how they manage their disagreements, children can be exposed to the same kind of bitter and damaging conflicts that marked the relationship before it broke down.

Jenny Reynolds, Senior Research Officer, One Plus One

Most children of divorced parents seem to cope with life as well as those from non-separated families two to three years on, provided they do not experience continued or increased bitter conflict or stress.[31]

Of course all families argue sometimes and this needn't be a bad thing for our children to witness (see Conflict between Parents, p.259). But exposure to frequent and intense conflict is confusing and distressing to a child, especially if they believe they are the cause or subject of the rows. It is our responsibility as parents to reduce our children's exposure to this as far as humanly possible.

Certainly research indicates that if separation takes place without too much high emotional conflict or without the child being exposed to it, the child can get through without too much distress. And it does seem that after about two years the range of disturbance among children of divorce is average rather than it being higher than the rest of the population.

Gill Gorell Barnes, Honorary Senior Lecturer Tavistock Clinic, family therapist, researcher

Understand behaviour changes

We have to accept that children are distressed when their parents break up, but that does not mean they are necessarily psychologically disturbed by it. It seems to be quite a small minority of children who are.

Gill Gorell Barnes, Honorary Senior Lecturer Tavistock Clinic, family therapist, researcher

Most children cope well in the long term, but distress and problematic behaviour are common in the first two years following parental separation or divorce.[32]

Some may find school and school work a sanctuary from the stresses of home life, but others find it hard to concentrate when their thoughts are elsewhere. It is important that teachers and others involved with their care are informed of what is happening so they can respond with understanding.

Children may display an increase in problematic, aggressive or argumentative behaviour, often directed towards brothers and sisters and sometimes towards their peers. Some children develop emotional difficulties, becoming anxious, withdrawn or excessively concerned about a parent's well-being. Understanding the feelings that underlie these difficulties, while keeping to family rules about acceptable behaviour, may help parents remain supportive, consistent and constructive.

If a child is behaving badly or doing something to attract attention, it is very important to say that you understand this is difficult for them and that if they want to talk about it you are happy to listen, but how they are behaving isn't acceptable. This allows the child to know the parent does understand and that the parent is also holding the boundary on behaviour. It encourages the child to communicate their feelings as opposed to acting them out.

Cheryl Walters, psychoanalytic psychotherapist and Head of Research at Parentline Plus

Understand children's feelings Children may feel confused, guilty, anxious, scared, rejected, angry, desperate – and not want to burden their parents further by talking about it. As far as you can, make time to listen to your child and to discuss worries (see Feelings and Fears, p.124 and Communication, p.89).

If you find this too distressing or you are worried about breaking down, try to find another trusted adult friend or relative whom your child might talk to about their feelings and concerns. Some children also like talking to other young people in similar situations. It can encourage them to talk more freely and reassures them that they are not the only ones experiencing family change.

Allow children to love both parents

Children are particularly vulnerable when they are caught in loyalty traps –
pressed to take sides against the other parent – or when they are used as
go-betweens or vehicles for the dispute.

Jenny Reynolds, Senior Research Officer, One Plus One

Distinguishing between your child's feelings and your own is central to how well a child survives major family problems, including parental separation. You feel one thing and your child may feel another. You may hate your ex and your child will still love them; you may feel liberated at the prospect of separation and your child may feel devastated.

Allow and respect your child's emotions and try not to impose your own feelings or use your child to 'get at' your former partner. By being clear that the family is made up of separate individuals with different experiences and valid but different views and emotions helps children see the split as a problem between the parents. They are not to blame.

As adults we must accept that children love both parents and that they need to be
able to feel good about each parent in order to develop and mature naturally and
feel positive about themselves.

Cheryl Walters, psychoanalytic psychotherapist and Head of Research at
Parentline Plus

Keep daily life as normal as possible Children generally feel more secure if their daily routines are disrupted as little as possible.

Keep children informed

If separation is on the cards, then giving children a false sense of security
isn't going to help. Parents may need to work hard at reassuring the child
that his or her relationship with each parent is safe but that how they live
together may change.

Jenny Reynolds, Senior Research Officer, One Plus One

Through good intentions, parents may fail to give children the information they need to feel safe. Intuitively, children are often well aware of emotional realities but can't make sense of their feelings because parents are 'protecting' them from the truth. Although it can be painful to talk and to allow difficult emotions to surface, it is generally far better for children to be sensitively informed than left in ignorance.[33]

So how can you tell children about separation or divorce in a way that helps them most? Using simple words and explanations is important. If possible, arrange for both parents to tell a child together or at least try to agree on the wording between you or have access to each other's version. If moving into a stepfamily, it helps if a child's natural parent first tells the child without the prospective step-parent present.

Be clear and up front with appropriate and necessary information: that your child is very loved by both parents, not to blame for the split in any way, and that you understand how strange it must feel. Give as many details as you can about the practical aspects of life. Explain what is going to change and reassure about what will stay the same – will you be staying in the same house, will they be attending the same school, have the same friends, toys, pets? If one parent is moving out, where are they moving to and when can the child visit? If you are moving to a new house, what does it look like? What are you taking with you? Basic and concrete information helps children feel more secure about their new family life.

Then be prepared to censor. Children do not need to be burdened with gory details about the breakdown of the parental relationship, or act as their parent's emotional prop and confidant.

We must speak and act with children age-appropriately. I always feel short and simple explanations are best, but with the option for the child to come back and ask questions, so they know this isn't a one-off chat but an ongoing process of understanding. Little children, up to about ten years depending on the child, do not need details. They have a right to know what is happening to them and it is important to keep them updated. But think in terms of giving them the basics they need in order not to be fearful of what is going to happen, and then try to answer their questions as they arise.

Cheryl Walters, psychoanalytic psychotherapist and Head of Research at
Parentline Plus

Let children be children Children can appear very capable and resilient at times of family distress. They often are, but they remain our children and need us to be the primary carers in the family. If children take on too much responsibility for practical and emotional care, supporting us, their siblings or others in distress, they may become unable to express or prioritise their own emotional needs. This can have long-term consequences to how they feel and how they relate to others.

Of course, there'll be times when we may need extra help from our children to get to the end of the week. This can be a positive experience if children feel genuinely appreciated for showing consideration to others. The danger comes when children carry responsibilities beyond their years on a regular basis, or are treated more as adult friends, expected to listen to and support their parents through emotional distress.[34] It can be very disturbing for children to feel they, not their parents, are in control at such a painful and confusing time or that they have responsibility for a parent's emotional well-being.

Overt allegiances between one child and one parent tend to fuel further conflict and mistrust in families, particularly between siblings.[35] We've enough to cope with, so for everyone's sake, it makes sense not to add these to the heap.

When parents separate, it's common for children to take on a more caring role, looking after the distressed parent, siblings, themselves and others. If this is acknowledged and openly discussed, if the child doesn't feel typecast or trapped in the role and feels valued when they do help, this can produce a sense of competence which in the long run enhances a child's self-esteem. However if the parent is so preoccupied that they can't acknowledge, appreciate or even see what's happening, or if the child feels trapped in the caring role, this can be damaging.

Dr John Byng-Hall, Consultant Child and Family Psychiatrist,
Institute of Family Therapy, London

Encourage questions Let children know they can ask any question they need, now or later. Also understand that how children make sense of the information they are given will change as they grow, so they may have to ask the same question many times.

Books about family change can help children begin to think and talk about what is happening in their lives. Building in a special time for questions – perhaps before bedtime – may also help.

One thing that was really helpful for my son, who was seven at the time and would not ask questions, was my devising a questionnaire by imagining the questions he might want answers to. I then answered the questions and wrote on the bottom that I was sure these weren't all the right questions but could he tell me what I had got wrong and any gaps he had found. The extraordinary thing was how well this worked. It offered a matter-of-fact focus at such an emotionally painful time.

Jim Wilson, systemic psychotherapist and director of the Centre for
Child-Focused Practice at the Institute of Family Therapy, London

Show it is OK not to have all the answers Better to say, 'I don't know what's happening with that yet, but as soon as it's a bit clearer, I'll let you know,' than get it very wrong, say nothing at all or close down communication.

Negotiate problem times Some events are more stressful than others in separated, divorced or step-families. These 'problem peaks' may include times of marriage, death, Christmas or other religious festivals, birthdays and holidays. Advance warning may at least help you plan accordingly; doing something or going somewhere completely different may help avoid heartbreaking comparisons with happier times.

Don't forget your needs

Much of the support that primary school children seem to benefit from need not come directly from the parents. Trusted grandparents or friends of the family can be very important.

Supporting Children Through Family Change, Joseph Rowntree Foundation[36]

Practical and emotional support from trusted friends and relatives may help reduce some of the many pressures on parents. This, in turn, may help them feel less distracted and more emotionally available for their children. For the children themselves, relationships with trusted adults outside the immediate family can provide comfort, understanding and distraction from the pressures of home life.

Pride can sometimes stand in the way of accepting genuine offers of support, but it can be a very positive step, easing pressure on the parent and making it a little easier for all to negotiate the days ahead.

Work at making it work

Regardless of the children's social class background or the structure of their family, the most important thing to them was the quality of their relationship with significant adults in their lives.[37]

Amanda Wade and Carol Smart, Centre for Research on Family,
Kinship and Childhood, University of Leeds

Much of what children experience in their new family structure(s) will be down to you and your ex-partner. It is the responsibility of every parent to try to make the new way of life work for the child – and to keep on trying.

Divorce involves adults sitting down and saying. 'What piece of hard thinking do I have to do to make things go well for the kids, however much I am in emotional turmoil? How am I going to keep a structure going which doesn't upset their lives fundamentally?' It feels artificial but it has to be done to ensure the kids' lives don't end up in a mess. You don't stop being a parent and anything that helps parents think that way will help the children.

Gill Gorell Barnes, Honorary Senior Lecturer Tavistock Clinic,
family therapist, researcher

Lone parenting

It is hard. Just the day-in-day-out slog of doing it on your own is pretty exhausting. But, for me and my son, it really is better than life when me and his mother were a couple. This is hard, that was hell.

Patrick B

My husband died suddenly, so we were plunged into life as a lone parent family with no warning. My advice is to treasure the people who are there for you and your kids. It may surprise you who is – and who isn't.

Helen M

It is perfectly possible to raise children successfully and happily as a lone parent, but the demands are huge. Lone parents are not only caring for their children but, very often, also juggling home and work life and managing contact with the other parent. Looking after yourself and occasionally prioritising your own needs as well as those of the children is essential if you are to have the physical and emotional resources to cope.

Let's be clear. Happy families come in all shapes and sizes. More and more children are experiencing life with one parent, even for a short time, and most cope well. Very many lone parents raise their children happily, often despite financial difficulties and other hardships. Certainly, the latest research suggests that children being brought up by one parent are less likely to suffer physical punishment than those whose parents are unhappily married.[38]

Yet studies – and parents themselves – tell us that certain factors make the hard job of raising children on your own even harder. Parents who are in conflict with a former partner or other family members, or who are very young, poor, unsupported, socially isolated or depressed[39] are less likely to feel happy in their relationships with their children or to feel they are managing the job of being a parent well.

Some of those factors are beyond parents' control, but lone mothers and fathers may be able to ease some of the pressures on them and their children by seeking and accepting extra support. This may be from friends or family, it may be from outside organisations. It may be offered, you may have to ask for it. It may be practical assistance, emotional support, regular or occasional help. Whatever form it takes, it can make a crucial difference to your resources and your family life. Try not to let it slip from your list of priorities.

I felt so overwhelmed and tired I even resented her wanting attention and cuddles when I got home from work. I just wanted to flop and have a bit of time for me. I've now come to an arrangement with a friend, so we have each other's daughters to stay over occasionally. I've also asked my mum if she can give her tea once in a while. It doesn't sound much, but it's made a difference.

Laura S

Stepfamilies

Adults in stepfamilies have less chance to be alone and establish the partnership as the touchstone of the family; on the other hand, they may be more pragmatic in their approach to the new family, and readier to make adjustments to the presence of children.

Not in Front of the Children, One Plus One[40]

Forming new families can take considerable emotional and social skill. Understanding the issues stepfamilies often face and imagining how each member may feel can help parents explore what works best for them and the children in their new family group.

Be aware Joining a stepfamily is a huge transition. Children are becoming part of a new and often unfamiliar unit, each member of which will bring their own temperament, habits, experiences, values, jealousies, expectations and prejudices.

Some children may only spend part of the time in the new household. Some will be sharing their lives with new step-siblings as well as a new step-parent. Some may be struggling with their relationship with an absent parent. Some may still be reeling from the effects of their parents' break-up. It's not uncommon for children to dislike their step-siblings or step-parent. Equally complicated, they may like them and feel disloyal to members of their birth family. They may share time between two new stepfamily units and feel they 'fit' in neither. They may be unfamiliar with the everyday routines of their new home. They may feel scared, jealous, angry, confused, ignored, rejected, replaced, betrayed, powerless.

The very fact of living with a person you don't know is difficult. All their habits are different, their expectations are different, their understanding of the child is limited, they smell different, they don't feel the same as the person who's gone. These things are tremendously important and powerful, especially for little children, and we have to recognise that. The child is very often outraged by this replacement and the early days of stepfamilies are often very difficult times. There is often a lot of envy and rivalry.

Gill Gorell Barnes, Honorary Senior Lecturer Tavistock Clinic,
family therapist, researcher

Give it time The parenting support charity Parentline Plus estimates it can take between two to ten years for relations in a stepfamily to stabilise. Do not blame yourself and especially do not blame the child if all is not sweetness and light – there is much to work out and work through. Given time and understanding, stepfamily relationships can work well.

Understand behaviour

The child is saying, 'Are you going to leave like my mother or father left? Is it safe to care about you? Is it safe to rely on you? Are you going to be there or are you going to leave if I am bad?' It is also about the child, in its own way, trying to heal that part of themselves that says 'I must have been really bad for my parent to leave', because somewhere in a child there is that sense that if they had been better, kinder, if they'd done their homework, whatever it might be, this wouldn't have happened.

Cheryl Walters, psychoanalytic psychotherapist and Head of Research at
Parentline Plus

When children become part of a stepfamily, their feelings are often reflected in their behaviour as both parent and step-parent are, quite literally, put to the test.

Relationships with siblings and step-siblings can suffer, too. It may

---

Reviews, routines and rules

Gill Gorell Barnes, Honorary Senior Lecturer
Tavistock Clinic, family therapist, researcher

We're a stepfamily and my own parents divorced when I was in my teens so I know the feelings as well as the theory of the feelings, as it were. I think the Pandora's Box issue – the fear that everything will flood out uncontrollably when you lift the lid and begin to talk – is a very big one in stepfamilies. I do think it stops people talking.

This is where discussion of house rules helps hugely – saying to children, 'When you come here let's think about how it is going to be different from when you are at Mum's. Let's see how we can make it go as smoothly as possible for you.'

It helps to talk about 'house' rather than 'family' rules because it is often an easier concept to buy into. It gets away from the child objecting because 'This isn't my family'. It also helps if adults are aware they are setting up a new organisation, a new habitat, and to think about its principles and rules and how these could be established. Talk these through with the children.

Think ahead: should you agree telephone rules between the natural parents, such as no phone calls between 7 or 8 p.m., or agree telephone times when the child is available to speak to the other parent? In families where everything can be more open, such rigid rules aren't needed, but in situations where everything is very suspicious and 'hot' it is very useful.

help to reassure yourself, your partner and all children in the family that in time, as relationships grow and new family routines and customs develop, aggression between brothers and sisters tends to decrease to levels found in families generally.

Realistic expectations of our children's behaviour and a recognition of their powerful and often conflicting emotions as they adjust to their new lives may help us maintain the mix of firm, clear parental guidance and warmth, responsiveness and understanding that they need.

Get together Family 'meetings' can help all the children have a say in discussions and decisions about everyday stepfamily life (see Reviews, Routines and Rules, p.274). This needn't involve anything heavy. Who clears the table, borrows toys without asking or hogs the bathroom can be very important to how a child feels about their new environment. It can also practise and develop family communication, so tougher issues may be discussed more easily if the need arises.

Encourage tolerance This can be crucial to stepfamily survival. Be open about the fact that your stepfamily is made up of people from different pasts but hopefully a shared future. You will have many different ways, ideas, attitudes and loyalties, but 'different' doesn't mean 'right' or 'wrong', simply other valid ways of behaving and feeling. Explain to children that differences in behaviour and belief can co-exist if you all try to be tolerant and understanding and talk matters through.

If there are children from two different birth families, it helps to give them all a chance to get to know each other better. Arranging outings, activities and time together in different and changing pairs can stop damaging allegiances and battle lines forming.

Know your role

A step-parent can put themselves under such pressure to be a super-parent, yet a very big part of failure in stepfamilies is unrealistic expectations of oneself and of others. It helps to recognise that things change over time. As a step-parent you actively have to build a relationship with children. You can't, for example, just come in and discipline children who are quite right to say, 'Who the hell are you?' Knowing where to draw the line involves putting yourself in the child's shoes, imagining how what you are doing or saying might feel to the child.

Cheryl Walters, psychoanalytic psychotherapist and Head of Research at
Parentline Plus

If you are a step-parent, you can be loving, supportive and caring but you are not a replacement parent, especially when the stepfamily is relatively new. This knowledge may save you and the children involved a great deal of heartache. You will have to work at establishing a relationship with each child, but until that is done, it is best to leave tough parental duties such as discipline to the parents.

You may also be the parent of children who spend most of their time in another family unit, with a former partner. Studies have shown that this dual role – of parent and step-parent – may result in fathers in particular developing more detached and distant relationships with children in both their 'old' and 'new' families.[41] Yet most children still want and need both their parents to be involved and committed to their well-being (see Divorce and Separation, p.262). There is no easy answer, but an awareness of children's experiences and needs may help parents stay 'connected' with their own children after they establish a stepfamily elsewhere.

In our study[42] we found it was much harder for stepmothers than stepfathers. Dads tend to be brought in more as mother's partner, to get to know over time. Stepmothers are expected to do much more in relation to the children and tend to be brought in to take on the kids and run the house. Children have much more direct exposure and stepmothers often have a much more difficult and resistant time. They can be treated with incredible hostility.

Gill Gorell Barnes, Honorary Senior Lecturer Tavistock Clinic,
family therapist, researcher

Avoid preferential treatment Preferential treatment of one child or group of children will fuel conflict in any family, but the impact of favouritism in stepfamilies is particularly marked. Of course you will love your own child or children with an intensity reserved just for them, but try to be fair, kind and understanding to all children in the new family. Rules of expected behaviour should apply to all. Avoiding obvious shows of favouritism and long-term differences in the amounts of affection or irritation shown to each child will help all family members.

Stay positive Everyone involved in a stepfamily has to work to make it a success, but they can work incredibly well. When they do, stepfamily children can journey into adulthood with a wider network of supportive relationships and with skills that will benefit them for the rest of their lives.

When it is a successful stepfamily, children learn to compromise in a way they often wouldn't have had to in a first-time family. They also learn to negotiate and they learn about the concept of getting something of what they want but perhaps not all, of things being good enough, so they are not always striving for the impossible.

Cheryl Walters, psychoanalytic psychotherapist and Head of Research at Parentline Plus

Grandparents

My tip for my mother: butt out. I cannot believe she still makes comments and drops hints about how things should be done. I'd love her support but I don't want to bring up my children like she brought up hers.

Clare T

Being a parent has made me appreciate and understand my own parents. It's brought us much closer.

Mark C

Grandparents are children's main carers in some cultures and play a central role in very many children's lives, supporting families with child-care, babysitting, household chores, outings, trips and treats and, crucially, offering another trusted source of time, patience and unconditional love.

This relationship matters to children: in an NSPCC survey, 78% of children said their grandparents were important to them.[43] Grandparents often have the opportunity to share relaxed time and it is this that children tend to treasure far more than material gifts. However, the shift towards dual-income families means increasing numbers of grandparents are now looking after children on a regular basis while parents work. This may reduce the 'relaxed' time they have available (see Grandparents and Grandchildren, p.278).

I believe I appreciate my grandchildren more than I did my own children. Is that a terrible thing to say? Because they are not around me all the time, I don't take them for granted. I can see just what wonderful little people they are.

Margaret R

Grandparents and grandchildren

- About 1% of grandparents in the UK have grandchildren living with them.[44]
- The value of childcare by UK grandparents has been calculated at more than £1 billion a year.[45]
- One in five children under 16 years old are looked after in the daytime by their grandparents.[46]
- Children in two-parent families where both parents work are the most likely to receive daytime care from a grandparent.[47]
- More than a third of grandparents spend the equivalent of three days a week caring for their grandchildren.[48]
- Three-quarters of UK adults believe that 'With so many working mothers, families need grandparents to help more.'[49]
- 39% of grandparents would like to have a life 'free from too many family duties'.[50]

My grandmother was my link to my family's past. Her words, stories, cooking, even her laugh had more to do with St Lucia than Hertfordshire where I grew up. She was a bridge from the past to my present.

Martin P

A new child in the family means many changing roles. The transition from child to new parent and from parent to grandparent isn't always smooth. Like any new territory, it may take a while to become familiar with the new boundaries.

Yet a much more fundamental process is also taking place which is likely to have an even greater influence on your life and that of your child. Having children, especially your first, throws your relationship with your own parents into sharp relief. Suddenly you can see life from a parent's perspective and how that affects you will depend on your own experience of childhood. Many people find their understanding and respect for their parents increases dramatically. For others it is a disturbing time, when old wounds are opened and memories revisited. For many more it is a mixture of both.

Children learn from example and as far as parenting is concerned you become a parent from the dysfunctional family you grew up in.

Cheryl Walters, psychoanalytic psychotherapist and Head of Research at
Parentline Plus

Whatever your experience, you can use your heightened awareness of your own parents' strengths and weaknesses to consider how you would like to raise your child. What was it about how your parents raised you that you enjoyed or benefited from in your childhood, and how could you give the same gift to your child? What would you like to do differently?

I think most of the problems do come from an adult's own parenting as a child. So when you are faced with a tricky situation you will often say exactly what your mother would have said to you, for better or worse. It can be quite a shock. In the absence of parent education what else do people have to base their parenting on?

Eileen Hayes, parenting advisor to the NSPCC

It helps to be aware that the areas of our upbringing that we found most difficult are often the areas we find difficult to negotiate with our own children. If you were disciplined harshly, for example, you may repeat this instinctively or avoid even necessary firmness. Addressing this balance and breaking away from old patterns and reactions may demand honesty, courage and strength. At the very least, it may require us to consider new approaches to help us raise our children as we wish.

If you think your upbringing wasn't that bad you'll do something similar yourself. Some people with unhappy memories will be fairly determined to make it different for their children. Others repeat the things that were painful to them as children and say things like, 'I got hit and it didn't do me any harm.' I find the most useful thing to do in these situations is ask the parent how they actually feel when they smack their child now. Nine times out of ten they will be honest and say they feel wretched and then they begin to see there is little to gain from repeating it.

Carol Ann Hally, health visitor, clinical practice teacher

Siblings

When I first saw him I thought he was great. Now he's bigger I'm not so sure.

Josie, aged eight

My two brothers are really irritating but they can be funny. Sometimes I'm quite glad I've got them.

Fiona, aged eleven

How siblings get along matters to our children and to us. Their relationships with each other are often the longest of their lives. The bond between them can determine the nature of our family life and help shape their experiences of childhood and the people they'll become.

Groundbreaking research over the last two decades offers new insights into how parents can help their children fight less, flourish as individuals and develop happy, supportive relationships as they grow. This is a huge subject – so huge we've written a book on it (see p.450). Clearly, we can't distil its entire contents into one section. But we can consider many of its key messages, that families themselves and those who work with them say really make a difference.

A new baby

You have to do more for the baby because he needs more doing, but in the other children's eyes you aren't being fair. However hard you try, in their eyes they're losing out.

Dan L

The arrival of a new baby will turn a child's life upside down. Children often find change disturbing (see Feelings and Fears, p.124) and there aren't many periods of family change more significant than this. Yet there are many things parents can do to ease the transition and to help the older child feel better about the baby's arrival.

Prepare the way

All I remember was my mother holding this thing in her arms that was lying in my place. I was the youngest of seven and known as 'Baby Maloney'. My mother said, 'Come here, you can hold her', and I really didn't want to and said so. That morning the shopkeeper greeted me with 'And you're not Baby Maloney any more!' I felt so confused. I thought, 'Who am I? I am Baby Maloney, I haven't changed.'

Brigid Treacy, parenting advisor

Talking to our children about what life may be like and how they might feel when the baby is born – the ups and the downs – won't eradicate distress and jealousy but can really help. Most children love to reminisce about their own infancy and look at photographs and their own 'baby things'. This can help them understand that they had their time being 'babied' even though they can't remember.

Wherever possible, other changes in their lives (in childcare, daily routine etc.) are best kept to a minimum. Involving older children in preparations for the new baby can help, as can understanding when they've had enough 'baby business' and need some attention focused on themselves. Crucially, we need to give older children the chance to ask questions and air anxieties, and we need to explain the nature of love. Many young children think of love as finite, almost like a cake. If a baby comes along, will their slice of love get smaller? Assuring our children that our love for them grows every day and no one could ever take any of it away can help allay very genuine fears.

Use whatever methods you can muster to help your child feel loved and appreciated

Tips suggested by parents include:

- Avoid holding the baby when your child sees you both for the first time after the birth.
- Ask friends not to go straight to the baby when they visit, but first to acknowledge the child.
- Nudge close friends to bring a little gift for the child as well as or instead of one for the baby.
- Involve the child in the day-to-day care as much as age, ability and inclination allow. Carrying nappies and pushing the buggy can make a child swell with pride one day and feel taken for granted the next.
- Share jokes about the baby – how little they can do, the funny faces they make. It's harder to feel threatened by something you can laugh about.
- Make a scrapbook of photographs and mementoes of when the child was a baby. Tell them lots of tales of what they did and how you felt, how you first held them, when they first smiled, so they realise they had this special time, too.
- Go easy on the 'big brother', 'big sister' routines. Children sometimes resent their identity being interwoven and dependent upon the new baby. They are still who they always were, thank you very much.

- Think of things that your child likes doing and that you can do together when you are feeding the baby, so they don't feel pushed away. Perhaps a special book to look at, a special video or a bag you can have nearby containing favourite toys and activities.
- Keep to old routines and habits as much as possible. Insisting a child now dry themselves because you've got your hands full may be perfectly reasonable to you but may feel like rejection to them.
- Put the child first sometimes. There will be many times when the baby requires immediate and preferential care, but there will also be times when they can wait. By sometimes attending to our older child first, we can help redress the dramatic drop in parental attention that most children experience when a new baby's born.
- Have times together without the baby so your child can be heard and feel special and loved.

Understand upset

I was completely unprepared for the anger being directed at me. I had thought so much about how my son needed help when the twins arrived, and how they would need protecting. I hadn't realised that it was me who would need protecting!

Kate K

Almost all children feel some distress and confusion at the arrival of a new brother or sister, and acknowledging this is important: 'It must feel strange sometimes having a new baby in the family. Would you like a cuddle?' (See Feelings and Fears, p.124.)

Many children do resent the baby's arrival and some parents find this hard to understand. If you're one of them, consider this tale, told to many parents in many versions: 'A man comes home to his beloved wife and says, "Darling, I love you so much and life with you is so good that I've decided to have a second wife. She's arriving soon, she'll be sleeping where you used to and we'll be one big happy family. Won't it be fun!"' Accepting a new and unrequested family member can be tough.

Understand behaviour changes Sleep problems and regressive or testing behaviour are very common. That's the bad news. The good news is that for most children, the peak of unco-operative or disruptive behaviour passes in the first two or three months.

Children feel more secure when they know what's expected of

Brothers and sisters

A study of the calls to ChildLine showed that 14% of children ringing about their family relationship problems discussed anxieties about siblings.

Some 6% of those calling about family problems believed their parents favoured a sister or brother.

them, so testing behaviour needs handling kindly but firmly: 'I know life feels a bit strange with a new baby and you know you're not to shout.' Regressive behaviour – slipping back in toilet training, wanting to be carried, have a bottle, be treated 'like a baby' – tends to diminish over time, and does so more quickly when parents are understanding and calm. It's often easier on everyone to go along with 'baby' behaviour until it fades.

I thought there would be no fallout because he was so much younger and because they obviously adored him, but it comes out in other ways. They have never taken it out on him but my younger daughter became much more clingy, desperate to be a baby, even saying she wanted her arms and legs cut off to make her small. My eldest daughter became a manic tidier, quite obsessive.

Marina C

Nurture the new relationship

This idea helped us so much. We'd planned for the rivalry, but we hadn't really thought about how the children could enjoy each other.

Kate W

Encouraging affection and showing older children that there's fun to be had in their relationship with the new baby can begin in their first days together. Talking about how the baby might be feeling, chatting about how babies show emotions and commenting on the baby's responses to the child will help develop affection and interest between them: 'Look, he's watching you.' 'He sounds upset. Maybe he's tired or needs a feed.' 'She's smiling! She loves you stroking her like that' (see Understanding your Baby, p.9).

Many children find joint 'play' with the baby hilarious, such as 'reflecting back' the baby's noises and expressions. This can begin in their first weeks. We can help by showing them how to do it and noticing when they do it themselves: 'Look, can you see how she sticks her tongue out when you do? She's copying you!' As ever, if we show appreciation of the child's sensitive or caring responses to the baby, we're likely to get more (see Positive Power, p.115).

Look after ourselves Looking after a new baby is physically and emotionally demanding and looking after a new baby *and* an older child or children is even more so. Yet only by looking after ourselves – eating regularly and well; catching up with sleep and rest when we can; accepting offers of genuine help and support – will we have the reserves we need to care for our children and their developing relationships.

Build bonds

Encourage play Fun and fantasy play helps children feel good about themselves and their brothers and sisters. It develops understanding of siblings' feelings – the bedrock of considerate relationships. We can encourage shared fun, first by showing the older child what games the young child enjoys then, as they grow, creating opportunities for free play to unfold.

Appreciate property principles Children do not like other children messing with their things without permission. Especially if that person happens to be a younger brother or sister. Precious possessions can be accorded special status and this can be explained to siblings and friends: 'This teddy is her very special toy, like your fireman's hat is to you, and no one can play with it unless they ask her first.'

Remember, turn-taking with toys is often an easier concept for children to grasp than sharing (see Refusing to Share, p.186).

Encourage concern and co-operation Talking about feelings as a family helps children understand each other's feelings and views (see Feelings and Fears, p.124). We can also treat our children as we would like them to treat each other. Fun joint activities, such as building a camp or making a cake, can help them see the benefits of co-operation. We can also help them build their skills to problem-solve, compromise and sort out their own disputes: 'I know this is your car, but Daniel's really upset. Can you think of anything else he might like to play to cheer him up?'

Notice the good times Even children who fight often will have occasional flashes of co-operative play or considerate behaviour. Our job is to spot those moments and comment on them, rather than focusing our attention on the grotty behaviour. Descriptive praise (see p.115) is a very powerful tool in promoting positive relationships.

Establish family rules And explain when these are applied differently because of age. Once children realise they are not being singled out for unfair treatment, they may moan a little less (see Rules and Boundaries, p.199).

Let all voices be heard Every child in the family should be able to express their feelings and views. We can help by encouraging family discussions, asking opinions of all, educating our children to listen to others and making talking and listening more comfortable for children who find direct communication hard (see Communication, p.89).

Explore emotions

Understand feelings between brothers and sisters A child may tell a sibling 'I hate you!' and the next minute be playing happily together. Because brothers and sisters know each other so well, they know precisely where to aim when putting the boot in. This means they can wind each other up more effectively than possibly any one else on earth. Intense, volatile, fast-changing and often negative emotions are not a sure sign of a problematic relationship but rather the flip side of an intense and intimate relationship.

Acknowledge how children feel This is the surest way of letting children know we've got the message: 'You seem a bit sad. Are you feeling left out?' They are then less likely to 'act out' their feelings in their behaviour.

Encourage constructive expression 'How can you let her know you don't like that, in a way she'll understand and won't get you into trouble?' From a young age, children can be encouraged to express their views, and reminded that they haven't got free rein to express them however they choose. Chucking the contents of the toy box around the room is no substitute for stating opinions.

Explore our feelings as parents We will have different bonds with our different children. We should take care this doesn't translate into overt and long-term preferential treatment. A child who feels less loved or favoured will resent their siblings, possibly for life. Some one-to-one time with each child can work wonders, helping them feel treasured and appreciated. Perhaps you could read together while the other child sleeps, go shopping together while their brother or sister is cared for by a trusted friend or relative – anything to give you a chance to spend relaxed time with each of your children on their own, simply enjoying each other's company.

Tackle sibling conflict

It's so easy to think of sibling rivalry as abnormal behaviour. It might be maddening but it's perfectly normal. I'm 32 and a mother myself, yet my 35-year-old brother has the ability to annoy me to a greater extent and in a shorter time than anyone else I know. And I think we both still watch the amount of concern, time and attention our parents give us, just to check we're not missing out.

Lucy D

Parents used to be advised to leave battling siblings to it. Extensive research – tried and tested by parents themselves – now indicates that it's much more helpful for parents to intervene constructively when children can't sort out disputes. This doesn't mean acting as our children's referee. If we act as judge and jury, deciding guilt and what happens next, our children won't learn to handle disputes on their own. Rather it requires us to help our children consider both sides of any argument and search for solutions that make everybody happy, rather than caving in or battling to the death over every contested toy (see Searching for Solutions, p.222).

Of course, this won't eradicate sibling conflict. Any attempt to quash all squabbles between children is doomed to failure. Yet children can be astonishingly creative, resourceful and capable of problem-solving when given the chance. Teaching them how to negotiate and compromise gives them skills for life, and helps us by reducing the number and intensity of sibling rows.[51]

Look behind the scenes Only when we've looked at the possible causes of conflict can we judge what needs to be done to solve it. What are the triggers? How our children behave towards each other, or how we behave? Are their arguments a symptom of other stresses or worries? We may have to attend to other aspects of our children's lives before we can expect their behaviour towards each other to improve.

Test the temperature Assessing the temperature of any conflict can help us decide when and how to intervene. Is the argument cooling down without our help? Is it getting heated, so children need a prompt to think the problem through? Is it so boiling with anger and aggression that they need to be separated and allowed to calm down before any talking starts?

Be constructive Intervention should be adapted to suit the heat of the moment (see above) but follows the same basic structure:

> **Define the problem** 'We've got one bike and you both want it.'
> **Describe the feelings** 'Looks like you're both getting angry.'
> **Search for solutions** 'How can you sort this out so you're both
> happy?'

Children often come up with compromises themselves, but if they're struggling or too young to think the situation through without our help, we can suggest options to choose from: 'You could take turns, perhaps a minute each; or maybe one of you would like to use the roller skates; or you could play something else [suggest ideas they may both enjoy]?'

Talk Once tempers have cooled the real work starts. Encourage children to think through what they did, the effects it had and how they could behave differently next time. If you are pleased at how they resolved the problem, say so.

Beware of bullying Disputes are a normal and healthy part of growing up with a brother or sister. One child habitually dominating or bullying the other is not. Bullying between siblings can cause life-long damage to all children involved. If we see such patterns emerging, it's vital that we support each child, help them break free from their roles as 'aggressor' and 'victim' and work out more constructive ways of behaving (see Assertion v. Aggression, p.368 and Bullying, p.374).

Parents are not always effective at sorting out the envy and jealousy between siblings. Yet if you do not recognise, say, that one child is being bullied by an older sibling, or do nothing about it, you are being deficient as parents. The basic message must always be that everyone in the family is valuable and treated with respect. Children will often not complain about being bullied in the family because they know they will not be heard or they are aware that the parents have favourites. As a parent you do need to look at what you are doing and be honest about that. We have to work at getting along with each other and accepting our differences.

Dr Dorothy Rowe, psychologist and writer

Avoid pigeonholes

The very fact that they are children in the same family makes siblings vulnerable to comparison and labelling: 'He was a good baby, she's a nightmare'; 'She's the sporty one, he's more academic'; 'He's just like his dad but she's more like me.' All labels are limiting, but if a child is compared to a sibling and found lacking too often, they can feel crushed (see Ripping up Labels, p.119).

Respect each child's individuality We need to respond to each child as a unique individual, distinct from siblings and stereotypes and from their or our past.

Avoid treating siblings 'the same' Our children have different experiences, strengths and vulnerabilities. They will need us at different times and in different ways.

I learnt from experience that 'the same' is not necessarily fair or helpful. I used to treat my children identically and it never worked – only the one whose needs I happened to meet was happy. I'm amazed I did this for so long because as a child I remember wanting to be treated differently from my sister but I forgot completely when I became a parent. House rules are applied equally to all, but beyond that I love them all differently but equally and consistently.

Brigid Treacy, parenting advisor

Beware comparisons and labels Pigeonholing children or judging them in relation to their brothers and sisters can crush a child's sense of worth and fuel sibling resentments.

Celebrate difference If, as a family, we tolerate and respect the differences between our children, and help them see that no one person has a monopoly on any particular trait and that most of us are a mixture of many, we'll help them clash less often and cope better when they do.

Let each child shine

I've got twins and in one school assembly my daughter was a star turn, reading the story and sitting centre-stage. Her twin brother's job was to bang a chime. Once. I could have cried for him. But when I met them both afterwards he was brimming with pride saying, 'Did you see me? Did you see me? I banged it!' He knew his sister could read when he couldn't but he was more concerned with what he'd done right. The worrying thing was that if he hadn't said it I might have been full of sympathy and said, 'Never mind'. He didn't want that, he wanted praise for what he had achieved, not attention and sympathy for what he hadn't.

Jane P

By appreciating each child's special qualities and interests, we can help each experience 'success' in their own terms. This reduces the risk of damaging rivalries and resentments.

Praising without reference to anyone or anything else – 'That's great. You must be so pleased' – can encourage a reticent or considerate child to admit pleasure in their own efforts and achievements. Ask children what they feel best about or what they most enjoyed, rather than what they achieved, did 'right' or got 'wrong'. Look for what you appreciate about each child, and let each child know 'you are special to me because you are you'.

Childcare

It's easy to underestimate the difficulties of getting childcare right. Some parents find looking after children quite easy and don't realise that not everybody does, so they will leave their child with someone who is too young to cope on a full-time basis. Some others are just scared. A lot of first-time mothers put off doing anything about childcare until not long before they are due back to work. They are scared of handing their child over at all, so end up doing something at the last minute. Choosing childcare is a very difficult process and the sooner you start it the better for you and your child because you will increase your options.

Sue Monk, Parents At Work

One morning I heard my daughter absentmindedly call the childminder 'Mummy'. It hurt, but then I knew she felt relaxed and secure.

Claire T

Childcare is a big one. Tears, disturbed nights, anxiety. And that's just you. Choosing someone to care for your child in your absence is one of the most important decisions parents make, yet the right care can be hard to find and even harder to finance.

If you don't go back to paid employment when your child is young, let no one say you have 'given up work': raising children is one of the most important and valuable jobs any person could undertake. If you do need to return – and that need could be for financial or personal reasons; both are valid and important to recognise – your task is to find the very best deputy your finances and circumstances allow.

No one route is the only right one. Each has advantages and drawbacks and which you eventually choose will depend on your needs and those of your child and family, where you live, how much support you have from others and how much you can afford. But remember that money is not the only determinant of quality: much reasonable-cost care is excellent, some high-cost care is no good at all.

All young children need to feel they are truly 'cared' for in their parents' absence, so search for a caregiver who recognises your child's emotional as well as physical needs. This is your child's most important relationship outside the family in the early years, and it is the responsibility of every parent to give it their very best shot.

Childcare and child development

Many parents, particularly mothers, still seem deeply anxious about whether the care of children outside the family home, however good it is, can be good enough. Yet the main conclusion of researchers is that good quality services are not harmful. More than this, good quality childcare can bring positive benefits: both parents are able to work and the family enjoys a better standard of living. And children may end up with the best of both worlds — the love and uniqueness of private family life, and being part of a community of adults and other children.

Peter Elfer, Elinor Goldschmied and Dorothy Selleck[52]

Surprise, surprise. Research shows that children require sensitive care, appropriate to their age and needs, from a small number of people.

'The idea that very young children can only develop healthily if they have one and only one caretaker, the mother, throughout the day, has now been clearly rejected by research,' explain respected childcare research specialists Peter Elfer and Dorothy Selleck. 'However, the importance of reliable, responsible and responsive adults is still strongly supported by research as well as clinical evidence.'

This view is echoed in the recent review of relevant research over 40 years by the Institute of Education.[53] The key, the review states, is not whether it is the mother or another who cares for the child but rather the *quality* of the care. 'Family life,' it adds, 'continues to be the most important influence on young children's development, even when they receive substantial amounts of non-parental care.'

One of the most important things is that care is sensitive and responsive to a child's needs. Children need to know that the person looking after them cares about them, is interested in them and respects them as an individual. This can be done in so many ways, for example sharing their pleasure by smiling and laughing with them; talking to them about what they are doing; not forcing them to eat when they don't want to; showing them how to button their coat; recognising when they are feeling a little under the weather and would probably prefer a quiet time rather than a trip to the playground.

Ann Mooney, researcher at the Thomas Coram Research Unit, Institute of Education, University of London, author of *Choosing Childcare*

One-to-one or nursery care?

I work in a relatively affluent area, where many parents seem to view childminders as a poorer choice of childcare than a nursery. Yet the nature of the relationship with a childminder, where they build up a one-to-one relationship in a family environment however different from yours, is still usually more natural for a young child.

Carol Ann Hally, health visitor, clinical practice teacher

Would your child fare better in a home environment or at a nursery? With one-to-one care or in a group setting? Different children respond differently to the same surroundings and your child's age, character, particular needs and ability to interact with other children will all influence your final decision.

If you are considering a nursery, check out its ability to care for your child's age group. Some take babies from as young as six weeks, but babies and very young children need be looked after by one, or at the most two key carers throughout the day. This 'key person' system should in effect offer your child a parent substitute – someone who has the time, concern and dedication to get to know your child well, focus on their emotional and physical needs, understand their 'signals' (see Understanding your Baby, p.9) and develop a caring and responsive bond.

Clearly, carers need sufficient contact time to respond to and play

Choice and circumstance

Childcare provision has improved in recent years but still has a very long way to go. At least 58% of women with a child under five[54] and 78% of women with children aged 6–13 work outside the home, yet the cost of good quality childcare in Britain remains among the highest in Europe.[55]

The traditional model of the family, comprising two parents, only one of whom goes out to work, now accounts for less than a quarter of all UK families with dependent children.[56]

Two out of three working mothers in one recent study relied on family and friends to look after their children.[57] Three-quarters of parents say that working parents cannot find enough childcare. Almost 40% of employees have dependent children but only 5% of workplaces offer nursery places.

with children of any age (see Building Relationships, p.298). Yet this is especially important for babies and children who are too young to ask for what they want or make their needs clear in a group setting.

Preparing the way

He had to be pulled off me, limb by limb. He found it traumatic and so did I, but this was the only nursery in our area and it was this or nothing. It had to work because I had to work and, I think especially with your first child, you feel powerless to do things differently.

Fiona M

Those initial few weeks are probably the most important period in building the childcare relationship. For everyone's sake, especially the child's, parents must try to manage them as well as they possibly can.

Sue Monk, Parents At Work

Most children are unsettled when their parents go back to work and will show it. View the situation from their perspective and it is easier to understand their upset and anger: they are having to adjust to times without you. Yet also understand that their distress does not mean they will suffer lasting damage. Separation anxiety is a perfectly normal reaction and can usually be negotiated successfully and sympathetically (see Separation Anxiety, p.140). If parents and carers are patient, loving and understanding, most children settle into their new routine.

If you have any choice about when you go back to work, it may help to remember that children tend to become more wary of strangers and new situations at around one year old. This process can begin as early as nine months, and can last until the child is about three. Whatever time you return to work, there is much you can do to minimise your child's distress:

Prepare well Spend as much time as you can with your chosen carer before leaving your child in their charge. Once you've all got to know each other better, go slow. First leave your child for just a short while and increase the time away gradually, reassuring your child each time that you will return. Good individual carers and nurseries should allow time for this. If they don't, ask why not.

Options and questions

The lessons from recent high-profile cases are that no amount of protection is a 100% guarantee of safety. Parents have to be aware that choosing childcare is one of the most important things they will do in their lives. This requires them to get well-informed, to allow as much time and to ask as many questions as possible.

Sue Monk, Parents At Work

If your childcare falls apart, everything else falls apart. It's as simple as that. If I know anything now it is that it is essential to ask all the questions up front, to see as many people and places as you can. Because if it does break down, or if it's just not good enough, it can be damned hard to pick up the pieces.

Diane T

Your basic childcare options are

— **Childminder** Usually a mother herself. Care based in her own home and may look after other children. By law, must be police-checked, registered and vetted by social services staff.
— **Day nursery** Quality, availability and fees vary hugely. Most are not suited to the needs of babies or very young children (see One-to-one or Nursery Care?, p.292).
— **Nanny** Care based in your home. Most have childcare experience and/or qualification. Expensive, although nanny shares are sometimes possible. Don't rely on nanny agencies to check references. You must do this yourself.
— **Au pair, mother's help** Generally young, untrained and inexperienced; not recommended for sole charge, particularly of pre-school children.
— **After-school clubs** Quality is very patchy, ranging from excellent to poor. Visit and judge for yourself.
— **Relatives** Will this be as reliable as you need? Do you share similar views on caring for children?

Issues to raise when questioning potential carers

— Relevant training and experience.
— Their attitudes to childcare, including issues of discipline (What behaviour is expected? How is this encouraged? What happens when children 'misbehave'?); distress (How do they comfort children when upset? etc.); food; free and structured play, and safety.

— The structure of your child's day.

— Continuity of care. This is very important for young children. How long do carers expect to remain in post? If you are considering a nursery, how long has it been open? What is its staff turnover rate?

— Availability of/access to facilities.

— Age and number of other children in their care.

— How will any questions and concerns you have be respected and addressed?

Questions to ask yourself

— How did the care environment look? Feel? Sound? Atmosphere is important. Did children there seem happy? Did it appear to be child-centred, relaxed and friendly? Did the carer(s) seem happy, approachable and sensitive to children's needs?

— Do they welcome discussion of your child's individual development, needs and care? Children fare best in settings where carers adapt their schedules to children's individual rhythms, where parent involvement is welcomed and information is shared with parents on a daily basis.

— Will your child be given the care, affection and individual attention they require? How will the carer respond to their particular needs and habits? Will your child be read to? Cuddled? Taken to the park? Allowed to draw and paint and enjoy messy play?

— Respect your instincts. Do you like her?

Trust her? Feel confident your child will be fine in her care?

References

You must personally contact the parents of children cared for by your prospective carer, preferably over the last three to five years. Be wary of any gaps in CVs.

Have you seen all relevant certificates and checked registration details, including terms of registration (including numbers and ages of children permitted and, for nurseries, staff/child ratios)? Your local social services department should be able to supply these.

Information

Full details of options, questions and the latest regulations can be obtained from support groups such as the Daycare Trust and Parents At Work (see Contacts, p.429).

The under-eights officer at your local social services department can provide advice and information on childcare options in your area. Talk to other parents, staff, carers.

Let your child meet their potential carer and watch how they behave together before you make any final decision; you will know much from their responses to each other.

Ask as many questions as you need to be reassured. This can feel strange, even rude, but it is very important that you do. No carer worth the name would take offence at what is only evidence of parental concern and care.

Give the carer as much information as possible about your child's routine, likes and dislikes, medical information, emergency numbers, etc. Also share what you know of your baby or child's communication 'signals' (see Understanding your Baby, p.9) and how they like to be comforted. Taking along your child's favourite comfort toy may help. Some parents like to write down important information in a notebook to give to the carer. Whatever you choose, try to get into the habit of exchanging information about what your child has been doing, and about their responses and feelings, and aim to build time for this into your routines.

Information exchange is especially important when children are too young to speak for themselves. It is also fundamental to establishing the triangle of trust and communication between parent, child and carer.

Babies can sense who is familiar and who is not, and they need to get to know a small number of carers, which takes time. They need exclusive relationships with these people who know them very well and who can understand how they express themselves. Toddlers also suffer if someone they are close to, whether parent or carer, suddenly disappears. They are very sensitive to disruption in the routines of their care, and the rhythm of their day should be respected.

Royal College of Paediatrics and Child Health[58]

Try to separate your anxieties from your child's Children will be OK if the care is good and they are supported through these early stages. They need to know their parents have confidence in the new care arrangements, so do your best not to crumple.

After settling your child, perhaps engaging them in an activity with their carer, reassure them that you'll be back later, say goodbye gently and go. Returning on a piece of elastic for yet more hugs and kisses is likely to make them more anxious if they think you are unsure about leaving them. Children look to us for cues about how to interpret situations. If we act worried, they'll worry and have a harder time separating from us. If appropriate, we can let our children know we understand how they feel and that we know their carer will comfort them after we have gone.

Your response as a parent needs to be sensitive and accepting that your child feels like that, to let them cry and to not try to shut them up or to get angry. Ensure the carer is sympathetic to the child's feelings, too. Those feelings are not going to damage the child. What may be damaging is the response of the parent or carer to those feelings. To be cross, unkind, dismissive or cold is going to do the damage.

Linda Connell, trainer in communication skills for parents and health professionals

Be honest It may seem easier in the short term to sneak out on occasions without saying goodbye, but this is likely to create insecurity and backfire big-time. Children experience this as a breach of trust. Many find it frightening. It also sends the message that parents find it hard to face up to the separation, that it's somehow 'wrong'. It will be far better all round to give a clear message that they'll be fine and that you look forward to seeing them when you come back.

Reassure yourself No carer worth the name could object to you phoning during the day to check your child's progress. Arrive a little early for pick-up sometimes; wait where you can hear or watch your child unseen. You needn't feel embarrassed about checking all is going as it should – your child's happiness and safety depend on your vigilance.

While it is true that a small child who separates reluctantly may seem 'fine as soon as you've left' nobody should assume that it will be, or was so. Someone who knows the child well should, ideally, look in after a few minutes, without being seen by him. And however happy he seems, the childcare worker or teacher should stay in close contact and try to ensure that the child's private experience does not belie his public armour.

The Commission on Children and Violence[59]

He always cried when I left, which was turning me inside out. So my childminder suggested I waited outside the front door, where he couldn't see me but I could hear him. It didn't stop immediately, it took a minute or so for him to settle, but at least I went to work knowing he was OK. After that, I'd phone from work. I would hear him in the background, jabbering away quite happily. It made me feel much better about the whole thing.

Laura B

Establish routines and rituals Adherence to familiar routines and set times for arrival and pick-up help children feel more secure; and this may require home routines adapting slightly if the caregiver's ability to adapt is limited. Very young children may find comfort in having something of their mother's with them, especially to sleep with (a T-shirt or a pyjama top that smells of you is perfect!). With older

Building relationships

Our children need close relationships and attachment to those who care for them in our absence. In a nursery setting, one 'key person' should be responsible for our child's emotional and physical care, getting to know them very well, helping them manage through the day and spending time together, playing and enjoying each other's company. Whenever possible, this should be the same person who greets your child when you drop them off in the morning.

'Most nurseries will have a key-person system, but the important issue is whether the nursery has really thought through what this means in terms of the relationship between that person and your child,' explain childcare researchers Peter Elfer and Dorothy Selleck. 'Some staff view it as an entirely administrative system while, at the other end of the scale, some nurseries take it to mean somebody who is key in your child's life.

'As parents you may have mixed feelings about this, due to the difficulty for you of your child becoming very attached to another. But this is desperately needed by a young child or baby. They need someone reliable who they are familiar with and who they can count on, who will make a relationship with them.

'So look closely – is there someone who will spend most of their time with your child, who will receive your child in the mornings, manage most of his physical needs throughout the day and build a relationship with him? Times when your child is anxious or in need of emotional reassurance will be frequent throughout the day, and the ability of the key person to "tune in" and be emotionally available most of the time is very important.

'It would be quite inappropriate for nurseries to make close relationships with children unless parents are very much part of that triangle, otherwise it may lead to all sorts of feelings of envy, jealousy and exclusion on the parents' part.

'Parents need to be involved and they have a right to a regular flow of information about what is happening while they are at work. If your child is cared for by many people in the day, it is more difficult for any one member of staff to give you proper feedback, and this is no good for you or your child.'

children, try to explain clearly what is going to happen and when you will be back, and stick to it.

Some children respond well to parting rituals such as waving out of the window – it helps them feel they are part of a process that ends with their parent's return.

Watch and listen to your child – and encourage others to do the same

When you drop your child off at nursery and they're crying and the teacher says, 'Don't cry, it will only upset Mummy,' that child will generally keep crying. If instead they say, 'It feels sad to say goodbye' the child relaxes because they feel understood. The mum or teacher can then say, 'It's also nice to say "See you later."'

Susie Orbach, psychotherapist and writer

If your child doesn't seem to be settling, talk to the carer about why this may be. Distress is normal, and children feel most reassured when this is acknowledged rather than ignored (see Feelings and Fears, p.124). If, however, you feel that the chemistry between carer and child just isn't right, it is time to look at other care arrangements. Also be aware that you may need different sorts of care as your child grows or your circumstances change. Respect your instinct as well as your intellect to tell you when arrangements need to change – what 'feels' right is as important as what is right in theory.

Parents mustn't let their feelings be crowded out by all the anxieties of going back to work and being professional to the extent that they become insensitive to the signals coming from the child. If you know in your heart of hearts that it is not right and your child is unhappy, there is no magic solution but you do need to get out as quickly as possible before it escalates. If the childcarer herself doesn't seem to be handling it, it probably isn't going to work either. That's the time to put your energy into looking for alternatives.

Sue Monk, Parents At Work

When you find childcare you are pleased with, remember to tell the carer. Happiness is infectious and a happy, appreciated carer is a great asset. Treat her with all the admiration due someone who is looking after your child as you wish and as your child needs. You will still need to keep her informed about how you like things to be done for your child, but if she is helping make your life work and your child feel loved, she deserves your praise and respect.

Important relationships: a quick reminder

We can extend our care for our children by recognising the importance of other relationships in and around the family, showing concern and regard for their bonds with others and the role we play in these.

- **Our relationship with our partner** Parenthood changes relationships. Recognising this, and occasionally prioritising your needs as a couple, will help all family members. Some conflict is a fact of family life. How we handle this shapes how our children feel about themselves and how they handle conflict in their own lives.
- **Role of fathers** Working patterns, economic pressures and changing family structures mean many fathers don't spend the time with their children they'd wish. But the more involved that caring dads can be, the greater difference they will make to their sons and daughters.
- **Lone parenting** One parent can bring up children happily and healthily, but it's hard work. The support of trusted friends, relations and others can ease some of the pressures and provide children with important role models and, importantly, someone else to talk to and to listen to them.
- **Divorce and separation** Be alert to the difference in children's emotional needs and your own. They need to know they are not to blame for family breakdown, and be allowed to love their mum and dad whatever changes in the parental relationship.
- **Stepfamilies and family change** Happy families come in all shapes and sizes. Take care to support children with understanding, respect and patience. Step-parents will need to work at establishing a relationship with each child, but until that's done it is best to leave tough parental duties such as discipline to the parents.
- **Grandparents** They play a central role in many children's lives, providing practical support and unconditional love. Thinking through their strengths and weak spots as parents can help us clarify how we would like to raise our own children.
- **Siblings** Brothers and sisters can influence how children feel about themselves for life. Siblings resent each other, fight, fall out, and also

share affection and fun. All are opportunities for us to help them learn about sharing, caring and coping with conflict in the family and beyond.

- **Childcare.** One of the most important decisions we ever take. A carer who knows a child well and can recognise and respond to their individual needs is important at any age, but essential for babies and young children. If you choose a nursery setting, ensure they have a key-person system in place.

CHAPTER NINE

GENDER AND DEVELOPMENT

How we relate to our children as boys or girls, and how they view their own gender, will influence the rest of their lives and their future relationships. That much is obvious. What's been far less clear over recent years, as parents are bombarded with new information about gender differences and development, is how we can best use this information to help our kids.

A different look at difference

It's really important with all children to let them be who they are. If we've learned one thing from 30 years of feminism, it's not to put kids in boxes according to gender. If a girl wants to play soccer, or a boy wants to write poetry and look after young children, then that is wonderful. At the same time, we have also been learning lately what all parents always knew – that most boys and most girls are different. Knowing the differences actually makes our parenting more individual and sensitive.

Steve Biddulph, psychologist and author

Children explore and examine gender roles throughout their growing up, almost trying them on for size to see how they fit and feel. If you are reading this while your pre-adolescent son is booting a ball or your daughter is applying nail varnish, or if your young daughter is attacking a bush with a water pistol or your son is swathed in glitter and netting, you won't have much time to muse on the latest twists in the gender and genetics debate. So let's cut to what the most recent and valuable research tells us. Which, as so often happens, is what most parents knew in the first place.

Boys and girls are born different Small genetic differences appear to influence how boys and girls think and behave. Other biological differences between the genders, including brain chemistry and even pre-natal hormonal influences, could also affect behaviour and development.

Biological differences need to be recognised but kept in perspective Blaming genetics alone for children's behaviour is not only daft but also potentially damaging as it lets adults off the hook. 'It's all in the genes' or 'Girls will be girls' may make headlines but don't make for constructive social policy or successful parenting.

At different times over recent years, public concern has focused on one gender or another. What is clear is that both genders need our love, support and informed understanding as they grow. Boy and girls thrive in homes where there is acceptance and acknowledgement of feelings and views, good communication, understanding of development, constructive guidance and emotional warmth.

Parental responses

Susie Orbach, psychotherapist

Much of the modern genetics debate is just a way of not taking responsibility. In fact, we do have an enormous influence as parents on what kind of relationship is possible with our children. Our children are a set of possibilities with which we engage, bringing all of who we are to our parenting.

Every way in which we bring ourselves to infants is imbued with a sense of our and their gender. Whether we realise it or not, most parents coo in a different pitch and tone depending whether the infant is male or female. We hold baby boys for longer periods of time than baby girls. We tend to breastfeed boys for longer, wean them later and each feeding period is longer than it is for girls. We potty train boys later.

On the other hand, we have proto-conversations with girls earlier and for longer periods of time. We encourage boys' physicality while bringing a certain reticence to girls, still. Differences such as these are based on our internal sense of what masculinity and femininity mean, what they elicit in us and what we try to confirm about our own sense of gender through the unconscious imposition of nuanced behaviour towards baby girls and baby boys.

Differences in how boys and girls are treated, by parents and society in general, will have a huge bearing on each child's self-image, expectations, aspirations and actions. Whether 'masculine' and 'feminine' behaviour traits have their roots in nature or nurture, they are certainly moulded by parental influence and cultural learning – how children are brought up, what they are exposed to and how they are expected to be.

Gender stereotypes are just that: sweeping generalisations. At various times in their growing up, some girls may like frocks; others are happiest in leggings climbing trees. Some boys like football or to shrug rather than talk, others are great communicators or cringe at the thought of competitive games. Tying our children to our own expectations of gender-related behaviour helps no one. As our knowledge of gender differences and similarities increases, parents have the chance to use this information sensitively, sensibly and constructively – to understand our own children's development better and thus respond to their needs.

We know from research and experience that boys tend to be more physically active, more action-oriented, less reflective and less receptive than girls. It is not, however, the prerogative of boys to be active or girls to be reflective, but there are trends that way and these can be exaggerated by parents' expectations. There are also differences in the pace at which they grow up. But we should be careful to remember the huge similarities between the genders. Children of both sexes are growing up with common experiences and common anxieties and as human beings we share a lot more similarities than differences.

Peter Wilson, child psychotherapist and Director of Young Minds

Understanding parental influence We are sending our children messages about what it is to be male and female all the time, whether we know it or like it or not. Some of these are glaringly obvious: the toys we buy, the clothes we choose, the behaviour we notice and praise, even the names we give our children all speak volumes about our own understandings of masculinity and femininity. Our children will also be acutely aware of the nature of our own gender roles and how we relate to adults of the opposite sex, so be wary of those jokes and throwaway remarks: 'Just like a woman', 'He wouldn't understand, he's a man,' etc. Young children, especially, can take them very seriously.

Other parental messages may be equally powerful but subtle and much harder to identify and evaluate (see Parental Responses, p.303).

Yet an awareness of them, along with an honest acknowledgement of our expectations and prejudices, will help us understand our influence on our children's self-image and behaviour and how we can use that most constructively.

Parents can teach children respect for the opposite sex and their own gender and abilities. The father who shows respect to the mother, for instance, is also teaching his child respect for women generally, and vice versa. This is important not only to help lessen the impact of gender rivalries but also to help children grow into healthy, happy adults capable of happy, healthy relationships.

I do treat them differently even though I try my hardest not to. If I'm honest, I'm tougher on him and I think my wife's stricter with our daughter.

Mark F

It is hard to know where to draw the line. I was never allowed Barbies when I was a kid because my parents considered them sexist. Which they were. But that made me want them all the more. I've let my daughter have them and we've had lots of laughs about how if she was real her ridiculously big boobs would make her fall over, but whether that's a sensible compromise or a cop-out I've no idea.

Megan T

Helping boys

Childhood can seem complicated enough without gender issues thrown in, but they exist and it is only common sense to recognise and deal with them effectively. The first important step for parents is to keep these issues in perspective.

There are genuine concerns about boys' abilities and opportunities to express how they feel, and there are known developmental differences that may make boys' early years at school harder to negotiate. Girls, once the object of boys' derision, are outstripping them academically and seem increasingly able to take their place and state their case. At the same time, facets of 'masculine' behaviour once considered positive, such as physicality and emotional reserve, are increasingly viewed as problems to be negotiated or overcome.

As adult men deliberate the latest media constructs of modern

It's different for boys

Steve Biddulph, psychologist and author

We are discovering some really important differences that can help us raise boys better. First and foremost has to be the difference in the rate at which boys' brains grow. In a word, they're slower. At birth most boys make less eye contact, smile less at their mum or dad, and we have to be really determined to chatter to them, be social with them, and help them learn to talk and communicate as they grow through to be toddlers. By the age of six, the average boy is still six to 12 months behind the average girl in fine motor skills – holding a pencil or scissors, sitting still to write or read, etc. Boys also develop in a different order to girls.

Girls may need more help to run around, ride bikes, throw a ball and so on. Little boys need help to learn to love. That means chatting, cuddling and playing with them. Not leaving them in front of a TV set. Not putting them in a crèche for long periods if you can avoid it – they are much more prone to separation anxiety and depression than girls. Fathers playing with them, being present and teaching them things is a proven boost to their ability and confidence.

Around the age of six fathers actually become the primary parent in a little boy's eyes. So doing things and going places with Dad really matters. A single mum can raise boys just fine, but trustworthy grandfathers, uncles or teachers taking an interest are very important.

Always allow boys to have their feelings. Give them a hug, and tell them 'Yes, it is very sad' when they are missing a friend who has left, or a pet dies. We want boys who can feel, because then they will be more resilient and less lonely as men. Boys especially love to talk while doing some activity. Teach them housework and do it alongside them, so they can chat about their day. Girls will tend to talk more directly, but boys (and men!) prefer to talk sideways, while sharing a task. We like to do something with our hands while we get our sentences together.

masculinity – are they New Man, New Lad, New Dad or Old Confused? – boys are also bombarded with conflicting messages about what it is to be male. All these issues overlap and, if not managed properly, can combine to make boys uncertain of what is expected of them.

Yet there is much we can do to support boys, negotiate the difficulties and reduce the risks.

Social and learning skills Different speeds and patterns of development between the genders mean many young boys' social and learning skills lag behind girls' of a similar age.

The heavy emphasis on literacy skills in many nursery and primary classes can also create a sense of bias in girls' favour, leaving boys with a misplaced sense of underachievement (see Gender and Schooling, p.312). How our sons negotiate this will depend partly on the sensitivity and ability of their school and teachers, and partly on our support (also see Play and Learning, p.324 and Feelings and Fears, p.124).

Recognising boys' difficulties can lead us to some obvious but often overlooked ways to help. When they start school, many boys still find it hard to sit still. They are bursting with physical energy and want to play with their whole bodies. Some enlightened schools now help by giving children bursts of physical exercise throughout the day to help them settle down and concentrate in class. Because their 'fine motor' skills (their ability to hold and use small objects such as pencils and scissors) lag behind girls, many boys find it easier to use bigger pens and pencils and to use bigger bits of paper in their early school years. They may also find it easier to draw on the floor, rather than sitting at a table for long stretches.

Boys tend to be more competitive and give up more readily if faced with initial 'failure'. In their primary years, they often respond best to lessons that involve short bursts of concentration followed by activities and action to build on skills and give them an experience of success, rather than long periods of sustained concentration.

Communication

The kind of man we want now is changing. We don't need men who can wrestle buffalo. They need to be able to talk!

Steve Biddulph, psychologist and author

Many boys find it difficult to talk about how they feel or to ask for help when they need it. Helping them is one of the most important tasks any parent of a boy can undertake. Boys especially may recoil from intense, face-to-face 'How Do You Feel?' conversations and benefit most from 'sideways' talk: doing an activity together and feeling comfortable in each other's presence while talking (see 'Sideways' talk, p.105).

The expectations and images we transmit to our children in their earliest years are also crucial here – we can't expect our sons to be emotionally literate if we suggest that 'big boys don't cry' and that stoicism is always a virtue. If we respect our children's feelings, they

Boys' talk

Research into the calls made to ChildLine indicates that the feelings and problems boys and girls experience are similar, but that the way they respond to and talk about those problems are very different.

The study[1] found that:

1: Boys appear to find it hard to talk. They think people expect them to look after themselves.

2: All children find it difficult to ask for help but boys especially so. Some seem to see it as a sign of weakness and a failure of their masculinity: 'If I said what I feel, they would call me a wimp'; 'I can't tell anyone about this, they'd laugh at me'; 'If I told my dad, he would just say, "You've got to stand up for yourself."'

3: Boys were more likely to be self-critical about having a problem at all – as if a 'real' boy would have prevented or put a stop to the bullying, assault or domestic violence, or been able to handle loss or family difficulties without feeling overwhelmed. They view the very thing they need most – emotional support and the freedom to talk about their feelings – as yet another aspect of failure.

4: For many boys, confiding in friends is unthinkable.

5: On the whole, girls are encouraged to share their problems. Their concept of self-reliance includes asking for help, while boys' appears to exclude it.

'As boys begin to grow they get more and more affected by what it is to be a boy,' says Mary MacLeod, ChildLine's former Director of Policy and Research and now chief executive of the National Family and Parenting Institute. 'It is as if they consider asking for help and being a boy is a contradiction in terms. There is an expectation in themselves that they ought to handle problems that of course they cannot, for example physical abuse from their fathers.

'It is important not to generalise too much. Some boys, for example, just want the chance to say what they are feeling and both girls and boys need attention given to their feelings. Rather than waiting for children to tell you, you may have to look for other signs that they are not coping, such as not wanting to go to school, becoming short-tempered, nastier to a sibling or parent or simply being on a short fuse.

'When talking to boys about problems, you probably need to get into a more active discussion about options and manage the discussion about feelings in a different way than you would manage it with girls. "How does that feel?" will be far too direct for most boys. You have to give them permission for their feelings, saying for example, "I've heard from lots of other boys in your situation that . . ."'

are more likely to respect their own and those of other people.

A recent ChildLine report detailing a 71% rise in suicide by young men in ten years shows with chilling clarity the pressures on boys and how dangerous it can be for them to bottle up distress.[2] Research also indicates that boys find it especially hard to ask for advice (see Boys Talk, p.308) and are far less likely to use helplines or even their GPs or other health services in adolescence and adulthood. Encouraging our boys to talk about difficulties and seek support when they need it is something that begins in the home and has far-reaching implications for the rest of their lives.[3]

> *Strategies to ensure that boys can communicate their problems should be a priority.*
>
> NCB: *The Forgotten Years*[4]

Physicality Many boys need exercise in the same way that a Labrador needs a walk every day. They have surges of testosterone throughout childhood and adolescence, but it is very high at around four and a half years – just when many are starting school in the UK. Testosterone makes them want to run around, be loud and be active, yet physical exuberance is now often seen as a problem to be contained rather than a childhood joy to be encouraged.

Nowadays, fewer children of either gender are allowed to play out in the street or to roam and run until they come home tired for tea. Boys tend to enjoy team games more than girls, yet in some schools, understandable concerns about boys' physical domination of play spaces[5] have led to ball games such as football being banned or discouraged without the provision of necessary alternatives. Playground space in many schools remains pitifully small and time for exercise and sport has been squeezed out of the school day by other pressures on the curriculum. Which all means that if our sons need action and exercise, it may be up to us to organise it. Try to aim for a kick about in the playground, a walk instead of a car ride, a swim or some other vigorous exercise at least once a day.

Schools can be more or less boy-friendly – it's important to check when choosing a school. Check teachers are comfortable around boys and don't just want to squash them. Boys need firmness and rules, and also they need chances to get exercise and run about, have lessons that are practical and have outdoor sessions. A school we know has 15-minute exercise breaks in the morning before classes start, because so many kids come by bus or car. The boys love it, and it helps them to be calmer in class. The girls love it too.

Steve Biddulph, psychologist and author

Self-image

I was thrilled when he started loving football because I knew he was a gentle child who'd found a way to hold his own in any male peer group.

Madeleine M

While many parents are aware of the inherent dangers of expecting or encouraging 'macho' behaviour in young boys, many still feel ambivalent towards them showing their gentler, more sensitive side. Many still find it easier to be the parent of a 'tomboy' girl than a gentler, less stereotypically 'masculine' boy, perhaps because they still equate emotions with 'feminine' responses and behaviour, and worry their sons will be teased and vulnerable. Recognising our own attitudes and prejudices is the first step to accepting and appreciating our sons for who they are, not who we might find it easier for them to be.

Boys encouraged to bury their feelings and identity may shut down their ability to express them. This will make them less resilient, less assertive of their own needs, and less able to deal with life's knocks constructively (see Feelings and Fears, p.124). Bringing up our boys to be themselves and to talk about feelings will make them less vulnerable, not more so. We can help them view emotional awareness as a strength, not a weakness.

Boys are not helped by the paucity of effective role models in their early years – a working father may see little of his children during the week, most pre-school children mix mainly with women and most primary schools have few male teachers (some have none at all). Try to consider what masculine input your son has in his life and remember that he will have to get his ideas of what it is to be male from somewhere. If it is not from trusted adult males inside and outside the home, it may be from television, videos or the big oik in Year Six.

If there's no good father figure to help the boy learn right from wrong, he'll take his ideas of being male from watching videos and from the gangs he hangs out with. So you can get this artificial sense of what is male.

Steve Biddulph, psychologist and author

Aggression

Violence is overwhelmingly a male problem, and the roots for this appear to be primarily social rather than biological, highlighting the inadequacies of current socialisation of male children, and the promotion of macho male attitudes and models in society . . . Both men and women [should] take trouble to separate ideas about masculinity from the concepts of personal 'toughness' that often relate to violence . . . If boys are taught that they can't cry when their sisters can, it's not surprising if they hit instead. 'Boys will be boys' only if we permit, even encourage, macho attitudes and behaviour.

The Commission on Children and Violence[6]

The male sex hormone, testosterone, increases the tendency towards violent behaviour, but does not mean boys have to be violent. Testosterone levels peak at various stages in a boy's development but the violence to which boys are exposed seems the greatest influence on whether those levels stay high. Boys brought up in non-violent households and in non-violent environments have been found to be no more violent than girls brought up in similar circumstances[7] – parenting and experiences count for much more than gender.

A parent can help a boy be non-violent and more effective in getting what he wants and needs by:

— Listening to him and enabling him to communicate his feelings constructively, so frustration, sadness, apprehension, embarrassment and other emotions do not turn into aggression because they festered without expression (see Feelings and Fears, p.124).
— Building his self-esteem and ability to talk issues through so he doesn't feel he has to hit to have influence (see Communication, p.89 and Friends, p.362).
— Helping him understand the difference between assertion and aggression (see p.368). Assertion involves expressing opinions and needs clearly and effectively, in ways that respect other people. Aggression means expressing them in ways that intimidate, threaten and often backfire.
— Helping him develop his social skills so he can interact with his peers and others more sociably and effectively (see Growing Independence, p.362).
— Role-modelling non-violent behaviour. If our sons see us being aggressive, they'll copy.

Gender and schooling

We are continually seeing in the media that girls are doing brilliantly and boys are doing hopelessly. This kind of reporting is one-sided and can often sound hysterical. There is an equally clear message from research that boys are ambitious and they hit the job market running and never look back. You need to break down the statistics further to make sense of them.

Bethan Marshall, lecturer in Education, Kings College, London

Groundbreaking new research offers fascinating insights into how boys and girls generally respond to schooling. Cutting through the hype to the core messages beneath will help us understand how best to encourage and support our children through their primary school years.

The core messages

— **There are identifiable differences in early years achievement between the genders** Boys lag behind in early literacy skills when they first enter school.[8] Girls tend to outperform boys in every subject in the early school years.[9]

— **The reasons lie in our children, our schools and our homes** Boys' learning skills develop more slowly. This 'gap' is compounded by other factors, including:

1: *The lack of male role models*[10] There are few male primary teachers. Mothers tend to read with their children much more than fathers.

2: *The age at which formal education begins*

There is increasing evidence that starting schooling at four rather than six, as in many other European countries, may disadvantage boys in particular.[11] There seems to be no advantage in terms of general academic achievement to starting so young, and it risks school seeming a struggle from the start, especially for boys. This can be a huge 'turn off'.

3: *Teaching and testing styles* The ways our children are taught tend to favour girls. Influencing factors include teacher expectations, assessment techniques, curriculum bias and what and how teachers reward and discipline.[12]

— **The 'gender divide' continues throughout their schooling** There continues to be a marked difference in performance and subject choice at secondary school.[13] But boys generally go on to perform better in the job market.

— **Some boys seem particularly disadvantaged** A minority of boys are very disaffected by their early learning experiences. They tend not to reach their potential at school and leave at the

These [disaffected] boys are falling by the wayside. What happens in this country is that we start education before most children are ready for it and they find it difficult. Some begin to feel a failure very young and this then creates a fear, a mental block about learning. This is where the problems start.

Bethan Marshall, lecturer in Education, King's College, London

earliest opportunity. The number of boys permanently excluded from school outnumbers girls by more than four to one.[14]

What can parents do?

There is a huge amount parents can do to help both girls and boys.

— **Avoid pushing children too far too soon** Respecting your child's capabilities is crucial, especially in the early years of schooling. No young child should be made to feel a failure. Aim to light the spark, not extinguish it by fanning too fiercely (see Play and Learning, p.324).

— **Provide role models** This is important for any child, but particularly boys. Fathers, uncles, grandads, etc. reading to boys in the early school years will provide a tremendous boost to their literacy and learning skills.

— **Let children experience success**

Praising what your child is good at is a powerful motivator. This may be counting, reading, drawing, telling jokes, caring for a pet, kicking a ball (see Play and Learning, p.324).

— **Build children's sense of worth** (see Feelings and Fears, p.124) It is important that parents let children know they are loved for themselves and not because of the speed with which they pass a developmental milestone or achieve a certain grade. All children, but girls in particular (see Helping Girls, p.315) may need to be reminded that life doesn't begin and end at academic achievement. This balance will boost their confidence to tackle new challenges and will help them cope better with schoolwork, especially when they are struggling.

— **Be observant, supportive and understanding** Parental awareness of children's development and needs is crucial if they are to reach their potential happily and healthily.

Children are individuals but we need to be careful not to push them too young, boys especially. This can cause so many problems, including the feeling of failure which can set up a vicious circle that puts them off education and learning for life.

Clare Mills, co-author of *Britain's Early Years Disaster*[15]

— Providing opportunities for exercise and physical release.
— Being tolerant of rough-and-tumble play. This can be a great way for boys to learn where to draw the line – when boisterous behaviour is OK (when all participants are enjoying it) and when it is not OK (when someone is feeling threatened or hurt by it).
— Setting clear boundaries about what is acceptable behaviour and what not (see Co-operation and Discipline, p.196).
— Ensuring family rules apply, whatever toys are played with. Whether you let your son have toy weapons such as swords and guns is a personal decision but most boys, at some stage in their childhoods, will make pretend weapons out of whatever they have available, whether or not we approve.

We can make it very clear that all toys are to be used for play and not to hurt or threaten. Anything used as a real weapon (whether it is a toy gun used to hit a sibling or a ball thrown at a friend's head) should be removed immediately (see The Weapons Rule, p.216). Playing is fine, fighting is not (see Effective Discipline, p.215).

Also remember that young children, especially, will act out the role of the costume they are wearing or the toy they are playing with. Do not expect a boy in Action Man combat fatigues or with a plastic Kalashnikov to sit drawing for an hour. If you are happy to encourage army games, let him have army toys. If it bothers you, don't.

Boys have one increase of testosterone at four and a half and again at 13–14. But again the environment we provide for them can make huge differences to what we see as their nature. Their testosterone level automatically rises during exposure to violence, and can stay elevated if the exposure continues. Studies in schools where there is a lot of bullying have shown the boys to have constantly higher levels of testosterone. If anti-bullying programmes were then effectively introduced, the testosterone levels throughout the school dropped. When you have situations of high stress, testosterone levels rise and this leads to more masculine behaviour and the whole thing feeds itself. If you have a safe environment, then boys are more like girls in their biochemical make-up.

Steve Biddulph, psychologist and author

Helping girls

There is an admirable 'We can do it', centre-stage feeling about girls' play which simply wasn't there 10 years ago.

Elizabeth Grugeon, senior lecturer in teacher education[16]

From the research I have done I would suggest it is better for girls to be a bit rebellious and question what you tell them. The girls in our study[17] who took more initiative and answered back more were more resilient, whereas the girls who were very obedient and did everything parents said were also more likely later on to do what a boy said or what their peer group suggested.

Adrienne Katz, Young Voice

Recent shifts in girls' sense of potential provides compelling evidence of the way children's behaviour is influenced by the attitudes and expectations of those around them. After centuries of little girls being undervalued and limited by society's low expectations of their capabilities, female propensities are now considered important and valuable and, in very general terms, girls do seem to be having a better time than boys (whether women are having a better time than men is, of course, another issue entirely).

One study[18] into the rising number of confident, motivated and

---

Can-do girls

from *The Can-Do Girls – A Barometer of Change*[19]

This study [into confidence, motivation and optimism in girls] suggests that what goes on within a family, even more than its structure, has a particular influence on a girl's confidence and belief that she can do things.

Ways in which parents communicate with their daughters appear to be the key. Listening to their views, treating daughters fairly and encouraging initiative emerged as particularly important to girls. Many girls equate listening with fairness – if your voice is not heard your sense of self is lessened. Having a trusted adult providing emotional support is another vital element When this family support is present and the school and community environment contributes, those girls living in a positive climate for women develop a 'Can-do' outlook that enables them to live life to the full.

optimistic young women in Britain highlighted various factors that had affected children's self-esteem, from material circumstances to health, education, even pop music and 'girlpower', but the key factor identified by girls themselves was supportive and understanding parents who 'listened' (see Communication, p.89).

Girls generally have greater social skills, become conscientious earlier and develop cognitive and fine motor skills sooner than boys. Yet it is important that these apparent 'advantages' do not blind parents to girls' needs. Just because girls commonly display less anti-social behaviour does not mean the problems they face affect them any less deeply or require less parental support.

Girls are self-motivated, conscientious and tend to set themselves high standards. This can spill into a stressful drive for perfection.

from *Understanding Our Daughters*[20]

Many young girls may be more good than is good for them. Their culture is changing, but the risk remains that many still value-judge themselves by their ability to please others, at school and at home. Conformity and blind obedience do not breed self-reliance, self-confidence or self-awareness. Children too hooked on pleasing may forget to consider their own needs or what they want from life.

Because girls are more conformist and schools under more pressure to get results, girls are increasingly being pushed through exam hoops. This can disadvantage them when they leave school. In the real world and the job market they may need to be more risk-taking, original and creative. These are not the qualities that necessarily get you through exams.

Bethan Marshall, lecturer in Education, King's College, London

This desire to 'be good' may spill into communication between girls and their parents. While girls want parents to listen, the evidence is that girls tend to tell parents what they think they want to hear. Even very young girls often wish to protect parents or not disappoint them. At best this inhibits a parent's ability to parent; at worst, it is potentially dangerous.

We can help our daughters avoid the 'too good' trap by:

— Building their self-esteem and showing that we love them unconditionally for who they are, not what they achieve (see Feelings and Fears,
p.124).

— Encouraging their physical confidence through sports, exercise and
physical fun, so they enjoy their bodies more, feel happier with their
body image and feel less fragile and vulnerable (see Rough and Tumble,
p.332).

— Encourage them to state their views, argue their case and see mistaks
as an important and necessary part of learning (see Play and Learning,
p.324).

— Let them know they can tell us anything (see Communication, p.89).
Listening to what girls have to say is very important, but so is an awareness that they may not be communicating all they need to tell.

On the flip side of the positive statistics about girls' achievements is
the less publicised data about the number of girls struggling with
mental health problems. High suicide rates for young men have
grabbed the headlines and tended to obscure research indicating
worrying rates of self-harm, depression and eating disorders among
young women. If nothing else, this should alert us to the active support
and understanding children of both genders need as they grow.

Gender and aggression

Dr Michael Boulton, child psychologist, Keele University, specialising in research
into aggression, bullying and victimisation

There is evidence that the type of bullying differs between the sexes. There is lots of evidence to challenge the view that males are more aggressive. What they do seem to differ on is the forms of aggression and it is exactly as you would predict – boys tend to be less subtle and more physical. They will kick and use action to victimise another peer. Girls will use more subtle psychological forms, such as social exclusion, manipulation of friendships, spreading nasty rumours, etc. There seems to be no difference in levels of aggression in verbal bullying by the two sexes.

However, these are general trends. There is a wide degree of difference within any one sex. So any one boy may be less phys-ically aggressive than any one girl. It is fair to emphasise that there is a wider range within each sex than between the sexes. It is dangerous to think only of male and female types of aggression because it blinds to the possibilities of girls being physically aggressive and boys being more subtle and psychological in their abuse.

Recent studies also show that increasing numbers of girls are now hit by their parents (see Smacking isn't the Solution, p.241) and are involved in physical bullying, while young women's convictions for violent crime continue to rise. As girls begin to shake off the passivity and vulnerability displayed by previous generations we should grab the chance to teach all children, girls and boys, the difference between aggression and assertion (see Growing Independence, p.362). The sooner all children are shown more effective ways to state their case than physical intimidation, the better for us all.

The great explorers

I was always laid back about what my children did with their own bodies and I never attempted to stop them, I'd just pretend not to notice. Then when my daughter was five she was reading on stage at her class assembly, in front of the school and parents, and halfway through thrust her hand down her knickers. There it remained for the next half an hour as she absentmindedly played with herself. Everyone pretended not to notice, but I realised that maybe I'd gone too far and a little awareness of appropriate public behaviour would be no bad thing!

Jenny P

Learning about their bodies Young children, from babyhood onward, fiddle with their genitals because it feels good. They are sensual beings who like touching themselves and it is important for their sense of self and gender that they be allowed to do so. We need to respect a child's right to enjoy and explore their own bodies and also, as they grow up, equip them with the knowledge of what is appropriate behaviour in public.

Our emphasis can be what is desirable where, not on there being anything wrong with what a child naturally enjoys doing, whether it is stripping off in the sunshine or playing with themselves (see Talking about Sex, p.386 and Understanding Development, p.397).

The simple physical possibility of excitement is there from the beginning. Children are discovering their own bodies and finding out what touch is nice and what isn't and in what types of ways, and I think it is very easy for adults to be intrusive of that process in a completely unnecessary way, saying, for example, 'Don't touch yourself'. It is much easier and more sensible to say, 'That feels nice but generally you do that on your own.'

Mary MacLeod, chief executive, National Family and Parenting Institute

Children go through phases of more or less inhibition about their bodies but generally, over time, they like to take their clothes off less and less in front of people outside the family. This often occurs once they start school.

If your child shows no inhibitions and this concerns you, you could gently bring their awareness to what your boundaries are by showing where you enjoy and need privacy, for example, by shutting the bathroom door and explaining why. Also respect children's boundaries once they begin to emerge – bursting into a pre-adolescent child's room

---

Respect, respect, respect

José von Bühler, sexual and relationship psychotherapist

Children are developing sexual beings and parents' attitudes towards this natural development should be one of total respect and absolutely no interference or abuse.

It can be difficult for parents to see their child as a sexual being in his or her own right, so we can deny this exists. Children have a huge amount of sexual behaviour. It is not helpful to reject this or pretend it is not there. Parents should remain emotionally supportive whilst being very clear about boundaries.

Any attitudes parents have towards sexuality are going to be noticed and used by the children. If parents feel in some way the body is indecent, for example, the children will pick this up pretty quickly.

Adults in general need to respect that the child's process of sexual development is a strongly personal one. Hence, the role of the parent should simply be a nurturing one: to inform when asked, support when in pain, guide gently when appropriate. Parents have a responsibility to explain where the boundaries are. These may vary a bit between families and cultures but in our society, there are clearly defined social norms about sexuality the child must learn sooner or later. It is vital this is seen as a learning process, not a punishing, non-permission-giving process. Expressions that are invasive of a child's sexual self-discovery such as 'That's dirty', 'Don't do that', 'What's the matter with you?' – are to be avoided. Negative intrusions may not be seen as damaging now but they may possibly be later in life, when the child establishes their adult relationships.

Remember, there are always specifically qualified professionals able and willing to help you if you are not certain.

announcing 'Don't be embarrassed' will not give a child necessary privacy. It is important for parents and children not to confuse privacy with secrecy: a child exploring their own body should not be a shameful or furtive act but rather private and personal.

You need to differentiate as a parent things that are done in private and things that are secret. They may look the same but they are not. You need to show the child that he can have a private life as we all do but it is not secret. This is key. It helps for a child to be free to talk about these things within the family and us as adults set a model which children can take in. So our communication as adults is important, both verbally and non-verbally.

Domenico di Ceglie, Consultant Child and Adolescent Psychiatrist, Tavistock Clinic, Director of the Gender Identity Development Unit, Portman Clinic, Honorary Senior Lecturer, Royal Free Hospital School of Medicine, London

Tutus and swords

From two years to four years Joe just loved dressing up in dresses. Always Snow White, never the prince and he had a fabulous eye for accessories. I remember him and Jack going to playgroup and both coming out dressed in frocks. Jack looked like Eddie Izzard but Joe looked stunning. I did in moments of madness wonder if it meant he would be gay but generally it didn't bother me. I chose not to encourage or discourage him.

Maggie T

Parents have a huge influence on how their children feel about themselves and their bodies. Being relaxed and realistic about boys playing at girls and girls playing at boys helps children explore, develop happily and healthily and keep their self-esteem intact. For parents to do otherwise risks much more harm than good.

'By the age of three, four, five you can already have a sense of where a child feels he or she belongs as a boy or girl,' explains Domenico di Ceglie, Consultant Child and Adolescent Psychiatrist at the Tavistock Clinic. 'Parents should know that gender exploration is not the same as atypical gender development. The first is much more flexible, the latter is much more fixed, with the child insistent that he or she actually *belongs* to the other sex. This is uncommon.

'As parents you need to recognise your child's behaviour and accept it exists in a non-judgemental way. By denying the behaviour exists you are communicating to the child he shouldn't be feeling these things or behaving in this way. What normally happens then is that the child stops showing

With young children it is hard to get the message across that we as adults need boundaries, for example when we go to the toilet, but children do learn it and it is essential to this process that we respect their need for privacy, too. This is a reciprocal thing.

Dr Dorothy Rowe, psychologist and writer

What and when you tell your child about their body and about sexual development and sex will vary between families and cultures (see Sex Talk, p.388), but it is important for the child's healthy development and safety that your child feels OK about asking you questions and telling you things you may rather not hear or deal with. Without true understanding children will lack the ability to know what is OK in their own behaviour and that of others.

---

these behaviours and pursues them in a secret way. The behaviour or interest does not disappear.

'The child then has to develop two aspects of himself or herself at a very young age – one for public consumption and one that is private. These problems remain and explode at adolescence. In the meantime, the child will continue to behave this way but secretively.

'There are two problems with this. Firstly, they will become worried about disapproval and being found out and could become quite isolated. Secondly, the secret can become quite exciting and this can sow the seeds of developmental problems. In a sense you start with an issue and then, depending on your behaviour as a parent, you can develop two or three problems as the child grows up.'

My eldest boy had a doll called Baby he would carry around everywhere. Over time we became more and more aware of other people's reactions. They would say it's unusual or ask me if it was good for him. As he got older he changed his favourite thing to a black and white bull and then a Fireman Sam hat. I feel pleased we were comfortable with his Baby. He is particularly kind with young children and I do sometimes wonder whether it is linked.

Claire S

I've always lived in jeans and trousers so it came as a shock to have a girl who loves pink and frills. But that's her. I could gag at some of the clothes she chooses, and at six she's got a greater range of lipsticks than me and wears them often. But she thinks she's beautiful, and that's fine by me

Debbi O

Gender exploration

The most important thing a parent can do is accept a child for how he or she is.

Dr Dorothy Rowe, psychologist and writer

Gender exploration can cause parental consternation but is a very natural and normal part of children's development as they try to establish their identity and how they fit into the world.

Very young children can be downright sexist as they try to impose order on their universe. Comments like 'Mummy, do that' or 'Daddy, fix it' may make us wince, but are only an indication of their increasing awareness of gender and roles and their desire for rules and predictability. Our own behaviour in the family can soon give them a more balanced view of the world and our many roles within it.

Once a child begins imaginary play, they can begin actively to explore gender roles and behaviour for themselves. Whether a boy or girl dresses up or plays out macho roles or more 'feminine' ones is irrelevant – some will be drawn to what is familiar, others to what seems exciting and different. The exploration is a form of learning, like any other. Parents tend to be overly fearful of behaviours that are nothing more than exploration and imagination. For the record, it does not indicate or determine your child's final sexual orientation. Letting boys and girls role-play and dress up as different characters and different genders does not make them gay.

Some children will explore through role play, some through dressing up, some a little, some a lot, and the best thing to be is relaxed about it. What little evidence there is indicates that discouraging exploration or pressurising a child to hide such behaviour could itself have long-term consequences. Adult cross-dressers tell researchers that being forbidden to 'dress up' as children increased it fascination and made them more determined to do so in adulthood (see Tutus and Swords, p.320). At the very least, 'banning' very normal play behaviour may give our children a strong message that exploring sexuality and identity is something secretive and shameful. This is not going to help our children live happy lives or develop happy relationships.

Gender and development: a quick reminder

- Boys and girls are born different – and biological differences need to be kept in perspective. All children need to be loved and listened to. We have a huge influence on how our sons and daughters feel about themselves, their gender and their place in the world.
- Boys' social and learning skills often lag behind girls', especially in their early years. Recognising these different patterns of development can alert us to areas where they may need our focused support. How we talk and listen to boys can encourage them to open up and communicate more easily. We can raise the next generation of men to be confident, considerate and emotionally literate.
- Girls often develop learning and social skills sooner, yet we should take care this apparent advantage does not blind us to their needs. Some girls may be too 'good' than is good for them. They may need our active support to encourage physical activity, risk-taking, speaking their mind and seeing mistakes as an inevitable part of life and learning.
- We need to respect our children's right to enjoy and explore their own bodies and gender and equip them with the knowledge of what is appropriate and safe behaviour in public.

CHAPTER TEN
PLAY AND LEARNING

We are exploring these two essentials of childhood in one chapter because they are so closely entwined.

Play boosts children's physical health and their emotional, mental and social development. Through discovery, exploration and imagination they begin to find out about themselves, their world and the important people around them. All while having fun.

Children also learn better if they are enjoying themselves. Interest in learning can be crushed under the weight of dull teaching, parental pressure and criticism. Yet if our children discover that learning can be fun, that spark of interest can be lit for life.

Play

One of my happiest memories as a child is splatting about in the mud in our back garden. I was a very happy squelcher.

Catherine F

Essentially children see play as the time they are not being organised or told what to do by adults. Having this time is important to them as it gives them a chance to feel they have some autonomy and control in their otherwise frequently controlled lives.

Issy Cole-Hamilton and Tim Gill, National Children's Bureau[1]

As a society we've become so obsessed with educational toys and speed learning that the whole point of play is sometimes lost in the rush for the flash cards. So it is worth stating the obvious. Play is meant to be fun and childhood should be a time for having as much of it as possible.

Guiding principles

Young children often find great pleasure in exploring objects and discovering for themselves what toys and play materials can do. At other times they need our help. From dough to construction bricks, we can show children the possibilities, spark their enthusiasm and imagination, then watch them take it from there.

'Take a rattle,' explains Professor Hugh Foot, specialist in child psychology and social development. 'While you and I know that a rattle is for shaking, a child who's never seen one doesn't. By shaking it and smiling the parent is telling the child what this object is for.

'The same applies until the child is old enough to read instructions or work out a game for themselves – you can't simply open the box and expect them to enjoy the contents, you first have to show them how.'

Through play and fun children develop increased self-esteem, an appreciation of life, greater ability to cope with its ups and downs and even enhanced relationships. For adults, too, an ability to find fun in life and humour in difficult situations often tips the balance between us having a good day or a bad.

Play is also a powerful tool for learning – a child having fun is absorbed and engaged and soaking up experiences from their very first infant games (see The Pleasure Principle, p.15). But it is much, much more besides. Strip the fun out of play and its potency is lost, so try to back-pedal on well-intentioned worthiness and see fun for fun's sake, as an end in itself.

Children enjoy humour from an early age. Very little ones will smile when you pull a funny face. Slightly older ones will love pee-po games. Many six-year-olds will have a fine set of puns and corny jokes. A child looking very serious as they stick their fist in and out of a plastic cup may be having a great time. A seven-year-old with a construction toy is not going to whoop with joy but is still having great fun. It's all important. Many studies show that the richness of a child's early play behaviour and interactions correlate with their social and emotional adjustment later in life.

Professor Hugh Foot, specialist in child psychology and social development,
Department of Psychology, Strathclyde University

Our responses to our children's play can boost the pleasure they find in it, from their first baby games on. Just as parents can give children

What your child may enjoy

	Big movements (Gross motor skills)	Small movements (Fine motor skills)
0–1 Year	Exploring safe environments. Crawling, reaching, being held to stand when ready.	Safe things to hold: rattle, bricks, our hands. Exploring objects with their hands and mouths.
1–2 Years	Slow walks, running on grass, climbing stairs with you, roly poly play – learning control of body, etc. Push and pull toys.	Increasing their control: building block towers, basic tasks, e.g. stirring. Using play materials: paint, play dough, crayons.
2–4 Years	Pedalling and steering tricycle/ riding bike with stabilisers. Simple ball games. Chasing games, rough-and-tumble, pillow/pretend fights. Climbing frames. Jumping, balancing, bouncing games.	Using scissors, painting, crayons, play dough, basic cooking, etc. Jigsaws, different size boxes to tower, bead-threading, turning pages of books.
5–11 Years	Vigorous sports and exercise: e.g. rhythmical dance, skipping, climbing, cycling, skating, football, swimming.	Drawing, painting, sewing, cooking including measuring ingredients, computer games, junk modelling, increasingly complex construction kits.

Relationships with people, environment, themselves

Thinking and understanding

Developing senses (mothers and carers holding them, responding, talking, laughing, etc.). Mobiles (close to infant's gaze), different light, colours, sounds. Interactive and imitative games. Familiar routines; peek-a-boo (from a few months enjoys gentle teasing and begins to understand things appearing and disappearing).

Looking at picture books/simple stories. Interacting with children and adults and watching what others do.

Nursery rhymes and actions. Rolling balls back and forth (interactive play). Naming/pointing to body parts, putting on hat and shoes. Exploring nature. Rituals and routines in play with friends. Imitative play; watering plants, dusting, cooking, etc. Hide and seek, piggyback rides, etc.

'Reading' picture books together. Having time to absorb (going at their pace). Large construction bricks, pegs in holes, safe household items; kitchen cupboard to empty/fill, etc. (working out how things fit together and come apart). Exploring and discovering objects.

Kicking balloons (big effects of small actions). Blowing bubbles, etc. (how things appear/disappear). Increasingly elaborate and collaborative play with other children; throwing/catching ball (give and take). Visiting farms, etc. (looking at the world around them). 'Helping'. Dressing-up games and imaginative play with friends, siblings, parents, on their own. Doing things for themselves.

Ordering objects into size/colour order. Building a tower then knocking it down (small steps achieve big task). Discovering distance, measurement, time (fascinated by watches, height charts, tape measures, etc.). Stories about themselves, photographs, etc. (their place in the world). Large construction bricks/models. Filling a dolls' house, parking toy vehicles, etc. (using spatial sense).

Choosing own friends and play: uninterrupted free play to build dens, create dance routines, etc. Team sports, games with rules, clubs they enjoy. Story-telling, drama, creating own shows, characters, etc. Funny poems, stories, simple jokes. Music.

Designing and making models (talk with them about how they do it. What do they like about it? What might they do differently next time? Planning and problem-solving). Simple experiments, e.g. gravity with a feather and heavy ball, guessing weights, measuring siblings, etc. (discovery). Looking after a pet. Expressing opinion in games, creating games. Word games: Scrabble, I-spy, etc. Strategy board games.

the message that play is an irritant of little worth, other than to entertain them elsewhere – 'Just go outside and play' – so we can also
express the value we place in fun by responding to their enthusiasms,
and showing interest and pleasure in their enjoyment.

If you are losing the battle against the rising tide of primary
coloured plastic in your home, it may help to know that most play
specialists recommend parents provide more play *materials*, not more
toys. Toys with limited function have limited appeal and life span.
Sand, water, paints, paper, clay, dough, cake mixes, old containers and
old clothes for dressing up are all potentially messy but provide far
greater opportunities for imagination and discovery – and cost less.
You might also try packing some toys away for a while. Rotating what's
available can make even old toys seem fun all over again when they
are brought out and others packed away.

*It is important not to let emphasis on material provision lead to under emphasis
on the child.*

Tina Bruce, *Time for Play in Early Childhood Education*[2]

Where's me?

*I have strong childhood memories of playing with white dolls and
reading about white men making history happen. Of course, as a black
child you grow up wondering where you fit into all this. Adults too
easily forget the powerful message in omission.*

Amanda N

Children as young as two have been shown
to recognise differences in skin colour.[3] As
children play and explore their own identity
and their place in the world, it's important
they have access to play materials that reflect
the diversity around them and their own
ethnic background.

Black dolls, crayons that match various
skin tones and books with positive images
of children and adults from various ethnic,
cultural and religious backgrounds are
more readily available in shops than was
the case even 10 years ago. Parents, carers
and teachers may also want to contact
specialist suppliers for play materials that
respectfully and positively build children's
self-image and reflect their world (see
Contacts, p.429).

Encouraging play can be as simple as providing the space and TV-free time for it to happen. But it also involves knowing when to join in and when to butt out. Help children get a game started, join in if they want, but resist the temptation to impose your own idea of the best, quickest or only way of doing it. They will be much more proud of a misshapen biscuit or a rickety tower they made themselves than the perfect one you created, and the experience will be a far greater spur for their future self-reliance and curiosity. Let children take the lead and show us when they want our assistance, knowledge or companionship. Allow them to make 'mistakes', imagine and do things their way.

If a child is absorbed in what they are doing I do not think it is right to interfere. Wait until they look up and want to share. The timing is important. A lot of parents try to explain what is going on when a child may not want or understand it. Verbal explanations can be more useful later if the child chooses to talk about it. There are different phases for children and it is not always helpful to strip the magic out of things with logical explanations.

Angela Gruber, transpersonal psychotherapist

Free and quiet times Getting the balance right between parental involvement and children's freedom also means allowing them time for free, quiet or unstructured play and daydreaming.

Recent studies have confirmed the obvious: that young children's outdoor play has changed radically in less than a generation. Fuelled by exaggerated fears of abduction and other harm (see Protection v. Exposure, p.379), it is now heavily dependent on safe public spaces where they can play in view of their parents.[4] As their lives become ever more restricted and organised, it becomes even more important that we create opportunities for free play inside and outside the home and, once they are old enough, experiences of play away from constant adult surveillance.

The idea that every minute has to be gainfully occupied is the antithesis of childhood.

Adrienne Katz, founder and executive director of Young Voice

We live in a very busy world and we need to create serenity rather than just 'doing'. I believe in silence as well as talking. Children need calm.

Christine Fahey, Montessori teacher

Freedom in free time

Our unusually early start to formal education in the UK makes our children's opportunities for free play even more important.

'It is children's right to childhood,' says educational psychologist Corinne Abisgold. 'The progress children make in play is very hard to quantify and therefore we are losing sight of some of the benefits, in a culture in which teachers have to say exactly what they are doing with the children and why.

'It is easy to say they know 20 letters and x numbers but this approach can become like a disease. Even children's leisure is becoming pressurised – how well can they do? How much can they do?

'It is really easy to destroy the joy in children's abilities to explore things for themselves. When I go to playgroups I have to bite my lip when parents talk about the need for tasks to be set for the children. I think we are becoming quite frightened of letting children play naturally.'

Structured activities and adult-style games with rules are fine in short measure, but only when left to their own devices can children truly revel in the silly, the competitive, the fantastical, the funny, the dreamy and the just plain daft games that adults so often understimate or misunderstand.

These free times allow children to develop self-awareness and the capacity for reflection, both crucial to their emotional development and learning. Even being bored on occasion and having to find something to do will build children's resourcefulness and creativity. A baby allowed to stare absent-mindedly into space for as long as they're happy or take gentle pleasure in the simple, sensorial things around them has a good chance of growing into a child who can run round like a mad thing but also stare up at the clouds, fiddle with their belly button, relax and reflect. Which seems a healthy and happy combination.

It is in free play that the children's culture takes over. It is hard to see they are playing sometimes but children really do make the most of the spare time, spare objects, spare corners and space left over from adult activities. I do not think they have lost their own play culture, but I do think there is less opportunity for them to play unsupervised.

Dr Pat Petrie, senior research lecturer, Thomas Coram Unit, Institute of Education, University of London

Play with other children

Through playing with other children a child learns how to negotiate and bargain, make compromises, control aggressiveness and assertiveness in others, constrain and confine their own aggressiveness, when and how to be assertive, to caretake other children, begin to handle rejection, bullying, loneliness, to join in games, seek company and strike out on their own, to enjoy humour, and so many other social skills they couldn't possibly learn by playing with an adult who, by their very presence, is in the controlling, restraining or caretaking role.

Professor Hugh Foot, specialist in child psychology and social development

The sooner children have opportunities to interact and play with others in their early years, the easier and more natural this will seem. Only children will reap obvious rewards, but even children of large families can benefit hugely by being liberated from their role as 'the little one' or 'the responsible one' (see Ripping up Labels, p.119).

Babies and toddlers are sociable and curious about other children, and can delight in interactive play and simply watching others. By their second year, they may begin to develop intricate play rituals and routines with friends. Even at this young age, they're learning basic lessons in social understanding with each other's help: how to start, join in and sustain joint games; how to stop when play becomes boring or uncomfortable; when and how to seek out company or go it alone.[5] Play with others helps children develop self-awareness, self-esteem, self-confidence and self-respect as well as their ability to make and keep friends.

Of course, play sometimes deteriorates into squabbles and fights, yet even these can provide important lessons in how to get along. It makes little sense to encourage a child to play with another who is continually domineering or aggressive, but disagreements and disputes will arise even among children who get on well. Problem-solving and negotiating small but sticky situations help children learn some of the basics of children's culture before they start nursery or school and to practise its finer points once they begin. It can also boost their language skills and ability to express emotions and opinions constructively.

We need to monitor how our children are doing and if we believe it is going too far, we do need to step in. But we shouldn't make their social environment so sterile and safe that they never fall out with one another because then, when they do come across the inevitable conflict, they would not be able to sort it out.

Dr Michael Boulton, child psychologist

We can encourage children's co-operative play and problem-solving by:

- Noticing and praising it when it happens.
- Providing plenty of opportunities to practise. We can play simple turn-taking with younger children: 'You roll the ball to me, then I'll roll it to you', 'You have a go then I'll have a go.' Older children may enjoy family games: board games, sports, etc. We can show through our own behaviour how to win without gloating and lose without blowing a gasket. Some children find losing very hard, and may need our help in thinking through ways to cope (see Feelings and Fears, p.124 and Searching for Solutions, p.222).
- Encouraging children of pre-school age upwards to think through problems and disputes with siblings and friends: (see Searching for Solutions, p.222, and Tackle Sibling Conflict, p.286).

Some children find play with others relatively easy, some need more encouragement and support, some need firm guidance on appropriate behaviour, or to be shown ways to play co-operatively, but all children need opportunities to develop and practise social skills, find fun and feel comfortable around others.

> *Rory* (age six): 'Bye bye you ballerina' (giggles).
> *Louis* (also six): 'Bye bye you ballerina's wife' (giggles).
> *Rory:* 'Bye bye you bossy army captain' (laughs).
> *Louis:* 'Bye bye you captain of pooh!' (both laugh so much they can't speak).

Rough and tumble

You want your children to be joyful and exuberant creatures. If a child is going to make secure physical as well as emotional attachments then the more general physical play that isn't too boisterous, the better. Children get this from each other but they also need it from their parents. I often think that young adults who don't form sound interpersonal relationships themselves may come from homes in which they were not often touched by their parents. They were touched for dressing perhaps when younger, but not touched in a jovial and playful manner when they were small.

Professor Hugh Foot, specialist in child psychology and social development

Rough and ready?

Steve Biddulph, psychologist and author

How fathers play has a bearing on their children's future. Fathers tend to stress their children, from toddlerhood on. They tend to wind them up a little bit, for example by tickling and chasing them. It would seem children learn from this stress within safe limits and develop some emotional immunity (see Reviewing the Role of Fathers, p.253).

Girls, particularly, can become more physical and confident in their play. Later this positive role model seems to delay sexual relations and help the choice of healthy partners for girls. It may remove the high need for male approval. Girls without this seem to get more confused when choosing a partner and if they muddle needing a father with a partner they may choose an authoritarian male who will tell them what to do.

For boys, rough-and-tumble play can be the way they learn to control their temper. Playing with them like this can teach them to stop and calm down if they get out of control, teach them to stay safe, and not to hit or hurt. It's an important lesson.

Children's rough-and-tumble play may not do a lot for their parents' mental and emotional well-being but, if it's any comfort, it is very healthy for theirs. Through it, children learn to be physically confident and know what they can cope with and what they can't. They test the limits of their bodies and their tempers, experience competing, winning and losing, and learn how to control their aggression and when to stop.

Whether it is rough and tumble with parents, relatives, siblings or friends, clear ground rules help. Precisely what these are will vary according to family beliefs and circumstance, but you may want to make a very clear distinction between rough and tumble and fighting. For example, rough and tumble is fine as long as no one is harmed or inflicting harm, all participants are enjoying it, and there is no risk of damage to people or property.

Not all children enjoy rough play, of course, so try to take your child's lead. Some become easily overwhelmed and this needs to be explained to siblings and friends. We can help develop the physical confidence of more shy or anxious children by gently introducing physical exercise and fun – swimming, dancing, playing with a ball – and watching out for signals that they've had enough. Clear and agreed family signals for rough play to end – perhaps saying 'time out' – can give the child a greater sense of control and safety and act as a clear stop sign to family and friends.

Encouraging imagination games

Euan (aged five, in tea towel cloak and waving inside of toilet roll): 'You are under my power. My po-weeeeeeeeer.'
Amanda (also five, in tea towel and crown): 'But I have THIS!'
Euan: 'What?'
Amanda: 'Magic fingers!'
Euan: 'Yikes!'

Through fantasy play children transform their world and their part in it (see The Developing Imagination, p.334). Make-believe and 'pretend' play often begins in later toddlerhood as children begin to understand that objects and even people can represent other things. By four, they may enjoy acting out roles, dressing up and exploring what it would be like to be someone else. By six and seven, they may be constructing long and complex dramas, interweaving their roles with those of their toys. At any age, these games will help them develop communication

---

The developing imagination

Professor Hugh Foot, specialist in child psychology and social development

From about 12 months, a child moves on to using pretend objects, e.g. 'drinking' from an imaginary cup. A child of, say, 15 months may hold an imaginary cup up to a doll's lips. These tasks can become welded together in a sequence, for example, undressing, bathing, putting a doll to bed.

The child may ask the parent to do something for her while she is washing the baby – turn on the tap, hold the towel and so on. It is healthy when parents participate in this way, when the child is in the driving seat.

Children can be quite upset if you do things out of order, if you break the rules of the game. It is very ritualistic.

Children close on two can have imaginary play friends. Something like a fifth to a quarter of children do, for a short time at least. It is more likely to happen to solitary children but of itself is not really anything to worry about. Playmates of this kind are usually 'there' when the child is playing on their own but forgotten when the child is called by their mother.

skills, increase their understanding of others and explore and express their emotions. It may help to remember this next time the sofa is turned into a pirate ship.

Our role is to spark our children's imagination through stories, books, games, thoughts (see Stories and Games for Thinking, p.351), by providing props, joining in when requested and even initiating games occasionally. The key task, though, is simply to let children play.

Screen time

All [adults should] make it their business to be familiar with the material to which children have access; to enforce all regulations designed to protect children from 'unsuitable' material; to discuss violent or otherwise disturbing stories and images with children, and to offer non-violent equivalents wherever they can. There are legitimate arguments against censorship, but there are none for leaving children to cope, unsupported, with whatever material comes their way.

The Commission on Children and Violence[6]

Parents know the power of example and exposure to TV – that's why my boys went World Cup crazy, that's why TV advertising's so effective. How can we know that, and at other times delude ourselves that they don't learn from what they see?

Simon P

While there's been much debate about what screen images do to children, a far bigger problem may be what screen time *stops them doing.* Heavy screen use (TV, videos and DVDs, computers and so on) cuts into the time children have for activities essential to their healthy development, such as talking and playing freely with others.

Too much screen time is anti-social and presents children with a very restricted view of the fun to be had in the world. 'Lack of contact with other people', fuelled by the increase in TV watching, has been pinpointed as the main cause of an apparent recent increase in shyness among people in general and adolescents in particular.[7] Delays in development of selective attention and an increase in language problems in very young children have been linked to over-use of television and videos (see Communication, p.89).

Research in the US[8] also indicates a strong link between childhood obesity and TV use, particularly when children have televisions in their bedrooms. Lead researcher Barbara Dennison caused a storm by suggesting that children under two shouldn't watch television at all. 'It has to do with how children learn by interaction with adults,' she commented. 'They don't learn well passively. They need you to talk to them and respond. Young children don't learn a lot from television.' The report concludes: 'Because most children watch TV by age two, educational efforts about limiting child TV/video viewing and keeping the TV out of the child's bedroom need to begin before then.'

We don't need to get too po-faced but we do have to face facts. Too much screen time can be damaging to children's development and tends to backfire if used as a child pacifier. Of course, some children's small-screen entertainment is inspiring, educational or just great fun. Watching TV programmes with older children can also prompt family discussions around important issues such as sex and sexuality, HIV/Aids and drugs misuse. But let's be realistic. Parents often allow children to switch the TV or computer on so they can get on with other things.

Unrestricted view?

One survey[9] of UK primary pupils aged 9 to 11 found that two-thirds had watched violent 18-rated videos such as *Pulp Fiction*, *The Terminator* and *The Silence of the Lambs*, suggesting that many children have few restrictions imposed on their viewing. Some of these films were likely to have been seen by much younger children. Four in 10 said they had watched the films with their parents' permission.

The average US child is estimated to have seen 32,000 murders, 40,000 attempted murders and 250,000 acts of violence on television before the age of 18 (UK figures not available).[10] Print and television news coverage of war and other events means many young children are viewing scenes of unimaginable horror (see Protection v. Exposure, p.379).

In a recent UK survey, a surprisingly high 20% of parents said they thought television had more influence on their children than they do.[11] On average, 8–15-year-olds in the UK spend over two hours a day watching TV and videos. Computer use is rising fast, with most UK schoolchildren now having access to a computer at home. A small but rising number of children (between 1 and 2%, predominantly boys) admit to using a computer for over five hours a day.[12]

A timely burst of a favourite video or game may keep fractious children quiet for long enough to get their meal on the table, but use the screen as a babysitter or child-distracter too often or for too long and no one benefits. Children can become restless, fizz pop around the house like demented puppies or explode in frustration or temper. Alternatively, they may turn into human blobs, too lethargic to raise themselves from the sofa while they whinge about being bored. Neither makes life easier.

It does seem that the happiest children watch the least TV. Favourite, repeated videos, chosen for their beauty and excitement and appropriate to the kids' ages, are better than the randomness of TV. And I suggest never more than an hour a day unless it's a special situation.

Steve Biddulph, psychologist and author

The same dilemmas and contradictions surround children's use of computers. Interactive teaching software has been shown to boost development of literacy and numeracy skills – as long as computers are properly used, supported *and limited*. One recent study into the effective use of information and communications technology in schools recommended that on-screen time be limited to fifteen to twenty minutes, three times a week.[13]

We should also be aware that children have access to more negative, violent and potentially damaging images than we would care to admit (see Unrestricted View?, p.336 and Protection v. Exposure, p.379). The debate continues between those who believe violent screen images and games increase violent behaviour in children, and those who challenge them to come up with the proof. Yet no one argues that a heavy diet of violence does a child any good. How much harm it does, in what way and to whom, is still in dispute, but while the academics argue, why take the risk?

Young children, especially, are still trying to make sense of reality and may find it hard to separate fact from fiction. For children of any age, repeated exposure to scenes of negative and anti-social behaviour may, in real but subtle ways, make aggression seem 'cool' and acceptable and make children wary or frightened of the world outside.

Clearly, the greatest influence on children's beliefs and conduct are their families and their own experiences – what they come to recognise as norms of behaviour.[14] Screen time and other media are only one source of the messages they receive about values, behaviour and aspirations. But by monitoring screen time and viewing, we can reduce any risks and broaden our children's opportunities for other types of fun.

We've not talked about banning anything, but simply agreed to watch favourite programmes instead of any old rubbish and set time limits on computer games. The kids agreed the times, and it seems to be working OK. They're actually less bored, not more.

David I

In all this, four key messages emerge. TV, DVDs, video games and computers are great tools and great fun if handled with care. Parents can encourage this by:

1　Limiting the time children spend before TV and computer screens. We now have enough electronic gadgetry to keep children quiet for hours, but a virtual childhood is a waste.
2　Monitoring the content of what children are watching and playing and who they are 'talking' to online (see Protection v. Exposure, p.379). The advent of videos, the Internet and other technological advances mean parents can no longer rely on the law and film classifications to restrict children's access.
3　Talking to our children about advertising. Most parents are aware of the 'pester power' of advertising aimed at children and its heavy influence on what children and families buy, from junk food to toys.[15] Research now confirms that younger children are unable to distinguish advertising from programming.[16] If we explain to our children how it's different, what advertisers try to do and how they try to do it, they may develop a little more ad resistance.
4　Watching with children – and talking to them about what they see and do. This can increase the value of what they see and help them separate fiction from fact. It also helps parents judge what effects programmes or games may be having on how their children feel and think.

It is clear that the context in which a child views violent images, and the presence or absence of a critical commentary not approving of violence, is likely to influence whether or how the child is affected.

The Commission on Children and Violence[17]

Learning

Affectionate relationships are essential for the full vitality of teaching and learning.

Colwyn Trevarthen, Emeritus Professor of Child Psychology and Psychobiology, University of Edinburgh

Parents play a crucial role in inspiring their children to learn and in supporting them when they find it a struggle. But it's not only what our children learn that matters, but what they come to associate with learning: whether it's enjoyable; whether their efforts are appreciated; whether they risk harsh criticism or encouragement.

All evidence points to the fact that encouragement and fun, not force, is the most effective way to unlock children's potential in their pre-school and primary years.

Encourage enjoyment

Good education is not really the information they have but rather the encouragement of their desire to learn.

Camila Batmanghelidjh, psychotherapist, Director of Kid's Company

---

Between the lines

To be beneficial, home learning needs to be enjoyable . . . rigid and structured home learning and pre-school education directed solely at teaching a child to read, write and do sums is unhelpful for pre-schoolchildren, whose self-esteem can easily be dented.
Royal College of Paediatrics and Child Health[18]

'Parents need to spend time on anything that sparks their child's interest,' says Adrienne Katz, founder of the children's charity Young Voice. 'Children have to be interested in the story to enjoy reading it. Some are forced through boring reading schemes then expected to make a huge effort to learn. It does not make sense. If you take time to find out what books they really like and why they don't like others, it will help enormously.

'One little girl I know hated reading books about animals because they so often got lost. It was putting her off. We all need to be more sensitive to these things.'

Children learn better if they are enjoying themselves. Right back in ancient history children were taught to read with enjoyment – for example Jewish children were allowed to lick the honey off the letters they were learning. If you are not enjoying yourself you are usually obsessed with failing. With enjoyment you want to go on because you are having a good time.

Nicholas Tucker, educational psychologist and Honorary Senior Lecturer in Cultural Studies, University of Sussex

This obvious point is often the first to be forgotten. Parents can make learning fun. The pleasure principle can begin from your child's earliest encounters with play materials and books; if they begin to associate these with cuddles and good times, you're off to a great start.

Young children's brains grow at an astonishing rate. At birth, the brain is 25% of its adult weight (the whole infant body is only about 5% of its adult value). By six months, the brain is nearly half its adult weight and by age four, psychologists suggest, 'substantial intellectual growth' is accomplished.[19] Hardly surprising, then, that children exposed to 'home learning' tend to perform better when they start primary school.[20]

Crucially, though, that learning only helps in the long term when it's enjoyable for both parent and child. Children's responses develop through experience, so if they have repeated experiences of 'learning' being dull or stressful they are likely to display bored or anxious behaviour around 'learning' situations in future.

To help our children learn happily, our task as parents in the preschool and primary years is to enjoy, encourage and engage our children's interests. Importantly, we need to allow and encourage our children to play freely (see Play, p.324). We can also play games together: nursery rhymes in the car, I Spy in the doctor's waiting room. Try looking at books together. Share silly and funny books as well as fascinating or inspiring ones that whet children's imagination and interest (see Between the Lines, p.339). Encourage confidence and pleasure in numbers: let children dial a grandparent, add up till receipts, count the cars on the way to the shops or the stairs on the way to bed. Allow them pleasure in the means as well as the ends: weighing and measuring, playing shops, cooking, making junk rockets, drawing, painting, exploring, imagining. If it's fun, they'll do it.

Doing it for themselves

My five-year-old got a real buzz out of doing his own shoelaces, being allowed to be more responsible for himself and knowing I'd notice. There are parents who throw themselves like saints into looking after their children in every way. It comes as a great surprise to them to see how children thrive when given the chance to do it themselves, what a boost it is to their self-esteem.

Kate K

Allowing children to decision-make and do things for themselves increases their confidence and pleasure in discovery (see Encouraging Enquiry, p.348). A child who is allowed to problem-solve and tackle situations in life is going to be better equipped to do the same in the classroom.

You can begin this process from babyhood on by letting your child experiment and work things out for themselves. Let your baby reach for things on occasion instead of always handing them to them, let them attempt to feed themselves, even though much of it ends up in their ear. As your toddler begins to insist 'Me do it, me do it', let them try whenever possible. As they grow, involve them in simple decision-making; 'If we stay in the park we won't have time for a play at home before bathtime. Which would you like?'

As a rule of thumb, try not to do things for your child that your child can safely do without you. Next time they want to go one rung higher on the climbing frame, ask yourself whether you want to hold on to them because it is best for them or best for you. If they can hold on well and you are there to catch them if they slip, letting them explore and test their own limits will increase their understanding of potential dangers and of their own capabilities.

When we teach children a new skill, let them try it again for themselves so they fully understand what to do and why. Whether it's cooking, swimming, writing a school report, tackling a maths problem, this is how we can equip our children with the confidence they will need to tackle new challenges, test their capabilities and 'think on their feet' even when we are not there to guide and support.

One of the most effective ways in which children learn is when a more able person helps them to see what they can achieve with a little help. Psychologists call this 'scaffolding', suggesting that a structure is put up to help build new skills, and then the scaffolding is gradually removed, allowing the child to consolidate their new-found skills for themselves.

John Oates, developmental psychologist

Let each child shine

Your small child's view of himself is based almost entirely on what you tell him. So try to praise him not just for achieving things but for trying.

Eileen Hayes, parenting advisor to the NSPCC

Every child needs to experience success and the pleasure of doing something well, and there's no greater motivator to try harder and learn more. So how could we help each child feel they shine? What are they particularly proud of that we could notice? What special qualities do they have? What have they enjoyed doing? What have they worked hard at? If we can notice and genuinely praise these (see Descriptive Praise, p.115), we'll boost our children's sense of their own worth and capabilities.

Correct without crushing

We can crush children's wonder and curiosity if we are not careful. The other day I heard a little boy say to his dad, 'WOW! That is the biggest car in the whole world!' and he said, 'Don't be so stupid, of course it isn't.' There is often no need to correct, just agree with the sentiment. The father could have said, 'Gosh, that is a big car.' There is no need to be over-conscientious about every word when your child is learning to read, for example. If you feel relaxed and want to enjoy the story I think children pick this up and can take risks in what is for most children a bit of a risky business.

Angela Gruber, psychotherapist

Children may need to have their mistakes pointed out to them so they know where they are going wrong. But not always.

If a child is corrected for every misread word or badly formed number or letter, they will quite understandably stop wanting to show you what they can do. Focus on what is most important at that time.

If it is their first attempt at writing words with finger spaces in between, praise them when they get that right. If they are working on capital letters and full stops at school, concentrate on those rather than every spelling. When they are reading, quietly and

If nothing springs to mind, keep searching. Look beyond 'learning' to other important areas of life. Perhaps your child has a beautiful smile, or can do fantastic cartwheels, or showed kindness and consideration to a friend, or remembered to pack their school bag. Parents may need to widen their own view of childhood 'success' – beyond the confines of classroom and sports field – if their children are to gain a sense of all they can bring and be in the world.

Ultimately, our aim should be to make each child feel special and appreciated for being themselves, and for trying as well as achieving. This is what will help them flourish, take pleasure in success, cope with life's knocks and not be crushed when a sibling or friend does 'better'.

It is really important to keep looking for things your child can excel in and enjoy, whatever that may be, and to focus on that. It may be that he loves to laugh, or that he loves to tell stories, or that he's great at drawing, whatever. Competition is in the air at school and I don't think one has to foster it at home. This is the place to focus on the strengths of the child.

Vivienne Gross, family therapist

---

simply say a word they are struggling with but try not to interrupt their 'flow'. If they are writing a story or working out a sum, make a mental note of any numbers or words they need to practise later but try not to interrupt the task in hand.

Remember to praise application as well as attainment. Also beware overuse of 'But', as in 'That's lovely, but next time see if you could do it more neatly', or 'Those are very good, but those ones are wrong.' Praise doesn't count if it is only used to sugar-coat criticism.

It is very easy to always end on a high note, with praise for something your child can do. So if he fails on one word, make sure you end on a word they do know and say 'Oh, good'. You can always end positively.

Nicholas Tucker, educational psychologist and Honorary Senior Lecturer in Cultural Studies, University of Sussex

I watched my child's teacher go through a spelling test with her and it was fascinating. She pointed out every word my daughter had got right or very nearly right and said, 'Well done'. She didn't have to point out the mistakes, because they were obvious – they were the ones that didn't get praised. It was the same information, just delivered in a positive way.

Jane P

Avoid criticism If we are too concerned that our children 'get it right' we may spend too much time showing them what they've done wrong.

Research evidence confirms that while some children's ability to learn is determined by genetic make-up or developmental disorder, many more reach adulthood falling far short of their potential because their early efforts at learning were met with humiliation and criticism rather than encouragement.[21] This can be a disincentive to learn, for life. It's far more constructive to praise what they do well than to criticise errors (see Correct without Crushing, p.342).

Take your child's lead

Try to understand imaginatively how it all seems from the child's point of view. Without this, how is it possible to appreciate the help that the child needs?

Margaret Donaldson, *Human Minds: An Exploration*[22]

Accept children for their own unique mix of strengths and vulnerabilities, and be guided by them. Observe what and how they are doing and encourage them to build gradually on their abilities. This way, you'll more accurately match your support to their needs.

Aim to keep them stimulated enough to want to take the next step. This requires us to be aware of their emotional and physical needs, as well as their educational development. Perhaps your child is developing quickly in one area but needs to work a little more slowly in another; perhaps they've had a bad day and can't concentrate for the moment.

Children develop different skills at different rates and do not achieve like rungs on a ladder. Look at your child and respect those skills he is developing. He may be desperately interested in nature or science and you are ramming reading down his throat. He may choose to do things in a different order.

Adrienne Katz, founder and executive director of Young Voice

Make it manageable Bite-sized tasks are generally easier than a seemingly insurmountable mountain of learning. They also provide more opportunities to succeed. Writing four words three times each, for example, can bring a much greater sense of progress and success than writing one word twelve times.

Show that it matters We can help our children feel valued, and that we value their efforts, by listening to them when they talk about learning and by sharing and showing pleasure in their enthusiasms. We also need to show our appreciation through our actions – taking time to look and comment on what they've done, attending events, sticking their pictures on the fridge door.

Keep a sense of proportion It's very natural to want our children to reach their potential and do as well as they are happily able, but if support tips over into heavy pressure and anxiety, children generally learn less, not more (see Easing School Pressures, p.357).

Parents have natural fears about how children are going to cope in the world but they need to keep some limits on their anxiety. The moment you get anxious, children pick that up and this will just lead them to make more mistakes.

Angela Gruber, transpersonal psychotherapist

Teach children about learning Explaining how people learn can boost a child's confidence to try.

It is our responsibility to make clear to the child that you cannot learn unless you make mistakes. Parents and teachers should also be big enough to say, 'Oh, you didn't understand that. I didn't explain it well enough, let me explain it again' – i.e. it is my duty to explain it better rather than 'You've got it wrong'.

Corinne Abisgold, educational psychologist

A child who is never allowed to fall over will not learn to walk; a child who is protected from making any mistake will not learn how to make a decision.

Anuradha Vittachi, *Stolen Childhood*[23]

Reminding children of something they can now do – perhaps reciting the alphabet or drawing a shape – will help them see how they have already achieved what they once found difficult.

Remember, also, to state the obvious: that different people learn different things at different speeds; that everybody is good at something and no one is good at everything; that everybody makes mistakes, and these can be a good thing if we learn from them. To a child, this can be revelatory.

All of us learn in very different kinds of ways. People have not thought about this enough in schools or in homes: some children like to learn alone, others learn better through interaction with others, some learn through words, others through visual or musical cues, some learn by doing. I think many parents are very aware of how their child learns just by trying different ways.

Professor Katherine Riley, Director of the Centre of Educational Management, Roehampton Institute, London

Positive examples Clearly, books, play things and other learning materials that reflect positive and authentic images of a child's ethnic background are important in developing their view of themselves, their culture and their own potential. Books and materials that reflect a wide range of racial and cultural groups will help all children better respect and understand the diversity around them (see Where's Me?, p.328).

Children soak up messages about who does what in their family and the world around them. If Mum or Grandma always reads to the children, what message does that give our sons? If Dad or an uncle is always turned to for help with maths or science homework, what message does that give our daughters? Recent research shows how boys' reading confidence and skills can rocket if read to by their fathers or other trusted male friends or relatives. Girls still tend to see science and related subjects as 'boy zones', and parents as well as teachers need to help them break through the gender barriers (see Gender and Development, p.302).

Learning to concentrate Sitting and concentrating does not come naturally to all children. If a child is having difficulty, we can encourage them to practise while doing something they enjoy (painting, cooking, construction kits, etc.), with us sitting alongside if that helps. Keep practice sessions short, and praise any progress.

High-energy children of all ages often find it easier to sit and think after physical exercise. If a young child finds it hard to sit still with a book, for example, try a burst of football or musical statues or silly dancing before settling down together. Older children may happily get down to schoolwork once they've had some full-throttle physical play. Try turning off the TV, radio or other distractions. Reducing consumption of fizzy drinks and high-sugar foods may also help children who experience 'sugar rush' energy surges.

Board and card games can help older children stay put and concentrate for increasingly longer stretches. If a child can't cope with a full-length game, do it in stages, keeping a note of where you left off the previous day.

Changing tack

I'm not the patient parent I thought I was. I got so wound up, it was like I couldn't believe she couldn't do it. I went over it again and again, getting madder and madder, and she still made the same mistake.

Helen P

If a child doesn't understand an explanation, repeating it may simply mean they get bored and you become frustrated. Sometimes shifting from abstract to concrete examples can work wonders. A child who shows no interest in adding six plus five may happily calculate the number of footballers needed to make an eleven-man squad.

Maybe explain the problem another way. Acknowledge how hard it can be and ask the child to think through other ways they might try again. Crucially, remember that parents often don't make great teachers. If our child isn't 'getting it', it may more down to our explanations than their lack of concentration!

If you are still getting nowhere, take a break and let the matter drop. The child may well want to try again after a bit of TLC. Even if they don't, a few days' rest will do much less damage than either of you getting cross or exasperated.

If the child can't do something, try not to get cross. Parents are not very good actors, and if you are going to show disappointment you are doing more harm than good. Children hate disappointing their parents and easily lose confidence.

Nicholas Tucker, educational psychologist and Honorary Senior Lecturer in Cultural Studies, University of Sussex

Avoid comparisons Telling children they are performing better or worse than their peers or siblings simply fuels anxiety. Our children are bombarded with comparisons to other children once they start school; home should be a comparison-free zone (see Ripping up Labels, p.119).

Teachers will be able to tell you how your child is progressing and whether they are attaining levels expected for their age and stage so you can pinpoint any areas where they might need extra support.

Yesterday I was talking to children who had been taken out of mainstream school for a few weeks to learn some of the basic skills they were struggling with. It saddened me how they all talked of being bullied. Children who are struggling may also have to cope with what goes wrong around that, feeling left out, being called names and so on. It is very important for parents to know how their child is doing.

Professor Katherine Riley, Director of the Centre of Educational Management, Roehampton Institute

Be honest Slightly older children, especially those who know from experience that school isn't always a fun factory, may appreciate a parent's acknowledgement that it's sometimes a slog. Let them know that hard work and application do make a difference – that sometimes you do have to work at something that seems boring just to be able to move on to the next, more interesting stage.

Talk about times in the past when they achieved through persistence. If they're finding it hard to stick with a problem, offer to be their partner, sitting by their side and encouraging them to the next step. Notice and praise effort, and explain that there would be no need for teachers and schools if learning was always easy.

It is often helpful for parents to explain the process of learning and how the mind works. Explaining how memory works, for example, that sometimes it is easy, sometimes we forget, that we have short- and long-term memory and how normal it is to find some things harder than others can be very reassuring.

Camila Batmanghelidjh, psychotherapist, Director of Kids Company

Encouraging enquiry

I've been thinking. I think Father Christmas is God's cousin.

Joshua, six

Shall I tell you why I'm glad I'm not a porcupine?

Holly, four

Education of the young that fosters enthusiastic learning will be collaborative. It will be more like an expedition to explore in the company of experienced and interested guides; or like a craft fair where creative people show to others what they

have discovered and made – not a competitive race over an obstacle course to win predetermined goals, watched over by judges with score pad ready.[24]

Colwyn Trevarthen, Emeritus Professor of Child Psychology and Psychobiology, University of Edinburgh

Learning, for children of the information age, will be less a matter of memorising facts and more a matter of knowing what to do with them. This ability to think, rather than be a receptacle for received information, can be aided even at pre-school and primary level, by encouraging children to ask questions, enquire, explore, and to think creatively and courageously.

Whether it is new initiatives to encourage mental calculation in maths classes[25] or new research into 'thinking skills', the message is clear: encouraging children to think can have remarkable benefits for their education as a whole.

Questions, questions

Children's natural desire to enquire is blossoming around the age of five and you are simply tapping a natural resource. The questions a child formulates for himself will be incredibly motivating and often remarkable – 'Does the wind have a mind?' We can close this question down because it is difficult to answer, or close down further enquiry by answering it, but our role as a parent is to facilitate the enquiry. This is not about giving a quick answer but about the trying to understand and keeping the enquiry open. The ability to ask original questions, enquire and be adaptable becomes even more essential now with the speed of technological change.

Robin Freeland, educational psychologist

Parents can help by keeping a sense of perspective and humour. Get too intense and your child's eyes may glaze over. 'The worst thing to do is make something the child has expressed interest in into a really big deal,' explains Nicholas Tucker, an educational psychologist and honorary senior lecturer in Cultural Studies at Sussex University.

'Try not to be too heavy, and take the lead from the child. There is this old story where a little boy says to his mother, "What is lightning?" and she says, "I'm not sure. Go and ask your father," and the little boy says, "I don't want to know that much!" Children do not want lectures. Unfortunately, parents often see an opportunity and then squeeze it to death.'

At its simplest level, this requires parents to focus on active enquiry rather than passive learning – to welcome questions, to admit when they don't know the answers and to fuel their child's interest in wanting to know more. Recognising a few common parental bad habits may help:

Child: 'How does the jam get in a doughnut?'
Parent: 'Pass me that cup would you? Thanks.' (Child ignored)

Child: 'How does the jam get in a doughnut?'
Parent: 'What are you on about now?' (Child treated as an irritant)

Child: 'How does the jam get in a doughnut?'
Parent: 'Ask your mother.' (Child fobbed off)

Child: 'How does the jam get in a doughnut?'
Parent: 'Well, I'm pleased you asked me that. After first being deep-fried in extremely hot oil the soft dough rises until it is the familiar doughnut shape. Once cooler and firm, it is pierced by a long needle and . . .' (Child asleep)

The remedy is relatively simple.

Child: 'How does the jam get in a doughnut?'
Parent: 'That's a good question. How do you think it might?' (Child encouraged to think for themselves)

If the response is, 'I don't know', you can still encourage them to think it through by giving them a series of possible answers to choose from. Throw in a few funny ones for good measure.

On a deeper level, we need to recognise the importance of enquiry, the doing and the discovery rather than simply the end result or final mark – and to explain that to our children. We can encourage the enjoyment of enquiry through games and stories (see Stories and Games for Thinking, p.351) and also by explaining how the things they learn link to the world around them.

We also need to recognise the impact of our own example on our children's attitude to learning. If we are open, enthusiastic and constructive about our own opportunities to learn and problem-solve, the chances are our children will be, too.

Stories and games for thinking

It is important for parents to give children as wide an experience of life as is possible, including music, art, 'finding out', sports and so on. Talk through things that interest them, reflect with them on what learning means and build on their talents. This can be done through stories (see below) and thinking games (see p.353). They ought to be fun, not work. Part of the fun for both of you is finding out what and how your child really thinks.

Robert Fisher, Professor of Education, Brunel University, and director of the Centre for Research in Teaching Thinking

A story for thinking: The Timid Hares

(Folktale from India, which also appears in similar versions in Europe and Africa)

Adapted, with kind permission, from *Stories for Thinking* by Professor Robert Fisher

There was once a timid hare who was always afraid that something terrible was going to happen. He was always saying: 'What if the sky were to fall down on us? What if the earth were suddenly to fall in? What would happen to me then?'

One day after he had been saying this to himself many times, he heard a loud noise. Bang! The ground seemed to tremble. The hare almost jumped out of his skin. 'What was that!' he cried. 'The earth must be falling in!' So he ran off as fast as he could go. After he had gone some way he met another hare. 'Brother hare,' he said, 'run for your life! The earth is falling in!'

'What's that?' cried the other hare. 'Hey, wait for me!' So he ran after the first hare, who told another hare, and soon all the hares were running as fast as they could. And each one cried, 'Run, run, the earth is falling in,

the earth is falling in!' Soon the larger animals heard and they began to run, crying: 'The earth is falling in! Run for your lives!'

A wise old lion saw them running, and heard their cries. He looked around. 'I cannot see the earth is falling in,' he said. So in his loudest voice he roared, 'STOP!' At this all the frightened animals skidded to a halt.

'What are you saying?' asked the lion. 'Haven't you heard?' trumpeted the elephant. 'The earth is falling in!'

'What makes you think so?' enquired the lion. 'The tigers told us,' said the elephants. 'What makes the tigers think so?' 'The bears told us,' growled the tigers. 'What makes the bears think so?' 'Why, the deer told us,' said the bears. 'Why do the deer think so?' 'The monkeys told us,' murmured the deer. 'And how do the monkeys know?' 'The jackals

continued overleaf

said so,' chattered the monkeys. 'And how did the jackals find this out?' 'The hares told us,' yelped the jackals. 'And how do the hares know?' One hare said that the other hare told him, and so on, until finally they came to the first hare. 'I know,' he said, 'because I saw it happen.' 'Where?' 'Under the big coconut tree.'

'Well, come and show me,' said the lion. 'Oh no, I'm too scared! It might happen again!' squeaked the hare. 'Well, climb on my back and I'll take you,' said the lion. So, still trembling, the hare jumped on the lion's back, and slowly they plodded to the big tree. Just then . . . BANG! A coconut came crashing to the ground. 'Run, run,' cried the hare, 'we're all going to be killed!'

'Stop and look!' said the lion. 'Well, what is it?' 'I . . . I think it's a coconut,' said the hare. 'Then you'd better tell the other animals that the earth falling in is only a coconut falling from a palm tree.'

One should not always believe what one hears.

Thinking about the story

Key question: What does the story mean?

1 What made the hare almost jump out of his skin?
2 What did he think the noise was?
3 Which animals joined the hare in running away?
4 Which animal did not run, and stopped the other animals?
5 Why did the animals think the earth was falling in?
6 What did make the noise? How did the animals know?
7 What advice would you give the hare?
8 Can you think of a time when you believed something that turned out to be wrong?

Thinking about knowledge

Key question: What do knowing and believing mean?

1 What do you know for sure? Can you give examples?
2 What does 'knowledge' mean?
3 If you know something does it mean it must be true?
4 If other people say they know something, does it mean it must be true?
5 If you read about something in books, does it mean it is true?
6 Are there some things you believe in but are not sure you know about? Give an example.
7 Do you believe everything you see? Why?
8 Do you believe everything you are told? Why?
9 What do you know that nobody else knows? Can you give an example?

continued

Further Activities

Make up a play about someone who was very scared of something that was not true.
Make a list of things you know and things you believe but are not sure of.

A game for thinking: Improve the Human Body

How to play

Players are given paper and pencil and told to design and draw some improvement or improvements to the human body. At the end of a given time, say 15 minutes, each player shows their drawing and explains what improvements they have designed. Players may then vote to find out whose design was thought to be the most creative and original.

If a family solves problems with democracy their children will show good problem-solving abilities whereas if they see us shouting or becoming depressed if there's a problem, these children become very poor problem-solvers. The kind of things we model in the everyday are absolutely crucial to what our children learn and how they learn it. People do not seem to be aware how critical these things are in the forming of children's thinking.

Robin Freeland, educational psychologist

Preparing for school

Preparing for primary school Imagine. You are starting a new job tomorrow. You can't remember where it is or what the office building looks like and how or even whether you'll get back home again. You don't know where you'll sit. You don't know who you'll be working with, who your boss is or what you're expected to do. You have no idea when or whether you'll be able to eat or even go to the loo. Everything you know well and love deeply will be somewhere else – and everyone's telling you you'll have such a wonderful time. No wonder many children find starting school so hard.

Acknowledging those fears and anxieties is the most effective means of helping children cope with them (see Feelings and Fears, p.124).

You can also help by gently and calmly giving your child as much preparation and information as they need. Make sure they know the sorts of things they may be doing and the rough structure of the day

If you have a chance to chat to the teacher before the first day, try to find out what will be expected of your child. Don't just think of schoolwork: how do they like children to ask to go to the loo? Will they be expected to shut the loo door? Will they be expected to sit at a desk? Simple things like this can throw a child, especially if they risk being chastised for something they are allowed to do at home. Reading books together about going to school, even playing school with their toys, can help familiarise children with new routines such as assembly or going to the school canteen for lunch. If your child will be taking a packed lunch, have a few 'practice' lunches at home, so opening the box and unwrapping the food doesn't seem so daunting.

Let them play with crayons, paper, scissors and books and, crucially, let them mix with other children before they start school. Meeting up with children who may be in your child's class before school begins can also ease the transition. The school or local playgroups and nurseries may be able to put you in touch with other parents in your area.

If possible, discuss in advance the school's attitude to you staying

---

Smoothing the way

Adrienne Katz, founder and executive director of Young Voice

Easing the transition to school is one of the most important boosts you can give a child. Their first impression and their feeling of coping with it will colour their view of school for a very long time. The happier you can make this transition the more positive the child feels about it.

It is the little things that matter, the sort of shoes you choose – laces or Velcro for ease, trousers that are easy to take down in the toilet, etc. Another important preparation is helping your child understand and follow instructions. Teach them prepositions – underneath, on top of, behind – because teachers are forever giving instructions such as 'Stand behind Jonathan', 'Put your books next to my table, please'. If young children do not understand these, and not all do, they may appear unco-operative or hesitant and the child feels nervous and unsure.

Using these words in a fun way yourself will help – 'Put teddy on the table. Where has he gone? On the table.' It only takes a few minutes here and there and is, I believe, even more valuable than teaching children the alphabet.

for a while in the mornings until your child is happy without you (see Separation Anxiety, p.140). Many children respond best to a gradual introduction, others may be happy with a clean break. Some schools welcome parents' support in the early days, others see it as unnecessary interference. There is little way of knowing how your child will respond until you get there, but thinking through the school's preferred approach and your possible responses will help.

Also think about your own attitudes to your child starting school. If you are very anxious or simply not ready to let them go, they will pick this up. Try to communicate positive messages about school, and your faith in the fact that they will be OK. If your child knows you feel relaxed about it and sees you relaxed in the presence of their teacher, they will expect to feel the same. It is a big step and most children stumble a little when they begin. But they get there in the end.

I have seen children going from almost solitary reclusiveness at age five going into primary school. They have never experienced playgroup, they have never experienced nursery, they have never had brothers and sisters or anyone else to play with and the first few months of integration into the school is traumatic. Parents should never allow children to be divorced from others of the same age. But even children as deprived as one or two I've seen coming in to primary school, within a few months will settle down and will be OK. It can be achieved, so never despair.

Professor Hugh Foot, specialist in child psychology and social development

The parent-school relationship

A good relationship between a child's teacher and parent(s) benefits children at a number of levels. For younger children, there is a connection between different parts of their lives, so what happens to them at school is not a completely different world but very much linked to their home life. This is enormously important to a young child. What parents know about how their child learns best is also very useful when fed back into schools, but this will only happen when the relationships are good.

Professor Katherine Riley, Director of the Centre of Educational Management, Roehampton Institute

Hone your diplomatic skills. When parents develop rapport with their children's school and teachers, they often get more information on the child's progress and needs and their own input and opinions get a better hearing. This may be crucial if a child encounters difficulties with schoolwork or other children (see Bullying, p.374).

Try to attend parent-teacher meetings and other opportunities to see your child's work. If you can't attend, the school may be able to arrange another appointment. Ask for information about how your child mixes and communicates with other pupils as this will help you gauge how they are coping.

If you've bad memories of school life it can be hard to think positively about your child's school, but try to unshackle their experiences from your own. The more positive your attitude, the more positive your child is likely to be.

Aim for an open and constructive relationship with teachers. Presuming your child is always in the right may limit your chances of productive discussion and blind you to possible problems and solutions. On the other hand, always defending teachers' actions in the hope of presenting a 'united front' may force your child to question their own feelings and experiences and make them reluctant to tell you when they encounter difficulties (see Feelings and Fears, p.124 and Communication, p.89). School life isn't always straightforward or fair, and recognising this can help parents and children discuss ways forward.

If you wish to draw the teacher's attention to a serious issue, agree a time to talk. It may help to write down the main points you wish to make. If you are not satisfied with the outcome of the meeting, ask for another meeting to explore the matter further or arrange to see a more senior member of staff. The school's administration office can inform you of its usual procedure for discussing problems if you're not sure who to turn to next.

If your child gets told off for something somebody else did at school and they feel an injustice has been done, I would advocate talking with the child about unfairness, acknowledging that it is unfair and upsetting, and thinking together about what you want to do. I wouldn't advocate taking every single case to the headteacher. Some children who feel their parents are going to write a letter or go marching up to the school about every single thing will then hide things because they fear their parents are a loose cannon.

Vivienne Gross, family therapist

Preparing for secondary school Starting secondary school can be a daunting prospect. Children will be moving to an unfamiliar environment with new faces, new rules and expectations, and different teachers for every subject. They will also be adjusting to life as the youngest children in the school. How they cope can depend very much on the kind of support they receive, and this can begin before they leave primary school.

The family support charity Parentline Plus (see Contact, p.429) suggests:[26]

- Giving children some say in which school they attend. This may help them feel committed to making a go of it.
- Visiting the school beforehand to meet teachers. Attend 'taster days' if offered.
- Remaining calm and cheerful. If you are anxious, your child's anxiety may be increased.
- Acknowledging any feelings of nervousness the child may have. Try saying, 'It's only natural to feel nervous' rather than 'Don't be silly, there's nothing to worry about.'
- Discussing any worries. Help your child think about who to ask for information or advice if needed e.g. 'What happens if you get lost?'. 'How can you get hold of me if you miss the bus?' Is there one particular teacher they should or could contact if they have problems or questions while at school?
- Looking through the school prospectus together to check rules and regulations and school uniform requirements.
- Where possible, practise the journey to the new school before term begins. Try to find another pupil in your area so your child has a travelling companion.
- In the last week of the holiday, gently reintroduce some routine of getting up, having breakfast and earlier bedtimes. Helping a child establish a routine can reduce distress.

Easing school pressures

I have seen seven-year-olds having anxiety attacks before their tests – actually shaking and hyperventilating – and this is at a school where we try to be so low key about tests at this young age they'd hardly know they are happening. In each case, they had picked up their parents' anxieties. Parental aspiration is understandable, and children do need parental support. But all parents, especially those of children who require extra help, need to be skilled in not transferring their anxieties on to their children.

Carol Munro, primary headteacher

Almost every schoolchild will now sit school assessments and tests. How well these are handled will vary hugely from school to school, but our children's ability to cope will be greatly influenced by our own anxieties and attitudes.

We can encourage our children's enjoyment of learning, and ask their school where and how we can best support them at home, without overloading them. This is crucial. Pushing our children too far, too fast, can harm family relationships, damage children's sense of their capabilities and achievements, distort priorities and seriously backfire.

Hothousing, where children are bombarded with tasks in an attempt to push them to some adult-ordained peak of performance, does not help them learn willingly and effectively in the long term. It is actively discouraged by leading educationalists and child support professionals.

Recent history is peppered with tragic examples of parents who have pushed their children too forcefully and ultimately to breaking point, sometimes with good intentions, sometimes to compensate for their own unfulfilled ambitions, sometimes out of raw competitiveness. Our society seems increasingly obsessed with speeding development and achievement: we have French for tots, baby gymnastics, 'pre-reading' tapes to play while toddlers sleep, homework videos, support books, websites and a whole raft of school assessments and tests to feed parents' neuroses.

Sometimes, it's essential that we actively support our children's learning at home (see Homework, p.359). At other times, the very best thing we can do is give our children a break, allowing them to relax and recharge. Be guided by each child's individual needs, and remember that:

Pushing children too fast denies them the experience of success Every time they reach the top of one mountain they are faced with another to climb rather than being allowed to draw breath and admire the view. It allows them no time to feel great about what they have achieved – the greatest motivator of all.

Pushing too hard makes failure inevitable There is no surer way to undermine children's confidence than to push them beyond their natural capabilities.

Homework

Homework varies hugely between schools, children and families. The following suggestions help in most circumstances.

- Check your child has sufficient space, equipment (pencil, rubber, etc.) and time to do what they need.
- Some children prefer to work alone, others like to work in the same room as other family members or friends. Try to keep background noise low and turn off the TV. Younger siblings may keep quieter for longer if you read or play with them.
- If space and/or quiet aren't available at home, perhaps your local library or child's school runs a homework club?
- If your child has regular homework, try to build this into the afternoon/evening routine. Some children prefer to get the work done as soon as possible, others like to play first. It doesn't matter as long as it gets done.
- Be available to help – sit with them if they like – but do not hang over your child's shoulder or interfere unless requested. If you help, tell their teacher, who needs to know their true ability levels.
- Give feedback rather than criticism. For example, 'Any ideas of another way to tackle that?' or 'That's hard. What might help?' rather than 'That's wrong.' Remember to praise application and effort as well as achievement.

- Check your child gets the sleep and exercise they need to sit down and concentrate.
- Encourage your child to note homework instructions: what is the task? when is it to be handed in?
- Explain how they could best organise and present their work if they seem unsure. Uncertainty of what is expected creates unnecessary pressures, and children have enough of these already.
- If a young child doesn't want to do homework, why not switch roles and play schools, with the child playing 'teacher' and you being the 'pupil'? This can ease tensions, enables the parent to discover what the child knows, and allows the child to learn and have fun.
- Show an interest. If you don't know much about the subject, ask questions. Try not to bombard them with questions, however, especially straight after school. Allow them some 'down time'.
- If your child is struggling or skipping work, let the teachers know so they can provide appropriate support and encouragement.
- Let older children take responsibility for their homework. Encourage, take an interest, provide an environment in which they can work, then let them get on with it. If they don't, let them take the consequences.
- Keep homework in perspective. Other activities matter, too, especially playing with family and friends. Homework shouldn't soak up too much of children's free time in the primary school years.

It does not equip children to learn without external pressure Exceptional performance at an early age does not mean exceptional performance later in life. A child's own motivation is the key to their future success, not their parents' demands.

Some people who work in selective schools talk about a syndrome that occurs around the age of 13 – the children peak. They have had their finest hour because they have had tutoring and parental squeezing for years and have been working flat out at their limit for so long they simply cannot keep it up. Their performance has had to be impressive to get into certain schools, but it is not a true reflection of their learning – more of the incredible input they have had. They come out of the hothouse and are expected to grow at the same rate and they simply cannot do it.

Robin Freeland, educational psychologist

A child may reject later what you force now Encourage when you can, coax when it helps and be firm when you need to, but avoid force. Force fuels resentment. Resentment fuels resistance and the likelihood of rejection.

I knew a boy who was an exceptionally gifted pianist at a very young age. His parents forced him to practise long and hard. Then, when he was 18, he announced he was leaving home and leaving the piano behind, too. I don't think he's touched one since. What is the point of destroying a child's pleasure? Surely it would have been better for him to have not been so pushed, perhaps not achieved such excellence so young, and still be playing music today?

Jane Cutler, Head of Music, Da Capo School of Music

Stress can harm health The effects of stress on health are well documented. A child's anxieties may find expression in very real physical symptoms, from stomach cramps to headaches, skin disorders to other chronic and debilitating conditions. If you feel your child may be suffering from school-related stress, it is important to inform teachers so they can consider appropriate support and solutions.

I see so many stressed children. London is full of them. Often their natural ability to learn is blocked because there is a difference between hammering information in and allowing the child to acquire learning skills.

Camila Batmanghelidjh, psychotherapist, Director of Kids Company

Hothousing takes time This time could be spent doing things that are much more important to a child's healthy development, and much more likely to inspire their desire to learn.

Hothoused children rarely have sufficient free time to just potter around, follow their own leads and learn that it is OK to be still, relaxed and quiet. Children I see are so often zoomed around from school to class. Taking this quiet time away at an early age will have important consequences for them as adults because they will have difficulty relaxing and being on their own.

Corinne Abisgold, educational psychologist

Play and learning: a quick reminder

- Play boosts children's physical health and their emotional, mental and social development. But most important of all, it's fun.
- We can take our child's lead, letting them show us when they'd like our assistance or companionship and when they'd like to play on their own. Free, quiet and unstructured play lets children's imaginations soar.
- Experience of play with other children helps develop their self-awareness, self-esteem, self-confidence and problem-solving skills. Rough and tumble play encourages physical confidence and develops self-restraint.
- Too much TV and screen time discourages physical and social play and is a waste of childhood. We need to monitor the content of what our children see, and be alert to its influence on how they think and feel.
- Children learn best when they are enjoying themselves. Allowing children to decision-make and make mistakes increases their pleasure in discovery and their confidence to risk-take and rise to challenges.
- It is far more constructive to praise what children do well than to criticise errors.
- Children of the information age need our active encouragement to think and enquire, rather than simply soak up facts like a sponge.
- Starting any new school is daunting. Preparation and information will increase children's confidence. Acknowledging their fears and anxieties will boost their coping skills.

CHAPTER ELEVEN

GROWING INDEPENDENCE

I never know who I'm going to meet – the six-year-old going on 16, or the six-year-old going on three.

John S

He's 10 now and I can't believe how much he's changed. He seems so grown up, it can take me by surprise how much he needs me.

Jenny T

This chapter deals with issues most children face as they progress through their primary years. As our children grow, their increasing independence will bring great change and opportunities to their lives and to ours. They are venturing out into the world, often into unfamiliar territory without us alongside, yet we are still the central figures in their lives. How we support them will profoundly affect their ability to cope and enjoy new experiences to the full, now and in their future.

Friends

I wince when I hear my daughter and friends' conversations about who's bestest friends with whom. It can be so cruel.

Carolyn P

After I lost my baby I heard my daughter talking to her friend about it with such brutal honesty. It was so matter-of-fact and what she obviously needed to say but in a way she would never have said to me. In that way kids do support each other, even when they're young.

Helen O

Friends matter. Our children's general happiness, behaviour, language, sense of worth, safety, aspirations and achievements are likely to be greatly influenced by their peers in general and their friends in particular.

As any adult knows, friends can help you through the toughest of times and falling out with friends can make even good times hard to bear, yet the intensity and importance of childhood friendships are often overlooked. Strong friendship bonds can develop from nursery and reception age on and often increase in importance over time.

Children's friendship styles vary. It doesn't matter much whether your child has one particularly special friend, or many; whether they form very close bonds, or seem happier with less intense relationships. Certainly, the wider circle of friends a child develops, the more support they can draw on and the more options they have, which is no bad thing in life. But what matters most is that each child has at least one friend, ideally at the same school.

Having a good friend will lessen the harmful effects of bullying. If you are excluded by the general peer group but you have a friend who is saying, 'You are not so bad as they say you are', this can be enough to satisfy your need to belong. You will not be damaged if somebody special is valuing you, even if you are not valued by everyone.

Dr Michael Boulton, child psychologist, Keele University, specialising in research into aggression, bullying and victimisation

General social skills matter, too. Much research has shown that being assertive rather than aggressive, and having good self-esteem and communication skills diminishes the likelihood of being bullied[1] (see Communication, p.89, Assertion v. Aggression, p.368 and Bullying, p.374).

Our role is to help our children develop the skills they need to get along with others while also encouraging their confidence, resilience and personal values, so they know when not to run with the pack. We can do this by:

Providing opportunities for our children to play with others We can't force friendships but we can encourage them by asking our children who they would like to get to know better and inviting them home to play. Out-of-school activities can widen a child's circle of possible friends and boost their social confidence.

We can also practise what we preach and show our children the benefits of friendship and social contact in our own lives.

My son was having a tough time at school. Nothing major, but he didn't seem to have any real friends. So we started playing football in the park on a Saturday morning and asking other dads and kids along for a kick about. Nothing formal, just for fun. It's been great and he's got pally with a couple of boys in particular.

Mike C

Boosting children's self-esteem Most children occasionally fall out with friends. Many will make up again soon after but for the time in between, they may feel devastated. We can help by acknowledging

Peer pressure

Most of our lives are spent in peer groups which exert a powerful influence over us for good or for ill. We're better equipped to retain individuality and good judgement as we grow older if we have a background of self-confidence . . . Early experience in the family influences the child's ability to develop relationships in later life that are built on tolerance, respect for others and socially responsible behaviour.

Royal College of Paediatrics and Child Health[2]

Parents worry about peer pressure, and it's hardly surprising they do. Who our children choose as friends will impact on their behaviour and safety and influence how others behave towards them. Yet it is not all out of our hands. Quite the contrary, children's friendships and their behaviour within them will be shaped by their experiences within the family and their relationships with their parents. So there is much we can do to help.

The potency of peer influence is clear from children's first weeks at school. A craze may sweep through playgrounds in a matter of weeks; a six-year-old may start talking playground-speak or develop a deep hatred of carrots for no other reason than that their best friend doesn't like them. Such manifestations of peer influence are relatively insignificant and often funny, yet others are key to our children's futures.

Many of the most serious issues around peer influence (such as anti-social behaviour and drug use) become apparent later in our children's lives, but now is the time to lay the foundations of social competence and decision-making that will help see them through.

As Dr Gavin Nobes, senior lecturer in Developmental and Forensic Psychology at the University of East London, explains:

their feelings and talking together about how friendships come and go, that some last a lifetime and others a day. We can also try to boost our children's sense of their own worth (see Feelings and Fears, p.124). Children who feel better about themselves tend to be more confident in forming friendships and also cope better when friendships go wrong.

Friendships can become crucial out of desperation that at least somewhere a child has an affirming relationship. This creates a fragile situation because when peers don't respond the child can feel desperate. They then try too hard, which backfires, and they are then vulnerable to behaving in any way to be acceptable to their peers.

Camila Batmanghelidjh, psychotherapist, Director of Kids Company

'Peers are very important. They are likely to be every bit as important as parents in, for example, the development of delinquency. And it is likely that these sorts of influences begin very young, possibly pre-school.'

Yet parents have a large part to play in influencing children's attitudes and behaviour, and thus their choice of friends. 'Importantly, parents should avoid being authoritarian, harshly punitive or aggressive,' says Dr Nobes (see What's Your Style, p.205). 'These parental styles lead children to develop anti-social behaviour and to then becoming attracted and attractive to other aggressive, deviant peers who, in turn, encourage and reinforce that anti-social behaviour.'

Parents can also help their children resist pressures to follow the crowd by encouraging them to value themselves, their feelings and their own decisions as they grow. 'There's no doubt that parents play a role in friendship choice and that those who are most influenced by the peer group tend to be those who don't get the support at home,' says Dr John Coleman of the Trust for the Study of

Adolescence. 'I don't think there's a single shred of evidence to show anything but that the most powerful support and influence for children and young people is the family.'

Importantly, we shouldn't allow our concerns about peer pressure blind us to the benefits that children's friendships bring. 'Peers have something unique and significant to contribute to development because they are equals: they tend to be equally knowledgeable, skilful and strong, and have similar interests,' Gavin Nobes explains.

'Negotiating rules with peers might well be an important first step in the process of learning about the rules that regulate social behaviour. With peers, children have almost unique opportunities to develop social skills, such as those of negotiation, co-operation, competition and conflict, in ways they usually cannot when with parents or teachers because adults are too big and too powerful.'

Developing social skills

It is not the kind of world where shy people get noticed. So all children, but especially shy children, need to be encouraged in the basic skills of communication and being sociable to get them started. You start the rollercoaster by practising with your children at home: 'Hi, my name is . . . what's yours?' Tell them about eye contact if someone talks to them and about asking how someone is, and practise these until they don't find them a problem any more. From this, they will find people are nicer to them and they can learn the next response until it becomes more natural.

Steve Biddulph, psychologist and author

Social skills matter

We are teaching and equipping our children for life so it is essential to teach them how to communicate and interact with people. A friend of mine's child went through a stage of never smiling at anyone and looking very sulky, so she actually told him to smile. She explained it was a signal to other people. It may not mean you want to be their friend but it is saying 'I'm friendly', so you then have the opportunity to find that out. It is about socialisation and survival in the real world.

Pat Elliot, psychotherapist

'People are waking up to the fact that children's social relations are just as important as their cognitive development,' says child psychologist Dr Michael Boulton. 'Many children are adept at socialising from an early age with very little coaching, perhaps because parents are providing these learning opportunities in the home. A small proportion of children lack these social skills.

'Some kids are happy being on their own. Others, however, may be on their own against their wishes, which may make them vulnerable to bullying. They just simply don't know how to join in, hover on the periphery of a game and are ignored.

'Some are outgoing but tend to make statements that put the peer group off: "I can do that better than you", "Don't do it that way, do it this", "Don't play that play this". They are then rebuffed. It is far better for a child to actively fit in with what's going on: "That's a good game, whose side shall I be on?" They assume they are welcome and accept the rules of the game. A parent can help a child develop these skills.'

We can help children negotiate social life and playground politics by encouraging and praising those social skills they have and working on those they don't (see Social Skills Matter, p.366). Think together of different ways to start a conversation: 'I liked your drawing. What do you like drawing most?', 'Who do you think's going to win the Premiership?' Talk together about different ways to join in or start up a game, and what children can do if they are rebuffed. Try to keep conversations short, light and focused on the child's needs rather than our own anxieties or experiences.

If a child is having difficulty making or keeping friends, try to spot any aspects of their behaviour that may be making them vulnerable to being picked on, excluded or ignored. Try not to 'fix it' or focus too intense a light on the issue, but ask them what they think might help (see Communication, p.89). Talking together about what makes a good friend can encourage children to think through what they might do differently. Drawing pictures or making lists of what children like in their friends and their friends like in them can help keep discussions positive.

It is key to listen to your children's feelings without dismissing them, or giving solutions. It is helpful to let them tell you what is going on. Even young children are amazingly resourceful at finding their own solutions given the opportunity – 'I understand this is difficult (e.g. best friend won't play with them). What do you think would help?'

Kitty Hagenbach, child psychotherapist

Encouraging children to think for themselves We can show our children that their opinions matter, both in their learning and their home life (see Respecting Opinions, p.103). They will carry this confidence into their relationships with their peers.

In America where the problem of drugs is much more prevalent, schools do projects with younger children to show them the value of their own thoughts and decisions. One example was a group of children who had to choose between two boxes, one of which contained something the children really wanted and they had to guess which one by placing a counter on it. After a while the children just placed their counter on the box that had most on. This was used to demonstrate to the children that it wasn't always the best option to go with your peers, i.e. you have to think for yourself.

Corinne Abisgold, educational psychologist

Assertion v. aggression Our children need to value their own opinions and express them constructively. Fundamental to their ability to mix happily with other children will be their understanding of how to give and take, how to consider other people's feelings and how to express their own needs and wants clearly, appropriately and effectively.

All children benefit from understanding the difference between assertion and aggression but it is especially helpful for those who seem to cave in to pressure or use force or threats to get their way. We can begin by explaining, in words suited to the child's age and stage, that there are three ways of responding to situations:

- **Aggressive** Aggressive people think their needs matter more than anybody else's. They will do whatever it takes to get what they want. Push. Grab. Manipulate. Say horrible things. They will get some of the things they want this way, but lots of people won't like how they behave. Their behaviour is likely to get them into trouble.

- **Passive** Passive people think other people's needs matter more than their own. They have trouble getting what they want or standing up for what they believe is right. Their behaviour doesn't resolve underlying problems and can lead to low self-worth and simmering resentment. And simmering resentment can lead to low self-esteem and/or explosive anger.

- **Assertive** Assertive people know their needs matter and other people's do, too. They try to get what they need or want by being clear and firm when necessary, in ways that don't hurt other people's bodies or feelings. They listen to other people's point of view and make their own views clear. This tends to make situations better because all those involved feel respected and understood.

This is sophisticated territory, yet even young children can begin to grasp the basics. Thinking through different situations together may help clarify the issues.

You want to use your friend's pen. What's the best way to get it?

1   Grab it or shout, 'Give me your pen'? (Aggressive)
2   Decide to use a pencil instead? (Passive)
3   Ask calmly and clearly, 'May I use your pen, please?' (Assertive)

Assertion skills

Adapted, with kind permission, from *Preventing Bullying!*
A Parent's Guide by Kidscape (see Contacts, p.429)

The children's charity Kidscape has compiled a list of skills to help children who are bullied or bullying become more assertive. The points will help children in most social situations, so are worth discussing with them.

Making requests

— Be clear about what you want.
— Plan ahead and practise.
— Make your request short and precise ('That is my pencil and I want it back').
— Decide what you want to say and stick to it ('I would like my pencil back'). You don't have to be rude but don't get sidetracked.

Saying No

— When you say No, say it firmly.
— If you don't want to do something, don't give in to pressure. Be firm. Remember we have the right to say No.
— If you are not sure and somebody is bugging you for an answer, say 'I need more time to decide' or 'I need more information'.
— Don't make excuses: keep your body posture assertive (don't stand all hunched up in victim mode) and look the person in the eye. The other person will know from the decisive way you are speaking and standing that you mean business (If you find looking people in the eye hard, practise keeping eye contact within your family).
— Offer an alternative: 'No I don't want to play football. Let's go for a walk instead.'
— When we say No to someone, we are only refusing the request. We are not rejecting the person.

Someone in your class has taken two books and there isn't one left for you. You've asked him to give it back and he won't. What would be the best thing to do next?

1 Hit him? (Aggressive)
2 Keep quiet and let him keep the book? (Passive)
3 Calmly explain to the teacher that you have a problem and ask for their help in sorting it out? (Assertive)

We can talk together about different ways of being assertive (see

Assertion Skills, p.369) and aim to illustrate its effectiveness in our own responses – by not caving in to aggressive behaviour, by listening and by being firm but not threatening (see Effective Discipline, p.215).

Teaching children how to sort out differences This is as effective for battling siblings as it is for fighting friends (see Siblings, p.279) and even young school-age children can grasp the basics of negotiation and the importance of resolving disputes fairly and peacefully. We can begin by setting out a situation clearly, acknowledging the feelings of those involved and expressing our confidence in the children's ability to sort it out.

1 **Define the problem** 'I can hear you both shouting but nobody seems to be listening to what anyone else is saying.'
2 **Describe the feelings** 'It's upsetting you both – and me.'
3 **Search for solutions** 'How can you sort this out so you're both happy? Let's hear a few ideas.'

Many children will come up with their own solutions. If they are young, or struggling to think of ways forward, we can make suggestions but still leave them to make the final decision: 'Maybe you could agree to listen to what each other is saying, then swap so everyone has a chance to be heard. Or maybe you could think of something else to play that you'd both enjoy. Which would help?' Our role is not to referee but to encourage the children to negotiate constructively and sort out disputes themselves.

   With enough practice, children can learn to do this without adult help. Recent studies show that children encouraged to resolve conflict in this way tend to sort out more disagreements before they reach boiling point, so have fewer and less bitter fights than those whose parents leave them to it or who constantly 'referee' their disputes.[3] So it helps them and it helps us.

   If differences in age, confidence or ability mean one child tends to dominate and get their way, we may have to become more actively involved to ensure everyone is heard. The following conflict resolution technique is straightforward, positive and fair. It looks like a lot of effort, but will make our lives easier in the long run. As before, our role is to guide rather than impose solutions, and to let the children themselves decide how to change their behaviour and make better choices in future.

1 **Explain** Tell the children that everyone needs a chance to speak. Express confidence in their ability to help sort the matter out.

2 **Take turns to identify the problem** Each child takes a turn to speak, describing the problems as they see it. No one interrupts. Encourage each child to talk about how they feel, not simply what has happened. We can suggest ideas, too: 'I can see you're angry because he took your toy, but I'm wondering if Jack's also feeling left out? Might that have something to do with it?'

3 **Suggest solutions** Let everyone have a turn to propose solutions. If they are struggling, suggest some.

4 **Agree a solution** Ideally, the children should do this between them.

5 **Review** Once agreed, express your confidence that the children will follow it through. Agree to get together again to discuss how the solution has worked out (in an hour, a day, two days depending on the dispute and the ages of the children).

You are aiming to educate to find solutions, ways to do things that suit everyone. We are not aiming for frozen, compliant children but children who can decide for themselves, learn from life and interact. The aim here is to have a child with heart and backbone. You do want a child to be kind to other children and they will do this if they have been shown enough kindness, but you also want a child who can be themselves and not just give in to others, who has the discipline to move through life, make decisions, get things done and make the best of their abilities.

Steve Biddulph, psychologist and author

Know what's happening If family communication is generally good, it is much easier to know when our children need extra support with their friendships (see Communication, p.89 and Feelings and Fears, p.124). Aim to have some idea of the friends our children play with and what they do in class and at break. If we know their school timetable, it is easier to talk about the specifics of the day rather than generalities. 'How was today?' may be shrugged off much more easily than 'What did you do in PE?'

Beware after-school activity frenzy It can backfire. If we over-stuff our children's days, we may leave too little time for relaxed chat to unfold. One recent survey[4] identified a 'critical time' after school when children want to talk through their day. The person they talk to need not be a parent, but children should be able to speak to someone they know and trust about how they feel. Some organised activities are fine and fun; too many may exhaust everyone and limit opportunities for real communication.

Help our children 'fit' Some children are happy to have very different clothes, haircuts and interests to their peers, but most like to appear sufficiently similar to feel they belong. If they want to strike out, be individual, do their own thing in their own way, that's great. But it should be their choice, not ours. Equally, if they want to fit in with their friendship group, we can help them conform enough to be accepted without turning them into class clones.

Parent's eyes can be so closed to this. I am not recommending parents having to buy the best trainers etc. but being aware of the impact that fitting in has on a child. You have to be alive to what it is like to be your child in that environment.

Mary MacLeod, chief executive, National Family and Parenting Institute

Modern manners

There is this view that with strangers we should be on our best behaviour but at home you can do whatever you like, which is wrong. Those closest to us deserve to be treated with respect and dignity and common politeness.

Dr Dorothy Rowe, psychologist and writer

Teaching children the basics of courtesy and generally accepted 'manners' equips them with useful social tools. If they know how to ask for help, show they have something to say, express pleasure and behave in ways that are generally appreciated, they are more likely to be viewed kindly by teachers and their best friend's mum. And this counts.

Let's be realistic. Social convention is often arbitrary and often broken. What are considered 'good' manners will vary widely between families, cultures and communities, so it is hardly surprising that children often forget what they are supposed to do when. But the more we explain what behaviour is expected and effective in particular circumstances, the sooner children grasp the nuts and bolts: 'Have you noticed how teachers ask people who put their hand up, not the people who shout out?'; 'If you've had a good time at a friend's house, it's great to tell them and their mum or dad.'

I'm a special needs teacher in primary schools and I know some children who have learned to say 'Excuse me' when they want to be heard and others who just blurt out what they want to say. Those who blurt out tend to get told off by the teachers and not heard, while those who say 'Excuse me' get praised and listened to. Like it or not, these social conventions make a difference to how children are treated.

Alison P

Children as young as six are often able to understand that expected and accepted behaviour varies between families (see Swearing, p.193). Explaining this clearly will help them when they come across other children and families doing things differently to their own – as they almost inevitably will.

Clearly, children pick up most of their habits through observation, but they will need more active guidance along the way if they are to survive and thrive in school and other social situations. Unfamiliar or more formal situations can be chatted through beforehand so the child isn't thrown off balance: 'When we go to see the teacher, she and I have a lot of talking to do. It would really help if you could wait quietly. What could we take along, so it's not so boring for you?' As ever, explaining expectations and praising positive behaviour rather than criticising mistakes is far more likely to produce positive results.

My partner, Shaaron, noticed that at about the age of four our little girl needed help to know how to wait. She was so concerned she would forget what she was going to say, she would get more and more frantic to be heard, especially if Shaaron was on the phone. She needed a task to begin to learn a new skill of waiting for the right time to speak, so we asked her to repeat silently in her head what it was she needed to say, until the right moment to tell us. This is more helpful to the child than saying 'Be patient' or 'Wait there'. Other skills to build on from waiting are listening, joining in on conversations on the right subject, noticing pauses in the conversation and asking permission to change the subject.

Steve Biddulph, psychologist and author

Bullying

In my experience most victims are sensitive, intelligent, gentle children. They don't come from homes full of conflict and shouting so when a bully comes at them they don't know quite what to do.

Michele Elliott, Director of Kidscape, the charity for bullied children
and their families

Younger children with less developed social skills and means of communicating and managing feelings are bound to be involved in nasty and mean behaviour towards each other. Prevention of bullying has to start here.

from *Why Me?* A ChildLine Study[5]

Bullying is a fact of school life and most children will experience it some time in their primary years. There is much we can do to help our children become bully-aware and bully-resistant. The first is to know the facts.

Bullying can be physical or psychological Professional definitions vary but children themselves consider bullying to incorporate everything from serious physical harm to teasing, name-calling, malicious gossip, destroying property, humiliation, rejection and exclusion.

Of all forms of bullying, psychological bullying can cause the greatest long-term damage to a child's view of themselves and their world. It can also be the first step on a downward spiral of intimidation that ends in physical attack.

Any form of bullying, however 'mild', must not be ignored If left unchecked, bullying can result in depression and other mental health problems, poor academic achievement, truancy, self-injury and, very rarely, suicide. It can also seriously damage those doing the bullying, who learn that aggressive, threatening behaviour gets them what they want, which in turn increases their chance of violent behaviour and relationship problems in adulthood.[6]

Listening and talking helps We need to listen to our children and discuss issues with them: what bullying is (i.e. not only physical threat or attack); where it might happen (are there any 'hot' spots – school cloakrooms, etc.?); how to minimise opportunities for bullying (not carrying valuables, staying in groups, walking on if confronted, etc.). Crucially, children need to understand that anyone can be bullied and it is not a child's 'fault'. Sometimes a child is picked on because of differences of race, gender, class, accent, appearance, disability, hair colour, academic ability, height. Sometimes because, for any number of reasons, they find it hard to stand up for themselves. Sometimes there seems no discernible reason at all.

Let your child know that showing bullies you are upset or frightened may encourage them to carry on. It often helps to ignore a bully (see Dealing with Taunts and Insults, p.376), but bullying itself should never be ignored.

Be direct. Say something like, 'I think you are being bullied or threatened and I'm worried about you. Let's talk.' If your child doesn't tell immediately, say you are there night and day, whenever she is ready to talk. Then keep a watchful eye.

Michele Elliott, Director of Kidscape

Children need to tell We need to give our children a very clear message that they *must tell* us, a teacher or another trusted adult as

Bullying – the hard facts

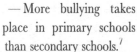

—More bullying takes place in primary schools than secondary schools.[7]

— In one ChildLine study[8], 64% of primary school children said they had been bullied at some point at school, 50% in the last year.

— A quarter of parents in one recent survey[9] said their child first encountered bullying at five or younger.

— 10% of calls to the Parentline Plus helpline about schooling related to children being bullied, mainly by peers but also by teachers, parents or a parent's partner.[10] Bullying included verbal

abuse, physical abuse and racial abuse. Reactions included refusing to attend school; running away; bullying behaviour at home, refusal to do homework, panic attacks, low self-esteem, unhappiness and depression; stealing; refusing to eat.

— Around 16% of 10–11-year-olds say school playtime and lunchtime cause anxiety.[11] About a third of Year 5 (nine to 10 years) and slightly fewer Year 6 (10 to 11 years) had experienced aggression or annoyance from other young people often or every day in the past month.[12]

Dealing with taunts and insults

Adapted, with kind permission, from *Preventing Bullying!*
A Parent's Guide by Kidscape (see Contacts, p.429)

When other people make hurtful remarks, don't argue and try not to become upset. Imagine that you are within a huge, white fog-bank: the insults are swallowed up by the fog long before they reach you. Nothing touches you.

Reply to taunts with something short and bland: 'That's what you think.' 'Maybe.' Then walk away. This might seem very strange at first and very hard to do but it does work and it can help you blot out insults.

soon as a situation feels difficult. Be explicit about this – children are bombarded with stories that suggest it is wrong to 'tell tales' but the sooner adults know what's happening, the sooner they can help.

Supporting children's friendships Even one friendship at school can reduce the risks of bullying. Children often need our active support to make and keep friends (see above).

If children find themselves without a friend time and time again they might not only begin to feel less liked by others, but begin to take that message on board and begin to dislike themselves. The child may then become the outsider, who becomes an easier target for bullying. Friendship can protect our minds and our bodies. That is why we need to take children's friendships very seriously and really go out of our way to help.

Allan Watson, National Pyramid Trust

The role of the bystander An estimated 70% of bullying is done in groups rather than by individuals acting alone.[13] We can discuss with our children what they might do if they are part of a crowd in which bullying takes place. Who could they tell? We can also make it clear that bullying does not pay. This can be the hardest point to put across to children, especially if they have seen bullies succeed where non-bullies have not. It may help to explain that boy or girl X will know they have not behaved well and so will other people. That is not a good feeling.

If a child is being bullied

If our children tell us they are being bullied, or we suspect they may be, we need to act:

- **Offer praise** ('It is very brave to tell'), **support** ('I will help in any way I can. There is much we can do together') **and reassurance** ('I love you very much. Always have, always will').
- **Check back** that our understanding of the situation is the same as the child's. This will help clarify the situation and prove to the child that the message has been received and understood.
- **Act** Bullying is complex and we need to consider a range of options. Ask for the child's suggestions, let them air any concerns and agree a joint plan of action. If the bullying is school-based, it is important the school is informed. Ask to see the school's anti-bullying policy, keep a record of any bullying incidents and contacts with school staff. Write to the school to avoid misunderstandings. Follow up every agreed step until you are satisfied the issue has been dealt with and your child feels safe.

Advising a child to get their own back or to hit back harder if physically threatened could make matters much worse.

— It may not work and the child could get seriously hurt.
— It reinforces the idea that might is right (when the child has been the victim of it).
— It can make children feel abandoned to fight their own battles.
— It can turn the bullied into a bully.

Yet also be aware that children do need to keep themselves safe. This may mean them running away, asserting themselves verbally, seeking adult help immediately or sometimes – when all other options have been tried or circumstances are extreme – defending themselves physically. Not all children can do this or want to, and parents should be aware of the dangers of telling children they should. Yet children who are expressly forbidden to use force in any circumstances may feel exposed. Talking to children about self-defence in the context of safety rather than revenge or tit-for-tat exchanges and emphasising that it is something they may feel they need to do in emergencies as a last resort, may help them feel less vulnerable (see Skills for Safety, p.381).

It is hard to know the balance. Quite often parents advise children very strongly 'You mustn't hit' and I am not advocating that we urge frightened children to take a stand against bigger, more threatening ones. However, occasionally, if a child is capable of being physically assertive it can stop matters escalating. So, yes, I have talked to my own children about self-defence. One feature of bullying is that if the person finds out they can get away with it, they will repeat it and it can spiral out of control. Tackling bullying is about trying to get in there very early on, if possible, to stop it escalating. Either by the child himself saying I am not going to put up with this – 'You are not to hit me again' – or calling for help there and then and adults responding. Sometimes if the child is able, self-defence can put an end to it, too.

Mary MacLeod, chief executive, National Family and Parenting Institute

Bullying can take a long time to resolve, and the damage done to a child's confidence and self-esteem may last even longer, so be prepared to provide your child with considerable emotional support. Anti-bullying support groups and charities such as Kidscape, the NSPCC or ChildLine (see Contacts, p.429) offer expert support and advice.

If a child is bullying

Children's reasons for bullying are as diverse as they are. Some feel inadequate or unloved and bully to feel dominant and significant, others bully because they follow the crowd; some are unpopular among their peers, others are popular and misuse the power vested in them by other children; some are bullied or treated harshly at home, others have always had their own way and so have never learned to nego-tiate or compromise; some do it very infrequently, perhaps in response to a difficult or sad experience; others do it often.

If a child is bullying, they need our help to stop:

— **Keep calm** Becoming angry or defensive won't help.
— **Tell the child you love them but their behaviour is unac-ceptable** Describe the behaviour and why it is unacceptable, but avoid labelling the child as 'a bully'. If this becomes part of their self-image it can be even harder to turn around their behaviour (see Ripping up Labels, p.119).
— **Explain the basics** Some young children need reminding of exactly what bullying behaviour is and why it can hurt and frighten others.

— **Talk about feelings** Children often express distress through problematic behaviour.

— **Be constructive** Does your child need to develop skills to negotiate conflict and manage their emotions? Practise different ways of handling difficult or volatile situations. Some children need to be shown ways to get positive attention and how to assert themselves without being aggressive (see Assertion v. Aggression, p.368).

— **Be honest** Bullying behaviour can be reinforced by parents' behaviour. If you intimidate, humiliate or threaten your child, you dramatically increase the chances of your child using similar techniques.

— **Channel aggression** Sports and rough-and-tumble play can act as a release and also teach children self-control. It should be monitored closely so it does not become a vehicle for bullying behaviour.

— **Review recreational and academic stimulation** Children who bully sometimes need something better to do. Is it possible that your child is bored or insufficiently challenged?

In our research[14] we asked children why they bullied. They cited three major reasons: 1. They did not like the person. 2. They were bored. 3. They were taking their feelings out on someone else.

Mary MacLeod, chief executive, National Family and Parenting Institute

— **Ask for the child's ideas** on how they could stop bullying and improve matters. Aim for your child to propose or at least agree to an approach, rather than impose your own. This helps them feel a part of the solution rather than simply 'a problem'. Saying sorry, or writing a note to the victim, may help but wait until apologies are sincere.

— **Be patient** Breaking any habit takes time and often has to be done in stages. Monitor progress (keep in touch with the school if bullying is school-based). Praise your child for reducing bullying behaviour.

— **Don't struggle alone** A parent's role is demanding and draining. Seek professional help, support and advice from anti-bullying charities when you need it (see Contacts, p.429).

Protection v. exposure

So many parents are in this terrible state of siege where they believe monsters and paedophiles are behind every lamp-post so we mustn't let the children

out of our sight. That creates such a stifling, constraining atmosphere.
The child feels loaded with the parents' anxieties and almost feels as if he
or she is doing something wrong.

Peter Wilson, child psychotherapist and Director of Young Minds

As a result of media attention and peer culture some parents perceive the
world to be an extremely dangerous place for young children in terms of the risk
of murder, sexual assault and abduction. They may over-protect children from
these relatively rare events while unnecessarily exposing them to the more
significant risk of injury from accidents in the home or on the roads.[15]

Royal College of Paediatrics and Child Health

We are losing our sense of perspective. As a society we tend to warn
our children most about dangers that threaten them least and gloss over
or ignore those that are much more likely to do them harm. Parental
neurosis is good for media ratings but we must also be aware that children
are extremely sensitive to parents' panic and fear. We owe it to them
and to ourselves to look at the issues calmly.

Our fear of the outside world is pushing children indoors where,
ironically, many risks are higher. Most abuse takes place inside the home
by people children know. The full extent of problems caused by 'home-
locked' childhoods is only beginning to be recognised but can include:

— **Almost constant adult supervision**, which can delay development of social competence and resilience, and put unnecessary strain
on parent/child relationships.
— **Long periods spent in front of a TV or computer screen**,
which can delay speech and social skills.
— **Insufficient physical exercise**, which can turn our children into
couch potatoes.

These are not a good preparation for a full and happy life.

Parents must wise up about the dangers in the home. Let's be sensible about it —
you are not doing kids any favours if they are always in the car and they do not
learn to cross the road. The real risk to their children lies at home and not in the
street but it is far harder to think that the man you are just starting to go out with
may be more of a threat to your three-year-old than a stranger.

Caroline Abrahams, Director of Public Policy, NCH Action For Children

Skills for safety

We need to teach our children how to stay safe without frightening them unduly. In a recent survey,[16] around 30% of 10–11-year-olds report that they have been scared or upset by an adult stranger at some point. This percentage has been consistent for a number of years. Just over 20% say they ran away when approached by a stranger.

The Kidscape charity suggests all parents should teach their children:

1: **To be safe** Tell your children they have a right to be safe. No one can take that away.

2: **To protect their own bodies** Children need to know their body belongs to them.

3: **To say no** Tell your children it's all right to say no to anyone if that person tries to harm them. Many children are told always to do what grown-ups say.

4: **To get help against bullies** Tell children to get friends to help them, to say no without fighting and to tell a grown-up. Tell them to give up something a bully wants (e.g. money, a bike, etc.) if they are going to get hurt; you will not be angry with them and keeping themselves safe is the most important consideration.

5: **To tell** Assure your children that you want them to tell you of any incident and that you will not be angry. Children

can also be very protective of parents and might not tell about a frightening occurrence because they are worried about your feelings.

6: **To be believed** If your children want your help, they need to know they will be believed and supported. This is especially true in the case of sexual assault as children rarely lie about it.

7: **Not to keep secrets** Teach children that some secrets should *never* be kept, even if they promised not to tell. Child molesters known to the child often say that a kiss or touch is 'our secret'. This confuses the child who has been taught always to keep secrets.

8: **To refuse touches** Tell children they can say no to touching or kissing if they don't like it. If someone touches them and tells them to keep it a secret, they *must* tell you. Never force children to hug or kiss anyone.

9: **Not to talk to strangers** Tell your children not to talk to strangers when they are by themselves and to ignore any such approach. Explain that they can pretend not to hear and quickly walk or run away. Tell them you want to know if a stranger tries to talk to them.

10: **To break rules** Tell children they can break rules to stay safe. They can run away, scream, lie or kick to get away from danger.

Every parent has to negotiate their own route between equipping children with the skills they need to stay safe and not restricting or terrifying them unnecessarily in the process. In addition to safety messages recommended by child protection groups (see Skills for Safety, p.381), parents themselves suggest that:

- **We talk to children about how to stay safe** (very important) much more than we talk about the risks to their safety (very small). This helps them feel more secure, not less so. It may only be a shift in emphasis, but it's a crucial one.
- **We nurture children's sense of competence and confidence** This will help keep them safe in an unpredictable world.

How we behave towards our children sends loud messages of their worth and helps protect them. In many situations their knowledge of themselves and their self-worth keeps them far safer than any particular instruction we may repeat to them.

Eileen Hayes, parenting advisor to the NSPCC

- **Teach children their full name, address and telephone number** as early as possible. Explain how to dial the emergency services and check they know how to use the telephone.
- **Discuss what an emergency is and helpful ways to respond** Children sometimes think 'emergency' means great calamity or threat of death rather than a scary or dangerous situation.

My kids got stuck in the lift in BHS and shouted for ages before anyone realised they were stuck. When I asked why they hadn't pressed the alarm button they both said, 'You always told us not to touch it.'

Richard P

- **Explain the difference between surprises and secrets** Abusers often tell children they must keep the abuse secret. We can explain that it's OK for adults to ask children to keep a surprise (birthday gifts, etc.) but not OK for adults to ask children to keep secrets (see Skills for Safety, p.381). If our children are confused as to which it is, they need to check with us.
- **Discuss the difference between a stranger approaching a child** (strange behaviour, to be avoided) **and them asking a stranger for help** in emergencies (sometimes necessary). Explain

that strangers would not be sent to pick them up from school, provide transport or deliver messages, however urgent. They are to be ignored, avoided and reported to a known and trusted adult or teacher.

- **Practise road safety** Crucial yet too often overlooked. Twice as many children fear an attack from a stranger than are worried about being hit by a car while crossing the road, yet road accidents are the biggest cause of accidental death in children under fifteen.[17]
- **Discuss safe computer use** Children need reminding not to give personal details or arrange to meet anyone they have 'met' online. Parental control settings can limit access and track use. Information on suitability of games is readily available (see Contacts, p.429).
- **Only let children stay the night at friends whose families you know and trust** Let them know they can phone you day or night, at any time, if they need you.
- **Talk about what to do if separated in crowds** Advise children not to wander off in search of you because you won't know where to look. Ask them to stay where they are, shout for you and wait. If you don't come or respond after they have shouted and waited an agreed number of times, tell them to ask for help from a female shop assistant or an adult with children.
- **Accompany young children into public toilets** and changing rooms.
- **Talk about telling** Let children know they can tell you anything, any time, and respond positively when they do (see p.107).
- **Talk about a parent's role** Children need to know that part of a parent's role is to protect their child and to help them in situations that are too confusing or scary for children to work out without adult help. They won't be 'letting you down' if they need you. That's what you're there for.
- **Be clear and calm** The more clear, calm and matter-of-fact we are, the more likely our children are to listen and to understand.

I remember my dad pressing a coin into my hand as I left for my first scout camp, saying something like, 'Ring me if anyone dares to touch a hair on your head.' I spent the next week wondering why anyone would want my hair and whether I should take my hat off.

Rob C

- **Check back** Even when children are too young to comprehend or cope with the full facts surrounding a safety issue, there may still be much we can do to help. Posing occasional questions or acting out simple situations can highlight major gaps in their understanding. Just as we wouldn't simply tell a child once how to cross a road or cut with scissors, we should not presume they will know how to put our words into action in an emergency without a little practice.

Responding to news events

My children have seen unimaginable horrors on the TV news and in the newspapers and they take in much more than we'd like to think. You can see it in their drawings.

Helen T

Recent years have seen wars, terrorist attacks, genocide, famine and other atrocities played out on our screens and in our newspapers. Our children are exposed to images and information that even adults find hard to bear or comprehend. Some psychologists believe no young children should watch or hear the news because it focuses on horrors they are not equipped to deal with. Others believe such censorship does not equip them with a balanced view of life and is unnecessary if they are growing up in a loving home that shows them a very different view of the world.

Where parents decide to draw their line will depend on many factors, including their child's age and temperament. But total censorship is not a realistic option. We may choose to shield our children from the worst scenes and stories, yet a newspaper may land on our doormat, shops play radio news, children talk to each other in the playground. It is inevitable that our children will get to hear of some events and issues we would prefer them not to know.

Equally, total media exposure without any parental censorship or support can leave a child in emotional free-fall. They may develop a very distorted view of the world because good news rarely makes the front page. Access to information about the cares of the world can create feelings of fear and powerlessness unless balanced with information about what they can do and how they might respond.

My son came home from school like Chicken Licken because he'd been told the hole in the ozone layer was letting in all these rays that were zapping us. I told him there was a hole, but people now knew what we needed to do to keep it under control and that you can protect yourself from the rays by using sun cream. He was still concerned, but at least he wasn't terrified.

Anne I

Rather than blanket censorship or exposure, it may help to think in terms of constructive support. When and if children hear of a horrific event, it may help to:

- **Put the issue into perspective** Stress these incidents are very rare. Explain what grown-ups are doing to find the person(s) responsible and to ensure it doesn't happen again.
- **Listen** This lies at the core of supporting our children through any hard or confusing times (see Communication, p.89). We want them to trust us and to listen to us so we can support them. For this to happen, we must first trust and listen to them. If they are worried, upset or feel in danger because of stories they've heard or reports they've seen, these feelings need to be acknowledged, not dismissed (see Feelings and Fears, p.124): 'I can understand you feeling scared. It is a frightening story.' We can then explain and reassure. Simply telling a child not to worry won't make their fears go away, but may make them feel they can't tell us their concerns.
- **Talk** through issues together to help allay children's fears. Ignoring issues provides no such opportunity. Ask, 'What can we do to help you feel safer?' Children are very resourceful and thoughtful when given the chance, and can often come up with solutions themselves when they feel their feelings are understood and taken seriously.

My boys became very stroppy before our holiday and I couldn't work out why, they're used to travelling. Then one of them mentioned tower blocks, were there any tower blocks where we were going? And I realised it was the first time they'd been on a plane since September 11. All these things go very deep, much deeper than we realise. We chatted, I tried to really listen and to put it in perspective. They were still nervous, but I think if I hadn't listened they'd have been petrified.

Julie P

Talking about sex

I find the subject embarrassing but I'm also embarrassed by my inability to deal with it. I'm a mum with three boys and no man in the house and I didn't ever expect to have to deal with this myself. I just can't seem to find the right time or place or words.

Sandra T

What we say and how we say it will depend on our children's age and understanding and our particular cultural beliefs, but all children need basic information. They are bombarded with sexualised imagery from advertising and elsewhere and may end up with very odd ideas about what people do, when and why, unless we counterbalance it with some sensitive, age-appropriate information and support.

Ignorance is no protection Rather than encouraging sexual activity, good sex education and family communication about sex tends to delay first sexual activity and reduce the risk of teenage pregnancy or abortion.[18] Yet knowing what information our children need when isn't always easy.

Be child-led As ever, it helps to take our lead from our children. If we answer their questions simply and honestly, as they arise, we can generally keep in step with their needs and abilities and avoid over-loading them with unnecessary or unrequested details. If we realise we've sidestepped an important question or cue for conversation because of our own anxieties, it's always possible to refer back and pick up the threads: 'You asked me an important question the other day and I was too busy to answer. It was about babies/sex/periods [address the child's question]. Shall we talk about it now?'

As a basic rule of thumb, when children are ready to ask the question, they're ready to hear the answer. Giving them the information they need now can open doors to further questions later.

Start young The younger children are when we first start talking, the more basic the issues we address and the less embarrassed parents tend to feel. If we talk simply and naturally, giving information in small steps, the topic will become less of a taboo. Our children will also find it easier to ask questions and listen to the answers. If they don't raise the topic themselves – and not all do – it's our job to start the ball rolling. Television programmes and stories in the media can often raise issues that lead to relaxed chats about relationships.

Deciding what is age-appropriate information is not always straightforward. Every child is unique, as are their parents and family situation. The answer given a three-year-old to the question, 'Where do babies come from?' will be developed in more detail for the eight-year-old who may ask, 'How did the baby get into mummy's tummy?' By then, many children will be ready to learn how the egg and sperm meet.

David Kesterton, national manager, Speakeasy, an fpa (Family Planning Association) course to help parents gain confidence in talking to their children about sex and sexuality

Check back This prompts us to address the child's agenda rather than our own: 'Is this what you wanted to know? Is there anything else you're not sure of?' It can also stop us overloading them with unrequested information or going up the wrong track entirely.

My six-year-old daughter asked me what sex meant. I told her a little and she rolled her eyes. I thought she must know more than I'd realised, so started to give a bit more information. She looked bored. I gave a bit more, then she exclaimed: 'But I want to know what sex means. What do you mean when you say you'll be with me in two secs?'

Clare C

Ask your child what they think about issues. This tells you how much they know and helps you give answers they can understand

Talking to your Child about Sex, fpa[19]

Keep it relaxed

If your child asks questions about bodies or sexuality, be calm and gentle and do not overload them with too much information. Calmly teach, as you would in other areas of their life, what is acceptable. Avoid moralising and preaching or children getting the message that what they are feeling is wrong; such behaviour may have the opposite effect of what you intended.

José von Bühler, sexual and relationship psychotherapist

Many parents find it easier to talk 'sideways' – chatting while doing something else together such as cooking, washing up, fixing the car. Children also seem to appreciate relaxed discussion that feels a normal part of family life and conversation rather than formal, face-to-face 'sit-down' talks.

Having a serious sit-down chat isn't always helpful because it puts the subject into a different context. To the child, it can feel like a ticking off and raises all sorts of anxieties. If you are alert, there will be all sorts of times when the subject can arise naturally. It's important to choose the time that's right for the child rather than simply the time that's right for you.

Dr John Coleman, Trust for the Study of Adolescence

Sex talk

About 25% of young people get their sex education from their parents, but double that figure, around 50%, want to talk to their parents about it. Around 50% get their information from peers but only 20% say that's what they want. Basically, young people want more opportunity to talk about these things with their parents, there's no question about it.

Dr John Coleman, Trust for the Study of Adolescence

- Nearly half of sexually active 13–15-year-olds have never discussed the subject of sex with either of their parents.[20]
- The average age of onset of sexual activity tends to be later for young people brought up in families where sex is talked about age-appropriately and openly, from an early age.[21]
- Are we leaving boys behind? Research shows that at all school ages, girls know more than boys about puberty, fertility, contraception and sexually transmitted diseases.[22]

Parents report many different reasons for teaching their children about sex and relationships. These often reflect the family's cultural background or religious beliefs. The reasons include:

- Encouraging young people to delay sexual activity.
- Developing self-respect and an empathy for others.
- Learning the value of family life, marriage and stable loving relationships.
- Learning about contraception and the range of local and national sexual

Be honest Children have a knack of choosing inappropriate moments to ask questions, and if it's too hard to reply there and then, it helps to say so: 'That's a good question. We'll talk about it when we get home.' If we're not sure how to respond, it's generally best to admit it: 'I need a bit of time to think how to explain it in ways you'll understand, but I will.' These are all positive responses that leave the door open to future communication. Ignoring a child or crushing curiosity can slam the door shut.

You need to make it clear to the child that they can express themselves and ask questions and these questions will be listened to. The child should never feel that they should not have asked the question.

Domenico di Ceglie, Consultant Child and Adolescent Psychiatrist, Tavistock Clinic

---

health advice, contraception and support services.
— Only having sex within marriage.
— The avoidance of unplanned pregnancy.
— Safer sex and increased condom use.
— Learning the benefits of delaying sexual activity.
— Learning and understanding physical development at appropriate stages.
— Understanding human sexuality, reproduction, sexual health, emotions and relationships.
— Learning the importance of values, individual conscience and moral considerations.
— Develop critical thinking as part of decision-making.
— Learning how to recognise and avoid exploitation and abuse.[23]

Which of these issues matters most to you will depend on your own views and values, but the list highlights the significance of good relationship education in our children's lives and the opportunities it brings for parents to discuss their own beliefs. All children of all faiths and backgrounds are learning about sex from soaps, advertising, magazines, their friends. If parents want their children to understand their particular values, priorities and beliefs, they need to start talking or at least allow access to appropriate information.

Children and young people from all faiths and cultures have an entitlement to sex and relationship education (SRE) that supports them on their journey through childhood to adolescence and adulthood . . . for example even if religious doctrine forbids sex before marriage or the use of contraception, young people need to know and understand the legal and health implications as well as different religious perspectives.

Simon Blake and Zarine Katrak,
Faith Values and Sex and Relationship Education[24]

Talk about feelings

Children need to learn about the positive side of sex as well as being aware of risks and dangers. If you want your child to come to you for support when they are a teenager, then they need to grow up being comfortable talking to you about sex and about their feelings

Talking to your Child about Sex, fpa[25]

Teaching our children about sex doesn't just involve talking about biology. Talking about feelings in relationships is crucial. The importance of care and respect for bodies and feelings, other people's and our own, are issues that extend far beyond the realms of sex education, but are too often ignored when discussing intimate relationships. If children seem old enough – and at ten and eleven many will be – it may help to talk about the difference between love and lust. Young adolescents often muddle the two. Simply explaining the different feelings involved may save them a lot of confusion later on. Or at least help them identify their confusion when it arrives.

Talk about the importance of considering the feelings of others in relationships, and not just the biology

Time to Talk about Sex, Parentline Plus[26]

My 11-year-old daughter asked me why people have sex if they don't want babies. I replied that it was because it felt nice, like cuddles can feel nice. That got us into a conversation about when cuddling doesn't feel OK – when you don't like the person, when it's not the right time, when you're not in the mood. And that led to us talking about how important it is to say 'No' to touches you don't want. It felt like a very important conversation to have, but I'd not thought of talking to her about these things until she raised them herself.

Jane P

Avoid euphemisms Thankfully, few parents still talk about birds, bees and gooseberry bushes, yet many still use euphemisms without realising how confusing they can be to a child. Children need clear understanding, and that requires us to use clear language.

While I'm talking to my children, I always try to remember a story told me by a family friend, who's a midwife. She was with a young teenage girl who hadn't even realised she was pregnant until she started to go into labour. It turned out that her parents had warned her not to sleep with boys. She told my friend she hadn't slept with him, she'd stayed awake all night.

Janice R

Family nicknames for parts of the body are fine if that makes talking about them easier, but children do need to know the correct terms, too.

One of the hardest things for me has been finding words we're all comfortable with. Intimate body parts didn't have names when I was growing up. They didn't need to because they were never mentioned.

Naomi N

Books and leaflets help children go back over information and can fill in gaps in their knowledge and ours. Organisations such as Parentline Plus, Trust for the Study of Adolescence, fpa and the Sex Education Forum (see Contacts, p.429) either produce their own literature for parents and children or can advise parents where to find age- and culture-appropriate publications.

Parents' own confidence in sex education is greatly affected by their own level of knowledge – much of which may be patchy and acquired from poor sex education in school plus life experience. Being embarrassed about the topic is probably what hinders most parents and the concern that their own level of knowledge may not be good enough – or that their children may know more than they do!

David Kesterton, fpa

Talking about drugs

You can't talk usefully to five-year-olds about heroin, but you can talk to them about medicines. About the difference between their medicines and someone else's, about who they would take medicine from – their mother? Their teacher? Their brother? What if their friend offers them some? By six and seven, you can begin to talk about legal drugs such as alcohol and cigarettes. It's a question of gauging where the children are and working at their level.

Nancy Hobbs, drugs education consultant, Project Charlie

This is a controversial area and one that many parents find hard, but the weight of research evidence suggests that equipping children with basic information about drugs from an early age, when they are likely to be more receptive, does not encourage interest in drugs but rather delays experimentation and reduces the likelihood of drug misuse.

Simple key safety messages – about medicines, about leaving needles alone and reporting them to adults, about telling trusted adults

---

Reducing drugs risks

Alcohol is a much bigger threat to young people than illegal drugs.
The statistics are alarming.

Dr John Coleman, Trust for the Study of Adolescence

- Boys tend to experiment with alcohol earlier than girls. 20% of 10–11-year-old boys in one survey had drunk alcohol in the previous week.
- In some areas of the UK, one in ten 11-year-olds have already used an illegal drug[27]. Many of these had friends who were also involved in a range of problem behaviours.[28]
- Almost 20% of 12-13-year-olds say they've been offered drugs.[29]
- One survey[30] found children as young as eight taking drugs and drinking alcohol.
- At least 19% of primary-aged children say they might or will smoke when they are older.[31] First experimentation with cigarette smoking often takes place between the ages of nine and 10 years.[32]
- Around 70% of 10–11-year-olds say they would like their parents to talk to them about drugs.

Research worldwide confirms that parent-child relationships influence young people's resistance to drug use, from childhood to adulthood. A major review[33] of international drugs studies has confirmed that:

- Parents often underestimate the extent of their own influence, believing peer influence to be the decisive factor in their child's drug-related behaviour. At the same time, many lack basic knowledge about drugs and confidence in communicating with their children.
- A close parent-child bond may discourage drug misuse both directly and through the child's choice of non drug-using friends.
- The attitudes held by parents strongly influence those of their children. The behaviour of parents towards substance misuse is an influential model for their children.

The message couldn't be clearer. What we do counts. And we can further boost our children's resistance to drugs by teaching them important life-skills in their primary school years.

about any thing or any incident they are concerned or confused by – can begin in the early primary years (see Reducing, Drugs Risks, below). Alerting children so young to dangers that seem so far distant from their experience may seem inappropriate. One mother told us it felt like 'bursting another bubble of innocence'. Yet, like it or not, drugs are part of the world in which our children are growing up. If we want them to be safe, we have to face up to that reality and equip

Children who are encouraged to resist peer pressure, value themselves, make decisions and solve problems are less likely to have smoked cigarettes or tried drugs by the time they are 14, according to Home Office research[34] into schools-based drugs prevention.

Nancy Hobbs, a drugs education consultant with the programme Project Charlie, explains: 'Children need information but they also need the confidence to think matters through, to make decisions for themselves and to feel good about themselves. They need skills to reach out to other people and to cope with peer pressure.

'No teacher or parent can guarantee that a child will not experiment with drugs, but we can give them the skills that will help them as they grow. Feelings are what connect us with other people. If children can't understand and deal with their feelings – embarrassment, fear, anger, etc. – they are not in a strong position to cope with the pressures to take drugs.'

The project uses games to help children address these issues and express and explore how they feel (also see Feelings and Fears, p.124 and Friends, p.362). One game has a different emotion written on each side of a die. Children are encouraged to discuss whichever emotion the die lands on and to

say when they last experienced it themselves. Other discussions are tailored to the children's age, knowledge and experiences.

The project, operating in schools in Leeds, Newcastle and London at the time of the Home Office study, faces up to the fact that children are likely to come into contact with drugs, especially as teenagers. Nancy Hobbs suggests parents also wake up to reality.

'It is so important for parents to talk about these issues in an age-appropriate way, so it doesn't become a taboo subject. As children grow older they need to know they can talk to their parents about such matters, but the roots of openness and understanding can begin to be encouraged at a much, much younger age.'

As the Home Office report states: 'For a growing number of young people, it is too late to attempt early prevention at secondary school. If programmes aim to give pupils resistance and other life skills, they need to give young people these skills before they encounter situations [where they are offered drugs] and at an age when they are prepared to accept advice.'

them to cope. And that process begins, gradually and gently, long before exposure to drugs becomes likely.

I found a needle and syringe in my garden, right near where the children play. It must have been thrown from a window from the flats behind. My eldest is six.

Carolyn V

My son goes to a good school with an excellent reputation for pastoral care of its pupils. He was offered E [ecstasy] at 11, the age I was when I was offered my first cigarette.

Martin P

As our children grow, they will need more facts and will ask more searching questions. What we say when will depend on their age and stage, the neighbourhood we live in and the issues they raise. But by nine or ten years, most children can understand basic information about different types of drugs and the dangers they pose, including alcohol, tobacco, solvents and prescription medicines. Legal drugs such as cigarettes and alcohol harm far more children than 'street' drugs, so talking about nicotine addiction and the dangers of alcohol misuse are important conversations to have with children in their later primary school years.

Understandably, parents often feel they don't know enough about drugs themselves to answer children's queries effectively. Drugs go in and out of fashion, new ones arrive and the jargon changes. This is when information services for parents and young people, such as Drugscope and the national drugs helpline Talk to Frank, can be invaluable (see Contacts, p.429).

But information alone is not enough. Neither is high self-esteem. Although smoking rates and use of some illicit drugs are known to be higher among children with low self-worth, use of others (including cannabis[35]) appears slightly higher among more sociable, confident young people,[36] for the simple reason that they mix more readily with others and thus may come across drugs sooner. This is an important piece of information because it indicates that drug use among the young is not limited to children with 'problems'. It is not, as some parents would like to believe, something that only happens to other people's children, somewhere else.

To resist pressure to take drugs our children not only need to value themselves and their decisions, but also to think through the emotions such pressures may arouse and the different ways they might respond (see Reducing Drugs Risks, p.392). What if they are offered drugs by someone they don't know? Or by a friend? What if they were the only one of their group who didn't want to accept? These are tough questions with no simple answers, but chatting them through in a matter-of-fact and relaxed way within the family can help them begin to grapple with the issues involved.

Importantly, children need to feel OK about expressing themselves in tricky situations and to know they can talk to us if they are struggling. These are important life skills we can develop and practise as part of growing up in a caring, communicating family.

The inbetweenies

The parents we met described [the middle years] as a turbulent time during which children became increasingly independent, questioning and assertive, while at the same time open to influences from peers and from the media . . . the predominant emotion voiced by parents in our study was one of anxiety.

NCB, *The Forgotten Years*[37]

She's nearly 11 and has already perfected the Elvis-style lip curl when I talk. She's getting moody, slamming doors, spending time alone in her bedroom. I thought I had years to go before all this adolescent stuff.

Nicola C

The late primary school years are a rich and confusing mix for children and for parents. The pressures on children to grow up fast are great. 'Teen' magazines and clothing are now pitched at children aged ten and under; everything from music to fast food to hair gel is targeted at the pre-teen 'tweenies'. Big business has spotted the potential of pocket money, pester power and peer pressure and are bombarding children with advertising about how they should look, behave, dance, eat and even smell. Sometimes our children will look and act far older than their years; sometimes they'll act just as they are – children – and we'll often have no warning of which it's going to be.

Yet the pre-adolescent years are also an age of opportunity. Our children are old enough to understand complex issues and want to discuss them with the important adults in their lives. They may have passionate opinions and urgent questions on everything from politics to footwear. Their personalities and special qualities will be developing at a speed that can surprise as much as delight. If we appreciate and respect our children and their changing needs, our relationships with them can develop and deepen. If we listen and talk with them, and keep track of what's happening in their lives, we can support them in ways that will boost their resilience and help them avoid and negotiate problems as they journey through adolescence.

Significantly, parents and children tend to identify the key stresses of this age group differently. Parents are concerned about the dangers of the 'outside' world (see Protection v. Exposure, p.379) while children themselves seem much more concerned about personal relationships with friends and family.[38] Friendships and peer groups increase in importance and influence, yet the vast majority of children still prefer information on major issues such as drugs and sex to come from their parents than from any other source.

These years are a time in the life-cycle when problems and difficulties may be emerging but when it is still not too late to stop them in their tracks.

NCB, *The Forgotten Years*[39]

Lost in the middle?

The majority of children and families negotiate the 'middle' years between early childhood and adolescence well. When they don't, the consequences can be far-reaching.

- Many children are still facing preadolescence and beyond with scant understanding of what will happen to their bodies and their emotions as they grow. ChildLine reports that a significant proportion of 'middle childhood' girls who contact the charity have anxieties about growing up and about periods in particular, but don't know where to turn for information or support.

- Support for parents is focused on the early years and, to a lesser extent, adolescence. Little information and support is provided through the 'middle' years, yet there is much evidence to indicate the difficulties children and parents can face.

- Eleven years is one known 'peak' age for truancy from school (the peak truancy age for children who go on to become 'young offenders' is nine years).[40]

- The 9–13 years age group accounts for 37% of children running away from home.[41]

Understanding development

My son burst into tears this morning just because his hair was sticking up in a funny way. Heaven help us.

Justine N

My daughter is growing up with girls who are told they've got 'The Curse'. It's appalling. We need to talk to our children about their physical development as something fantastic and amazing. Yes, it happens to everyone, but it's still amazing, we can still help our children feel excited and appreciate the changes that are going to happen to them and the pleasures that are going to come.

Susie Orbach, psychotherapist

Our children are developing physically and emotionally. We need to understand and respect these changes, and our children may need our help to understand them, too.

Their view of the world and their place in it will be shifting. In their later primary years, and certainly as they approach eleven, most children are aware their lives are about to change. The relative familiarity and smaller scale of their primary school will soon be left behind and the world into which they are about to venture may feel a bigger and more daunting place than they'd previously realised (see Play and Learning, p.324). Many children will be increasingly confident, independent and assured but they can also sometimes feel lost and in need of understanding and support.[42]

Thankfully, most children feel they can turn to their parents. Most children aged between nine and twelve say their mother is the first person they would turn to if they had a problem about school, health or friends.[43] In a questionnaire study of nearly 40,000 school pupils aged nine to eleven, more than 75% of girls and 80% of boys said they wanted to talk to their parents about puberty and growing up.[44]

And there's a lot to talk about. At this age, our children are becoming preoccupied with bodily changes – what will happen and what's already happening. Signs of pre-puberty and even puberty itself may be apparent between nine and twelve years, but can take our children and us by surprise. Rapid mood changes, heightened emotions, worries about appearance, breast development, hair growth, sweating, shutting themselves away in their bedrooms and listening to CDs can all begin before our children have finished primary school. Even if

Are children developing earlier?

Many parents express surprise at how quickly children seem to be growing up. So is it happening earlier or are children simply looking older sooner? And should these apparent shifts in development affect how we relate to our sons and daughters?

The bottom line is that no one is absolutely sure. There needs to be more research in more countries before definite conclusions are drawn. But the growing consensus among scientists and researchers seems to be that children are not actually reaching puberty much earlier than previous generations, but that the process is starting earlier and taking longer.

'The best recent and large-scale study, carried out in the US, suggests there's no evidence that the age at which girls start periods has got younger,' explains Dr John Coleman, of the Trust for the Study of Adolescence. 'But it did show that the first stages of puberty, such as breast development, are occurring earlier. More girls of 8 and 9 were showing the first stages of pubertal development. One possibility is that the pubertal process is elongating, so instead of the whole thing being over in 18 months it might be taking $2\frac{1}{2}$ years.'

Which means our children will need our support and understanding through the rocky road of puberty for that much longer, and starting earlier than we might have imagined. Certainly by the end of their primary years, many children will be aware

they haven't, they won't be far off – and it's best to be prepared (see Gender and Development, p.302).

Clearly, children need to know of changes they'll experience ahead of them happening, especially periods for girls and wet dreams for boys. We need to be guided by our child's age and stage, but also to be aware that early maturers, the girls who start their periods and the boys who start growing substantial body hair in their primary school years, will need particular support. Girls seem especially vulnerable to being sidelined by their peer group if their physical development is racing ahead of the rest. This can lead to feelings of 'not belonging' to their former friendship group, which may in turn encourage friendships with older boys from a relatively young age. This increases the risks of early sexual behaviour, earlier alcohol use and other dangers.

All the research shows that early maturing girls are vulnerable and parental support is vital. Anything a parent can do to encourage friendships with other girls the same age is important, as is talking with them about growing up and the of physical and emotional changes.

Children are certainly getting taller and heavier. What many children wear and how they behave is also shifting down the age range, though that may have as much to do with marketing and peer pressure as developmental shifts.

'What is clear is that there's been a shift in social puberty, if you want to call it that,' says Dr Coleman. 'Girls are dressing up earlier, they are more sexually aware and there's more dating behaviour at an earlier age. For parents, this is hard. It seems so provocative. It just wouldn't have happened in our generation. But what's the effect on the child? The honest truth is I don't think anyone really knows. They are much more aware, but with good support at home I think most will deal with it without being pushed off course.

'It certainly puts a greater premium on communication and support for children in schools and at home. Like it or not, we can't turn the clock back, so as parents and educators we need to respond to the changes by providing more information and support at an earlier age.'

I was talking to my son about how emotions can sometimes feel overwhelming when you're growing up, especially when they take you by surprise or you're not sure where they're coming from. He seemed to appreciate the chance to talk about it, like it helped him feel a bit more understood. As adults we can forget how powerful those feelings can be.
Martin P

feelings it brings. In general, the more support they have at home, the more resistant they will be to pressures towards risky behaviour.
Dr John Coleman, Trust for the Study of Adolescence

Significantly, children of this age group say they need to be allowed to express their emotions, desires and thoughts and to be increasingly involved in joint decision-making.[45] This doesn't mean agreeing with all that our children say or desire, but it does mean listening and taking their views into account (see Communication, p.89). Respecting their feelings is key, too. A bad hair day or a minor disagreement with friends might not seem like the end of the world to us but to a pre-adolescent child, it can certainly feel that way. This is when they need us to be respectful, sensitive and supportive.

We do need to be sensitive as parents, for example acknowledging their concern about their spots but reassuring them they look fine.
Eileen Hayes, parenting advisor to the NSPCC

Respecting change As our children grow, they may want the ground rules of family behaviour to adapt. For example, as they move into pre-adolescence, they may no longer feel OK about parents or other family members seeing their developing bodies. By recognising the new boundaries children set themselves, and by respecting their feelings, opinions and changing needs, we will help them develop respect for their bodies and their decisions about them (see Skills for Safety, p.381 and Respect, Respect, Respect, p.319). Comments such as, 'Don't be daft, you've got nothing to hide', however well-intentioned, can give a child the message that it is not for them to decide what feels OK.

We can let our children know that they can tell us if we fail to notice when they want things done differently. We can also role-model respect for our own bodies and for others. Children learn by example and how parents consider and respect themselves are powerful lessons.

This respect should go right across the board. It makes me tremble when I hear comments like 'Let's dress you up to look pretty for Daddy' or 'Big boys don't cry'. These may reflect how unthinking adults can be when commenting on matters so fundamental to the balanced development of children.

José von Bühler, sexual and relationship psychotherapist

Balancing independence and safety

It's as much an instinctive thing as a rational one. If I don't feel OK about a situation, I tell my son that I can't agree to it. I don't think we should lose our instincts as parents just because our kids are older, but we've also got to keep questioning our decisions. I'm constantly revising the rules because his abilities are changing or because I realise my fears are unfounded.

Melissa B

Children and young people in their middle years need experiences to encourage their growing independence from their families . . . most would like more opportunities for activities outside their homes after school, at weekends and during holidays.

NCB, *The Forgotten Years*

Clearly, our growing children need us to keep track of what they are doing, with whom and where. And they also need opportunities to develop independence, capabilities and confidence. Achieving that balance is one of the hardest roles for parents of children in their 'middle years'.

There can't be any firm guidelines here. What's appropriate and safe will depend on many factors, from the children themselves to the neighbourhood they are growing up in to your family's experiences and beliefs. But what's clear is that many children are not given sufficient opportunities to develop independence safely and are reaching adolescence ill-prepared.

Experiences of childhood have changed radically in a generation. Researchers[46] have found that only half of nine-year-olds are allowed to cross roads on their own, only a third are allowed to go on non-school journeys without an adult and fewer than one in ten are allowed to use buses, yet thirty years ago most nine-year-olds would have done all these things. On the other hand, many primary-age children are still permitted to surf the net without parental controls blocking access to adult chat rooms and websites. It's a peculiar mix.

What to do? Again, this can't be a definitive list, but parents and professionals who work with families have suggested that we:

- **Encourage some out-of-school activities** Where children can get together under the care of a responsible, trusted adult but away from their parents' gaze.
- **Understand their need for autonomy** Children's lives are far more restricted in some ways than previous generations. For example, most have fewer opportunities for outside play with friends. Yet research confirms what parents themselves report: that children now make more decisions about what they wear and have greater control over their leisure activities, spending, access to information and the media, mobility and ease of travel than ever before. Perhaps this is how they are discovering and exploring some autonomy in their lives. If they are not allowed the freedoms we had as children, they'll find other freedoms elsewhere.

There are all sorts of areas in which autonomy is developing, and this raises a whole new set of issues for parents about what is appropriate and how they negotiate this with their children.

Dr John Coleman, Trust for the Study of Adolescence

- **Agree ground rules** and the importance of sticking to them. If, for example, your eleven-year-old wants to go to the shops with a friend, and you are happy about that, agree a time to meet. If they stick to the deal, they can go again. If they don't, the next visit is delayed until such a time as they show sufficient responsibility to handle their new freedoms.

- **Keep monitoring** Pre-adolescent children are still children. We need to know their whereabouts, activities and friends.
- **Familiarise ourselves with technology**, its uses and potential abuses (see Protection v. Exposure, p.379).
- **Mobile phones** Again, depends on your personal views, budget, neighbourhood. Some parents like their children to be able to get in touch. Others are concerned about health issues, or fear mobile phones increase the risk of mugging and may lull children into a false sense of security. Clearly, phones can never replace fundamental awareness, social competence and safety skills. If you and your children feel safer with them, it helps to go for cheaper models (less attractive to thieves). If using a pay-as-you-go scheme, give children a top-up card to keep in case of emergencies.
- **Question our decisions and stick to our guns** Children in this age group are often far more resourceful and capable than we realise. We need to ask ourselves occasionally, are we restricting their freedoms because of well-founded concerns or because we are viewing them as the children they were rather than the children they have grown to be?

However, if our knowledge or our instincts tell us that a situation is unsafe or inappropriate, we need to be clear and stick to our decision. Research confirms that children want their parents to maintain clear boundaries.[47] Yet they also need those boundaries discussed and explained, their views acknowledged and considered, and the rules revised when appropriate.

After you have had a big argument about something you don't want them to do you'll often hear them saying later to a friend, 'Oh, I can't coz my mum won't let me.' You get the feeling they didn't really want to do it anyway, that they needed an excuse for their peer group. Giving children a free rein can make them feel unsafe and uncomfortable. They expect us to provide an excuse sometimes, so it's important to follow your instinct about what feels right.

Eileen Hayes, parenting advisor to the NSPCC

Encourage the timid or unadventurous Not all children push the limits and press for freedoms. Some are quieter and more compliant by temperament; some are desperate to please. These children may nced to be encouraged to take more risks and make more decisions themselves. If we start the process gently in these middle years, they will be more equipped to cope with life at secondary school and through their adolescence.

Some children are too co-operative or introspective and you have to push them for them to find their feet. It is lovely to hold on to these hugely sweet and co-operative kids but they do have to find their own way in the world and live it. These children may need reassurance that it's OK to challenge, to disagree, to have different tastes to their parents.

Eileen Hayes, parenting advisor to the NSPCC

Understand the growing importance of friends

This is the age when you have to learn how to be social, how to make friends, how to manage more than one friendship. It really is not easy for many children, but the consequences of failing can be very big.

Allan Watson, National Pyramid Trust

Who our children mix with matters. The role of peer pressure in early substance misuse and anti-social behaviour is clear, and we can help our children resist pressures to follow the crowd by encouraging them throughout their childhood to value themselves, their feelings and their own decisions (see Reducing Drugs Risks, p.392). Having the courage to do what you believe to be right when your friends are doing otherwise is a tough call for anyone, and especially children. Discussing different ways to deal with tricky situations – who to tell, what to do, how to use humour to assert your views without putting yourself at risk – can help here.

Yet we shouldn't let our worries about peer pressure blind us to the support and full-throttle fun that children's friendships can bring. Important messages about health, social behaviour and school work come from peers as well as parents at this age. Through friendships, our children can learn how to share problems, conflicts and feelings and deal with a range of situations and emotions. Just as important, their social lives and important steps towards independence will depend to a large extent on having friends alongside.

If we don't know our children's friends, we need to try harder. We can encourage our children to invite friends round, take them as a group to the cinema or the swimming pool, help them feel welcome if they drop by. Only if we know them can we judge the appropriate balance of freedom and restriction in our children's lives.

Understand school pressures School teachers may become increasingly anxious about children's attainment as they reach the end of their primary years, partly because they want them to move on to secondary school well prepared, and partly because the tests results are made public and thus reflect on the school and their own teaching skills. Inevitably, some of this anxiety is transferred to the pupils. Our job is to support our children and reduce their anxieties wherever possible, not inflate them through unrealistic expectation or demands (see Play and Learning, p.324).

How we do this will vary according to our child's individual needs and particular circumstances. If the child and their school seem to be coping pretty well, the very best support may be to make home a test-free zone, where they can relax and get on with other important things in life. Like having fun. If, however, children are fretful because they feel they are falling behind, we might help ease their concerns by setting some time aside to run through parts of the curriculum they're finding tough. Many schools are happy to provide support materials for use at home. If not, ask the teacher what revision guides or websites they recommend. Bear in mind, this is for their benefit, not ours (see Learning, p.339). If home support becomes a source of conflict or anxiety, it's time to stop.

Expand children's range of skills Not all children are academic high-fliers, but all need to experience success and develop a range of skills for adulthood. We can help by encouraging our children to try a wide range of activities: cookery, art and crafts, music, sports and games, in fact anything that tends to be squeezed out of the school experience but which they may find useful and pleasurable. Once children master the basics of a new skill, their belief in themselves and their own ability grows. This confidence spreads into other areas of learning and life, and also helps them cope better with life's ups and downs.

As their skills develop so children believe more in their own competence, their self-doubt begins to fade, they are becoming 'able' and that is recognised by others and by themselves. Their self-esteem grows, they can see themselves as OK, likeable, worthy of friendship. If this is sustained by other positive things like a good relationship with an adult, recognition at school, a stable family that's not struggling against poverty and discrimination, then children learn to take the knocks in life as well, and bounce back. That resilience really helps through the teenage years.

Allan Watson, National Pyramid Trust

Keep connecting

At primary school age children tend to be more open about being unhappy and more willing to accept adult support or advice than they are in their teenage years. That is why it is the golden opportunity. If children are struggling, at this age it is easier to help.

Allan Watson, National Pyramid Trust

Our pre-adolescent children may start to focus on connecting with friends, but we need to focus on connecting with them. Our relationships with our children still need affectionate, playful times of togetherness to thrive. Family life may be changing as our children grow, but it's still where we support each other, share with each other, talk and listen to each other, care and have fun.

Of course, admitting any of this in public may be deeply uncool if you are eleven, ten or even nine. Many children of this age – boys especially – shrug off open displays of affection from their parents, but many still appreciate hugs and physical affection when out of view of their friends. If they don't, it's up to us to find other ways to express our love and appreciation.

Major research and parents' own experiences highlight the importance of communication with children in their 'middle' childhood years (see Communication, p.89). Good family communication ups the likelihood of our children telling us what they do at school and other times away from our supervision. Children need us to talk with them, discuss issues, provide information, acknowledge their opinions and choices, but most of all they need us to listen. Only when we've heard what life is like for them, what worries them and what doesn't, can we judge how best to support them.

We need to respect their views and choices to keep channels of communication open. This does not mean we have to share or approve of their choices, we just need to be careful not to embarrass, alienate or crush them when their choices are different to ours. If their opinion on music is squashed, for example, they are less likely to open up in other areas. So a parent could say, 'I know you like this CD but I struggle with the language he uses' or 'I can see his talent but it's not for me/in this house/ in front of your brother'.

Eileen Hayes, parenting advisor to NSPCC

The road ahead

We've just come back from a walk. We took a football, an instant barbecue, food, water and ourselves. Each of the kids – one 8, one 11 and one 14 – said it was the best day. We forget the simple stuff sometimes, but that's where many of the best memories are made.

Michael W

Now's a good time to reflect on how we'd like our relationships with our children to grow, and what might help along the way. One thing's for sure: as our children move towards adolescence, they will need us differently, but they'll still need us.

Young people themselves say they want their parents to 'be there' for them. Interesting, isn't it? No mention of expensive trainers or designer labels. When researchers ask adolescents what they most want from their parents, they say they want their feelings understood and their views heard. They want us to notice when they are hurting and to respond when they need us; they want to be able to turn to us for advice and they want us to acknowledge their views and development when setting limits on behaviour; they want warmth, respect and understanding.[48]

In other words, all we have learned through our relationships with our children up to now will help us in the new territory of their teenage years. Of course, we will have to adapt as they develop and allow them the independence they need to grow, but that's nothing new. We've been doing it for years. What matters most, the fundamentals of strong relationships, remain the same: warmth, trust, interest, concern, closeness, kindness and fun.

By responding to our children as individuals; acknowledging and respecting their feelings; listening and talking; understanding and guiding behaviour; supporting their abilities and enthusiasms; sharing times together and enjoying their company, our bond with our children can continue to grow. This will help us all appreciate the happy times and cope better when mistakes are made or things go pear-shaped.

As you'll know by now, this book is not about perfect children or perfect parents. It is about connecting with our children and developing happy, supportive and warm relationships with them that help them flourish, enjoy life and cope with its knocks. As parents, we can't know what the future holds, but by continuing to love, respect and appreciate our children as they grow, we will help them develop the competence and confidence they will need to be themselves, face the future and take their place in it. That's what we mean by 'raising happy children'.

Growing independence: a quick reminder

- Friends matter. They can shape our children's experience of childhood and school; they can buffer them from bullying and boost their social confidence and sense of worth.
- To mix happily with others our children need to learn how to give and take, consider other's people's feelings, to express their own needs and wants clearly and effectively, negotiate differences and cope with conflict.
- We need to be alert to bullying, in all its forms. We need to be available and listen when our children are struggling, and to act when our children need our support or intervention.
- We can help our children to stay safe, and encourage a sense of perspective about the dangers they face. Unfounded fears lead to stifling over-protection.
- Children need age-appropriate drugs information and sex education to equip them for real life. What they can absorb and understand will change as they grow. We need to respond to their questions and anxieties and guide appropriately.
- As children move through pre-adolescence, they still need our love, understanding and appreciation, even if it's deeply uncool for them to admit it. Children themselves say they still want their feelings understood, their views heard, and our active support to help them flourish.

APPENDIX 1

References

CHAPTER ONE
Baby's needs, your needs

1 *Helpful Parenting*, Royal College of Paediatrics and Child Health, London, 2002
2 Brazelton, T.B. and Nugent, J.K. (1995), *The Neonatal Behaviour Assessment Scale*, Mackeith Press, Cambridge
3 Brazelton, T.B. (1974), *Monographs of the Society for Research into Child Development*, University of Chicago Press, Chicago
4 Anderson, C.J., and Sawin, D. (1983), 'Enhancing responsiveness in mother-infant interaction', *Infant Behavior and Development* 6, (3) 361–8; Beal, J.A. (1986), 'The Brazelton Neonatal Behavioural Assessment Scale: a tool to enhance parental attachment', *Journal of Pediatric Nursing*, 1, 170–7; Beal, J.A. (1989), 'The effect on father-infant interaction of demonstrating the Neonatal Behavioural Assessment Scale', *Birth*, 16, 18–22; Britt, G.C. and Myers, B.J. (1994), 'The effects of Brazelton intervention: a review', *Infant Mental Health Journal*, 15, 278–92
5 Nagy, E. and Molnar, P., '*Homo Imitans and Homo Provocans: A theory of human imprinting*', 33rd Annual Meeting of the International Society for Developmental Psychobiology, New Orleans, Louisiana, November 2000
6 Van Rees, S. and de Leeuw, R. (1993), *The Kangaroo Method*, Video by Stichting Lichaamstaal, Body Language Media Centre, Scheyvenhofweg 12, 6093, PR Heythuysen, The Netherlands
7 Murray, L. and Trevarthen, C. (1985), 'Emotional regulation of interactions between two-month-olds and their mothers', in Field, T.M. and Fox, N.A. (eds.), *Social Perception in Infants*, (pp.177–98), Ablex, Norwood, NJ Trevarthen, C. (1993), 'The function of emotions in early infant communication and development', in Nadel, J. and Camaioni, L. (eds.), *New Perspectives in Early Communicative Development* (pp.48–81), Routledge, London
8 Stern, Daniel, *The First Relationship: Infant and Mother*, Harvard University Press, 1997

9   Cited in *Helpful Parenting*, Royal College of Paediatrics and Child Health, London, 2002

10 *Helpful Parenting*, Royal College of Paediatrics and Child Health, London, 2002

11 Source: Midwives Information and Resource Service (MIDIRS)

12 Bowlby, J. (1973), *Attachment and Loss, Vol. 2, Separation, Anxiety and Anger*, Hogarth Press, London

13 Shore, R., *Rethinking the Brain. New Insights into Early Development*, Families and Work Institute, New York; 1997, pp.7–47

14 Christensson, K. et al. (1995), 'Separation distress call in the human neonate in the absence of maternal body contact', *Acta Paediatrica*, vol. 84, pp.468–73

15 St James-Roberts, I. and Halil, A. (1991), 'Infant crying pattern in the first year – normal community and clinical findings', *Journal of Child Psychology and Psychiatry*, vol. 32, pp.951–68

16 As told to Dr Hawthorne by Betty Hutchon, Neonatal Behavioural Assessment Scale trainer and Head Paediatric Occupational Therapist at the Royal Free Hospital, London

17 As described in Stern, Daniel, *The First Relationship: Infant and Mother*, Harvard University Press, 1997

18 Trevarthen, C. and Hubley, P. (1978), 'Secondary intersubjectivity: Confidence, confiding and acts of meaning in the first year', in Lock, A. (ed.), *Action, Gesture and Symbol: The Emergence of Language* (pp.183–229), Academic Press, London, New York, San Francisco

19 Source: The Association for Post-natal Illness

20 *Helpful Parenting*, Royal College of Paediatrics and Child Health, London, 2002

21 Parr, M. (1996), *Support For Couples in the Transition to Parenthood*, PhD thesis, Psychology Department, University of East London

22 Cohen, D., *The Fathers' Book* (Family Matters Series), John Wiley and Sons, 2001

23 *Post-natal Depression*, The Association for Post-natal Illness, 2003

24 *Post-natal Depression*, The Association for Post-natal Illness, 2003

25 Cox, J.I., Holden J.M. et al., *Perinatal Psychology: Use and Misuse of Edinburgh Post-natal Depression Scale*, Gaskell, London, 1994

CHAPTER TWO

Sleep solutions

1   Anders, T., Keener, M., Bowe, T. et al. (1983), 'A Longitudinal Study of Nightime Sleep-Wake Patterns in Infants from Birth to One Year' in Call, J., Galenson, E. and Tyson, R. (eds.), *Frontiers in Infant Psychiatry*, Basic Books, New York

2   Quine, L. (1997), *Solving Children's Sleep Problems*, Beckett Karison, Huntingdon

3   Ferber, R., Boyle, M.P. (1983), 'Nocturnal fluid intake: A case of, not treatment for, sleep disruption in infants and toddlers, *Sleep Research*, 12, 243–9

4   Christensson, K. et al. (1995), 'Separation distress call in the human neonate in the absence of maternal body contact', *Acta Paediatrica*, vol. 84, pp. 468–73

5   McKenna, J., Mosko, S., Richard, C. et al. (1994), 'Experimental studies of infant-parent co-sleeping: mutual physiological and behavioural influences and their relevance to SIDS (sudden infant death syndrome)', *Early Human Development*, 38, 187–210

6   Source: Foundation for the Study of Infant Deaths and the Department of Health

7   Messer, D. and Richards, M.P.M., 'The development of sleeping difficulties', in St James-Roberts, I. Harris G. and Messer D., (eds.), *Infant Crying, Feeding and Sleeping*, Harvester Wheatsheaf, 1993, pp. 150–173.

8   Quine, L. (1997), *Solving Children's Sleep Problems*, Beckett Karlson, Huntingdon.

9   The World Health Organisation, Quality of Life Association (WHOQUAL, 'Development and General Psychometric Properties', *Social Science and Medicine*, 1998, vol. 46, pp. 1569–85)

CHAPTER THREE

Feeding and food wars

1   Source: MIDIRS (the Midwives Information and Resource Service)

2   *Infant Feeding Survey 2000*, Department of Health, London

3   National Childbirth Trust, UK, 2003

4   *Infant Feeding Survey 2000*, Department of Health, London

5   National Childbirth Trust, UK, 2003

6   Advice from the government's Committee on Toxicity of Chemicals in Food, Consumer Products and the Environment (COT), 1998

7   Douglas, J. (1991), 'Chronic and severe eating problems in young children', *Health Visitor*, vol. 64. no. 10: 334–6

8   Stein, A., Wooley, H., Cooper, S.D. and Fairburn, G. (1994), 'An observational study of mothers with eating disorders and their infants', *Journal of Psychology and Psychiatry*, vol. 35, pp. 733–48

9   Stead, M. and Goodlad, N. (1996), *Promoting Consumption of vegetables; A qualitative Exploration Study of Women's Knowledge and Attitudes – Practice*, University of Strathclyde Centre For Social Marketing, Glasgow.

10 The Feeding Clinic, the Children's Hospital, Birmingham

11 Wardle, J. and Huon, G. (2000), 'An experimental investigation of the influence of health information on children's taste preferences', *Health Education Research*, 15(1), 39–44

12 *Guardian*, September 11, 2002

13 *The Observer*, May 10, 2003.

14 Food Standards Agency, 2003.

15 Food Standards Agency recommendations, based on reports by the Scientific Advisory Committee on Nutrition, issued May 2003.

16 Waterston, A. (1994), 'Effect of deprivation on weight gain in infancy', *Acta Paediatrica*, vol. 83, pp.357–9

17 Gregory, J. et al. (1995), *National Diet and Nutrition Survey*, HMSO, London

18 Children attending the Feeding Clinic, the Children's Hospital, Birmingham

19 Petter, L. P. et al. (1995), 'Is water out of vogue? A survey of the drinking

habits of 2-7 year olds', *Archives of Disease in Childhood*, vol. 72 (2), pp. 137–40

20 *Food for the Growing Years*, Paediatric Group, British Dietetic Association, 1990

21 Dennison, B. A., Erb, T.A. and Jenkins, P.L. (2002), 'Television Viewing and Television in Bedroom Associated With Overweight Risk Among Low-Income Preschool Children', *Pediatrics* 109: 1028–35, American Academy of Pediatrics

22 *The Couch Kids* (2000), British Heart Foundation

23 American Academy of Pediatrics

24 Prentice, A. M. (2002), 'Food, lifestyle and the global obesity epidemic: what are the targets for action?', *Weight Management*, 7–10

25 Hoek, H.W. (1991), 'The incidence and prevalence of anorexia nervosa and bulimia nervosa in primary care', *Psychological Medicine*, 21:455–60

26 Patton, G.C., Selzer, R., Coffey, C., Carlin, J.B. and Wolfe, R. (1999), 'Onset of adolescent eating disorders: population based cohort study over 3 years', *British Medical Journal*, 318, 765–8

CHAPTER FOUR
Communication

1 *Children and Violence*, Report of the Commission on Children and Violence, convened by the Gulbenkian Foundation, Calouste Gulbenkian Foundation, London, 1995

2 Kuhl, P.K. (1998), 'The development of speech and language', in Carew, T.J., Menzel R., and Shatz, C.J. (eds.), *Mechanistic Relationships between Development and Learning* (pp.53–73), Wiley, New York:

3 Lacerda, F., von Hofsten, C. and Heimann, M. (2001), *Emerging Cognitive Abilities in Early Infancy*, Erlbaum, Mahwah, NJ, cited in Trevarthen, C. (2002), 'Infant Development and Communication', *Zero to Three*, National Center for Infants, Toddlers and Families, Washington

4 Trevarthen, C. and Malloch, S. (2002), 'Musicality and Music Before Three: Human Vitality and Invention Shared With Pride', in *Zero to Three*, National Center for Infants, Toddlers and Families, Washington

5 Mehrabian, A. (1969), *Tactics in Social Influence*, Prentice-Hall, New Jersey

6 Ward, S. (1992), 'The predictive validity and accuracy of a screening test for developmental language delay', *European Journal of Disorders of Communication*, Vol 27. Ward, S. (1999), 'An investigation into the effectiveness of an early intervention method for delayed language development in young children', *International Journal of Disorders of Communication in Young Children*, July

7 *We Know It's Tough to Talk*, ChildLine, 1996

8 Zimbardo, Professor Philip, Stanford University, to the British Psychological Society, 1997

9 Ghate, D. and Daniels, A. (1997), *Talking About My Generation: a survey of 8–15 year olds growing up in the 1990s*, NSPCC, London

10 *Listening to 10-year-olds: A ChildLine Study*, ChildLine, 1996

11 *Children and Violence*, Report of the Commission on Children and Violence, convened by the Gulbenkian Foundation, Calouste Gulbenkian Foundation, London, 1995

CHAPTER FIVE
Feelings and fears

1   *Helpful Parenting*, Royal College of Paediatrics and Child Health, 2002
2   Newson, J. and Newson, N. (1989), *The Extent of Parental Punishment in the UK*, Approach, London; Patterson, G.R., Reid, J.B. and Dishion, T.J. (1992), *Antisocial Boys: A Social Interactional Approach*, (Vol. 4), Castalia, Eugene, OR; Loeber, R. and Stouthamer-Loebar, M. (1986), 'Family factors as correlates and predictors of juvenile conduct problems and delinquency', in *Crime and Justice: An Annual Review of Research*, vol.7, Tonry, M. and Morris, N. (eds.), 1986
3   *Children and Violence*, Report of the Commission on Children and Violence, convened by the Gulbenkian Foundation, Calouste Gulbenkian Foundation, London, 1995
4   Gottman, John with Declaire, Joan, *The Heart of Parenting*, Bloomsbury, 1997
5   *Managing to Change: Play and Learning*, National Children's Bureau, 1995
6   *Helpful Parenting*, Royal College of Paediatrics and Child Health, 2002
7   Dunn, J. (1993), *Young Children's Close Relationships: Beyond Attachment*, Sage
8   Roberts, R., *Self-esteem and Successful Early Learning*, Hodder & Stoughton, 1995; Elfer, P. (1996), *Building Intimacy in Relationships with Young Children in Nurseries*, Early Years
9   Elfer, P. and Selleck, D. (1999) *A Three-year Study of Care and Learning of Children Under Three in Nurseries*, Esmel Fairbairn Charity Trust
10 Puckering, C. et al. (1994), 'Process and evaluation of a group intervention for mothers with parenting difficulties', *Child Abuse Review*, 3, 299–310
11 Hunt, Candida, in consultation with Mountford, Annette, *The Parenting Puzzle: How to Get the Best out of Family Life* (a practical guide for parents, based on the Nurturing Programme), Family Links, 2003
    Candida Hunt, Family Links
12 Hunt, Candida, in consultation with Mountford, Annette, *The Parenting Puzzle: How to Get the Best out of Family Life* (a practical guide for parents, based on the Nurturing Programme), Family Links, 2003
13 Walsh, F. (1996), 'The concept of family resilience', *Family Process*, 35(3), 261–81
14 Montgomery, S. et al. (1997), 'Family conflict and slow growth', *The Archives of Diseases in Childhood*, vol. 77, no.4
15 Katz, A. and Buchanan, A. (1999), The Tomorrow's Men/Women at the Millennium Projects: Factors associated with high and low self-esteem. A study for the Mental Health Foundation
16 Bullock, R. et al. (1995), *Child Protection: Messages from Research*, HMSO
17 The Tomorrow's Men/Women at the Millennium projects (*op. cit.*), confirming the findings in *The Can-do Girls – A Barometer of Change* by Adrienne Katz, research based on the *Express on Sunday* Girlstalk Survey and further work in association with Ann Buchanan and JoAnn Ten Brinke, University of Oxford
18 *Helpful Parenting*, Royal College of Paediatrics and Child Health, 2002
19 Gorell Barnes, Gill, Thompson, Paul, Daniel, Gwyn and Burchardt, Natasha, *Growing Up In Stepfamilies*, Oxford University Press, 1998
20 Listening to 10-year-olds: a ChildLine study, ChildLine, 1996

CHAPTER SIX
Horribly normal

1 Brazelton, T. Berry, *Touchpoints: Your Child's Emotional and Behavioural Development*, Perseus Books, USA, 1992
2 *Children and Violence*, Report of the Commission on Children and Violence convened by the Gulbenkian Foundation. Calouste Gulbenkian Foundation, London, 1995
3 Baumrind, D., 'Rearing competent children', in *Child Development Today and Tomorrow*, Damon, W. (ed.), Jossey, New York; 1989
4 Whaley, K.L. and Rubenstein, T.S. (1994), 'How toddlers "do" friendship: a descriptive analysis of naturally occurring friendships in a group child care setting', *Journal of Social and Personal Relationships*, cited in Goldschmied, Elinor, and Selleck, Dorothy, *Communication Between Babies in Their First Year*, National Children's Bureau
5 *Children and Violence*, Report of the Commission on Children and Violence, convened by the Gulbenkian Foundation. Calouste Gulbenkian Foundation, London, 1995
6 Commission on Children and Violence convened by the Gulbenkian Foundation. Calouste Gulbenkian Foundation, London, 1995.

CHAPTER SEVEN
Co-operation and discipline

1 *Helpful Parenting*, Royal College of Paediatrics and Child Health, 2002
2 Simpson, A. Rae (2001), *Raising Teens: A Synthesis of Research and a Foundation for Action*, Centre for Health Communication, Harvard School of Public Health, Boston
3 Baumrind, D. 'Rearing competent children', in *Child Development Today and Tomorrow*, Damon, W. (ed.), Jossey, New York; 1989
4 *Children and Violence*, Report of the Commission on Children and Violence convened by the Gulbenkian Foundation. Calouste Gulbenkian Foundation, London, 1995
5 *Helpful Parenting*, Royal College of Paediatrics and Child Health, 2002
6 *Managing to Change: Play and Learning*, National Children's Bureau, 1995
7 Bullock, R.et al. (1995), *Child Protection: Messages from Research*, Dartington Social Research Unit, HMSO
8 *Children and Violence*, Report of the Commission on Children and Violence convened by the Gulbenkian Foundation. Calouste Gulbenkian Foundation, London, 1995
9 Gershoff, E.T. (2003), 'Parental Corporal Punishment and Associated Child Behaviour and Experiences: a Meta-analytic and Theoretical Review', *Psychological Bulletin*
10 *Helpful Parenting*, Royal College of Paediatrics and Child Health, 2002
11 *Children and Violence*, Report of the Commission on Children and Violence

convened by the Gulbenkian Foundation. Calouste Gulbenkian Foundation, London, 1995

12 Reiss A.J. and Roth, J.A. (eds.), *The Development of an Individual's Potential for Violence: Understanding and Preventing Violence*, National Academy Press, Washington DC, 1993

13 Pfeiffer, C. and Wetzels, P. (2000), *Physical Punishment of Children and Young People and its Consequences*, Lower Saxony Institute for Criminological Research, Germany

14 Bullock, R.et al. (1995), *Child Protection: Messages from Research*, Dartington Social Research Unit, HMSO

15 Straus, M.A. (1994), *Beating the Devil out of Them*, Jossey-Bass Inc., San Francisco

16 Straus, M.A. and Paschall, M.J. (1998), *Corporal punishment by mothers and child's cognitive development*, longitudinal study paper, presented at the 14th World Congress of Sociology, Montreal, Quebec, Canada; Family Research Laboratory, University of New Hampshire, Durham, NH

17 Straus, M. and Stewart, J.H. (1998), *Corporal Punishment by American Parents: national data on prevalence, chronicity, severity and duration in relation to child and family characteristics*, Family Research Laboratory, University of New Hampshire

18 Scottish Executive, 2002

19 Smith, M. (1995), 'A community study of physical violence to children in the home, and associated variables', presented at International Society for the Prevention of Child Abuse and Neglect, Fifth European Conference on Child Abuse and Neglect, Oslo

20 *Children and Violence*, Report of the Commission on Children and Violence convened by the Gulbenkian Foundation, Calouste Gulbenkian Foundation, London, 1995

21 Smith, M. (1995), 'A community study of physical violence to children in the home, and associated variables', presented at International Society for the Prevention of Child Abuse and Neglect, Fifth European Conference on Child Abuse and Neglect, Oslo

22 Newson, E. and Newson, J. (1963), *Infant Care in an Urban Community*, Allen & Unwin, London

CHAPTER EIGHT
Important relationships

1 Parr, M. (1996), 'Support for Couples in the Transition to Parenthood', PhD thesis, Psychology Department, University of East London

2 Snarey, J. (1993), *How Fathers Care for the Next Generation: A four decade study*, Harvard University, Cambridge, MA

3 Pruett, K. D. (1997), 'How Men And Children Affect Each Other's Development', *Zero to Three*, 18

4 Fathers and Fatherhood in Britain: Findings', Joseph Rowntree Foundation, *Social Policy Research* 120, July 1997

5 *Helpful Parenting*, Royal College of Paediatrics and Child Health, London, 2002

6 La Valle, I, et al. (2002), *Atypical Work and its Influence on Family Life*, Joseph Rowntree Foundation, The Policy Press

7 Ruhm, C.J. and Teague, J.L. (1995), *Parental Leave Policies in Europe and North America*, National Bureau of Economic Research, Cambridge, MA

8 Lamb, M.E. and Oppenheim, D., 'Fatherhood and father-child relationships: five years of research', in Cath, S.H. et al. (eds.) (1989), *Fathers and their Families*, the Analytic Press, New Jersey
Burgess, A. and Ruxton, S. (1996), *Men and their Children: Proposals for public policy*, IPPR, London

9 Anderson, A.M. (1996), *Journal of the Society of Pediatric Nurses*, vol. 1, no. 2, Jul–Sep, pp. 83–92, cited in *MIDIRS Midwifery Digest* (Mar 1997), 7, 1

10 Parr, *M. (1996), 'Support for Couples in the Transition to Parenthood'*, PhD thesis, Psychology Department, University of East London

11 Lewis, C., 'Fathers and Preschoolers' in Lamb, M.E. (ed.) (1996), *The Role of the Father in Child Development* (3rd edn), Wiley

12 *Helpful Parenting*, Royal College of Paediatrics and Child Health, London, 2002

13 *Helpful Parenting*, Royal College of Paediatrics and Child Health, London, 2002

14 La Valle, I. et al. (2002), *Atypical Work and its Influence on Family Life*, Joseph Rowntree Foundation, The Policy Press

15 Survey by Mori, commissioned by the NSPCC, published April 1997

16 Survey by Mori, commissioned by the NSPCC, published April 1997

17 Ferri, E. and Smith, K., *Parenting in the 1990s*, Family Policy Studies Centre/Joseph Rowntree Foundation, 1996

18 'Fathers and Fatherhood in Britain: Findings', *Social Policy Research*, 120, Joseph Rowntree Foundation, July 1997

19 'Fathers and Fatherhood in Britain: Findings', *Social Policy Research*, 120, Joseph Rowntree Foundation, July 1997

20 Ghate, D. and Daniels, A. (1997), *Talking About My Generation, a survey of 8–15 year olds growing up in the 1990s*, NSPCC

21 Catan, L. and Coleman, J. (1998), *Communication in Adolescence*, Trust for the Study of Adolescence and BT Forum

22 Edwards, J. (ed.) (2001), *Not in Front of the Children: How conflict between parents affects children*, One Plus One, Marriage and Partnership Research, London

23 Edwards, J. (ed.) (2001), *Not in Front of the Children: How conflict between parents affects children*, One Plus One, Marriage and Partnership Research, London

24 Brody, G.H. (1998), 'Sibling Relationship Quality: Its Causes and Consequences', *Ann. Rev. Psychol.*, 49, 1–24

25 Cited in Edwards, J. (ed.) (2001), *Not in Front of the Children: How conflict between parents affects children*, One Plus One, Marriage and Partnership Research, London

26 Smith, A., *'A Community Study of Physical Violence to Children in the Home, and Associated Variables'*, Thomas Coram Research Unit, presented at International Society for the Prevention of Child Abuse and Neglect, Norway, 1995

27 Hawthorne, J. et al. (2003), *Supporting Children Through Family Change: a review of interventions and services for children of divorcing and separating parents*, Joseph Rowntree Foundation (Family Change series), YPS

28 Sources: Parentline Plus; *Children in the UK*, 2002, Office for National Statistics; 'Fathers and Fatherhood in Britain July 1997: Findings', *Social Policy Research*, 120, Joseph Rowntree Foundation.

29 Wade, A. and Smart, C. (2002), *Facing Family Change: Children's circumstances, strategies and resources*, Joseph Rowntree Foundation, YPS

30 George, C. and Solomon, J. (2003), *Babies' Attachment to Parents Affected by Overnights*, Mills College, Oakland, CA, and Early Childhood Mental Health Programme, CA, cited in the *Daily Telegraph*, April 4, 2003

31 Hetherington, E.M. (1988), 'Parents, children and siblings six years after divorce', in Hinde, R.A., Stevenson-Hinde, J. (eds.), *Relationships Within Families: Mutual Influences*, Clarendon, Oxford; Gorrell Barnes, G., Thompson, P., Daniel, G. and Burchardt, N., *Growing Up In Stepfamilies*, Clarendon, Oxford, 1998

32 Hetherington, E.M. (1988) 'Parents, children and siblings six years after divorce', in Hinde, R.A., Stevenson-Hinde, J. (eds.), *Relationships Within Families: Mutual Influences*, Clarendon, Oxford; Gorrell Barnes, G., Thompson, P., Daniel, G. and Burchardt, N. (1998), *Growing Up In Stepfamilies*, Oxford University Press

33 Hawthorne, J. et al. (2003), *Supporting Children Through Family Change: a review of interventions and services for children of divorcing and separating parents*, Joseph Rowntree Foundation (Family Change series), YPS

34 Byng-Hall, J. (2002), 'Relieving Parentified Children's Burdens in Families with Insecure Attachment Patterns', *Family Process*, vol. 41, no. 3

35 Hetherington, E.M. (1988), 'Parents, children and siblings six years after divorce', in Hinde, R.A., Stevenson-Hinde, J. (eds.), *Relationships Within Families: Mutual Influences*, Clarendon, Oxford

36 Hawthorne, J. et al. (2003), *Supporting Children Through Family Change: a review of interventions and services for children of divorcing and separating parents*, Joseph Rowntree Foundation (Family Change series), YPS

37 Wade, A. and Smart, C. (2002), *Facing Family Change: Children's circumstances, strategies and resources*, Joseph Rowntree Foundation, YPS

38 Leach, P. (1999), *The Physical Punishment of Children: some input from recent research*, NSPCC

39 *Helpful Parenting*, Royal College of Paediatrics and Child Health, London, 2002

40 Edwards, J. (ed.) (2001), *Not in Front of the Children: How conflict between parents affects children*, One Plus One, Marriage and Partnership Research, London

41 Simpson, B., McCarthy, P. and Walker, J. (1995), *Being There: Fathers after Divorce*, Relate Centre for Family Studies

42 Gorell Barnes, G., Thompson, P., Daniel, G., and Burchardt, N., *Growing Up In Stepfamilies*, Oxford University Press, 1998

43 Survey by Mori, commissioned by the NSPCC, published April 1997

44 Clarke, L. and Cairns H., 'Grandparents and the Care of Children: the Research Evidence' in Broad, B. (ed.), *Kinship Care* (2001), Russell House Publishing

45 Research for the Abbey National by the Future Foundation, 2002

46 Clarke, L. and Cairns, H., 'Grandparents and the Care of Children: the

Research Evidence' in Broad, B. (ed.), *Kinship Care* (2001), Russell House Publishing

47 Clarke, L. and Cairns, H., 'Grandparents and the Care of Children: the Research Evidence' in Broad, B. (ed.), *Kinship Care* (2001), Russell House Publishing

48 Prasad, R., 'Lynchpins' of family spend three days a week with grandchildren', *Guardian* Dec 14, 2000

49 Bryson, K. and Casper L.M., 'Co-resident Grandparents and Grandchildren', in *Current Population Reports*, May 1999, US Department of Commerce

50 Research for the Abbey National by the Future Foundation, 2002

51 Perlman, M. and Ross, H.S., 'The benefits of parent intervention in their children's disputes: an examination of concurrent changes in children's fighting styles', *Child Development*, 1997, 690–700

52 Elfer, Peter, Goldschmied, Elinor and Selleck, Dorothy (2003), *Key persons in the Nursery: Building relationships for quality provision*, David Fulton Publishers, London

53 Mooney, A. and Munton, A.G. (1997), *Research and Policy in Early Childhood Services: time for a new agenda*, Thomas Coram Research Unit, Institute of Education, University of London

54 IDS (Incomes Data Services Ltd), study 630, July 1997

55 *Childcare Facts*, 2003, Daycare Trust

56 Mooney, A. and Munton, A.G. (1997), *Research and Policy in Early Childhood Services: time for a new agenda*, Thomas Coram Research Unit, Institute of Education, University of London

57 Ferri, E. and Smith, K. *Parenting in the 1990s*, Family Policy Studies Centre, Joseph Rowntree Foundation, 1996

58 *Helpful Parenting*, Royal College of Paediatrics and Child Health, London, 2002

59 *Children and Violence*, Report of the Commission on Children and Violence convened by the Gulbenkian Foundation. Calouste Gulbenkian Foundation, London, 1995

CHAPTER NINE
Gender and developments

1 MacLeod, M. and Barter, C. (1996), *We Know It's Tough To Talk: Boys in Need of Help*, ChildLine

2 MacLeod, M. and Barter, C. (1996), *We Know It's Tough To Talk: Boys in Need of Help*, ChildLine

3 Coleman, J. and Dennison, C. (2000), *Young People and Gender: a Review of Research*, Trust for the Study of Adolescence, on behalf of the Women's Unit in the Cabinet Office and the Family Policy Unit in the Home Office

4 Madge, N. et al. (2000), *The Forgotten Years*, NCB

5 Armitage, A. (1998), Report to the Children's Oral Culture Conference, Sheffield University

6 *Children and Violence*, Report of the Commission on Children and Violence

convened by the Gulbenkian Foundation. Calouste Gulbenkian Foundation, London, 1995

7 Archer, J., 'Male violence in perspective', in Archer, John (ed.), *Male Violence*, Routledge, 1994

8 Lee, B. et al. (1998), *Gender Research in Educational Achievement*, National Foundation for Educational Research

9 *Children in the UK*, National Statistics, 2002

10 Brooks, G. et al. (1997), *Trends in Reading at 8*, National Federation for Educational Research in England and Wales

11 Warwick, B. and Elley, W.B. (1992), 'How in the world do students read?', *IEA Study of Reading Literacy*, the International Association for the Evaluation of Educational Achievement;
Schweinhart, L.J. and Weikart, D.P. (1997), *Lasting Differences: The High-Scope Preschool Curriculum Comparison Study Through Age 23*, High-Scope Press

12 Lee, B. et al. (1998), *Gender Research in Educational Achievement*, National Foundation for Educational Research

13 Girls on average continue to do better than boys. In 2000/01, 57% of girls gained five or more GCSEs, compared with 46% of boys. *Social Focus in Brief: Children 2002*, Office of National Statistics

14 *Children in the UK*. National Statistics, 2002

15 Mills, C. and Mills, D., *Britain's Early Years Disaster*, Channel 4, November 1997, prepared for the National Task Force on Mathematics (formed the basis of Channel 4's Dispatches *Too Much Too Young*, January 1998)

16 Grugeon, E. (1998), Report to the Children's Oral Culture Conference, Sheffield University

17 Katz, A. (1997), *The Can-Do Girls – A Barometer of Change*, based on the *Express on Sunday* Girlstalk Survey and further work undertaken at the Department of Applied Social Studies and Research, Oxford University

18 Katz, A. (1997), *The Can-Do Girls – A Barometer of Change*, based on the Express on Sunday Girlstalk Survey and further work undertaken at the Department of Applied Social Studies and Research, Oxford University

19 Katz, A. (1997), *The Can-Do Girls – A Barometer of Change*, based on the *Express on Sunday* Girlstalk Survey and further work undertaken at the Department of Applied Social Studies and Research, Oxford University

20 Katz, A. (1988), *Understanding Our Daughters*, Exploring Parenthood: part of the Women at the Millennium Project

CHAPTER TEN
Play and learning

1 Cole-Hamilton, I. and Gill, T. (2002), *Making the case for play: Building policies and strategies for school-aged children*, National Children's Bureau

2 Bruce, T. (1989), *Time for Play in Early Childhood Education*, Hodder and Stoughton

3 Witter, B. (1993), 'Childs play', *Child*, December, January, 67–8, 114–15

4   Whewa, R. and Millward, A. (1997), *Child's Play: facilitating play on housing estates*, The Chartered Institute of Housing

5   Paley, V.G. (1992), *You Can't Say You Can't Play*, Harvard University Press; Dunn, J. (1993), *Young Children's Close Relationships; beyond attachment*, Sage

6   *Children and Violence*, Report of the Commission on Children and Violence, convened by the Gulbenkian Foundation. Calouste Gulbenkian Foundation, London, 1995

7   US psychologist Professor Philip Zimbardo, to the British Psychological Society, University College Cardiff, July 1997

8   Dennison, B.A., Erb, T.A., and Jenkins, P.L. (2002), 'Television Viewing and Television in Bedroom Associated With Overweight Risk Among Low-Income Preschool Children', *Pediatrics*, 109, 1028–35, American Academy of Pediatrics

9   A *Sunday Times* survey of more than 2,250 children, June 1996

10 *Guardian*, April 27, 1998

11 McCarraher, L. (1998), *Family Viewing: A report on parents, children and the media*, Parenting Education and Support Forum/National Children's Bureau, London

12 *Social Focus in Brief: Children 2002*, Office of National Statistics, London

13 Recommendation by Peter Avis, director of the British Educational Communications and Technology Agency, following research by Nottingham University psychologist Professor David Wood, May 1998

14 See, for example, *Violence – Directions From Australia*, National Committee on Violence, Australian Institute of Criminology, Canberra, 1990; Philo, G. 'Children and Film/Video/TV Violence' in Philo, G. (ed.) (1998), *Message Received, Glasgow Media Group Research 1993–1998*, Longman

15 McCarraher, L. (1998), *Family Viewing: A report on parents, children and the media*, Parenting Education and Support Forum/National Children's Bureau, London

16 Dibb, Sue (1996), *A Spoonful Of Sugar – Television Food Advertising Aimed At Children: An international comparative survey*, Consumers International, London

17 *Children and Violence*, Report of the Commission on Children and Violence, convened by the Gulbenkian Foundation. Calouste Gulbenkian Foundation, London, 1995

18 *Helpful Parenting* (2002), Royal College of Paediatrics and Child Health, London.

19 Brierly, J. (1987), *Give Me A Child Until He Is Seven. Brain Studies and Early Childhood Education*, Falmer Press

20 'The effective provision of pre-school education', Institute of Education, as quoted in *Helpful Parenting* (2002), Royal College of Paediatrics and Child Health, London

21 *Helpful Parenting* (2002), Royal College of Paediatrics and Child Health, London

22 Donaldson, M. (1992), *Human Minds: An Exploration*, Allen Lane/Penguin Books, London

23 Vittachi, A. (1989), *Stolen Childhood – In search of the rights of the child*, Polity Press

24 Trevarthen, C. (2002), 'Learning in Companionship', *Education in the North*
25 Recommendations for good practice in the government's Numeracy Task Force's preliminary report, *Numeracy Matters*, January 1998
26 *Helping Children Learn: Changing Schools*, Parentline Plus, 2002

CHAPTER ELEVEN
Growing independence

1 *Children and Violence*, Report of the Commission on Children and Violence, convened by the Gulbenkian Foundation. Calouste Gulbenkian Foundation, London, 1995
2 *Helpful Parenting*, Royal College of Paediatrics and Child Health, 2002
3 Perlman, M. and Ross, H. S. (1997), 'The benefits of parent intervention in their children's disputes: an examination of concurrent changes in children's fighting styles', *Child Development*, 690–700
4 O'Brien, M. and Jones, D., 'The Absence and Presence of Fathers: Accounts from Children's Diaries', in Bjornberg, U. and Collind, A. (eds.) *Men's Family Relations*, Almqvist & Wiksell, Stockholm, 1996
5 MacLeod, M. and Morris, S., *Why Me? Children Talking to ChildLine About Bullying: A ChildLine Study*, ChildLine, 1996
6 Reiss, A. J. and Roth, J. A. (eds.). (1993), *The Development of an Individual's Potential for Violence: Understanding and preventing violence*, US National Academy of Sciences, National Academy Press, Washington DC
7 Smith, F.K. and Sharp, S. (1994), *School Bullying – Insights and perspectives*, Routledge, London; MacLeod, M. and Morris, S. (1996), *Why Me? Children talking to ChildLine about Bullying*, ChildLine, London
8 MacLeod, M. and Morris, S. (1996), *Why Me? Children talking to ChildLine about Bullying*, ChildLine, London
9 Commissioned by *Family Circle* magazine, published January 1988
10 Parentline Plus (2000), Report on Analysis of Calls Concerning Schooling
11 Balding, J. (2002), *Young People In 2001*, Schools Health Education Unit, Exeter
12 Balding, J. (1997), *Young People In 1996*, Schools Health Education Unit, Exeter
13 MacLeod, M. and Morris, S., *Why Me? Children Talking to ChildLine About Bullying: A ChildLine Study*, ChildLine, 1996
14 MacLeod, M. and Morris, S., *Why Me? Children Talking to ChildLine About Bullying: A ChildLine Study*, ChildLine, 1996
15 *Helpful Parenting*, Royal College of Paediatrics and Child Health, 2002
16 Balding, J. (2001), *Young People In 2001*, Schools Health Education Unit, Exeter
17 Child Accident Prevention Trust, June 1998
18 *Promoting the Health of Teenage and Lone Mothers: Setting a research agenda* (1999), Report of a Health Education Authority Expert Working Group, chaired by Kaye Wellings
19 *Talking to Your Child about Sex*, fpa, 2001
20 Hill, C. and Boydell, P. (2001), *Does Your Mother Know? A study of underage sexual behaviour and parental responsibility*, The Family Matters Institute, Bedford

21 *Promoting the Health of Teenage and Lone Mothers: Setting a research agenda* (1999), Report of a Health Education Authority Expert Working Group, chaired by Kaye Wellings

22 Winn, S., Roker, D. and Coleman, J. (1995), 'Knowledge about puberty and sexual development in 11–16 year olds: implications for health and sex education in schools', *Educational Studies*, 21, 2

23 Blake, S. and Katrak, Z. (2002), *Faith, Values and Sex and Relationship Education*, Sex Education Forum, National Children's Bureau

24 Blake, S. and Katrak, Z. (2002), *Faith, Values and Sex and Relationship Education*, Sex Education Forum, National Children's Bureau

25 *Talking to Your Child about Sex*, fpa, 2001

26 *Time to Talk about Sex*, Parentline Plus, 2003

27 McKeganey, N. and Norrie, J. (1998), *Pre-Teen Drug Users in Scotland*, University of Glasgow, Centre for Drug Misuse Research

28 Madge, N. et al. (2000), *The Forgotten Years*, NCB

29 Statistics from the Schools Health Education Unit, Exeter, 2002

30 Community-based research into drug and alcohol abuse and misuse by young people in Belfast, published by Radical, 2002

31 Balding, J. (2001), *Young People In 2001*, Schools Health Education Unit, Exeter

32 Health Education Authority, 1992

33 Velleman, R., Mistral, W. and Sanderling, L. (2000), *Taking the message home: involving parents in drugs prevention*, Home Office

34 McGurk, H. and Hurry, J. (1995), *Project Charlie: An Evaluation of A Life Skills Drug Education Programme for Primary Schools*, Home Office Drugs Prevention Initiative
    Hurry, J. and Lloyd, C. (1997), *A Follow-Up Evaluation of Project Charlie*, Home Office Drug Prevention Initiative

35 Balding, J. (1999 and 2000), *Young People In 2000* and *Young People in 1999*, Schools Health Education Unit, Exeter

36 Regis, D. (2001), 'Self-esteem and health risky behaviour', *YoungMinds*

37 Madge, N. et al. (2000), *The Forgotten Years*, NCB

38 Borland, M. et al., *Middle childhood. The perspectives of children and parents*, Jessica Kingsley, 1998

39 Madge, N. et al. (2000), *The Forgotten Years*, NCB

40 Lewis, E.J. (1995), *Truancy: The partnership approach*, Home Office Police Research Group

41 Abrahams, C. and Mungall, R. (1992), *Runaways: Exploding the myths*, NCH Action for Children

42 *Listening to 10-year-olds: A ChildLine Study*, ChildLine, 1996

43 Balding J. (1996), *Very young people in 1993–5: The health related behaviour questionnaire results for 18,929 pupils between the ages of 9 and 12*, University of Exeter Schools Education Unit

44 Madge, N. et al. (2000), *The Forgotten Years*, NCB

45 Rae Simpson, A. (2001), *Raising Teens: A Synthesis of Research and a Foundation for Action*, Centre for Health Communication, Harvard School of Public Health, Boston

46   Hillman, M., Adams, J. and Whitelegg, J. (1990), *One False Move: a Study of Children's Independent Mobility*, Policy Studies Institute

47   Rae Simpson, A. (2001), *Raising Teens: A Synthesis of Research and a Foundation for Action*, Centre for Health Communication, Harvard School of Public Health, Boston

48   Rae Simpson, A. (2001), *Raising Teens: A Synthesis of Research and a Foundation for Action*, Centre for Health Communication, Harvard School of Public Health, Boston

APPENDIX 2

Contributors

Corinne Abisgold is an educational psychologist.

Caroline Abrahams is Director of Public Policy at NCH.

Gill Gorell Barnes is an Honorary Senior Clinical Lecturer at the Tavistock Clinic London, a family therapist, researcher and author of: *Family Therapy in Changing Lives*, Macmillan, 1998; with Dowling, Emilia, *Working with Families through Separation and Divorce: The Changing Lives of Children*, Macmillan, 1999, and *You're Both Still My Parents*, Prestige Health Productions (video), 1997

Camila Batmanghelidjh is a psychotherapist with extensive experience of taking therapeutic work into communities. She campaigns for improved resources and increased access in child mental health. She founded the charities: The Place To Be and Kids Company.

Paula Bell is a health visitor.

Steve Biddulph is a British-born psychologist and bestselling author who lives in Australia. Further reading: Biddulph, Shaaron, *The Mother and Baby Book*, Leopard Books, 1997; Biddulph, Steve, *Raising Boys*, Thorsons UK, 1998; Biddulph, Steve and Shaaron, *More Secrets of Happy Children*, Thorsons UK, 1999.

Lisa Blakemore-Brown is an independent chartered psychologist, author and chairwoman of Promoting Parenting Skills, a national group of psychologists committed to the use of an empirical research base for parent programmes.

Dr Michael Boulton is a child psychologist in the Department of Psychology at Keele University. He has carried out extensive research on aggression, bullying and victimisation.

John Bristow is a psychologist working in organisations, a psychotherapist in private practice and, until recently, a Parent Network co-ordinator.

Elizabeth Mary Bryan MD FRCP FRCPCH is an Honorary Consultant Paediatrician at Queen Charlotte's and Chelsea Hospital, London, and founder of the Multiple Births Foundation. She was co-founder of the Twins and Multiple Births Association. She is Vice-President of the International Society of Twin Studies. Her books include: *Twins, Triplets and More*, Penguin, 1992; *Twins and Higher Multiple Births: A Guide to their Nature and Nurture*, Edward Arnold, 1992.

José von Bühler, RMN, CPN, Dip. Human Sexuality, BASMT Accred., MSc in Human Sexuality. He is a sexual and relationship psychotherapist, Director of von Bühler Associates, working from the Cardinal Clinic, Berkshire.

Dr John Byng-Hall is Consultant Child and Family Psychiatrist at the Institute of Family Therapy, London. He has published widely on topics such as family myths, stories, legends and scripts, the impact of chronic illness, and attachments within the family. He is author of *Re-writing Family Scripts*, Guilford Press, 1995.

Domenico Di Ceglie is a consultant child and

adolescent psychiatrist at the Tavistock Clinic and Director of the Gender Identity Development Unit, Portman Clinic. He is Honorary Senior Lecturer, Royal Free Hospital School of Medicine, London, and editor of *A Stranger in My Own Body*, Karnac Books, 1998.

Christine Chittick is an NCT ante-natal teacher.

Dr John Coleman is Director of the Trust for the Study of Adolescence. He is a clinical psychologist with a special interest in young people. He has an international reputation as a lecturer and author, and his publications include textbooks on adolescence, and books and videos for parents of teenagers.

Linda Connell is a counsellor, a trainer in communication and group work skills and a Parent-Infant Facilitator for PIPPIN (see Contacts, p.429).

Anne Cowling is an advisor for Leeds Healthy Schools, Education Leeds.

Mary Crowley is chief executive of the Parenting Education and Support Forum.

Jane Cutler is Head of Music at the Da Capo School of Music, London, 'committed to developing a new approach to music education'.

Barbara Dale is a parent of eight, a parenting counsellor and psychotherapist.

Sarah Darton works as a health visitor and parenting workshop facilitator.

Hilton Davis is Professor of Child Health Psychology at King's College London and Director of the Centre for Parent and Child Support, South London and Maudsley NHS Trust, based at Guy's Hospital.

Peter Elfer is Senior Lecturer in Early Childhood Studies, Roehampton, University of Surrey. The current focus of his research and writing is on the experience of children under three in nursery settings. His new book *Key Persons in the Nursery* (David Fulton, 2003) is written with Elinor Goldschmied and Dorothy Selleck.

Pat Elliot has wide experience as a teacher, bereavement counsellor, parenting educator and psychotherapist. She runs a psychotherapy practice, offers freelance consultancy and training on bereavement issues to schools and other professionals, and runs parenting groups. She is author of *Coping with Loss – for Parents*, Piccadilly Press, 1977 and a tutor and trainer at the Psychosynthesis and Education Trust.

Dr Michele Elliott is the Director of Kidscape children's charity and an author.

Christine Fahey is a Montessori nursery teacher and proprietor.

Robert Fisher is Professor of Education, Brunel University, and director of its Centre for Research in Teaching Thinking. He has published more than 20 books on education, including the highly acclaimed *Stories for Thinking* series (see *www.teachingthinking.net*). He is involved in research and training with schools and LEAs and is an advisor to the QCA and DfE on literacy and thinking skills.

Hugh Foot is Professor of Psychology at the University of Strathclyde, specialising in child psychology and social development.

Robin Freeland was a respected educational psychologist. He has, sadly, now died. We wish to acknowledge his contribution to this book and to the lives of very many children.

Edie Freeman is a homoeopath (LCH) who works from two clinics: the North End Road Practice, 8 Burghley Road, London NW5 1UE and the Viveka Clinic (see below).

Yehudi Gordon is a consultant gynaecologist and obstetrician, specialising in holistic health. He works at the Birth Unit of the Hospital of St John and St Elizabeth, London and at his clinic, Viveka, 27a Queens Terrace, London NW8 6EA.

Vivienne Gross is a family therapist in both the NHS and private practice, and a freelance consultant and trainer in Family and Systemic Psychotherapy. She is a member of the Institute of Family Therapy.

Angela Gruber is a transpersonal psychotherapist.

Kitty Hagenbach is a transpersonal psychotherapist and child psychotherapist working at Viveka, 27a Queens Terrace, London NW8 6EA. She specialises in working with parents regarding the emotional and psychological aspects of parenting.

Carol Ann Hally works as a health visitor and clinical practice teacher.

Dr Gillian Harris is Senior Lecturer in Developmental Psychology at the School of Psychology, University of Birmingham. She is a consultant clinical psychologist and head of the Feeding Clinic at the Children's Hospital, Birmingham.

Dr Joanna Hawthorne is a research psychologist at the University of Cambridge and co-ordinator and trainer at the Brazelton Centre in Great Britain (see Contacts, p.429).

Eileen Hayes is parenting advisor to the NSPCC, a Trustee of Parenting Education and Support Forum (c/o National Children's Bureau, 8 Wakely Street, London EC1V 7QE) and chair of its Media and Parenting Group. This forum brings together those concerned with or working in the field of preparation, education and support for parents.

Ann Herreboudt is a midwife and family therapist on the Birth Unit at St John and St Elizabeth's Hospital and at the Viveka Clinic (see above).

Dr Andrew Hill is a psychologist at the Psychiatry and Behavioural Sciences Unit, Leeds University.

Nancy Hobbs is a drugs education consultant with Project Charlie, a drugs prevention programme for primary school children.

Candida Hunt is Assistant Director of Family Links (see Contacts, p.429) and a national trainer in the Nurturing Programme, an emotional literacy programme for families and schools. She is the author of *The Parenting Puzzle – How to Get the Best out of Family Life*, Family Links, 2003, a practical guide for parents based on the Nurturing Programme.

Simon James, the Association of Post-natal Illness (see Contacts, p.429).

Noël Janis-Norton is the Director of the New Learning Centre, offering training workshops for pupils, parents and professionals who work with young people and parents.

Adrienne Katz is founder and executive director of Young Voice, a charity 'working to make young people's views count'. An author and journalist on issues of concern to families and children for 20 years, she has worked on social research projects in association with Dr Ann Buchanan of Oxford University since 1996.

David Kesterton, is national manager of Speakeasy, an **fpa** (Family Planning Association) course to help parents gain confidence in talking to their children about sex and sexuality.

Gez Lamb is an osteopath with special emphasis on the 'cranial' approach. He works from 1 Oldbury Place, London W1M 3AN.

Penelope Leach Ph.D is a research psychologist and advocate for families. She has recently published a new version of her classic *Your Baby and Child*, rewritten for a new generation (Dorling Kindersley, 2003). She is a principal investigator on the Families, Children and Childcare study and President of the National Childmind Association.

Mary MacLeod is chief executive of the

National Family and Parenting Institute. Prior to this she was Director of Policy and Research at ChildLine.

Doro Marden is a parent educator, freelance trainer and a trustee of the charities Parentline Plus and Young Voice.

Bethan Marshall is a lecturer in education at King's College, London, specialising in gender and literacy.

Peter Mellor is a counsellor and parent skills trainer.

Clare Mills is a qualified speech and language therapist and co-author (with David Mills) of *Britain's Early Years Disaster*, Channel 4, 1997, prepared for the National Task Force on Mathematics.

Sue Monk is former chief executive of Parents at Work (see Contacts, p.429).

Ann Mooney is a child psychologist and Research Officer at the Thomas Coram Research Unit, Institute of Education, University of London. Recent publications include: Mooney, A. and Munton, A.G., *Choosing Childcare*, Arena, Aldershot; 1997; Mooney, A. and Munton, A.G., *Research and Policy in Early Childhood Services: Time for a New Agenda*, Institute of Education, London; 1997.

Carol Munro is a primary headteacher and member of Brent SACRE (Standing Advisory Council on Religious Education).

Elizabeth Newson is Emeritus Professor of Developmental Psychology, University of Nottingham, an author and consultant to the Early Years Diagnostic Centre. She has researched and published extensively in child development.

Dr Gavin Nobes lectures in developmental and forensic psychology at the University of East London. His research interests include children's social development – especially the development of morality and anti-social behaviour – families, physical punishment and abuse, and children's understanding of science.

John Oates is a developmental psychologist in the Centre for Human Development and Learning, Open University. Further reading: Oates, J. (ed.), *The Foundations of Child Development*, Blackwells, 1994.

Jenny Oberon is a freelance pupil behaviour management consultant and trainer. She was a founder staff member of the Leeds Attendance and Behaviour Project, working with children, parents, schools and their communities. She has introduced parent/pupil groups into many schools around the country, as well as running staff stress management projects in schools and businesses. She can be contacted at *jenny@oberon.totalserve.co.uk*

Susie Orbach is a psychotherapist and writer. She co-founded the Women's Therapy Centre and has written many books on food, eating, women's psychology and emotional literacy.

Dr Pat Petrie is Senior Research Lecturer at the Thomas Coram Research Unit, Institute of Education, University of London.

Dr Greg Philo is Research Director at the Glasgow University Media Unit.

Judith Philo is an analytical psychologist and Jungian analyst. Before in-depth psychology training, she worked in nursing and midwifery, and later in social work and counselling. She has extensive experience of working with families in the health and social services, and as an advisor on a parent support advice line.

Christine Puckering is a clinical psychologist and Senior Research Fellow at the University of Glasgow. She is co-founder of Mellow Parenting, an intensive prevention and intervention programme for situations where there is grave concern about parenting. Recent publications: Puckering, C., et al. (1996), 'Taking Control: A Single Case Study of Mellow Parenting', *Clinical Child Psychology and Psychiatry*, 1, pp.539–50; Mills, M. and Puckering, C., 'Bringing about change in parent-child relationships,' in Trowell, J. and Bower, M. (eds.), *The Emotional Needs of Young Children and Families*, Routledge, 1995.

Jenny Reynolds is Research Consultant to One Plus One, the marriage and partnership research charity (see Contacts, p.429).

Martin Richards has, for two decades, carried out research on the effects for children of parental divorce. He has written widely on the issues and has been involved in government policy-making and development of supportive interventions for children and their parents. He is Director of the Centre for Family Research and a Professor at the University of Cambridge.

Professor Kathryn Riley is Director of the Centre of Educational Management, Roehampton Institute, London.

Penelope Robinson is Director of Professional Affairs, The Chartered Society of Physiotherapy.

Dr Dorothy Rowe has worked as a teacher, child psychologist, and clinical psychologist in the NHS. She has researched and written extensively. Her work is concerned with meaning and communication. Her books include: *Depression: The Way Out of Your Prison*, Routledge, 1983, second edition 1996; *Beyond Fear*, HarperCollins, 1987; *The Successful Self*, HarperCollins, 1988; *The Depression Handbook*, HarperCollins, 1990, reissued as *Breaking the Bonds*, 1991; *Time on Our Side*, HarperCollins, 1994; *Dorothy Rowe's Guide to Life*, HarperCollins, 1995.

Dorothy Selleck is a Senior Development Officer in the Early Childhood Unit at the National Children's Bureau.

Marjorie Smith is a psychologist, Deputy Director at the Thomas Coram Unit and Reader in the Psychology of the Family at the Institute of Education. She has been carrying out research on children and families for over 20 years.

Lolly Stirk is a child-birth educator who specialises in pregnancy and post-natal yoga.

Brigid Treacy is a parenting advisor and former Parent Network co-ordinator.

Professor Colwyn Trevarthen is a biologist specialising in the communication of feelings, purposes, interests and ideas. He is Professor (Emeritus) of Child Psychology and Psychobiology at the University of Edinburgh. Further reading includes: 'Conversations with a two-month-old', *New Scientist*, 2 May 1974; 230–5; 'Playing into Reality: Conversations with the infant communicator,' *Winnicott Studies*, Number 7, Spring 1993, 67–84, Karnac Books, London; 1993; 'The child's need to learn a culture', *Children and Society*, 9 (1), 5–19, 1995.

Nicholas Tucker, formerly an educational psychologist, is now honorary senior lecturer in Cultural Studies at the University of Sussex.

Peter Walker is a pioneer of baby massage and soft gymnastics for children. His new video *Baby Massage and Movement* is available for £13.99 (p&p inc., UK only) from Little Venice Films, PO Box 8293, London W9 2WZ. Further reading: *Baby Massage*, Piatkus, reprinted 1998.

Brian Waller is chief executive of Home-Start (see Contacts, p.429).

Cheryl Walters is a psychoanalytic psychotherapist in private practice working with individuals, couples and families, Head of Research at Parentline Plus and co-author of *All Together Now – what to expect when stepfamilies get together*.

Louise Walters is former chair of the Crysis helpline (see Contacts, p.429).

Dr Sally Ward, a specialist paediatric speech and language therapist, has sadly died after a long illness. She was the originator of the Wilstaar Programme (a preventative programme for speech and language disability and accelerated language development in all children) and author of *BabyTalk* (Century, 2000).

Stella Ward is a qualified nurse and parenting course facilitator.

Allan Watson is chief executive of the National Pyramid Trust for children.

Francis Wheen is a journalist and broadcaster.

Jim Wilson is a systemic therapist, author of *Child-Focused Practice: A Collaborative Systemic Approach*, Karnac Books, 1998, and director of the Centre for Child-Focused Practice at the Institute of Family Therapy, London. The centre offers a therapy and counselling service for children and their families.

Peter Wilson worked for many years as a social worker and psychotherapist, both in the community and residentially with emotionally disturbed young people. He is the Director of Young Minds, the children's mental health charity (see Contacts, p.355).

Gill Wood is an NCT ante-natal teacher.

In writing this book we have spoken to hundreds of parents from all walks of life in a huge variety of settings and situations. Those quoted have been identified in the text by their first name and first initial of their surname. Some parents have requested that their first names be changed.

APPENDIX 3

Contacts

Advisory Centre for Education (ACE)
1c Aberdeen Studios
22 Highbury Grove
London N5 2DQ
Tel: 020 7354 8318
General advice line: 0808 800 5793
Exclusion line: 020 7704 9822
www.ace-ed.org.uk
An independent advice centre for parents, offering information about state education in England and Wales for 5–16-year-olds. Offers free advice on many topics, including exclusion from school, bullying, special educational needs and school admission appeals.

Anti-Bullying Network
Moray House School of Education
The University of Edinburgh
Edinburgh EH8 8AQ
Info Line: 0131 651 6100
www.antibullying.net
Established by the Scottish Executive, for teachers, parents and young people to share ideas about tackling bullying.

Association of Breastfeeding Mothers
PO Box 207
Bridgwater
Somerset
TA6 7YT
Tel: 020 7813 1481
Support for breastfeeding mothers.

The Association for Post-natal Illness
145 Dawes Road
Fulham
London SW6 1BE
Helpline: 020 7386 0868
www.apni.org
Provides information, advice and support for sufferers of post-natal depression and their relatives/friends.

Barnardos
Tanners Lane
Barkinside, Ilford
Essex 1G6 1QG
Tel: 020 8550 8822
Helpline: 0845 7697967
www.barnardos.org.uk
The country's largest children's charity, offering a wide range of supportive projects in the following areas: disability, education, children needing families, disadvantaged communities, disadvantaged young people and families with young children.

Benefits Agency
Child Benefit – Central Helpline: 0845 3021444
Family Tax Credit – Central Helpline: 08456 095000
Your local benefits agency is listed in the telephone directory under B.

BLISS

68 South Lambeth Road
London SW8 1RL
Tel: 0870 7700337
Freephone helpline: 0500 618140
www.bliss.org.uk

The premature baby charity providing information
and support for families of premature and sick
newborn babies.

The Brazelton Centre

For training and information contact:
Dr Joanna Hawthorne
Box 226, NICU
Addenbrookes NHS Trust,
Hills Road
Cambridge CB2 2QQ
Tel: 01223 245791
www.brazelton.co.uk

The centre aims to provide an understanding of
infant development and foster strong infant-parent
relationships. Training programmes for healthcare
professionals are available.

**British Association for Counselling and
Psychotherapy**

1 Regent Place
Rugby
Warwickshire CV21 2PJ
Tel: 0870 443 5252
www.counselling.co.uk

Can provide a list of qualified counsellors in your
area.

The British Psychological Society

St Andrews House
48 Princes Road East
Leicester LE1 7DR
Tel: 0116 254 9568
www.bps.org.uk

Can provide directory of qualified chartered
psychologists and child psychologists by area.

**Centre for Counselling and Psychotherapy
Education**

Beauchamp Lodge
2 Warwick Crescent
London W2 6NE
Tel: 020 7266 3006
www.ccpe.org.uk

Offers individual, couple and child/adolescent
psychotherapy on a sliding-scale rate.

Child Growth Foundation

2 Mayfield Avenue
London W4 1PW
Tel: 020 8994 7625
www.heightmatters.org.uk

For parents who are concerned about the growth
of their children. Information and support groups.

Child Psychotherapy Trust

Star House
104–108 Grafton Road
London NW5 4BD
Tel: 020 7284 1355
www.childpsychotherapytrust.org.uk

Provides publications on request on a wide range
of subjects concerned with the emotional development of children.

ChildLine

Freepost 1111
London N1 OBR
Helpline (24 hr): 0800 1111
www.childline.org.uk

The 24-hour national helpline for children and
young people in trouble or danger. All calls are
free and confidential and children may call about
any problem.

Children 1st

83 Whitehouse Loan
Edinburgh EH9 1AT
Tel: 0131 446 2300
www.children1st.org.uk

Scotland's own childcare agency for prevention of
cruelty to children.

Children's Legal Centre

University of Essex
Wivenhoe Park
Colchester CO4 3SQ
Tel: 01206 872466 (office)
Adviceline: 01206 873820
www.childrenslegalcentre.com
Free advice by telephone or letter regarding legal
issues involving children and children's interests.

The Children's Society

Edward Rudolph House
69–85 Margery Street
London WC1X 0JL
Tel: 020 7841 4400
www.childrenssociety.org.uk
Independent charity working with children, young
people and their families throughout England and
Wales.

Contact-a-Family

209–211 City Road
London EC1V 1JN
Helpline: 0808 808 3555
www.cafamily.org.uk
Provides advice and information on all issues
affecting families of children with disabilities,
special needs, or rare disorders.

Cruse Bereavement Care

Cruse House
126 Sheen Road
Richmond
Surrey TW9 1UR
Tel: 020 8940 4818 (office)
Helpline: 0870 167 1677
www.crusebereavementcare.org.uk
Offers free help to those affected by bereavement
with opportunities for social support and practical
advice.

CRY-SIS Helpline

BM CRY-SIS
London WC1N 3XX
Tel: 020 7404 5011
www.cry-sis.com
Self-help and support for families with excessively
crying, sleepless and demanding babies from birth
to 18 months.

Daycare Trust

21 St George's Road
London SE1 6ES
Tel: 020 7840 3350
www.daycaretrust.org.uk
A charity promoting high quality affordable child-
care for all.

DFEE

www.parents.dfee.gov.uk
Provides information and ideas on how parents
can help at school. See the 'discover' section for
help with homework.

Disabled Parents Network

Unit F9
89–93 Fonthill Road
London N4 3JH
Tel: 0870 2410450
Information line: 0800 0184730
www.disabledparents network.org.uk
Offering peer support for disabled parents,
disabled people looking to become parents, and
family, friends and allies of disabled people.

Disability Pregnancy and Parenthood
International

Unit F9
89–93 Fonthill Road
London N4 3JH
Freephone: 0800 0184730
www.dppi.org.uk
Information for disabled parents, disabled people
looking to become parents, and family, friends and
allies of disabled people.

Drugscope
Waterbridge House
32-36 Loman Street
London SE1 0EE
Information: 0870 774 3682
www.drugscope.org.uk
The drugs information charity providing straight-forward information on drugs, the common terms, their effects and associated risks. Clicking on the 'Find a Drug Service' button links to a database of local drug treatment and help services.

Eating Disorders Association (EDA)
103 Prince of Wales Road
Norwich NR1 IDW
Adult helpline: 0845 6341414
Youthline:0845 6347650
Text phone service: 01603 753322
www.eda.uk.com
A charity offering a range of information on eating disorders (including anorexia nervosa, bulimia nervosa and binge eating disorder) and related issues including details of specialist treatments available throughout the UK.

Family Caring Trust
8 Ashtree Enterprise Park
Newry
Co. Down BT34 1BY
Tel: 028 3026 4174
Fax: 028 3026 9077
www.familycaring.co.uk
A Northern Ireland-based charity concerned with the care of the family. Resources for parents and parenting groups available via website.

Family Links
New Marston Centre
Jack Straws Lane
Oxford OX3 ODL
Tel: 01865 454004
Fax: 01865 452145
www.familylinks.org.uk
An Oxford-based charity promoting emotional literacy, nurturing and relationship skills in families, schools and communities. It runs the

Nurturing Programme parenting course, with a parallel PSHCE course for primary schools, and offers training courses for professionals working in education and in health

fpa UK (Family Planning Association)
2-12 Pentonville Road
London N1 9FP
Tel: 020 7837 5432
Helpline: 0845 3101334
www.fpa.org.uk
For advise on sex education, contraception and sexual health.

Family Welfare Association
501–505 Kingsland Road
London E8 4AU
Tel: 020 7254 6251
www.fwa.org.uk
Offers financial advice to families and individuals.

Fathers Direct
Herald House
15 Lamb's Passage
Bunhill Row
London EC1Y 8TQ
Tel: 020 7920 9491
www.fathersdirect.com
Provides a range of resources, research and training for working with fathers.

FSID (Foundation for the Study of Infant Deaths)
Artillery House
11–19 Artillery Row
London SW1P 1RT
Tel: 0870 7870885
Helpline: 0870 787 0554
www.sids.org.uk/fsid
Provides support to bereaved families, advice to anyone concerned about cot death and promotes infant health.

Gender Identity Development Unit
Portman Clinic
8 Fitzjohns Avenue
London
NW3 5NA
Tel: 020 7794 8262
Offers a service to children, adolescents and their
parents where there are concerns about the gender
development of the young person; a parents group
is available for parents of children who attend the
clinic.

General Osteopathic Council
Osteopathy House
176 Tower Bridge Road
London SE1 3LU
Tel: 020 7357 6655
www.osteopathy.org.uk
Provides information and list of registered
osteopaths.

Gingerbread
7 Sovereign Close
Sovereign Court
London E1W 3HW
Tel: 020 7488 9300
Adviceline: 0800 018 4318
www.gingerbread.org.uk
Runs a network of self-help groups for single
parents.
Gingerbread Wales
Tel: 0292 047 1900
Gingerbread Scotland
Tel: 0141 576 5085

Homeopathic Medical Association
6 Livingstone Road
Gravesend
Kent
DA12 5DZ
Tel: 01474 560336
Supplies a list of qualified homeopaths and an
information leaflet.

Home-Start
Central Office
2 Salisbury Road
Leicester LE1 7QR
Tel: 0116 233 9955
Helpline: 0800 068 6368
www.home-start.org.uk
Support, friendship and practical advice to families
with children under five in their homes, provided
through local schemes.

**Hyperactive Children's Support Group
(HACSG)**
28 Worple Road
London SW19 4EE
Tel: 020 8946 4444
www.hacsg.org.uk
Monthly workshops and clinics for parents of
children with behavioural problems or learning
difficulties.

**Information Service of the Early Years
Diagnostic Centre**
272 Longdale Lane
Ravenshead
Notts NG15 9AH
Tel: 01623 490 879
For parents of children with communication
disorders.

Institute of Family Therapy
24–32 Stephenson Way
London NW1 2HX
Tel: 020 7391 9150
www.instituteoffamilytherapy.org.uk
Couple and family counselling and mediation.

**The International Society for Twin Studies
(ISTS)**
www.ists.qimi.edu.au
The society aims to further research and public
education in all fields related to twins and twin
studies, for the mutual benefit of twins and their
families and for scientific research.

Kids Company

Arch 259
Grosvenor Court
Grosvenor Terrace
London SE5 ONP
Tel: 020 7703 1808
www.kidsco.org.uk

Provides caring adults to whom children can talk about their concerns and who can visit them in their schools or homes. It also has a children's centre where children refer themselves for support.

Kidscape

2 Grosvenor Garden
London SW1W 0DH
Helpline: 0845 104590
www.kidscape.org.uk

For parents of children being bullied.

La Leche League

LLGB Admin Office
PO Box 29
West Bridgford
Nottingham NG2 7NP
Helpline: 020 7242 1278
www.laleche.org.uk

Provides breastfeeding support, information, publications and local breastfeeding counsellors.

Meet-a-Mum (MAMA)

77 Westbury View
Peasdown St John
Bath BA2 8TZ
Tel: 01525 217064
Helpline: 0208 768 0123
www.mama.org.uk

Provides friendship and support to all mothers and mothers-to-be, and those suffering from post-natal depression.

Multiple Births Foundation

Hammersmith House Level 4
Queen Charlotte's Hospital
Du Cane Road
London W12 0HS
Tel: 020 8383 3519/20
www.multiplebirths.org.uk

Provides specialist professional advice and information to parents of twins and more, and to health professionals in the field.

National Association of Citizens Advice Bureaux (NACAB)

115–123 Pentonville Road
London N1 9LZ
Tel: 020 7833 2181
www.citizensadvice.org.uk

The national association of 1,400 Citizens Advice Bureaux, which provide information and advice on subjects such as housing benefits, immigration, finance, consumer complaints and family matters.

National Autistic Society

393 City Road
London EC1V 1NG
Tel: 020 7833 2299
Helpline: 0870 600 8585
www.nas.org.uk

A parent-led charity providing support and information for people with autism and their parents and carers.

National Childbirth Trust

Alexandra House
Oldham Terrace
Acton
London W3 6NH
Tel: 0870 444 8707
Breastfeeding Helpline: 0870 4448708
www.nctpregnancyandbabycare.com

The NCT offers information and support in pregnancy, childbirth and early parenthood and aims to enable every parent to make informed choices. It campaigns on behalf of parents for improvements in maternity and post-natal care.

National Childminding Association

8 Masons Hill
Bromley
Kent
BR2 9EY
Tel: 020 8464 6164
Advise Line: 0800 169 4486
www.ncma.org.uk
Help and advice to those looking after other people's children.

National Children's Bureau

8 Wakley Street
London EC1V 7QE
Tel: 020 7843 6000
www.ncb.org.uk
A charity concerned with making the voice of children heard.

NCH

Central Office
85 Highbury Park
London N5 1UD
Tel: 020 7704 7000
www.nch.org.uk
A leading children's charity running projects in the UK and abroad and campaigning on behalf of children and their families

National Council for One-Parent Families

255 Kentish Town Road
London NW5 2LX
Tel: 020 7428 5400
Helpline: 0800 018 5026
www.oneparentfamilies.org.uk
Information service for single parents.

National Family Mediation (NFM)

9 Tavistock Place
London WC1H 9SN
Tel: 020 7485 8809
www.nfm.u-net.com
Fostering the provision of independent family mediation services to couples experiencing separation or divorce whilst focusing on the children involved.

National Family and Parenting Institute

430 Highgate Studios,
53–79 Highgate Road
London NW5 1TL
Tel: 020 7424 3460
www.nfpi.org
Set up by the government in 1999 to support families in raising children. The institute wants to make it easy for parents to find out what help is available and to ensure that parenting services provided by small and large organisations are more widely publicised.

National Health Service Direct

Tel: 0845 4647
www.nhsdirect.nhs.uk
24-hour health information by phone or on the Internet.

National Newpin

Sutherland House
35 Sutherland Square
London SE17 3EE
Tel: 020 7358 5900
www.nationalnewpin.freeserve.co.uk
Peer support, training, individual counselling, group therapy and family play therapy for parents and children.

National Pyramid Trust

84 Uxbridge Road
London W13 8RA
Tel: 020 8579 5108
www.nptrust.org.uk
Helps primary school children fulfil their potential by building their self-esteem and resilience through clubs.

National Society for the Prevention of Cruelty to Children (NSPCC)
National Centre
42 Curtain Road
London EC2A 3NH
Helpline (24 hr): 0808 800 5000
www.nspcc.org.uk
The NSPCC is the UK's leading charity specialising in child protection and the prevention of cruelty to children. Their helpline provides counselling, information and advice to anyone concerned about a child at risk of abuse.

One-Parent Families Scotland
13 Gayfield Square
Edinburgh EH1 3NX
Tel: 0131 556 3899
www.opfs.org.uk
Scottish organisation for single parents.

One Plus One
The Wells
7–15 Rosebury Avenue
London EC1R 4SP
Tel: 020 7841 3660
www.oneplusone.org.uk
An independent research organisation whose role is to generate knowledge about marriage and relationships and uses the findings in a practical way, setting up working projects to support families and couples.

Osteopathic Centre For Children
109 Harley Street
London W1G 6AN
Helpline: 020 7628 2128
A charity providing fully qualified osteopaths for children (a donation is requested for each treatment).

Parenting Education and Support Forum
Unit 431 Highgate Studios
53–79 Highgate Road
London NW5 1TL
Tel: 020 7284 8370
www.parenting-forum.org.uk
An umbrella organisation for all groups and agencies involved in parenting education and support.

Parentline Plus
Head Office
Unit 520 Highgate Studios
53–79 Highgate Road
London NW5 1TL
Tel: 020 7284 5500
Adviceline: 0808 800 2222
Free textphone helpline: 0800 783 6783 (for hearing and speech impaired people)
www.parentlineplus.org.uk
Parentline Plus is a national charity dedicated to providing help and information to parents and carers via a free helpline, parenting courses, interactive website and information service. Parentline Plus also provides training to professionals working with families.

Parents at Work
1–3 Berry Street
London EC1V 0AA
Tel: 020 7253 7243
Helpline: 020 7253 4664
www.parentsatwork.org.uk
A charity supporting working parents and helping employers develop family-friendly policies.

Parents Information Network (PIN)
www.pin.org.uk
An independent service providing guidance for parents about computers and education, including advice on software and website evaluation, home learning and safety on the Internet.

PIPPIN (Parents in Partnership – Parent Infant Network)
Derwood
Todds Green
Stevenage
Herts SG1 2JE
Tel: 01438 748478
www.pippin.org.uk
A national charity providing structured parenting courses for expectant and new parents.

Refuge

2/8 Maltravers Street
London WC2 R3EE
Domestic violence helpline: 0870 599 5443
24-hour helpline for domestic violence.

Relate

Herbert Grey College
Little Church Street
Rugby
Warwickshire CV21 3AP
Tel: 01788 573241
www.relate.org.uk
This office will provide information regarding your
local Relate centre, offering counselling help for
marriage and family relationship needs.

The Royal College of Speech and Language Therapists (RCSLT)

2 White Hart Yard
London SE1 1NX
Tel: 020 7378 1200
www.rcslt.org
Information on speech and language therapy and
speech and language therapists.

Royal London Homoeopathic Hospital NHS Trust

Greenwell Street
London W1W 5BP
Tel: 020 7391 8833
Provides information on services including a chil-
dren's clinic. All services are free.

Samaritans

The Upper Mill
Kingston Road
Ewell
Surrey KT 17 2AS
Tel: 020 8394 8300
National Helpline: 08457 909090
www.samaritans.org
A charity available 24 hours a day to provide
confidential emotional support for anyone experi-
encing feelings of distress or despair, including
those which may lead to suicide.

Sex Education Forum

NCB
8 Wakley Street
London EC1V 7QE
Tel: 020 7843 6000
www.ncb.org.uk
An umbrella body of national organisations
working together to provide effective sex education
for all children and young people.

Society of Homeopaths

2 Artizan Road,
Northampton NN1 4HU
Tel 01604 621 400
www.homeopathy-soh.org
Provides information leaflet plus a register of
professional homoeopaths throughout the UK

The Speech Language and Hearing Centre

Christopher Place
Charlton Street
London NW1 1JF
Tel: 020 7383 3834
www.speech-lang.org.uk
A new centre for pre-school children with hearing
impairment and delay in speech or language.

TalkToFrank

(Formerly the National Drugs Helpline)
Confidential 24-hour helpline: 0800 776600
www.talktofrank.com

Trust for the Study of Adolescence

23 New Road
Brighton BN11W2
Tel: 01273 679907
www.tsa.uk.com
Registered charity and independent research and
training organisation, promoting knowledge and
understanding of young people. It stocks a range
of publications for parents and professionals.

Twins and Multiple Birth Association (TAMBA)
2 The Willows
Gardener Road
Guildford
Surrey GU1 4PG
Helpline: 01732 868000
www.tamba.org.uk
Information and support for families with twins, triplets or more.

Women's Aid Federation (England)
PO Box 391
Bristol BS99 7WS
Tel: 0117 944 4411
www.womensaid.org.uk
National Helpline: 08457 023468
Offers advice and refuge to women and children threatened by violence.

Working Group Against Racism in Children's Resources
Unit 63A Eurolink Business Park
49 Effre Road
London SW2 1BZ
Tel: 020 7501 9992
Information on books, toys and resources which provide positive representation of all children and communities.

YoungMinds
102-108 Clerkenwell Road
London EC1M 5SA
Tel: 020 7336 8445 (office)
Helpline: 0800 018 2138
www.youngminds.org.uk
National charity committed to improving the mental health of all babies, children, and young people. Parents' adviceline and information line for those concerned with the mental health of a child.

Young Voice
12 Bridge Gardens
East Molesey
Surrey KT8 9HU
Tel: 020 8979 4991
www.young-voice.org
A charity working to make young people's views count.

Youth Access
1/2 Taylors Yard
67 Alderbrook Road
London SW12 8AD
Tel: 020 8772 9900
Information on local contacts for counselling, advice and information for young people.

Republic of Ireland Contacts

Association for Children and Adults with Learning Difficulties (incorporating the Dyslexia Assocation)
Suffolk Chambers
1 Suffolk Street
Dublin 2
Tel: 01 679 0276
Fax: 01 679 0273
Email: acld@iol.ie
Website: www.iol.ie/~acld/
Promoting awareness of dyslexia and supporting adults and children with Specific Learning Difficulties.

Barnardos
Christchurch Square
Dublin 8
Tel: 01 453 0355
Email: info@barnardos.ie
Website: www.barnados.ie
Offers a wide range of services to children and their families including family support services, a national children's resource centre, a bereavement counselling service and adoption advice service.

Caint
Tel: 01 840 4349
Email: caint@indigo.ie
Website: http://indigo.ie/~caint/Default.htm
Parent to parent support and information for mothers and fathers of languages impaired children.

ChildLine
Tel: 1800 666 666
Free-to-use national helpline for children.

Childminding Ireland
The Enterprise Park
The Murrough
Wicklow Town
Tel: 0404 64007
Email: childm@indigo.ie
Website: www.childminding-irl.com
National organisation promoting high standards in family-based day care. Childcare vacancy service for parents wanting to find a registered child-minder in their area.

Children's Rights Alliance
13 Harcourt Street
Dublin 2
Tel: 01 405 4823
Email: info@cra.iol.ie
Website: www.childrensrights.ie
Protecting, promoting and advancing children's rights. Providing information, including an online Children's Rights Information Centre detailing children's rights and services in Ireland.

Cuidiú – Irish Childbirth Trust
Carmichael Centre
North Brunswick St.
Dublin 7
Tel: 01 872 4501
Website: www.cuidiu-ict.ie
Parent to parent community based voluntary
support group providing support for families
throughout all stages of parenthood – from preg-
nancy to adolescence. Branches and groups
nationwide.

Family Mediation Service
A free, state-run service, staffed by professionally
trained mediators, helping couples experiencing
separation or divorce address the needs of all
family members. Free information packs on issues
such as How Children React To Separation,
Managing The Stress Of Separation And Divorce,
Managing The Financial Issues.
Regional Offices:
    Dublin: 1st Floor, St. Stephen's Green,
        Earlsfort Terrace, D2. Tel: 01 634 4320
    Galway: 1st Floor, Ross House, Merchants
        Road, Galway. Tel: 091 509730
    Cork: Hibernian House, 80A South Mall,
        Cork. Tel: 021 252200
    Limerick; 1st Floor, Mill House, Henry Street,
        Limerick. Tel: 061 214310
Part-time offices:
    Athlone: c/o CIC, St Mary's Square, Athlone,
        Co. Westmeath. Tel: 0902 20970
    Castlebar: Family Centre, Chapel Street,
        Castlebar, Co. Mayo. Tel: 094 25900
    Dundalk: 3 Seatown Place, Dundalk, Co.
        Louth. Tel: 042 93594210
    Tallagh: The Rere, Tallaght Social Services
        Centre, The Square, Dublin 24. Tel: 01
        414 5180
    Tralee: c/o Kerry Family Resource &
        Counselling Centre, Balloonagh, Tralee,
        Co. Kerry. Tel: 066 7186100
    Wexford: Distillery Road, Wexford. Tel: 053
        63050

Gingerbread Ireland
Carmichael House
North Brunswick St
Dublin 7
Tel: 01 814 6618
Email: info@gingerbread.ie
Website: www.gingerbread.ie
Voluntary body providing practical, friendly advice
and support for single parents and their families

**Irish Association of Speech & Language
Therapists**
29 Gardiner Place
Dublin 1
Tel: 01 878 0215
Website: www.clubi.ie/iaslt
Helping parents locate and contact speech and
language therapists working privately in their area.

Irish Multiple Births Association (IMBA)
Carmichael Centre
North Brunswick St
Dublin 7
Tel: 01 874 9056
Email: twinsplusimba@eircom.net
Website: www.carmichaelcentre.ie/imba
Supporting families with twins, triplets and more.

**Irish Pre-school Playgroups Association
(IPPA)**
Unit 4
Broomhill Business Complex
Broomhill Road
Tallaght
Dublin 24
Tel: 01 463 0010
Fax: 01 463 0045
E-mail: info@ippa.ie
Website: www.ippa.ie
Promoting quality play-based early childhood care
and education.

Irish Society for the Prevention of Cruelty to Children (ISPCC)

20 Molesworth St
Dublin 2
Tel: 01 679 4944
Fax: 01 679 1746
Email: ispcc@ispcc.ie
Website: www.ispcc.ie

Ireland's leading children's charity specialising in the prevention of cruelty to children. Every year the Society works with thousands of children and parents to foster better relationships between parents and children while promoting better understanding of children's needs.

Mental Health Ireland

Mensana House
6 Adelaide St
Dun Laoghaire
Co. Dublin
Tel: 01 284 1166
Email: info@mentalhealthireland.ie
Website: www.mensana.org

Information on maintaining mental health and coping with mental health problems including stress, anxiety and post natal depression. Website carries support group listings.

National Children's Nurseries Association

12C Bluebell Business Park
Old Naas Road
Bluebell
Dublin 12
Tel: 01 460 1138
Email: info@ncna.ie
Website: www.ncna.net

Advice on how to choose a quality nursery. Lists of registered nurseries by area.

Parentline Republic of Ireland

Carmichael House
North Brunswick St
Dublin 7
Helpline: 1890 927277
Email: parentline@eircom.net
Website: www.parentline.ie

Parentline offers a confidential service to parents, grandparents, guardians, health care professionals, teachers and all concerned with parenting and family life, via a helpline, face-to-face support and parenting groups.

Republic of Ireland Department of Health and Children

Hawkins House
Hawkins Street
Dublin 2
Tel: 01 635 4000
Website: www.doh.ie

RollerCoaster

Website: www.RollerCoaster.ie

Website for parents in Ireland

Treoir

National Information Centre for Unmarried Parents
14 Gandon House
Custom House Square
IFSC
Dublin 1
Tel: 01 670 0120
Fax: 01 670 0199
E-mail: info@treoir.ie
Website: www.treoir.ie

The national co-ordinating body of both statutory and voluntary agencies providing services for unmarried parents and their children in Ireland. It is a voluntary organisation supported by Government, health boards and other agencies. It provides a free, confidential, accessible and up-to-date information service.

Index

443

Jan Parker and Jan Stimpson

Sibling Rivalry, Sibling Love

Voted Top Parenting Book by the *Independent*

'This is a valuable and important book. Parents – and professionals who work with them – should do all they can to get their hands on a copy.'
Eileen Hayes, Parenting Adviser to the NSPCC.

'A great book – well researched and full of useful, practical recommendations and real-life examples.'
Dr Mandy Byron, Consultant Clinical Psychologist, Great Ormond Street Hospital for Children.

'At last, a book for parents with more than one child! *Sibling Rivalry, Sibling Love* is warm, thought-provoking and packed with helpful ideas. I thoroughly recommend it.'
Belinda Phipps, Chief Executive of the National Childbirth Trust.

'Lively, thoughtful and full of ideas for us all to reflect on as we bring up our children.'
Peter Wilson, Director of Young Minds.

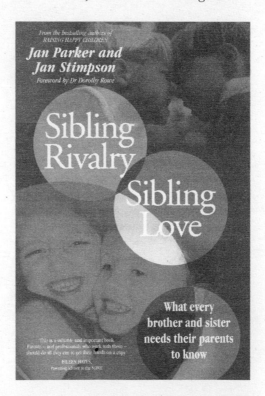